This book is a labor of love and [...] family. I started writing it in the fall of 2000 while deployed as the Command and Battle Group Chaplain on the nuclear aircraft carrier USS Abraham Lincoln (CVN-72) in the North Arabian Gulf. The Christian Apostle Paul wrote in I Corinthians 15:10 in the Christian New Testament, "But by the grace of God I am what I am, and his grace to me was not without effect". He felt that by grace God had taken him from being the worst of sinners, a Jewish Pharisee who persecuted the new Christian Church, to become the Apostle to the Gentiles who wrote most of the New Testament influencing billions for over two millennium. I feel the same on a much smaller scale. By grace the Lord has taken me from being a rebellious and angry pot smoking anti-war hippie and led me to become a United Methodist Minister and U.S. Navy Captain Chaplain who traveled the world. As a result, I have given this work the title "By the Grace of God". It is my hope and prayer that the Lord Jesus Christ will use this book to draw my entire family, dad, sister, wife, children, children-in-laws, grandchildren, future great-grandchildren, their families and all our friends and acquaintances closer to Him for His glory.

Rev. Dr. Douglas John Waite, Captain, Chaplain Corps, United States Navy (Retired). May 2016, Waikiki, Honolulu, Hawaii, douglasjwaite@gmail.com, www.howtoheal.org

Contents

1
Beginnings

I was born in Puyallup, Washington on June 21, 1950 to a young couple known affectionately as John and Jeri Waite. They were both from small towns in Eastern Washington close to the Idaho border, Clarkston and Pomeroy, Washington. They had met after my dad had returned from the Pacific in WW II, married and moved to Puyallup to be close to my mom's family who had settled there. Dad was attending school at the College of Puget Sound on his GI Bill and mom was working at Penny's to make ends meet. Mom became pregnant with me just before dad's senior year. He had to quit to pay the bills one quarter before he received his degree in Business. I believe he always regretted not hanging in there a little longer to finish that degree.

Soon after my birth, mom and dad moved to Spokane, Washington looking for work and wanting to be close to dad's family who lived there. Dad found a job in management with General Mills at their plant. They stayed there until 1955. I remember waiting for my dad to come home from work every night. I couldn't wait to see him come through the door. I also remember falling down the stairs playing a little guitar and putting my teeth through my lip. Mom was pregnant and thought she was going to go into labor.

My only sibling, a sister named Suzanne Lee, was born in Spokane in 1954. I missed my mom terribly while my sister was being born. I was very proud that I had a new sister and I remember showing her off to all my neighborhood friends one afternoon and knocking her bassinet over. She was wrapped in so many blankets she didn't get a scratch. I also vividly remember my dad crying his eyes out the night his father died that same year. Seeing him like that really disturbed and confused me.

Other memories I have during that time concern my grandma and grandpa Waite. Grandpa Waite owned a Texaco service station and my mom would often drop me off there when she had doctor's appointments. Grandma would bring us homemade potato soup to eat for lunch. I remember being at their home and watching my sister Suzanne play with all the things in grandpa's pockets in his work uniform. Grandma would take me shopping all the time. I always enjoyed being with her. We would go out to lunch together and shop.

One vivid memory I have was the week before grandpa died. He was an avid outdoorsman. He had come out to the Northwest from Little Falls, Minnesota during the depression riding the rails to find work. He wound up in a lumber mill in Lewiston, Idaho. He raised his large family of five kids in Clarkston, Washington until they moved to Spokane and he bought his Texaco service station. Short and strong, he had a mean temper. I heard a story of him chasing a man all over the lumberyard one time with a board in his hand. He loved to hunt and fish. My dad said he fed his family hunting during the depression. Dad said he never saw his dad ever miss a shot. When I was four grandpa, dad and I went fishing at one of the many lakes around Spokane. I can remember it like it was yesterday. Wherever grandpa put his line in, he would catch a fish. My dad could not catch a thing. Grandpa was really giving him a hard time. They would switch places and grandpa would still catch fish and dad would get skunked again. Grandpa just laughed and laughed.

Grandpa and I fell asleep in the car on the way home. He died the next week of a heart attack as a young man. He had broken his leg and would not stay off it. There was speculation that a chiropractor knocked a blood clot loose and it killed him.

The Christmas after grandpa died, I remember being at their home and staying the night on Christmas Eve. I was in the back bedroom and couldn't sleep. My Uncle Bob, my dad's youngest brother who was in the Navy, was saying that he could hear Santa's bells and if we didn't get to sleep he wouldn't come to our house. That year I got a cowboy outfit for Christmas.

Mom and dad tell a story of their church attendance during those years. My mother had been raised Methodist and my dad was raised with nothing. Dad attended church with mom at the Methodist Church. I would cry in church during those early years and the Methodist minister asked them to please put me in the nursery or not come back. They tried the nursery but I cried even more. They decided to try the Episcopal Church close by and the priest said they could let me cry all I wanted in his service. That was how my parents became Episcopalians and they have remained so most of their married life except the last few when they went back to the United Methodist Church in Sun City West, AZ. The Methodist Church lost many years of dedicated worshippers and tithers because of that minister who did not like a crying baby. I was baptized as an infant in the Methodist Church and my sister and dad were baptized together in the Episcopal Church.

In 1956 General Mills transferred my mom and dad to Lewiston, Idaho, close to the towns they grew up in. We moved into the Orchards on half an acre and my parents bought their first home. I started grade school there. I can still remember my mom taking me the first day of school and missing her when she left. I did not attend kindergarten. My mom spent time teaching me and getting me ready for first grade. During that year my dad brought home a little blond Cocker Spaniel named Princess. She would be my best friend for the next twelve years, dying finally in my senior year of high school. Princess once got loose and came all the way to school looking for me.

One Christmas Eve I remember looking out my bedroom window in the middle of the night and seeing the Christmas star. It was right there shining brightly in the sky. I told others later but they did not believe me. To this day I think I really saw it. I also had an experience early one morning while my dad was shaving and getting ready for work. I saw or dreamed that Satan came into my room and was floating around. It was very scary. I got up and told my dad but I think he just thought I had a nightmare. It seemed very real to me.

In 1957 we moved to Yakima, Washington and I finished the first grade there. Dad became the manager of the General Mills feed store in a little place called Union Gap. They bought their second house in Yakima. Across the street was a boy named Dick. We became good friends and eventually finished college together joining the same fraternity and later living in a house together. We are still friends to this day. Once Dick and I got in a fistfight and he had me down on the ground hitting me in the face. My dad was watching and later scolded me for not hitting him back in the face. I distinctly remember telling him that some people are made to fight and some are made for peace. I couldn't have been more than six but instinctively I knew what I was destined for, to bring peace to others. Later dad taught me how to fight back anyway.

We attended Saint Timothy's Episcopal Church in Yakima every Sunday. I remember they had a priest who was older, single and everyone loved him. His name was Father Baker. At Sunday school he would bring ice cream for all the kids. In about the third grade they had a contest to win a Bible. All you had to do was memorize the 23 Psalm and one other passage. I memorized the one psalm but lied to my two teachers about the other one, convincing them I had done it for the other. A few Sundays later my Bible was presented to me in front of the congregation. As the priest called me forward, I felt about as small as you could possibly be. I believe it was the first time I really experienced the conviction of the Holy Spirit. I knew I had done something very wrong. When I got back to my seat, I promised God I would make up for what I had done by reading that Bible. He never forgot my promise.

We were not a family that did much for vacations. Money was always tight. Once when I was in the third grade we went to stay at Twin Lakes in Idaho in a neat cabin with another big family my dad knew in General Mills. It was a great time. I did nothing but fish. I caught loads of crappie, perch and bass. Another time we drove to Merced Air Force Base in California where my uncle was a Colonel in the Air Force. We stayed with them and enjoyed the lifestyle of a senior officer. I distinctly remember having brunch at the Officer's Club and was very impressed. I loved the clubs and pools. It was so hot driving down there without air conditioning my sister got a bad heat rash. I always wanted to go to Disneyland but we never went. Once we went camping at Lake Chelan. We had just gotten set up when the State Patrol notified my parents that there had been a death in the family, my great grandmother. That was the end of that vacation.

One thing we did do as a family was travel to the ocean at Grayland near Aberdeen to my grandmother Chubby's store, the 'Treasure Chest', and her sister Ruth's resort, the 'Sea Anchor Lodge'. Chubby's real name was Alice. She was my mom's mom and had been married to the sheriff of Garfield County, Ransom or 'Dick' Gilliam. Grandpa Dick died as a young man from wounds received on the battlefields of France in WWI. While there he learned fingerprinting at the University of Paris and exported it to the Pacific Northwest. He became well known for this new technology in law enforcement. My mom was only fourteen when her dad died suddenly. It left a big hole in her and all the family. Chubby never remarried.

Great Aunt Ruth's lodge was a huge old house with many bedrooms that they would rent out to huge parties. Grandma ran both from her little apartment. From the time I was just a boy we would go there on weekends with all of our aunts, uncles and cousins. It was always a great time. We would dig razor clams, eat crab and go to Westport to watch the salmon boats come in. The parents would tuck us in at night and go out to the bars to party. I believe my love of the ocean started there. One thing I didn't love was sleeping with my cousin who always wet the bed.

One time mom and dad left Sue and me with grandma while they went on a trip. She was going out with a guy named Bill who was a big shot from Oceanspray Cranberries. He drove a big Cadillac. They took us down to the beach and left us to run and jump in the surf on an air mattress. The current moved us way up the beach from where they dropped us off. They came back and could not find us. They were frantic. When they finally did see us, Bill chewed me out royal. I was really upset at him. He was not my grandpa and had no business talking to me like that.

We stayed in Yakima until I finished the fifth grade. I have a lot of good memories of those years. I learned to ride a bike there and my uncle Bob bought me a BB gun. Dad had a lot of birds in his warehouse and would let me go down on Saturdays and shoot them. I think I spent more time shooting his big windows. Dad would also take me with him to hunt pheasants on the Indian reservation with Princess. She was one fine hunting dog. I would follow behind my dad and Princess with my BB gun. Princess would get the scent of a pheasant and start yipping and running. If you could keep up with her you would eventually get a shot. I distinctly remember dad shooting a big rooster one Saturday afternoon. As I ran to get it, I fell into a ditch that I did not see and went down flat on my face. We would road hunt on those gravel reservation roads on warm sunny fall Saturday afternoons and listen to the football games on the radio. Occasionally, we would find some good ripe Yakima apples to eat in one of the orchards we walked through. They were so crisp, juicy and sweet. The smell of fall would be in the air. Those were some of the happiest times of my early life and my best memories with my dad. I tried to build those memories with my sons too and now my grandsons.

Christmas was always a special time. My sister and I were in bunk beds. I can remember faking to be asleep and hearing my mom and dad taking the Christmas presents out of their hiding places. That was when I finally knew what I had suspected, they were Santa Claus. One Christmas I was having trouble going to sleep. It was some kind of insomnia. No matter how I tried, I could not get to sleep. I would be scared at night to go to bed because I would just lie there. I also had a scare with diabetes. They used to give tests at school with your urine. Mine came back positive. For weeks I had to go to the doctor and take blood tests. It was a nightmare. Everyone really thought I was sick. Finally, the tests came back conclusively negative. I was normal again.

Winter break was special. We would build snow forts and have snowball fights. Our house sat on the top of a hill. We would make a sledding path down the middle of it. I found out that if you took hot water and poured it on the snow, it would freeze into ice. It made a great slide. In the second grade I fell in love. I would walk her home and try to kiss her. In the third grade I got glasses. They wondered why I was always squinting all the time. It was a revelation to finally see clearly. I have worn glasses or contacts ever since except for a few years after I had Lasik surgery. In the fifth grade I was in love again. Her name was Barb. Years later I would take her to my junior prom.

My friend Dick's dad took him on a camping trip and taught him about the birds and the bees, sex. I was in the fifth grade. I was really envious. I had heard about sex from the guys in the neighborhood but I wanted my dad to take me out like Dick's did. I bugged dad and bugged him. Finally, he relented and we went up into the Cascades for a night. We camped at this neat lake and rented a boat the next morning to do some fishing. It was a good time. I kept waiting for my dad to start telling me about sex. He never did. I don't think that generation talked much to their kids about sex. We were supposed to learn it by osmosis. Instead, we learned about it on the street. I tried to make sure that all my kids had the same sex parent take them out for a weekend before the teen years to talk about sex and life.

Next, General Mills took my mom and dad to Tacoma, Washington. We bought our third house close to Puyallup where I was born. We had come full circle.

Mom and dad built this house from scratch. It was brand new and very beautiful with a fireplace that went through from the living room to the family room. I helped my dad put in the lawn. We would still go hunting in the fall with Princess but pheasant hunting was not so good in that part of Washington. One Saturday while hunting, dad told me that he was going to quit General Mills because they wanted him to transfer again to California. They were closing out the feed business and they wanted him to go to the flourmills.

Boldly, dad quit and went to work for Allstate Insurance as a salesman. He had a new home and a growing family but he took a gamble to change careers and it paid off. Dad was always honest, an extrovert and a hard worker. Soon he was one of Allstate's top producers. He began by going to training in Palo Alto, California that took him away from us for awhile. We all missed him terribly. In those days Allstate had booths in all the Sears stores. Dad would spend many evenings and Saturdays at Sears selling insurance. I began to see less and less of him.

We were attending the Episcopal Church in Puyallup in those days. I had become an acolyte or altar boy, helping the priest up in front. I also remember going through Confirmation there. We attended classes and finally the Bishop came and laid hands on all of our heads and said a prayer. I didn't feel any different afterwards.

Seventh grade was one of the toughest years of my life. I was short in those days, wore glasses and had an overbite. My glasses were even taped where they had broken. Today they would call me a geek. While I always was smart in school, I was not very athletic. We had a rough group of kids in our rural area that were into all kinds of trouble. We rode the buses quite a distance into Puyallup every day and back for school. I was taking music and would carry my cornet with me. This group of kids thought I looked like a good target to harass and make fun of. They were bigger and older and would get me in the back of the bus and threaten me. They would tell me that if I didn't pay them money they would beat me up. I was scared to death and paid them money for awhile from my lunch money. Eventually my parents found out. May dad was a boxer in high school and he began to try to give me some lessons. He told me that the only way this was going to stop was if I picked the toughest of the group and offered to fight him. I finally had enough and decided to take dad up on his advice. I told this guy I wasn't going to give him any more money and that I wanted to fight. One night on our way home we faced off when we got off the bus. Punches were traded and we wrestled around on the ground for awhile. Suddenly, he got up and walked off. I never had another problem with him or the others. This advice stayed with me my whole life. I learned that the only way to deal with intimidation and fear was to face it head on and stand up for yourself. When you did, often it would disappear. Also, bullies do not like it when people fight back and will go find someone else to bully.

I was really into scouting in those days and became the Senior Patrol Leader of my pack. The scoutmaster told me that I was a natural leader. I eventually quit because the girls started making fun of me at school in my uniform. It wasn't cool to be a scout.

My eighth grade year was one of the best. My closest friend Jim was the best athlete in school. He could run like the wind and no one could beat him. I had several girlfriends that year and finally wound up with a cheerleader, one of the prettiest and most popular girls in school named Carol. My buddy and I got invited to all the best parties. I thought I had died and gone to heaven. To top it off, Jim decided that I needed to run for school office. He became my campaign manager and put me up for vice president of this brand new junior high. I was running against the most popular girl in school. I didn't think I had a chance. Jim decided my campaign slogan would be, "It is not too late to vote for Waite". He plastered it everywhere and asked everyone to vote for me. I even gave a speech to the student body. My mom helped me with it and **we** decided to make it funny. It said something about postnasal drip. Everybody cracked up. All my other classmates' speeches were very serious. I think that clinched it. When all the votes were counted, I had won by one vote. I couldn't believe it. I had gone from being a geek to one of the most popular guys in school, the vice president, with a great best friend and a beautiful girlfriend. I could do anything if I just put my mind to it, or so I thought. Soon my life would take some drastic changes.

2
DOWN INTO THE DARKNESS

Once again my dad was being transferred. He had been promoted to become the District Sales Manager (DSM) for Allstate back in Yakima, Washington. We were moving, this time the summer before my ninth grade year. We sold our new house and headed back to Yakima. I was devastated. I had finally reached a social state of respectability and now I had to start all over. I would be a no-body again. I was angry with my parents.

We moved to Yakima and my mom and dad decided to get a place with a swimming pool. They thought the pool might help us make friends. It did help. I also decided I would give athletics a try again. I gained most of my height that year, 5' 10" and about 150 pounds, and I was actually big for a ninth grader. I decided to try football right off the bat. The junior high was seventh through ninth grade. Some of the kids I knew in grade school were there, including Dick. It gave me a little bit of an edge. I tried to pretend that I was fast like my friend Jim had been. The coach was a friend of my dad's so he tried me out for first string. I didn't know the first thing about football and most of these kids had been playing sports together for years. I was big and fairly quick but still had not gained my full coordination. Needless to say, I was not very good and I wound up playing tackle on the fourth string. I did last the whole season and lettered but cracked a bone in my arm.

I made some friends on the team but they were not the athletic and academically motivated kids. My old friend Dick was part of the second group. Ironically, he was the president of the junior high and thick with the 'in crowd'. He was friendly but busy with his social group. The friends I made were the ones who were smoking, drinking and partying with the girls. Steve was one of them. He took me in and introduced me to other kids doing the same thing from another junior high across town. We would hang out after school at this one guy's house, Jerry, smoke and listen to music. His mom was a single parent and worked most of the time. Jerry also was older and had a car. We all hung out with him for transportation and a safe place to crash. All of these kids came from good homes but were more rebellious in their orientation to life. I have told my own children when we moved around that when you are new in town you look for any friendly face to take you in. Often that face is the rebellious group that is always in some kind of trouble. That is what happened to me.

There was also a group of girls that went with this social group. They were friends with the academic popular athletic kids but more rebellious and into partying. I started going out with one of the cheerleaders from my school that went with both groups. We began to get invitations to the parties of both groups but my closest friends were the rebellious kids. As I look back now, I was very angry that I had lost all my social position from Puyallup and so I looked for a way to express that anger. I didn't realize this for years. At the same time, my dad's job took up most of his time. I saw him less and less.

That second summer I took my last vacation with the family. We rented a trailer and drove to Yellowstone, a real vacation. I was almost fifteen. I had started smoking that year and would hide my cigarettes in the back of my transistor radio. I would go on long walks wherever we stopped so I could smoke. My parents started calling me the camp prowler because I was always taking off on my own. We finally got to Yellowstone. I started fishing and caught some nice fish. Walking back to the trailer a bear started after me. It was scary as I ran for the trailer and threw the fish to him.

My friends and I began to get into alcohol, mostly from what we could steal from our homes. We also would sneak out of our homes late and meet in the park to smoke and talk on warm summer nights. Soon some of the guys started joy riding in cars. Sometimes it was their parent's cars that they would take late at night. At other times it was the cars of people they knew. They also started breaking and entering homes that were vacant to steal alcohol.

My family went back to attending Saint Timothy's Episcopal Church. They had a new young rector who was a Harvard graduate. I would go to church with my parents but I found it very boring. Sometimes I had been out all night. Once I even fainted I was so tired. Finally, I told my Mom I was not going any more. It just didn't mean anything to me. I couldn't relate. She went and talked to the rector who told her that when he was my age he did the same thing. His parents left him alone and look what happened to him. My parents decided not to force me to go and put the decision into my hands. Look what happened to me. I have reflected on this many times in raising my own children. All of them have become bored with church during their high school years and have stopped going. As adults some of them have come back to church as I eventually did.

By this time, all my friends were in the same high school together. We formed a tight social group of about ten of us. Others from the more academic/athletic or more rebellious, we called them hoods, would join us from time to time. On one occasion, a new recruit of ours decided he was going to run away. He was taking care of the grounds of a family who was traveling in Europe. They left him the keys to their house and cars. He would take their cars and alcohol late at night and come around picking us all up. We would stay out all night just driving around, drinking and smoking.

One night he came around for me. My dad just happened to be up using the bathroom when he came knocking at my window. I was asleep and didn't hear him but my dad did. When dad came to the window, he took off. He tried some other guys that night but didn't get anyone. That was the night he decided to run away. He got all the way to Oregon before they caught him. He gave up all of our names to the police. The next day at school we were all called to the principal's office and taken down in squad cars to the police station. They had us all in separate interrogation rooms. Miraculously, we all gave them the same false stories about our involvement in joy riding. I remember hearing my dad come into the station demanding to see me. When he finally got to me, he said, "I don't care what you've done, just tell the truth". I was really proud of him that night. When the detective talked to me he said, "Waite, I know you are guilty. If it is the last thing I do, I am going to see that they put you away for five years". He really scared me. From that day on, I was more careful about breaking the law. My dad hired a good lawyer, a friend of the family, who went with me to juvenile court and that was the end of it.

Later in life I had to do the same thing for one of my kids.

My friends were intelligent, most of them went on to graduate from college, but they were also rebellious party animals. There was a group of about ten or twelve girls who hung out with us too. Corey became my girlfriend and we went together throughout our junior and senior years. I drove a 1957 Ford with chrome reverse wheels, metal flake paint job, dual glass pack exhaust, and a 312-thunderbird interceptor engine. I wasn't a jock or academic but Corey and I were popular in many circles.

My dad got me a job at Sear's part time and that kept me going financially. I was good at academics but I didn't spend much time at it. All I lived for was the party scene with Corey and my friends. My relationship with my parents really deteriorated during those years. Many were the nights that my mom would be in tears worried about the way my life was going. I started really disliking my dad and we would fight and yell constantly. We never came to blows but we did come close. I was always intimidated by his boxing background, and rightly so. We quit hunting together. I would hunt with Steve and Princess or with Corey, Steve and Steve's girlfriend Kathy. I think Dad thought he was in the way but the truth was I really did miss going out with him.

Alcohol was a big part of our lives in those days. We came up with many clever ways to purchase it. Our next-door neighbor was a beer distributor. They had kids about our age or a little older. I would work for them sometimes when they had a big shipment come in at the warehouse. Some of our beer came from that arrangement. One of the guys, Rod, looked older and could sometimes purchase beer in the store without being carded. I had a bad temper when I drank and would often pick fights. Steve was a real fighter with a reputation and would usually get me out of them.

During those days, and many others, God protected my life. I attribute part of that to the fact that my parents prayed for me, had me baptized and presented to the Lord as a baby. Also, I had gone through Confirmation and been prayed over for God's anointing. I believe there is power in those things. God's hand was on me even when I was paying no attention to him. I have encouraged my children to commit their children to the Lord in the same ways.

One night Steve and I were at a party together as we often were and this time we were in his car. We had drunk too much as usual and Steve got in some kind of argument with a guy about whose car was faster. They decided to drag race. As we headed out to the cars, I started to get in the passenger side as I always did. Steve would not let me in. I couldn't believe it. I asked him what was going on and he just locked the door and drove off. As he was racing this guy, he went out of control and through a fence. A big 4X4 beam went right through the passenger side front window into the front seat. If I had been sitting there, it would have taken my head off. That kind of thing happened to me all the time. I seemed to always get caught when I was doing something I shouldn't, and I was always spared when I should have been arrested, seriously hurt, or killed. God and his angels were protecting me then as they do now. I reflect on this and pray God's angelic protection on my children, their spouses, future spouses, grandchildren, future grandchildren and all my family every day. I tell my children God has special angels who follow them around to make sure they get caught when they are out of line and to protect them always. I made sure they were all baptized and presented to the Lord as babies. All but one went through Confirmation when they were in about the seventh or eighth grade. Each one accepted Christ into their lives as young children in Vacation Bible School. Now I pray for their spouses and children.

Corey and I were off and on until her mother was diagnosed with cancer. I stayed close to Corey while we watched her mother die. At the funeral the family asked me to sit with them. That experience welded Corey and I together. I was sure we would get married. There was one problem. She wanted to stay in Yakima and I wanted to get out of Yakima and make something of my life.

My senior year I applied to college and was accepted at both of the two big state universities, the University of Washington (UW) in Seattle and Washington State University (WSU) in Pullman close to where my folks grew up. My mom had attended WSU for one quarter and my dad had always wanted to attend the UW. I chose the UW because of my dad and because I wanted to get out of Yakima and into the big city.

Steve and I had a dream of going commercial salmon fishing in Alaska. Towards the end of our senior year, we would drive all over Western Washington every weekend asking commercial fisherman to hire us. We pounded the waterfront talking to anyone we could find. Finally, a captain in Gig Harbor noticed us. He told us that if we would come over every weekend until we left for Alaska and work for nothing, he would take us. We agreed and came over every weekend sleeping on the boat. The boat was a purse seiner, the Bernice, over fifty feet long with a crew of six. We worked hard getting her ready, mending nets, and painting, you name it. Finally, the big day came. We had driven over the day after high school graduation. It was really hard to say goodbye to

Corey in my driveway. We pledged our love and loyalty to one another and soon we were separated for the first time.

It took us a week to go up the Inside Passage to Petersburg, Alaska from Gig Harbor. We arrived just in time for my eighteenth birthday. Steve and I celebrated by drinking all the beer we had taken onboard for the crew. When our skipper Wally found out, he was furious. Fishing was hard work. Steve was a lineman and I ran the power skiff. We would look hard for the salmon and when we found them we would make sets as long as the fish were there, often over 24 hours. It was really hard work. Steve and I always got all of the smelly stinky work pitching the fish out of the hold to the tender with a pew stick. That summer I saw some of the most beautiful country and experienced wildlife in some of the most extraordinary ways of my life. We would watch eagles swoop down and grab salmon, brown bears feasting on the shore, salmon rubbing against our legs as we walked up a stream and whales mating. The mountains coming straight down into the ocean were unforgettable.

Steve and I lasted until Labor Day and made a fairly decent wage for our labors. We both missed our girlfriends so much we ached. We would all write torrid love letters and make passionate phone calls. Finally we could take it no longer. We caught the first plane home. When I arrived home that first night and called Corey, I could tell something was wrong. I drove over to her house. She tried to explain to me that she had met someone else while I was gone, all the while telling me she loved me in her letters and phone calls. I was devastated. I couldn't believe it. How could she do this to me? It took me years to get over that girl.

After Corey, I began to turn my sights toward Seattle and the UW. I decided to go out for rush and pledge a fraternity. Most of the guys from Yakima were in one house, Alpha Tau Omega or ATO. My old friend Dick was going to the UW too and had already decided on ATO. He encouraged me to do the same.

My dad took me over and got me a place to stay at the Seattle Allstate DSM's house near the UW campus. I would take the bus in and visit the various fraternities during rush week. Since I had been in Alaska all summer, no one knew me. I was starting from scratch. It was scary but I decided to press on. I think the loss of Corey motivated me to try new things I may not have done otherwise. I finally was offered to pledge ATO and another house and I chose ATO because of Dick and all the guys from Yakima.

One of the first guys I met there was a sophisticated city boy from Seattle who was very streetwise. He took me one day to the local Dairy Queen, parked, and put a sign on the top of his car that said "Pharmacy". Soon kids from all over were coming over and buying drugs that he kept in his glove compartment with a gun. He was one of the biggest speed dealers in North Seattle and he was my fraternity brother. He used the fraternity as a cover for his drug dealing.

Drugs had just started to reach some level of popularity in Yakima about my senior year in high school. Like alcohol, I got involved with drugs because of peer pressure. I wanted to be one of the guys, to be accepted by my social group. When I got to the UW, drugs were preferred over alcohol and often combined. I got involved with them like everything else I did, with both feet.

My freshmen year I had many girlfriends but none who really took the place of Corey in my heart. I started to wonder if I could really love anyone again like I had loved her. My sophomore summer I was elected by the frat to become co-rush chairman with my fellow brother Mark. Together we bought a 1961 Lincoln Continental convertible as our rush-mobile. Our frat had a large group of the UW crew team in our house. Several members of the crew were working at a place next to the Ballard Bridge called Pacific Chemical. The co-rush job didn't really pay me enough so I asked them to help me get hired at Pacific Chemical. I interviewed borrowing one of my fraternity brother's shirt, coat, tie and an MGB GT. I had a terrible cold and my nose was running profusely. As I was waiting for the interview, I struck up a conversation with a good-looking young blond receptionist. She took pity on me and got me some Kleenex. After the interview, the manager asked this young woman, Gail Anderson, which one of the candidates she liked the best. She told him, "The one who wore the coat and tie". He hired me and I started driving an old oil truck and applying nitrogen fertilizer on lawns for a promotional. It was called Green Grass Fertilizer. Gail was also the dispatcher for the trucks and I saw her often. I heard my fellow frat brothers saying that they thought she was cute and were considering asking her out so I beat them to the punch and asked her out first.

We had our first date on July 4th 1969. I met her and her family at a resort close to the Canadian border called Birch Bay in my Lincoln Continental with a fraternity brother. She had a friend with her and the four of us drove to Stanley Park in Vancouver, British Columbia. We had a great time. I asked her out again to go sailing at night with one of my other fraternity brothers and his girlfriend out in Puget Sound. We started to date regularly and Gail began to accompany me to the many rush functions I was holding that summer. She was a big hit with the frat.

On one of those functions we were going to Spokane in Eastern Washington. I decided to take her home to Yakima and introduce her to my parents. When we arrived I immediately took her out to the pool to show off. The diving board was set up so I went up on it to show her the spring. What I didn't know was that my dad had set it there but not bolted it in. When I got to the end of the board to make a big bounce, I went down, clothes, wallet, cigarettes and all into the pool. I thought Gail would never stop laughing. When my parents finally got home, they met Gail standing there in the briefest bikini either of them had ever seen.

That night we went out with my best friends, Steve and Kathy. It was the first time Gail had met them. Steve had just bought a brand new Javelin. We did our usual date of parking and drinking and then headed into town. Steve was a speeder and before we knew it a policeman was on our tail with his lights flashing and siren blaring. Steve had too much to drink and whenever that happened, he was capable of just about anything. He decided to outrun the cop. We started racing through the streets and alleys with the police car right on our heels. Gail and I were in the back seat with no seat belts and feeling no pain. Suddenly we came to a stop sign onto a four-lane arterial. Steve went right through it into the approaching traffic. Unknown to us, there were two cars drag racing each other and coming directly at us from the right side. The first one missed us and the second hit us dead on at the firewall. We found out later that Javelin was spot welded in just four places in the front end. If it hadn't been, we would have all died. That racing car tore the Javelin right in two, taking the engine with it. Those two teenagers went through the

24

windshield and both of them lost their front teeth but lived. The rest of our car went up into the air and landed on someone's front lawn. I remember the whole thing in slow motion.

When everything finally stopped, I could not find my glasses. Somehow I got myself out of the car and tried to help the others. Everyone was conscious but Kathy. She had blood all over her. After I helped Steve and Gail get out through the window, Gail pointed at my shoulder and said, "Look". I glanced down and saw my right shoulder about four inches lower than it should have been. The pain hit me instantly like a hammer and I went down hard. The policeman was right there and had an ambulance on the scene quickly. They took us all to the hospital. Kathy had cut the aorta in her heart and was in critical condition. They had to air lift her to Seattle. I had dislocated my shoulder. Gail had hurt her leg. Steve had the radio come out and hit him in the head. Otherwise, the three of us were OK.

I prayed that night for Kathy. I always believed in God. I never stopped but I just did not have any time for him. The only time I turned to God was when I was really in a bad jam. Almost always, God heard me and came through. He healed Kathy and she survived to later marry Steve and give birth to two boys. They would later divorce. Their oldest son later served with me in the Navy.

My parents met Gail's parents over the phone that night as they told them about the accident. The next morning we were all in a daze. We went down to look at the car and it was in two mangled heaps. No one could believe that anyone lived through it. My arm was in a sling but I went ahead with Gail and attended the rush function in Spokane the next night. Another fraternity brother drove us. It took weeks before we felt comfortable riding in a car again without fear. The result of the whole experience was that Gail and I became welded together as a couple. I was falling deeply in love with her and her with me. The accident just cemented it and brought it to our attention. One afternoon I just woke up and realized that I loved Gail as much or more than Corey. Gail had filled my heart again and done what I did not think was possible, helped me to truly love another human being. I pinned her that fall with my fraternity pin before she headed off to college in Ellensburg, Washington. I didn't want her going out with anyone but me.

That summer I also had another close call with death. I was under the influence one night and up on the roof of the fraternity. It was a two-story building with a brick courtyard. Somehow I fell off to the bricks below with my cowboy boots on. I thought I had shoved my feet through my ankles. I was in tremendous pain and couldn't go to work. They put me on pain medications. There was a rock festival going on that weekend and all my fraternity brothers wanted me to go. They came and got me out of bed and took me to the concert. About 50,000 people were there to hear the likes of Chicago and Chuck Berry. We were drinking and someone gave me something else. The last thing I remember was sitting by the stage listening to Chicago. I woke up seventeen hours later. I had overdosed on pain medications, alcohol and who knows what else. I was just lying there on the ground and people were walking over me. No one stopped to see if I was OK that entire time. It was dark and all my friends were gone. I could have died that night but for the grace of God. I woke up and I could hear this deep laughing that seemed to be echoing over the entire area. I didn't know what it was then but today I believe it was the voice of Satan laughing at what he was doing to destroy my life. He would have succeeded if God didn't have other plans and his angels weren't watching over me. I also started to become disillusioned with the whole flower child love philosophy. It all sounded good but was not a reality. Drugs did not expand the mind; they just seemed to take you down. It would be a while longer before I would really see that.

Mark wrecked the Lincoln and rush was over. I was back to walking where I wanted to go. Almost every weekend that quarter I would hitch-hike over to see Gail or she would come home to Seattle and be with me. We couldn't get enough of each other. One night in her dorm room I asked her to marry me. She agreed and we considered ourselves engaged. It would be awhile before we had a ring or a date set.

About that time I had my first encounter with what became known as 'born again' Christianity. Somehow one of our fraternity brothers invited two members of Campus Crusade for Christ to dinner. After the dinner they gave a presentation in the parlor. I stayed for it. Each of them told how an encounter with Jesus Christ had changed their life. They said that this Jesus was still alive and would come and live inside of anyone who invited him. All we had to do was admit we were sinners, believe that Jesus died for those sins, and ask him to forgive us and to come into our lives. They said God's Spirit would then come to live inside us, forgive all our sins, give us power to live for God, and eternal life. It sounded good to me. Looking back I don't think I had ever heard anyone talk like this before but maybe I just never listened. What did I have to lose? When they had a prayer to receive Christ, I prayed with them. I went back to my room and didn't feel any different. I soon forgot the whole thing, but God never forgets.

27

I had started as a business major at the UW because that was what my dad was and wanted. There was much social upheaval and unrest in those days. We were involved in losing an unpopular war in Vietnam. Martin Luther King and Bobby Kennedy had just been assassinated. President Nixon and Spiro Agnew were at war with the youth culture. Haight Ashbury and the flower children hippies of San Francisco were in their prime. The Beatles were the most popular rock group in the world and protest music was everywhere. The Civil Rights Movement was at a crescendo. All the while, I was taking business classes and studying profit maximization. The world was coming apart at the seams all around me and all I was doing was burying my head in the sand, or so it seemed. The turning point came with the incident at Kent State where National Guard troops gunned down some students at a peaceful rally. The student movement was in shock and then galvanized. How could the government do this? It had to be stopped. We successfully closed down the campus of the UW. All classes were pass/fail the rest of the quarter. Thousands marched out into the main north south freeway, Interstate 5, and stopped traffic in both directions for hours, eventually facing off with the Washington State Patrol Tactical Squad. It was ugly all over.

I was taking my first philosophy class that quarter. I loved it. It seemed to relate so much more to me than my business classes. I decided then and there to drop out of business and major in philosophy. I became very interested in searching for truth. I distinctly remember calling my dad and telling him. His response was, "How are you going to make a living in philosophy?" I didn't have a clue but I just knew I could not study profit maximization another day when the culture was collapsing upon itself. One of the most popular leaders of the counter culture of those days was a college professor named Timothy Leary. I took his advice and tuned in, turned on, and dropped out. One of the first things I dropped out of was the fraternity. The frat was a brotherhood by vote. One ding and you were out. When I was rush chairman, I couldn't get anyone in who was black or had long hair. I believed that all were brothers and sisters by no one's vote. Dick and I and two other of our fraternity brothers moved out and we got our own big house at Green Lake. It was party time almost every night.

That summer we all split up. Dick went to Europe backpacking with another brother from the house and I went back to Alaska. I wanted to go to Europe too but Gail said if I did she would not be there when I got back. I had met a longhaired hippie named Frank who owned his own fishing boat, a troller. He was from Alaska and needed a partner to get his boat home. My Dad helped me invest in the venture. I think he thought that if I got back to Alaska fishing with the wind in my hair it might do me some good. Frank and the boat were to go ahead and I would join them in Yakutat when school got out. The boat never made it. It blew up on the way. I flew up anyway and we tried to make a go of hand seining from a skiff and living on an island, hippie style. I was very much into nature. I wore jeans, hiking boots, wool shirts, a backpack, wire rimmed John Lenin glasses and I had long hair. I lasted about two weeks and headed home.

By the time I got back to Seattle all the summer jobs were gone. I went home to Yakima and got my car, then a 1957 Chevy, and slept in it for a while. I searched the papers for a job and could only find one, selling encyclopedias door to door for Colliers. It was a tough job. They had all these applicants for the job and we had to interview. They asked each one of us why we wanted the job. Everyone said things like, "I want the experience". I said that I wanted to make money. They hired me immediately. My first couple of weeks was disastrous. I could not sell those books and I was living in my car. We would go out in teams of about four and canvass huge areas. Sometimes we would go over the mountains and be gone all week. A sales manager would drive us around, drop us off, and pick us up later. Many of the little towns were Green River Ordinance that meant no door-to-door solicitation. We would work those towns too but we had to be careful. If people turned us in we could get arrested.

Because I was a student at the UW and had a student ID, I decided to pose as if I was doing a student survey for the university. I started getting in more doors. The sales pitch was pretty good and if you could give it well and learn to close hard, you could get a sale. I made $100 on each set I sold.

One night we were in Eastern Washington and I had not made a sale all week. I was so discouraged and exhausted. For the first time in years I decided to pray. I asked God to help me sell encyclopedias. The next day I sold a set. The day after I sold a set. Each day that week I sold a set. I was the top salesman in the region that week. I took the money I made and bought Gail a beautiful diamond engagement ring at a mall in Portland, Oregon. I gave it to her but still didn't set a date. Back in Seattle at the sales meeting, they asked me if I wanted to be a sales manager. Managers got a percentage of every set their crew sold. I said yes and took my 57 Chevy on the road. I continued to sell books but not at the same rate I had done that one special week.

I forgot all about God except for one evening when we were in a small farming town about sunset. A full moon was out over the top of the dry barren hills.

It was beautiful. I remember sensing the creator's presence and just saying aloud, "What do you want with me? What do you want with my life?" I didn't hear any response but somehow I knew in the deepest places of my being that he was calling me to himself.

I had another experience selling books that hit me hard. I ran into a minister and his large family one day in a little town. They were very kind and invited me in for a cold drink and gathered the whole family. They believed that I was doing some kind of survey for the UW. As I began my presentation, the pastor got very quiet. In the middle he stopped me. He asked me how I could be so dishonest. How could I go around posing as a student surveyor when all I was really doing was selling encyclopedias? He said I should be ashamed of myself and he asked me to leave. It was the first time anyone had confronted me on my scam. I really felt convicted that what I was doing and what I had become were wrong.

My conviction didn't last long. I continued to sell books and ended the summer eleventh in the world for Collier. I was a natural salesman like my dad. I won a scholarship to college. By that time I hated my job and wanted to quit. I think it really hurt me for future sales work. I also won a free trip for two to Las Vegas. Gail and I went to Vegas without telling her parents. We called them from the hotel saying we were sleeping in separate beds. They were sure we would come home married but we had no intention. We ran out of money quickly and we weren't even gambling. I sweet-talked the girl at the front desk into loaning us some money. I was proud that I had that kind of persuasive power. I never intended to pay it back. Later I finally did. To this day I regret not taking Gail to see Elvis Presley. He was playing in town and Gail idolized him. We were low on money so we decided to see Joey Bishop instead. It was a good show but Gail has never let me forget that she didn't get to see Elvis before he died.

That fall I decided to move out on my own. I was really searching for truth and trying to find myself, and my place in the universe. Dick had come back from Europe acting really strange and had moved in with the guy he went to Europe with. I met a professor named Tom from the UW who had an organic farm in Woodinville where Microsoft is today. He was leaving to drive to South America to do some research and he wanted me to take care of his organic farm. It sat on a little lake there named Leota. I had this white Samoyed Husky named Jasper that I got from one of the book sales managers. He was a beautiful dog and we were inseparable. The house Tom lived in was really a chicken coop that the woman who owned the property had remodeled into a little apartment. I loved it and moved in for the next seven months. I was majoring in philosophy and taking heavy nineteenth century classes that were often Marxist in orientation. In fact, many of my professors at that time were Marxists. I was also deeply influenced by Emerson and Thoreau. I was doing my own experiment on the organic farm in getting back to nature. I also got a job at Nordstrom's selling women's shoes in Bellevue. It was a schizophrenic existence. On one hand I was the back to nature hippie philosopher and on the other a businessman in an upscale clothing retail business. I hated the job and loved the philosophy. I really wanted to know the truth. I was so into philosophy at that time that I quit smoking cigarettes, something I had done since I was about fourteen, because I couldn't stand the tobacco companies making a profit off a product they were addicting me to.

Gail hung with me through all of those changes. She got tired of us being apart and so she transferred to North Seattle Community College so we could be together more. I asked her to move in with me at the chicken coop but she refused. I was taking her for granted too in those days. One night we were at a party and there was a girl from my old high school. This girl admitted that she had a crush on me all through high school. We were talking intensely and Gail would come over and sat right between us. She was really gutsy, that is one reason I loved her so. Well, she caught this girl and me kissing in the kitchen. Later that night she found her phone number in my pants pocket and threw it away.

Soon Gail told me that she thought maybe we shouldn't be engaged anymore. I still had not committed to a date. Marriage scared me and I wanted to put it off as long as I could. I used to say, "Why do we need a piece of paper anyway? Who makes up those rules, some little old ladies?" Gail decided that we should take the diamond back and get two friendship rings. We found these two beautiful gold rings designed by a northwest artist. Hers had little diamonds on it. We started to wear them and quit talking marriage.

Gail had a wonderful mom named Shirley. She was beautiful inside and out. All of Gail's friends loved her mom and would come over to the house just to talk to her. Shirley loved me but she knew that my life was messed up. She had just gone through a real spiritual revitalization in her own life. Unbeknownst to me, she had put my name in a prayer group of women who were praying for me to find new direction in my life. Later she told me that she figured the best way to get to Gail was to pray for me. I have thought about this often with the boys and men my daughters have brought home over the years. I have also learned that when godly women get together and pray, there is tremendous power.

I was getting deeper into drugs and alcohol and my life was going down the drain. I would look in the mirror and not like the person I was becoming. I was filled with a lot of anger and hatred towards the establishment, policemen, people with short hair, the government and especially my dad. To me he represented everything I couldn't stand. Instead of being filled with love as the hippie philosophy promoted, I was filled with a lot of hate. I also do not think I knew how to love. I was very selfish. Everything revolved around me and meeting my needs. I rarely thought of doing something for anyone else unless I directly benefited from it. The thing is, I knew better. I had not been raised to be this kind of person and it was really bothering me.

From time to time some of my drug friends would come over and stay a few days. Some of them were bikers who drove motorcycles. We called it crashing. On one occasion I opened my place to them. After all, we were all supposed to be brothers and sisters. I gave them the run of my farm. After they left I discovered that they had stolen from me. I was devastated. What was this flower child philosophy anyway? It was turning out to be a farce.

My Marxist philosophy professors were always taking potshots at the Bible. In their lectures they would find some way to make fun of and discredit the Bible. On one such occasion I went to my professor after class and asked him if he had ever read the Bible. He said, "No". So I asked how he, a philosophy professor, could make disparaging comments about a book he had never read. He said, "Who the hell are you. Get out of my class". That day I determined I would read the Bible. I did not feel I could be a true philosopher and not check out this important work. It never ceases to amaze me that God can even use an atheistic philosophy professor to accomplish his purposes.

I had come a long way since the ninth grade and most of it wasn't good. Drugs, alcohol and rebellion were taking me down to the bottom of the pit. It seemed I was being smothered in darkness. Some of my friends went there and never came back. I sensed that I was in danger of the same fate.

3
Out into the Light

I did not have a Bible at the chicken coop. I remembered that once a long time ago I had been given a Bible in church. I went over to my parent's house looking for it. There it was in the bookcase, a leather King James Bible with a zipper around it. On the outside was stamped in gold, Douglas John Waite. Inside the cover it said Fr. Baker presented this Bible to me on June 12, 1960. It was the same Bible I had lied to get in the third grade and promised God I would read some day. When we make promises to God, we may forget, but God never forgets.

I took the Bible back to my house and tried to read it. I started in the New Testament with the birth of Jesus in Matthew. I knew that much from my Sunday school days. I tried to read it like I did everything else, high. I couldn't make any sense out of it at all. One night I decided I would try to read it when I was not high, we called it straight. The words just leaped off the page at me. This Jesus was really a neat guy. Why had I never read him before? He would have made a good hippie: long hair, robes, and outside in nature, telling people to love each other. I couldn't get enough. Every night after dinner I would read for a while. This went on for a couple of weeks.

One night I asked myself, "Why did Jesus go around saying he was God? Why didn't he just call us his brothers and sisters?" Recognizing each other as brothers and sisters on the planet was very important to the hippie philosophy. That night I read these words, "Whoever does the will of my father, the same is my brother, my sister, and my mother" (Mathew 12:50). You could have knocked me over. Someone was talking to me. As I continued to read, I became convicted in my heart that this was the truth. Jesus was the Messiah, the Christ. The Bible was true. Jesus died for my sins and rose from the dead. He was coming back some day.

Somehow a 'Four Spiritual Laws' booklet from the group Campus Crusade for Christ got into my coat pocket about the same time this was all happening. I do not know to this day where it came from. I was not attending church and did not associate with any Christians. I thought everyone who went to church was a hypocrite. I did not believe there were any real Christians anywhere. I found that little booklet one-day and began to read it. The same group put it out who had come to my fraternity to dinner that night a couple of years before. It explained simply that God loved me and had a plan for my life and there were spiritual laws that I had broken. Jesus came, lived and died to bridge the gap between God and man and was still alive. If I would personally invite him into my life he would come in, forgive my sins, and give me eternal life as a gift. It sounded like a pretty good deal to me then, just as it had that night at the frat. What did I have to lose?

I took the booklet and Jasper and walked out into my favorite place, the woods. There on a stump I invited Jesus to come into my life, to forgive my sins, and to give me eternal life. I didn't hear any bells or see any visions but when I walked back to the coop, I sensed a presence that was new, but familiar. It was a presence that had been with me all my life protecting me but now that presence was inside of me. I believe that is what it means to be a Christian. You shift from having God with you to having God in you. He is 'with' all of his creation but he is only 'in' those who

37

invite him in. He is the creator of all but only the father of those who are born again spiritually by receiving his son Jesus. God is a gentleman and only goes where he is invited.

When I got back to my apartment, I knew what I had to do. I took all the drugs I had in the house and flushed them down the toilet. It was one of the toughest things I ever did, to push down on that toilet handle, but it felt great once I did it. I also knew that I had to destroy any drug paraphernalia that I had: clips, pouches, pipes, etc. I knew I was not to give them away, but destroy them, which I promptly did. No one was there telling me anything. I simply had a new presence, authority, power inside that was suddenly directing my life.

I had said that I would never quit using drugs. I loved to get high. At once I knew that I was never to touch drugs again. The power of that attraction was immediately broken. I have never touched drugs from that day until now, over forty years as of this writing. Looking back I believe that mine was a supernatural attraction to drugs. It was almost demonic. When I invited Christ into my life, the power of that hold was broken. This is my story and not anyone else's. I have worked with many that have struggled with drugs over the years. They did not have this instantaneous release from the grip of drugs when they invited Jesus into their lives that I did. I do not know why or how this happened to me, I only praise God for it.

All of a sudden I went from the darkness of drugs and alcohol into the light of Jesus the Christ. It was night turned to day in my life. Jesus was living inside me and he started making some changes. Things that I was comfortable with before, I found I could no longer do. Over the years I had become a pretty good liar and I was not what you would call impeccably honest. I did whatever I had to do to take care of me. Now I found that I couldn't lie or steal without feeling really convicted.

Shortly after my conversion experience the Lord tested me. I went to the drive-in window at the bank and the woman who waited on me gave me too much money. I drove off thinking how lucky I was. My old self was exulting that I had taken the bank. They didn't need the money so why not keep it. My new Christ presence was telling me that God wanted me to be honest and tell the truth no matter what. Finally, I turned around and went back to the window. I explained to the woman that she had given me more money than she should have. She looked around to see if anyone was listening and said, "Thank you. If I would have had one more mistake, I would have lost my job". I went home feeling on top of the world. It was great being honest and true and it had its own reward.

I went and told Gail what had happened. She thought I had finally gone over the edge. She had known me as a pre law business major, a hippie philosopher and now a Jesus freak. Though I had taken her through many changes, she still loved me. This truth would later sink in and commit me to her for the rest of my life. She didn't understand this new change in my life but she decided to stay with me in it. I told her I wanted to stop having sex until we were married, kind of a second virginity. Now she knew that I had really flipped out. Though she thought it sounded nuts, she decided to go along. I wanted our relationship to become something that God could approve of and bless.

The next thing I did was to go to my old drug friends. I told them that I had invited Jesus Christ into my life and I didn't want to use drugs anymore. They laughed out loud. Now if I had told them that I had become a Buddhist, a Hindu or I was following the Maharishi, they would have thought that was really cool. But a Christian, they could not accept that. Only two of them remained my friends and accepted me for who I had become. I discovered they were my real friends. The others just associated with me as long as I was into drugs as they were. I discovered something about friends that day. True friends are those who accept you for who you are and do not try to force you into being anyone else.

I sensed I was beginning to love, really love for the first time. I was starting to think of others and not just myself. That was a totally new experience for me. The presence of Christ in my life, the Holy Spirit some called him, was turning me inside out and making me into a brand new person.

I didn't know any other Christians except Gail's mom. I told her what had happened to me and she went crazy with excitement. She just knew that God had answered the prayers of the group that was praying for me to find new direction in my life. It was a miracle. I would have to agree with her. When women pray, things happen.

One night I had a group of biker friends over to the chicken coop. I went for a walk while they were all doing drugs. When I returned I found them looking through my Bible and laughing their heads off. I just couldn't take it. I went down by the lake, stood on the dock, looked up into the starry sky and asked God to send me some Christians. I had to have some Christians to talk to.

The next day at the UW, I ran into a girl from high school I had a crush on that had been attending with me for three years yet I had never seen her there before. As we talked she began to tell me about how she had become a Christian. She was witnessing to me. I told her that I also had become a Christian. She invited me to some meetings she was attending at the Seattle Center that week. I called Gail and asked her if she minded if I went. She wasn't thrilled about another woman from my past but she relented and said yes.

We went to the Center with her parents who were attending too. It was Bill Gothard doing the Basic Youth Conflicts Seminar. There was an expensive cover charge for the conference and I did not have a ticket. I went to the doorman and told him that the Lord had sent me and I didn't have a ticket. He handed me a ticket and said, "Well here it is. I have been waiting for you". I walked in and sat down with Linda and her family. There must have been 15,000 people sitting all around me and learning how to live for Christ. All of a sudden I heard the voice of God inside, "Is this enough Christians?" I couldn't believe it. There really was something to prayer. God was awesome. That night I made a commitment to read the Bible for five minutes a day. It is a commitment that has taken me through the Bible many times.

I couldn't get enough of the Bible. I just devoured it. It was my lifeline to reality and truth. God was really speaking to me. My life was beginning to line up according to it. It was like God's love letter to me, or his owner's manual for how my life was to operate. As I obeyed his words, my life was blessed and I felt close to Him. When I ignored it, my life went sour and I felt far away from God. I have found this to be true to this day.

One day I was over at my parent's home when I ran into their Episcopal Priest, Father Jack. He was young and hip and I could relate to him. I sensed that God wanted me to talk to him so I called and made an appointment. I went over to the study in his house and told him what had happened to me. He told me that I had become born again or saved and now had the Holy Spirit inside. He said there was much more. He called it the baptism in the Holy Spirit. He gave me some books to read. They were The Cross and the Switchblade by David Wilkerson and They Speak with Other Tongues by John Sherrill. They were the first Christian books I ever read. Fr. Jack told me to read the books and get back to him.

I couldn't put them down. As I read about the work of the Holy Spirit in these people's lives, my heart burned within me. One day I was at the Student Union Building on the UW campus. I was reading They Speak with Other Tongues. Out of nowhere this attractive hippie looking girl asked me if I believed what I was reading. I said that I didn't know. She went on to tell me about a conference on the Holy Spirit that was going on at her Church, Calvary Chapel, in Seattle. She invited me to come. I went over to Gail's and asked her to come with me. She agreed and when we arrived at this huge church it was packed. The only seating left was in an overflow area with the sound piped in. We sat there for a while but I knew we had to get into the main sanctuary. I grabbed Gail's hand and headed in. The only seats left were up by where all the speakers were. There were two seats on the end. We went up and sat down.

The place was full of over a thousand people. The speakers were leaders from every major Protestant and Catholic denomination. They were all giving testimony to an experience they called the baptism in the Holy Spirit. It was the same experience the books I was reading talked about. Interspersed with the testimonies was praise to God like I had never experienced. People were standing and lifting their hands in the air with their eyes closed worshipping God with all their beings, some in languages I did not understand. Also, there were people speaking for God in the first person in English telling us that Jesus was coming back soon and we needed to all be ready. They called this prophecy. The presence of God in the room was overwhelming and electric.

Suddenly everyone stood and began to praise God together. Gail and I were seated gripping our armrests. I heard a voice deep down inside telling me to stand up and praise God. I resisted wondering what Gail would think if I did stand and raise my hands to God. Later she told me that she was worried who in the room recognized her. I could stand the urge no longer and I leaped to my feet, raised my hands and joined the chorus of voices offering verbal praise to God. That is the last thing I remember. The next thing I knew I was outside in front of the church with Gail. I felt like I was drunk and I didn't think I could drive home. Gail drove me back to my parents. I had this sense of absolutely no fear of anything. My whole being was filled with the most wonderful sensation of God that was beyond description. It was the highest high I was ever on and I had taken nothing. As I lay in bed I began to hear this beautiful language praying inside me. It just went on and on. Months and years later I would read in the book of Acts that when the followers of Jesus were baptized in the Holy Spirit on the day of Pentecost, many thought they were drunk. Also, they began to speak in languages they never learned. I had this experience and had never read those passages. I also read that perfect love casts out fear. The disciples also went out after that with new boldness and converted the Roman Empire to Christianity in less than 300 years.

When I awoke the next morning I was still as high as the night before though the language had stopped. I soon discovered that my faith had doubled

43

and all I wanted to do was read the Bible and praise God. I had a fire for the word of God that was unquenchable. I just burned it up reading through the whole New Testament in no time at all. I would go out into the woods by our house with my guitar and sing the Psalms in the Old Testament to God in tunes I would make up.

I went back to Fr. Jack and he sent me to a retreat on the Holy Spirit up in the Cascade Mountains. There was a Jesus blue grass band there by the name of 'The Heavenly Hills Brothers'. They were all former hippies who had been deep in the drug world and had come out through faith in Jesus Christ. They now lived in a Christian commune in Eastern Washington. The teacher for the weekend had a ministry in healing. He taught on the baptism in the Holy Spirit and the gifts of the Spirit. It was all new to me. They were praying for people to receive the baptism in the Holy Spirit by gathering around them, laying their hands on the individuals and praying, some in their new prayer language they claimed the Spirit had given them. Others called this 'speaking in tongues'. Eventually I went to be prayed for. They laid their hands on me and began to pray. They prayed for a long time. After awhile they asked me if I had experienced anything. I asked them what I should expect. What they described was the experience that I had that evening at Calvary Chapel. I was convinced that God had baptized me in his Holy Spirit in a sovereign move of his grace; in the same way he had brought me to faith in his son, just he and I with no intermediaries.

I came off that mountain on fire for the Lord. I tried sharing all this with Gail but she was not in the same place. Her mother was however. Shirley had a life changing experience with the Holy Spirit very similar to mine. We began to talk constantly about our faith. She was my first real Christian friend. I went through the motions of sharing the <u>Four Spiritual Laws</u> with Gail. She even prayed the prayer to receive Christ, similar to how I did that night in the fraternity. To her credit, she wanted to connect with what I was experiencing but her heart was just not into it. She still wanted to be involved in the party scene that I couldn't stand any longer. I would go with her and not participate. All I wanted to do was attend praise meetings and worship God. I don't know how we survived those days but we did.

Being a brand new Christian, I wanted to tell everyone what wonderful joy I was experiencing in Christ. Fortunately, I picked my dad to talk to first. I began by asking his forgiveness for all the times that I had hurt him. He asked me to forgive him also. We both shed tears and embraced. It was a special moment and a great healing. Later, I was helping him do some yard work digging a ditch for drainage on a Saturday. All day long I told him about my experience and asking Jesus into my life. He lovingly listened and put up with my constant jabbering about the Lord. If you are going to be obnoxious about your new faith, it is best to do it with people who already love you.

One night I was over at my folks and visited a vacant lot with Jasper that I used to go to before I met the Lord. The lot overlooked Lake Sammamish. It was a beautiful starry moonlit night and the presence of God was very real. As I prayed, I asked God what I should do about Gail. In those days it seemed I could hear God's still small voice within very clearly. He said to my heart, "Will you ever find another girl that will love you like she does? She loved you as a pre law business major, frat rat rush chairman, philosopher, hippie and now a Jesus freak. She loves you Doug, not any of the trips you are on at the moment. Will you

45

ever find another girl like that?" I said, "No Lord." Then he said, "Why don't you marry her and do it on August 28th." Picking a date had always been a problem for me but here God was giving the very day to me.

I jumped into my 57 Chevy and headed over to Gail's. Like me, she had moved home for a short time. I ran into her house and told her to sit down; I had something important to ask her. I said, "Gail, will you marry me on August 28th?" She gave me that look like I had gone over the edge again. After a pause, she said, "Yes." We went into the kitchen where her mom had her social calendar. Shirley was into everything in the community of Olympic Manor in Ballard. Every day on that calendar for months was filled, and it was only June, except one day, you guessed it, August 28th. It was also a Saturday.

We began to make plans for an August outdoors Seattle wedding in Gail's beautiful back yard in Olympic Manor. There was still a lot of hippie counter-culture philosophy in me and we decided to have it outside, no tuxes or wedding gowns, no formal invitations, sandals with flowers in Gail's hair. It was to be just a good old informal summer party. All invitations would be by word of mouth. Shirley secretly didn't listen to me and did an invitation anyway. Kentucky Fried Chicken, where Gail used to work, would cater it and we would get a keg of beer. I asked the 'Heavenly Hills Brothers' if they would come from Yakima and play for us and they agreed. I went to Fr. Jack and asked him if he would officiate. He agreed if we would go through premarital counseling, something we were glad to do. Gail and I had not had sex since the night of my conversion that spring. Though it was hard, and we came close to not making it, we lasted until our wedding night. I have counseled many couples to do this over the years and some have taken me up on it, to their delight.

That summer I worked as a roofer for the son of the woman who owned the chicken coop. I traded my 57 Chevy in for a light blue panel truck. I completely rebuilt the engine, put in a new transmission, installed Ford Galaxy bucket seats in front, wood paneled the back, laid carpet and used a tapestry for the headliner. It was really cool. We designed it to travel and camp. It had a fold down table and Gail's granddad let me use a camping bed with box springs that he had. On the back I painted in black a fist with forefinger raised to heaven, the sign of the Jesus people of those days, and the words "Truth Is Love". Our plan was to drive to Alaska for our honeymoon. I wanted Gail to see that wild and wonderful country. We even planned to take Jasper. In fact, we started toying with the idea of raising a dog team.

Finally the day came, August 28, 1971. I got up that morning at my mom and dad's the happiest man in the world. It was a beautiful day in Seattle with not a cloud in the sky. I wore a light blue flowered shirt, white jeans and sandals. Gail wore a beautiful long light blue dress with flowers she had made, sandals and a garland of flowers in her hair. She was radiant and looked gorgeous. All our families were there and many friends. Some were dressed formally and some informal. My old friend Steve from Yakima was my best man. Kathy was very pregnant with their first child. Gail's older sister Joan stood up for her. Gail's dad gave her away. Fr. Jack wore all his vestments and did a traditional Episcopalian wedding service. It was a real blending of old and new, traditional and contemporary. I was so full of the joy of the Holy Spirit I thought I would float away. It was truly one of the happiest days of my life. Right when Fr. Jack asked if anyone objected to this union, Jasper barked as if on cue. Everyone laughed. Gail and I used the friendship rings we were wearing as our wedding rings. Inside hers I inscribed 'We Are One' and in mine she wrote 'God Bless Love'. After the ceremony every one ate, drank, visited, enjoyed the beautiful day and listened to the unique blue grass Christian music of the 'Heavenly Hills Brothers' who showed up in a big truck at the last minute.

That evening Gail and I visited my folk's home at Tam O' Shanter by Lake Sammamish and a party they were hosting for family and friends. Dad bought us a night at the north Seattle Ramada Inn. Steve and Kathy came over to the motel and we had some Cold Duck, our favorite drink at the time. We drank a toast out of some engraved silver wineglasses that Joan and Joe had given us. That was the only drink I had all day as I had quit drinking on my 21st birthday in June. I always had everything backwards. Gail made up for both of us however.

We got up early the next morning with the panel truck packed to the gills. Gail, Jasper and I headed north to Alaska. We took the Canadian Yellowhead Figure Eight Highway up to Jasper and across to Dawson Creek. The scenery was unbelievable. Each night we would stop and camp for the night in some campground. We also picked up hitchhikers as it was very safe, popular, and the 'in' thing to do in those days. One hitchhiker traveled with us for several days.

One hundred miles above Dawson Creek the Al-Can (Alaskan Canadian) highway begins. Then it was a gravel road thousands of miles long through majestic mountains and forests with very few places to stop and get gas or food. It is also a very dangerous road as big trucks travel it at top speeds constantly. We were no more than a day onto that highway when the fall rains began to pour, and pour they did, in buckets. The rain came down in great sheets and that, combined with the wild driving truckers, made the journey very difficult.

At one point I needed a break so I pulled off the road onto a broad shoulder. What I didn't realize was that shoulder was pure mud. We got stuck right up to the bottom of the doors. I opened the door and my great white husky leaped out into the mud right up to his neck. I couldn't believe the mess we were in with no one around for miles. I went to the side of the road and tried to flag down a passing trucker to take me to the nearest service station for help. I had long hair and not one of them would stop. In those days truckers were shorthaired red necks. Today many have long hair, how things change in time. I looked up into the sky and prayed with all my heart, "Lord, please send us some help." I hated the thought of leaving my beautiful new bride in that mess with Jasper while I went to get help.

The next thing I knew, here came a couple driving a four-wheel drive vehicle with a big winch in front. They were from Alaska and prepared for anything. This couple was in the middle of a huge fight. The man rolled down his window and asked me what was wrong. As I tried to explain, he kept fighting with the woman. Finally he told me that if I would take the end of his winch down to my van in the mud, he would pull me out. I agreed and got it hooked up. As he and his companion continued their heated dialogue, they pulled us out of the mud onto the road and then they promptly left. I was saying, "Thank you Jesus", all over the place. I looked at Gail and said, "This is no way to spend a honeymoon". We drove back to Dawson Creek that night and got a motel. All three of us stood in the shower for hours trying to get rid of that mud.

We finished our honeymoon driving around the Olympic Peninsula to my Grandma Chubby's resort in Grayland. Soon it was time to go back to the real world. I had gone from the depths of darkness to the heights of the light, all in the space of a few short months.

4
Newlyweds

We moved into a little house Gail's dad found for us in the Fremont District of Seattle almost under the Aurora Bridge. The house rented for $60 dollars a month. It heated, cooked and made hot water all by wood. We were still into the 'back to nature' hippie philosophy of the time. The electrical system was 15 amps. We could not run the refrigerator and anything else that heated up without blowing the fuses. I borrowed Gail's grandpa's trailer to lay up wood for the winter and made many trips with the panel truck.

During these days I was trying to find someplace to have Christian fellowship. I didn't trust churches yet. Fr. Jack told me about a group of young men my age that were meeting from St. Luke's Episcopal Church in Ballard. This church was one of the leaders in the whole movement of the Holy Spirit that was becoming known as the Charismatic Renewal. Fr. Dennis Bennett was their rector and was becoming famous for a book he wrote about his baptism in the Holy Spirit called 'Nine O'clock in the Morning'. I started attending this group of young men. They would gather together and pray in the new languages that the Holy Spirit had given them. They called it their prayer language. Though I had an experience with this language the night I was baptized in the Holy Spirit, I had never audibly vocalized it. One night I shared this and they all laid hands on me and prayed that I would have a release in my prayer language. That night I began to pray in a language I had never learned. I read later that Paul talked about this language in his New

Testament book of Corinthians. Though I have had some spells when I doubted its validity, I have been praying in this language from God in my devotional life and ministry ever since and found it to be very meaningful.

We were not attending any formal Christian group at this time and I ran into one at the UW. It was made up of mostly students who were excited about their new faith. They followed the teachings of a man called Witness Lee from China. He believed that there was just one church in every locality. The group met on campus and had a strange way of studying the Bible. They would take a phrase of scripture and say it over and over together using different intonations each time. I went to a few meetings and even attended their building off campus one night with Gail.

There was also another prominent Christian figure at the UW. He was known all over campus as 'Holy Hubert'. Hubert came from Berkley and traveled up and down the coast preaching in the open air on college campuses. He was very unbecoming with with hair and missing teeth. For years I had heard and seen him and joined in with my fellow students in making fun of him. None of this fazed Hubert however and he would take on any heckler with a good deal of success. It was always good entertainment to watch 'Holy Hubert' in action. He drew huge crowds.

After I became a Christian I started listening to Hubert with new ears. It was at one of his gatherings that I met Linda who took me to the Basic Youth Conflict's Seminar. Hubert was right on and had so much confidence and boldness; no fear would be the best way to describe him. He claimed to be an apostle. I learned later that the Black Panthers at Berkley used to beat him up and he would just look at them and tell them he loved them. Eventually, the Panthers started protecting Hubert because of his love for them.

I had been praying for God to guide me in getting the right Christian fellowship. I needed it but didn't know where to turn and I was afraid of organized religion. One day I was attending a Witness Lee Bible study on campus when Hubert walked in. He began to challenge everyone in the room on their beliefs. Suddenly he looked right at me and said, "You are not one of these people are you?" I said, "No." He said, "Come with me", and I walked out the door with him. We spent the rest of the day together. He talked to me about many things. I believe God sent him that day to get me out of that group. I later learned that they had many beliefs that ran counter to mainline orthodox Christian theology. It seemed that God was taking me by the hand and leading me. I read in the New Testament that Jesus is the good shepherd who leaves the ninety-nine sheep to find the one who is lost. When he finds that lost sheep, he picks them up and puts them on his shoulders. For months I traveled on Jesus' shoulders as a new Christian. Eventually he took me back to the main flock and put me down in the midst of the others. Those first few months I will never forget. He showed me the way and used Hubert to do it. I believe Hubert might have been an apostle. Years later I ran into a book about Hubert's ministry.

There was a lot of crime in the Fremont District. It was known at that time as a drug center. It seemed like every other night the burglar alarm would go off in the businesses below us. One night we heard a woman screaming for help outside on our street. I grabbed an old baseball bat I had and headed out to the front door. Gail thought I had my shotgun and tried to stop me. When I got outside I heard a car door slam and the screaming stopped. Gail got very sick with a cold, fever and flu. It was just freezing in the morning in that house until you got the fire started in the stove. I decided I had enough and starting looking for a new place to live outside of Seattle.

I found a new place for us outside the city in Lynwood in an area known as Cherry Hill. It was a neat little house with an electric stove and oil heat. It sat right in the middle of an acre of wooded fir trees. We moved in on Christmas day. It was like living in a forest. I can still hear the wind blowing in those trees at night. It was awesome. We loved the place. One of the previous tenants had a horse and had made a big corral on the property. I closed it in for Jasper. We decided to buy a female Samoyed for him and to raise sled dogs. We named her Jennifer and she was as cute as could be. We tried to keep them both outside in the corral during the day while we were at work and school.

One very cold rainy day I came home and could not find the dogs. I heard some barking and looked over at my neighbors beautiful two story house. He was the head seismologist for the UW. Our dogs had dug under the fence between the houses. The neighbors had a doggy door for their two big dogs. You guessed it. Jasper and Jennifer were up in the picture window, covered with mud, hanging over my neighbor's couch and barking at me. They were having a ball. I was mortified and prayed the neighbors wouldn't come home before I got those dogs out of the house. Jasper was one of the smartest dogs I ever knew. He kept jumping out of the corral and I kept making it higher. At one point it was about seven feet high. One afternoon I saw another neighbor's huge dog walking by our house. Jasper saw him too. He loved to protect his turf and would attack a dog of any size with no fear. I watched in horror as he jumped up seven feet, hooked his front feet over the fence and pushed his back legs off the fence flipping him over to the other side. In an instant he was tearing that other dog apart.

Gail was still very much into our old party life style during those days. We went to a New Year's Eve party at one of her friend's house where there were lots of alcohol and drugs. I was very uncomfortable and quiet during the night. I didn't want to take any mood altering substances into my being. I was content to be high on the Lord. Gail however wanted to be with her friends and get high and party. I was vexed in my spirit. How were we going to make it when we were attracted to different worlds?

That winter it snowed very hard. One time Gail and I were snowed in. It was wonderful to skip work and school. We felt like we were in an Alaskan hideaway. We hooked up Jasper to the sled one moonlit night and had him pull us all over Cherry Hill. That was as close as we came to a sled team and one of the best memories I have of our first year of marriage.

I wanted to quit the UW that year and go to a Christian school at Seattle Pacific College. My professors at the UW were mostly Marxists. I tried everything to get away from their godless teaching. One quarter I took the class Philosophy of Aesthetics. I thought surely this is a class where I could get away from Marxism. The professor had been thrown out of the University of Warsaw for his Marxist teachings. He was teaching Marxist aesthetics and tried to tell us that the art of the ages represented man's alienation. I wrote him a paper saying that I agreed with his premise but I felt the alienation was caused by man's separation from God. He gave me the first and last 'D' I would ever receive. I wanted to quit on the spot and go to the Christian college. My dad was still helping me pay for tuition. He told me he would quit paying and Gail told me she would be very upset with me if I did quit the UW. They teamed up on me and I relented but I was grieved in my spirit in that department every day until I graduated.

As we got closer to graduation, I kept getting letters in the mail from the armed forces encouraging me to come down and join. I had been in the first draft in 1969 for the Vietnam War. It was a lottery by birthday. My number was 60 and that was very low. Everyone in college received a deferment until they graduated, then they went back into the draft with the number they held. The summer I graduated they were up into the 200's. I started getting letters saying they had seen my name on the list and to come down for an interview. I had three choices: run to Canada, try to flunk the medical exam, or go into the military. Many of my friends did the first two. I went to the Lord in prayer.

One of the things Basic Youth Conflicts taught was that God would guide us through the counsel of our parents. My dad was a WWII Navy veteran who was on the invasion of Okinawa in the Pacific. Gail's dad was also on that invasion as an Army machine gunner. One day I went over to my parents in Bellevue with Gail. I had prayed that God would guide me in the decision about the military through my dad. I asked my dad what I should do about the military. He told me he could not answer that for me. I told him I was not going home until he did. We stayed all afternoon. Suddenly, dad turned to me with a strange look on his face. He said, "Go into the military and get it over with." I said, "Thanks dad", grabbed Gail and headed home. As I prayed to God for additional wisdom on the military decision, I heard him say to my heart that I served in his Army wherever I was and whatever I did.

The next day I began to explore the military options. If I went in, I wanted to go Navy because I loved the ocean and that was where my dad had served. I also wanted to become an officer. I found the Navy officer recruiter and took the test for Officer Candidate School (OCS). I was a philosophy major and scored low on the math and science. They told me to come back in six months. I didn't have six months. I could be a grunt in the jungles of Vietnams with an M-16 by then. I looked at the Army program and scored high enough to become an Army artillery officer but I would have to commit to at least five years after the six months of Army OCS. I didn't want to give the military that much of my life. I also learned that Army artillery officers did not last long in Vietnam. I wanted to meet my military obligation and get more education through the full GI Bill. The Navy offered a two-year enlisted program with full GI Bill and a guaranteed service 'A' school.

My father-in-law was an electrical contractor who had his own business and no sons. He told me that if I would become an electrician he would give me a job when I got done which could later turn to ownership of the business. All three of my father's offered me a career and I eventually chose the one that had the best retirement plan.

I went with the Navy enlisted program and got a guaranteed Electrician's Mate 'A' School. I would have to go to boot camp and 'A' school in San Diego, about six months total, and then serve two years after that plus reserve drills, with full GI Bill. It sounded like a good deal all around. I enlisted in May of 1972 at the old Lake Union Navy Reserve Center for a July 4 boot camp. Gail would stay in Lynwood until I finished my training. We were soon to experience our first separation of many from Uncle Sam.

5
Enlisted Man

June 10, 1972 I graduated from the University of Washington with a Bachelor of Arts in philosophy. It was a college degree. I remember my family and Gail's family at the commencement cheering me on. I was the first in my family to graduate from college. The governor was our speaker that day. Within days I was on my way to San Diego. I never let the grass grow long under my feet.

On the plane ride down, I noticed a young man get on the plane in San Francisco who looked like me, long hair, and had a similar big manila envelope under his arms. When we got off the plane and were picked up by the white Navy bus that took us to the Naval Training Center (NTC), I saw him get on too. We wound up sleeping in the same barracks room that night. At about 4 AM the next morning some chief came through the place banging on a garbage can telling us that everything the recruiter told us was a lie. So began my eight weeks of boot camp.

Reed was the name of the young man I had traveled with. He was a senior from UC Berkley and was a Christian like me. We became instant friends. I was the oldest in the company at 22 and was the only one married and who had a college degree. They called me grandpa. The chief hated me because of my education and would get me in the back of the company and hit me in the stomach daring me to do something about it. I think he was demon possessed. He was also an alcoholic. The only time we could ever get away from him was to go to church on Sunday morning. Almost everyone did. One Sunday he wouldn't let us

59

go and made us run in place with our rifles over our head. He wanted us to all say, "Praise the devil" as we ran. I refused. They also made us put everything we came with in a box and send it home. They tried to make me take off my wedding ring and send it too. I refused. They started putting unbelievable pressure on me to take off that ring. I told them they could kill me and I still wouldn't take it off. Eventually they gave up. Today they could never get away with those abuses but it was rampant then.

I always got the highest scores on all the academic tests and became the Honor Man of the company. Reed was also honored. There were many young men there who were very scared. Reed and I started a Bible study that met at night in secret. That was the only free time we had. We took several of the young men under our wing and helped them through, pointing them to the Lord for strength.

Eventually graduation day came. It was a very proud day. None of my family was present but I marched proudly in my stiff sparkling whites and leggings in formation. Those days were very hard but they taught me to be proud of my flag, my country and the armed forces. The sadistic chief even cried as we left.

Gail had somehow conned her mom into driving her down for our first anniversary and to set up house in San Diego for my 'A' school. I couldn't stand to be without her. I was so lonely. She quit her job, gave Jasper and Jennifer away, sold the panel truck, put our household goods in her parent's basement and joined me in San Diego. My cousin Dick, he likes to be called Richard now, was also in San Diego on the carrier USS Constellation. I had no civilian clothes. He picked me up and took me home giving me some of his clothes to wear. We went all over San Diego looking for apartments that Gail and I could afford. Finally we went to meet Gail and her mom at a gas station. I couldn't wait. My head had been shaved and my face was sunburned except for a strip on my forehead where my ball cap sat. I looked pathetic, especially in Dick's clothes that hung on me. When I walked up to Gail, she could not even recognize me. Later she confessed that she was not sure she even wanted a husband who looked like that.

We celebrated our first anniversary and moved into our new little furnished apartment across the street from a Greek Orthodox Church and down the street from a strip club in North Park. Our managers were Christians and the couple next door was a Navy officer and his new wife. We loved it. There was also another married man who lived below us. He had come late to my boot camp company. His name was Eric and he was an African American who had been a Marine in Vietnam. He went home from the war and got in trouble with the law. The courts made him come back into the military. He decided to go Navy and wound up in my company. He bonded to me because I was married and he looked all over town for the apartment I had rented. He rented the unit under ours and moved his wife Willy Mae out. It was quite a little community.

I started 'A' school and learned about marine electricity. Gail stayed home and kept the apartment. One of her friends, Marilee, came down and stayed with us for a while. Eric would throw big parties and invite us all over. We were the only Caucasians there. It was a cultural learning experience.

I was just a Fireman Apprentice or FA (E-2), second from the bottom. They gave me one rank for my college degree. Gail would have some of my closest friends over who were single and now going to school. One of my duties was to usher at the base theater. On those nights Gail would come down and help me. The base theaters then had big comfortable lodge seats for the officers and their families. Gail and I would look at those seats and wish that we could sit there.

Gail had a Methodist background and the apartment managers were Methodist so we started attending their church. One afternoon Gail got a call from her dad. Her mother was diagnosed with cancer again. This time they thought it had spread. Gail was devastated. I remember taking her down to the beach, walking and crying. She decided to fly home and nurse her mother through her chemotherapy. I spent the last two months of school alone in the apartment.

Just before graduation Gail surprised me and flew down to drive our 1966 yellow Mustang back with me to the Pacific Northwest for Christmas while I was awaiting orders. We drove to Disneyland first. I had never been there. It was a night with low attendance and we just flew around the park going on every ride. We stopped in San Leandro near San Francisco and spent a night with Reed and his family touring the city. The next day we drove for twelve hours straight to Seattle. We arrived on Christmas Eve and stayed at Gail's house. Gail's mom was very sick and getting weaker and thinner every day. She had lost all her hair and was bed ridden.

Cancer is a terrible disease. Gail continued to care for her mother. One night Shirley told me to lead and Gail would follow, especially in spiritual things. She began to tell us about visions she was having. Gail would stay by her side at night and fall asleep. Shirley would wake her up suddenly and say things like, "Don't forget to tell Doug what I am about to tell you." These visions were of a river that she was to cross and loved ones now deceased on the other side calling her over. On several occasions she almost went but she came back to us because it was not her time. I remember her telling me, "I am ready to die and I am ready to be healed". Gail's mom taught me how to face death with courage and faith. She was glad that she had met two of her daughter's spouses but regretted not meeting her grandchildren. She would tell Gail and me that she regretted not seeing our first dark haired child. As it turned out years later, our first daughter had very dark hair. We prayed so hard for Shirley to be healed, as did all her Christian friends who were always coming over. I could not understand why the Lord did not heal her.

Shirley lasted past Christmas and New Year's. We tried the best we could to celebrate her 50th birthday. On January 7th Gail and I had gone to visit our old neighbors out in Lynwood. It was a typical cold snowy Pacific Northwest day. We came home and Gail was helping her mother into the bathroom. She died in Gail's arms. I called 911. As I stood outside on the porch listening to the approaching sirens, I heard that still small voice of the Lord speaking to me. He said, "Raise your hands up to heaven and worship me". With tears streaming down my face I began to praise him in that beautiful new language he had given me. A peace and calm that cannot be understood flooded my soul.

The church funeral service was very hard. Memories of Corey's mom came flooding back to me.

I recall singing Shirley's favorite hymn, "How Great Thou Art", with heavy tears streaming down my face. I wore my Navy blues in her honor. Gail was a mess as was all the rest of her family. I had never seen her this distraught. On top of everything else, I had to report soon to Treasure Island (TI) near San Francisco to receive my new orders for twenty-four months of active duty.

It was so hard to leave Gail and go to TI. While Shirley was still alive I had put in for a hardship location to be closer to Gail while she cared for her mom. I checked into the barracks at TI and began to wait. We would stand the duty at midnight under the Oakland Bay Bridge in the cold fog at a guard shack by the Admiral's house. I would do jumping jacks and pushups just to stay warm and awake. It was awful. Every day and night I would be talking with young men who would get their orders to Vietnam, go over to Travis Air Force Base and the next day they were in Vietnam. I did not want to go to Vietnam and I was scared. I missed Gail and wanted to be with her in her grief.

One night I just surrendered to God and told him I would do whatever he wanted. I was in his army and if he wanted me in Vietnam, I would go. The next morning my orders were in. As I slowly unfolded them, I was afraid to read what they said. Slowly I read the words USS Brinkley Bass DD-887, a destroyer. I was sure they were in Vietnam. I walked over to the chief and asked him to look up for me where this ship was. He just started laughing at me. He said, "Son, that ship is welded to the pier. It doesn't go anywhere. It is a reserve training ship in Tacoma, Washington." I ran to the phone to tell Gail. We couldn't believe it, two years in Tacoma, Washington. Once again the Lord had heard our prayers and kept us together. He used Gail's mother's illness to do it. That was one of the few good things that came out of Shirley's lost battle with cancer.

I flew home and we began to look for apartments in Tacoma, just thirty miles south of Seattle. We looked everywhere and finally found a small duplex in Lakewood by McCord Air Force Base on Meadow Road. We accepted the place and went back to Seattle for the night. All of a sudden, Gail wanted to back out. She thought we had made a mistake. I called the landlord and she was not happy. She was going to make us pay a month of rent anyway. We finally decided to try it.

Once we moved in, we liked it. One Sunday we drove around the block and there was a big church out on Steilacoom Boulevard. It was called Lakewood United Methodist Church. Since Gail was Methodist, we started attending. The pastor was a middle-aged man named Don. He was from Texas and had been a geological physicist for Shell Oil on the oil fields. Don had become an alcoholic and his wife and three daughters had left him. One night as he knelt in despair in his bedroom, the resurrected Jesus of Nazareth had personally come to him and called him to the ordained ministry. He went back to seminary, was ordained and got his family back. He had pastored one church previous to Lakewood in Eastern Washington.

Don was a man's man and had played football in college at Baylor. He dressed casual and preached practical down to earth sermons. He had also experienced the baptism in the Holy Spirit. When I told him my story we became instant friends. The church was close to two military installations and was full of young military families. We fit right in. They had a young married couples group called 'Roaring Twenties'. We started attending and became close friends with some dynamic young Christian couples. Many of the husbands were Air Force pilots. They took Gail and me in and began to disciple us. We learned about the importance of worship, fellowship, tithing, Bible study and witnessing. This church was on fire. It was just what we needed.

Gail's attitude towards spiritual things had drastically changed after her mother's death. She became very interested in the faith of her mom. That was one other good thing that came from Shirley's death. One night we went with some Christian friends from my new ship to a meeting where a missionary from Africa was speaking. He told some marvelous stories of the power of God while ministering in Africa. At the end of his presentation, he asked people to raise their hands if they wanted to accept Christ into their lives. I looked over and Gail had her hand up. She stood and prayed to receive Christ. I couldn't believe it. After all this time she really had committed herself to Jesus. I was overjoyed. Now maybe we could really fellowship together as one in Christ. To this day Gail does not remember that night, but I do. It was a turning point for us as a couple. Her mother's advice was right.

I bought Gail a little black Cocker Spaniel for her 22nd birthday. We named her Bridgette. I thought the dog could keep Gail company while I was gone on the ship. Gail also got a good job as a bookkeeper at the Tacoma Mary Bridge Children's Hospital.

The ship was different. It had a permanent crew of about two hundred. The rest of the crew was made up of the reserves that would come aboard for the weekends. When I first reported, the ship was gone on a trip. I checked into the local reserve center on the same site. They had me doing nothing and I was bored. I wanted to be a productive Christian and do my best at whatever I did. I asked my supervisor if there was anything I could do. He told me the only thing he could think of was to clean the venetian blinds. I went to every room in that two-story building over the space of the next two weeks and cleaned every venetian blind.

Finally, the ship came back. I reported aboard to R Division in the Engineering Department. I was an Electrician's Mate Fireman or EMFN (E-3) by then. My Division Officer invited me to his stateroom. He said, "Waite, I see you have a college degree. How would you like to be my secretary?" I said, "Sir, if I had wanted to be a secretary I would have become a yeoman." He said, "Fine." The next day I was doing ninety days mess cooking. Mess cooking was where all the new sailors washed dishes, cleaned up, threw out the garbage and sometimes helped the cooks. It was long miserable work and hours. I remember working in the scullery where you pressure washed the dishes. It was very hot, humid and we were rocking and rolling somewhere in the Pacific. I was seasick, washing dishes and vomiting into a bucket. It was my birthday. I hated it.

One day the chiefs, senior enlisted, found out I was a college graduate. They got me over to the chief's mess to clean and cook for them. Life there was much better and they had good liberty or time off. I met a Christian while I was mess cooking named George. He was from North Dakota. We would help each other throw out the garbage. Together we noticed that Christians often bowed their heads and prayed before they ate. In that way we found some other believers and started a small Bible study.

Eventually I made it to the Electrical Shop. It was run by a chief and had about four or five other electricians. I loved my job. You had to use your brain. I would put on my tool belt and go anywhere I wanted. If anyone asked me what I was doing I would just say I was tracing a circuit. Sometimes, when I got stumped, I would ask God to show me how to fix the problem. Almost immediately the answer would come. In time, I became known as one of the best electrician's on the ship. Often, when no one could solve the problem, the Commanding Officer (CO) would say, "Has Waite seen this?"

The guys in my shop soon found out I was a Christian. They would invite me to go drinking and womanizing but I was not interested. One day they put Rev. Waite by my coffee cup. Little did they know their joke was a prophecy. Often when I would walk into the space and they were telling a dirty story, they would stop. This bothered me until one day the Lord spoke to my heart and told me that it was not because of me but because of him that they stopped when I came in. He was living inside me and I took him wherever I went. They were embarrassed because of the presence of the Lord when I walked in. After that, it didn't bother me anymore.

I did not preach at them and just tried to live the Christian life in their presence, aiming to be the best electrician I could. The only time they would come to me were when they were really hurting and or drunk. In those times they would seek me out and ask for my advice looking for words of comfort. My guiding verses during those days were from Philippians 4:6-7. It said, "In nothing be anxious, but in everything with prayer and supplication with thanksgiving, let your requests be made known to God. Then the peace of God which passes understanding will keep your hearts and minds through Christ Jesus". I typed this out on my old Underwood typewriter and pasted it on our home kitchen wall and on the bulkhead of my rack where I slept on the ship. Its constant reminder got me through those tough days. As I write this, I am a Navy

Commander sitting in my stateroom on the nuclear aircraft carrier USS Abraham Lincoln CVN-72 speeding to the Persian Gulf on a six-month deployment. Those words are printed on the bulkhead by my rack as they were on my last carrier USS Nimitz CVN-68 during Operation Desert Storm. For over 30 years they were my guiding verses while undergoing hardship and separation at sea.

Probably the toughest guy on the ship was in my shop and my supervisor. He was big, ugly and mean. His name was John or Big John but everyone called him 'Animal' behind his back. The whole ship was afraid of him. One day Animal told me out of the clear blue sky that he wanted to have Jesus in his life. There was a young Hopi Indian electrician mate there too named Lyle and he said, "Yeah, me too!" I took them both out on the fantail and shared the Four Spiritual Laws I had read when I invited Jesus into my life. Both of them asked Jesus to come into their hearts. I was very overjoyed.

Animal was amazing. He started devouring the Bible when he was on watch, just as I was doing. At one point I was memorizing whole chapters including the Sermon on the Mount. I believe this helped heal my mind that was kind of fuzzy due to my drug days. Animal was doing the same thing. He read about how Jesus healed. He had some warts on his feet so he prayed one night that Jesus would take them away. To his amazement and all of ours, they disappeared. Big John was ecstatic. He was so excited he went around and told everyone on the ship what Jesus did. He had such a reputation for being mean and ugly that everyone listened, "Yes Big John, whatever you say." John got out of the Navy after that and the last I heard he was teaching Sunday school in a Baptist Church. John and Lyle taught me that the best way to witness to your faith is not with words but with your life. People have to see Jesus in you first before they will listen to what you say.

We decommissioned the USS Brinkley Bass DD-887 and crossdecked to her sister ship the USS Orleck DD-886. One day on watch in the Engine Room, the Messenger of the Watch came down and told me the Commanding Officer, CO, wanted to see me in his inport cabin. I couldn't believe it. As an Electrician Mate Third Class, EM3, I had never talked to the CO except to say, "Good morning sir". I didn't know he even knew who I was. I thought I might be in some kind of trouble. I reported to his cabin and he told me to sit down. "Petty Officer Waite, tell me how you met Jesus Christ", he said. So I gave him what later I learned was my testimony. He listened quietly to the whole story. When I got done he looked at me and said, "Waite, from now on you do Protestant services at sea. Dismissed." "Aye, aye sir", I said. How did he know? That was another thing I learned, CO's know a lot more than you think about what goes on around their ship.

From that day, on I did the Protestant Sunday services on the ship. My brothers in the Bible study, we only had men in those days, helped me with it. I was also learning how to play the guitar and one of the other Petty Officers named Mark played too. We would hold services in the helo (helicopter) hangar and pack it out. I started thinking about the Navy Chaplain Corps. I really did not like being enlisted. The officers treated us as second-class citizens. I had as much education and was the same age as most of them. They were allowed to teach classes with pay in a college degree program on the ship. I tried to teach a class too. I could certainly use the money. They turned me down because I was enlisted. I decided then and there that the only way I would ever stay in the military was as an officer.

Being enlisted wasn't all hardship. I had some good times too. We went to Hawaii twice. The second time Gail flew out to meet me with my friend Mark's pregnant wife Lynn. They met us on the big island of Hawaii in Hilo. We drove around the island, stayed in Kona and then flew to Oahu to meet the ship. In those days Ft. DeRussy down on Waikiki had a military place to stay for $5 a night with a mess hall or dining facility. It was great. Today a huge military resort hotel complex named Hale Koa, House of the Warrior, stands in its place. We also stayed in some bungalow cabins on the beach at Bellow's Air Force Base. It was the week that President Nixon resigned August 1974. Gail and I had another honeymoon on that trip. I have always encouraged other sailors, regardless of rank, to have their spouses meet them in far away ports whatever the cost. It is one of the benefits of the Navy to see the world and such rendezvous keep your marriage alive during difficult times. I think that is one of the secrets of the success of our marriage, now twenty-nine years as of this writing.

Our ship did not have a chaplain but I had met some at boot camp. Only one or two impressed me. We had one onboard once for two weeks active reserve duty. He just played the piano by himself the whole time. Another reserve chaplain had to be asked by us if he would lead a Bible study. He acted like he didn't know how. We showed him. I told the Navy I would like to be released from my active duty obligation to attend seminary and come back as a chaplain. The Navy agreed and I started to get excited about getting out of the military. I went to Pastor Don at the United Methodist Church and told him what I wanted to do. He took me before the District Board of Ordained

Ministry made up of a group of local United Methodist ministers. They interviewed me and had me wait outside for their summary. Don came out and told me that they had decided they didn't want me to become a chaplain at that time. They wanted me to finish my enlisted obligation and then come back.

I was really deflated. Why did they do that? I had talked the Navy into the whole thing and the church had let me down. Don talked to me and told me that maybe I was putting the cart before the horse. I was trying to go to seminary before I had ever been called to full time Christian ministry. Don asked me, "Have you been called of God to be a pastor?" I honestly could not say yes. Looking back, it was the right decision. God was putting the seeds of full time ministry and chaplaincy in my heart but the time was not right.

I was getting close to the end of my active duty service and a position opened on Don's staff as a youth director, so I applied. I thought that a year doing full time Christian work would let me know if that was where God wanted me. Don met with his Staff Parish Relations Committee and they accepted my application. I began part-time while I was still in the Navy and full time when I got out. The position included moving into the huge old two story church parsonage next door to the church as part of the salary package. I had a talk with my father-in-law who was hoping that I would start as an electrician at his business when I got out. I told him I needed a year to see if this was where God wanted me. He reluctantly agreed. I accepted the position. Gail and I moved into the old parsonage. One of the first things I did was paint it on the outside.

I started having the guys on the ship over on Saturday nights when we were home. At that time the only trips the ship took were to Hawaii in the summer for training reserves during their two-week active duty for training. One night we must have had thirty sailors over with special missionaries, Mom and Pop, who ran the Overseas Servicemen's Center in Australia. Many of the guys remembered them from when the ship came back from Vietnam and stopped in Australia.

At that time we had a guy onboard who was a Satanist. Wherever we would go onboard to study the Bible or pray he would find us and create confusion. We used to say, "The blood of Christ", to him and he would shake and leave. That night he showed up at the house. Mom and Pope were very knowledgeable in the gifts of the Holy Spirit. As soon as Mom saw this young man she said to him, "So how long have you worshipped at the Church of Satan." Mom had the gift of discerning of spirits. He began to talk to her. Later in the evening we were all together listening to testimonies, praying and singing. The presence of God was very powerful and real. As we stood and joined hands to close in prayer, the power of God knocked the young Satanist down to the ground with a loud bang. It was an amazing sight. We thought that Satan had sent him to break up our meeting but that God had gotten to him instead. Suddenly he got up off the floor and ran out the door. We all stood there in awe and praise of the power of God. Some of the sailors accepted Christ that night.

The Christian ministry on the ship grew very powerful. Part of me was sad to leave the fellowship we had there. I still keep in touch with some of the officers and crew from those days. I even attended a USS Orleck reunion a couple of years ago. I was the only person there still on active duty. I sat at a table with sailors from every decade from the 1940's to the 1970's. The ship was later sold to Turkey and was just recently decommissioned. It has now been returned to

Orange, Texas, the city it was commissioned in, to be set up as a museum.

I will never forget the day I was discharged from active duty as an enlisted man in the United States Navy Reserve. It was in January 1975 and was one of the happiest days of my life to that point. It was such a relief to walk away from the military for what I thought was the last time. As it turned out later, I was very mistaken. I was proud that I had served my country but I was ecstatic for it to be over. I never wanted to serve in the military again. I thought this was a chapter in my life that was finished and done with. We never know what plans God has for us. Everything God leads us into is preparation for what is coming. My enlisted time would prepare me perfectly for the career that was coming that I could not see.

6
Fulltime Ministry

I started working part-time at the church. I had junior high, high school and college age groups. I also functioned as the assistant pastor. Finally, I was discharged from Navy active duty January 12, 1975. I said I wanted nothing to do with the Navy ever again. God loves to challenge us on those 'ever' or 'never' statements we make from time to time. He likes to remind us that we are really not the bosses of ourselves anymore. Only he has the right to make decisions like that for us.

Don felt that Gail needed to quit her job and spend time with me while she could. If I were going to go into the ministry, we would have very little time together in the future. She felt like she was being lazy and doing nothing until she got pregnant with our first child. We had been married for almost four years. During that time one of us would want children and the other one wouldn't. Then we would turn around and reverse roles. Finally, we both wanted children. I believe that is one way you know when God wants you to do something, when you and your spouse both have peace about it. In fact, Gail and I have learned that God guides us that way. If one of us does not have peace about a major decision, either it is not what God wants us to do or it is not God's time yet. Eventually, we both wanted children and started trying. It still took us two years to get pregnant.

I threw myself into my work as I do everything I attempt in life. The senior high group was especially difficult. Before Gail and I moved into the old parsonage it had been the senior high youth house.

They had a single male youth director that many of the girls had crushes on. Gail and I took the house over and I was married. Some of the youth resented us. I found out later that when new kids would come to the youth group, these resentful youth would call them and tell them not to come back. It was a tough year. One night I had my fill. I went into the sanctuary and knelt down at the communion rail. I told the Lord I was through and going to quit. When God speaks to me, it has never been audible. It always has come as that still small voice in my heart followed by circumstances and confirmed by others. This was the night he spoke to me in my heart and said, "I want you to serve me full-time in the ministry". God had never said that before. It was the call that Don had been talking to me about.

That summer the senior's of the senior high group that had caused me so much trouble left and the new ninth graders came. It was a whole new ball game. Prior to this, I had brought the junior high group from Dennis Bennett's Ballard St. Luke's Episcopal Church down for a weekend with my junior high youth. By the end of the weekend their youth had prayed with most of mine to receive the baptism in the Holy Spirit. Those kids came alive in the Spirit. They were praying for healing for one another and some even spoke in languages they had never learned. These on fire new ninth graders became the foundation of a brand new senior high group. I also had a dynamic new college age group that was growing as well.

Gail's sister Beth used to stay with us a lot in those days. She was ten when her mom died. Beth was junior high age by the time we went to work for the church. She fit right into our junior high group. She would come down for the weekend and attend all the youth functions we did. She got exposed to the Lord and the Holy Spirit, especially at the retreat with St. Luke's. Those days left a permanent mark on her in two ways. First, she was very close to us then, almost like one of our own children. We are still very close, even though she is grown and married now with children of her own. Second, she developed a deep faith in God that is still with her. She and her husband Steve are very active in their United Methodist church today. All of that started in those days at Lakewood.

Don had me doing other things. I would go out and visit newcomers to the church. He also had me visit and preach in the local nursing home. I would accompany him to the local ministerial meetings and the hospital. He wanted me to experience everything that a pastor does. Don began to tell me I had the gifts to be a pastor. I had never heard that before. I was slated to preach my first sermon on a Sunday a few weeks away. I had some kind of an idea of what I wanted to say.

That Saturday night Don's wife Louise called me. She said he was sick in bed and I was going to have to preach in the morning. I was beside myself. What was I going to do? I stayed up half the night getting that sermon together while Gail went out to dinner with a couple from the church. The next morning I stood up there with what I had put together. I was so nervous I couldn't hold my head up. I preached the sermon and sat down. I was sure it was a flop. Afterward, people came up to me and said I had really spoken to them. They wanted me to preach again. I was amazed. This was the beginning of a lifelong lesson in preaching. God is the one who speaks through us in preaching. It is not us. We must prepare the best we can but the results are supernatural.

After my call from the Lord, I was ready to declare my intentions to pursue the ordained ministry. I was at a Full Gospel Businessmen's meeting and I told one of the leaders there about my call. He said, "But did God call you to be a United Methodist pastor?" I said, "No". He said, "Then don't you do anything until he tells you that specifically." This set me back for a while. While this brother meant well, I think he was sent by the enemy to slow me up.

Awhile later I was at a meeting with David Wilkerson, the evangelist who wrote The Cross and the Switchblade. He was there with the singer Dallas Holm and his band 'Praise'. I had brought the entire junior high group with me. We were there listening when David got to the end of the evening. He gave an altar call and asked people to come forward. I heard the Lord say quietly to my heart, "I want you to go forward and dedicate yourself to serve me in the ministry". I said, "Lord, I can't go forward. I'm the youth director and I have all these kids with me. What will they think?" Well, eventually I gave in and went forward. I looked behind me and the entire youth group had come forward too. David said later that he felt God was calling people into the ministry that night.

I wanted God to come and tell me face to face that he wanted me to be a pastor. One day I was riding my bike and talking to the Lord about this. I heard him say to me in my heart, "Take a look at your life, all of it has been pointing you to ordained ministry in the United Methodist Church." As I reflected on everything that had happened to me, I had to agree. I talked to Don and went forward one Sunday in the service and dedicated myself to serve the Lord in the ordained ministry. Don began by having me meet with the church Staff Parish Relations Committee. Ordination in the United Methodist Church wisely begins in the local church. If they don't endorse you, you can't continue. The people begin the process. They interviewed me and felt that I was genuinely called to be a pastor. Not only that, but they voted to support Gail and I in seminary for $250 a month until I graduated, big money in those days. Don and I couldn't believe it. He and I took this decision to the denominational District Board of Ordained Ministry, the same group that I had seen before. This time they voted to endorse me for ordination.

I applied to Fuller Theological Seminary in Pasadena, California and was accepted. Fuller was a nondenominational but evangelical seminary. Don felt that it was the best seminary in the country. I knew nothing about seminaries and just accepted his opinion. One of our ministerial friends, Sherman, had also gone there and said the same thing. I started getting excited about continued education in Christian Theology. Fuller had an extension in Seattle at University Presbyterian Church. I enrolled that fall quarter and took a class on Genesis. It was wonderful. I couldn't get enough. I was very impressed with the whole concept of scholarship and faith coming together.

Gail was about ready to deliver our first child. She had gotten pregnant just before I got out of the Navy. She had accepted Christ into her life but had not had the experience of the baptism in the Holy Spirit. I did not preach at her but just tried to lead. One night she woke me up from a deep sleep and said, "I need it." I said, "What do you need?" She said, "You know, the baptism in the Holy Spirit". Not long after that the Lakewood Church had a Conference on the Holy Spirit with the rector of St. Luke's Episcopal Church and the author of "Nine O'clock in the Morning", Fr. Dennis

Bennett. Don was really excited about having Dennis at Lakewood. He was known all over the world. He was even listed in the Encyclopedia Britannica as the first 'charismatic'.

Friday night of the Conference the church was electric with the power of God and our anticipation of what was going to happen. At the end of his talk about the baptism of the Holy Spirit, Dennis invited people to come forward for prayer. Over one hundred members of the congregation came forward. To my disappointment, Gail was not one of them. Later we were with our old Navy friends Mark and Lynn out in the parking lot when all of a sudden Gail turned around and went back inside. I followed her and she was up front with all the others. Dennis was praying with each one and laying hands on them. Many were praying in new languages they never learned.

Gail and I went back to the parsonage. We were getting ready to go to bed. I could not wait to find out what happened to her when Dennis prayed for her. I said, "Did you get your prayer language?" She said, "I don't know, I haven't tried it." She walked out of the room. A few minutes later she came back praying in a beautiful language she had never learned. After that Gail and I were on the same page spiritually. She began to grow in her faith like crazy. It was a wonderful thing to be married to a woman that was filled with the Holy Spirit and operating in the spiritual gifts, excited about the Lord. It was also wonderful to have this all happen while Gail was carrying our first baby. I have always felt that something wonderful also happened to that little baby growing in Gail's womb that night like the Holy Spirit did with John and Jesus in the womb.

That September our first child was born, a beautiful little girl with dark eyes and hair like me, just as Shirley saw in her spirit before she died. As we were parking the car at Tacoma General and walking into the hospital about midnight, Gail said to me, "Are you ready to become a father?" It really hit me. As most new parents, we were overcome with the miracle and wonder of the birth of a new human being. Birth is a spiritual experience as well as physical. When a child is born you feel close to God for days. We named her Briana Marie, the feminine of Brian, which means 'strong'. She is very strong and independent. We had her baptized by Don soon after.

The Roaring Twenties laid hands and prayed for me one night at our house for the ordained ministry and our seminary experience. The next day I started the drive in our little Orange Mazda to Fuller Theological Seminary in Pasadena, California. My mission was to check out the campus and find us an apartment. I located a great apartment in a fourplex on Orange Grove Boulevard. The couple next door was also going to Fuller, Barb and Charlie. Charlie was 6' 9" tall. Barb was an outspoken brash New Yorker. They showed me around and offered to look after my car if I left it. She drove me to the airport and I came back to Lakewood excited about what was ahead for us.

We got a U-haul truck and loaded it with everything we had. Gail, the baby and the dog were all in the front seat. As I was pulling out, one of the Air Force pilots that we had grown to love, Bernie, handed us his gas credit card. He said, "Here, put everything on this." I couldn't believe it. God was taking care of us. I truly did not know how we were going to make it financially to Pasadena. When you are doing what God wants, he pays the bills.

After a couple of days traveling on the freeway in a U-haul truck with a baby and a dog, we arrived in Pasadena. It was quite an adjustment from Lakewood.

We arrived just in time for New Year's Day. New Year's in Pasadena is unbelievable. Over one million people descend on this town for the Rose Parade and Rose Bowl football game. We went with our new neighbors, parking our U-haul at a service station and sitting on top to watch the parade. It was cold but wonderful.

I started classes that January. With my G. I. Bill and the support from the Lakewood Church, I didn't have to work. It was great to just focus on my studies without having to support my family as many of my classmates were doing. We had a little closet I made into a study. I studied hard six days a week and took Sundays off. Our neighbors Barb and Charlie had no children and loved Briana. We shared a deck on the second floor and Briana would go back and forth between us. Bridgette was also a hit and they adopted her too. Down below was an older woman named Alida who was widowed with no children. We adopted her as our grandma and she adopted us too.

Out the front window you could see the dry rocky San Gabriel Mountains when the smog would let you. They were beautiful at times. Out on the back deck you could see palm trees. It was warm most of the time. At night the police helicopters would fly over with their searchlights descending like knives in the darkness. It was not good to go out alone at night in our area. There were reports of some violent crime that had taken place close by but we never experienced it thank God.

I rode my bike to the seminary about two miles away every day, which gave Gail and Briana with the Mazda. Having a philosophy background really helped me in seminary. Some of my classmates came from science backgrounds and really struggled. I believe that God led me into philosophy even before I really knew him. He is at work in our lives every day we are on this planet whether we know it or not.

I loved my studies. I couldn't get enough. To just make the Bible, God and Jesus my total focus was fantastic. My grades were at the top of my class, unlike my college days. It really makes a difference when you are studying something that is your passion.

That first quarter we joined a small group of students and their spouses. The seminary assigned us to this support group. One couple was Marty and Elyse. Marty was a Jew who had accepted Jesus as his Messiah. He worked for an organization known as Jews for Jesus. They were radical in their evangelization of the Jewish community. Gail and I became close to this couple. Today Marty is a pastor in Santa Barbara. We are still close with them.

Though I didn't have to work, I found it hard to not be working in a church. There were local churches that posted part-time job openings at the seminary all the time. I saw one that was from the First United Methodist Church in South Pasadena. It was a huge old traditional church. They wanted me to teach a class. We started to attend there. Gail was not happy with me because she felt that God had provided for our needs so I would not have to work. I didn't listen to her. I later regretted it as I have most of my life whenever I charged off on my own ignoring Gail's advice. Later I saw that I was not in God's will there and resigned.

We began to attend Pasadena First United Methodist Church across from the seminary. It was a very large old traditional downtown church with a huge staff and endowment. They even owned their own retreat center up in the mountains. The choir had an orchestra and they played Bach for the anthem each Sunday. Many of the musicians were professionals in Hollywood. I felt it was important that I keep my

United Methodist ties if I was going to stay in that denomination. Many of my fellow students just attended what I call the 'what's happening now' church or the church with the most popular pastor, music or program. Many did not have a clue as to what denomination God wanted them to fit into. There were some students from the seminary that were on the staff at Pasadena First. One was a Methodist pastor and his family from South Africa. He was working on his doctorate.

There was also one of my seminary professors who attended there. He was a United Methodist, charismatic and taught classes on John Wesley and the Holy Spirit. He was also a dynamic preacher. I looked to him as one of my mentors. We started attending and got involved. This time I decided to just be an attendee and not get involved with the ministry though it was very hard. I was aching to roll up my sleeves and get to work for the Lord. Gail and the Lord had to keep telling me that I was there to learn and I would never get another opportunity like this. We got involved in a small group there too and met our good friends Tudor and Ceci who are co-pastors today. Another couple is teaching at a seminary now. The amount of spiritual talent was overwhelming. Many had come out of the drug and protest culture to Christ as we had. These people are Christian leaders all over the world today. I believe God called a special group of leaders during those days.

That summer we traveled back home with Barb and Charlie. They followed us in their car and we camped all the way up the coast. I had applied to be ordained as a Deacon at the Pacific Northwest Annual Conference. It was meeting that year at the University of Puget Sound in Tacoma, Washington where my dad had attended. We took Barb and Charlie to our old church at Lakewood. They loved the church and Don. I met with the Conference Board of Ordained Ministry. This is the third step in the process. They interviewed me and asked me about my theology and Christian experience. I gave them the story of my conversion. One senior pastor said that either I was the biggest liar they had ever heard, or I was for real. They discussed me while I waited outside for what seemed like an eternity. Finally they came out and informed me with a long sad face that I had been accepted and would be ordained that weekend.

The ordination on Saturday night at Conference was a very spiritual and moving experience. We were at a large United Methodist Church close to the University of Puget Sound where we were meeting. All my family and Gail's came. It was packed. About twenty of us were being ordained Deacon and Elder. In those days Deacon was a probationary ordination for Elder. We all robed up and got into a procession of the entire clergy in the Pacific Northwest Annual Conference that included Washington and northern Idaho. Our bishop resided in Seattle. As we all headed up the stairs toward the sanctuary, I had the strangest sense of being connected to all the apostles and clergy of all centuries. When it came my turn, the bishop and elders laid hands on me and prayed. I was given authority to be a pastor. From that day on I carried the title Reverend. It seemed strange but good, Rev. Douglas John Waite.

We drove back to school and I attended summer quarter. That summer I took twelve credits of nothing but New Testament or Koine Greek. The Christian New Testament was originally written in Koine Greek, now a dead language. For the entire summer I ate, drank and slept Greek. By the end of the summer I could read the Greek New Testament. I decided to go straight through summer quarters so that my G. I. Bill would not stop but keep going and I could get done sooner. There were usually breaks between the quarters where I was getting income but had no responsibilities. During those times we would usually pack up the Mazda with the baby, dog, bikes and gear to go camping up in the mountains and get away from the smog and the heat. Our favorite trip was to the Sequoias and Yosemite. We would ride our bikes in the evening with Bridgette running along. They had a donkey that we would take Briana around on a trail. It was a wonderful time together. Once on a hike into the woods, we ran into a couple involved in a Christian radio ministry. She claimed to see angels and to be a prophetess. She prophesied over Gail and me in a wooded meadow within thirty minutes of meeting. She said that God would use us mightily in ministry and that our way would be hard but God would see us through, he had prepared our way. It was very encouraging.

Gail used to work in the evenings for World Vision answering telephones to raise support through their telethons. She got $5.00 an hour, big money in those days. A few times we would come close to running out of money and we would turn to the Lord. On one occasion the rent and tuition was due and we didn't have it. I turned to the Lord and asked him to help me. We had learned at the Lakewood Church about tithing our income. In the beginning we were just '$1.00 a week in the plate' people. Pastor Don used to preach about giving a percentage of your income to God, start with 3-5% and work toward 10%. He would challenge us to just try it and see if God did not bless us. We did and God did. We always seemed to live at a higher standard of living than we made on paper. By the time we got to seminary we were even tithing our G. I. Bill and the gifts from Lakewood and individuals that sent us money from time to time. Other seminarians would ask me how I could keep from working. I would ask them if they tithed. Most would say they couldn't afford it. I would say back that they couldn't afford not to. Gail and I were the only people I knew who even tithed our gifts and the only ones I knew who were not always working two jobs and constantly worried about money, there had to be a correlation. I would encourage them to start tithing.

This time we were out of money. It has happened to me a few times as a Christian even though I did tithe. I cried out to the Lord. I said something like, "Lord, you sent me here, you wouldn't do that and let me fall on my face financially. Please help soon." Within a short amount of time after that prayer, we got a check in the mail. It was from a former member of my destroyer, Scott, who had started attending the Lakewood Church because of my ministry. He said in a note that God had told him to tithe his entire savings account that he had never tithed and to send it to me. It had happened about the time I had cried out to God. I have seen the Lord do this time and time again throughout my ministry and Christian life. When you are faithfully serving him and in his will, he will always come through when you need him to, in money as well as other areas. When I left seminary, I was the only person I knew who was debt free. I went to the most expensive seminary in the country, did not work most of the time and left with all my bills paid. Many clergy I have known were paying off college and seminary loans for years into their ministry. I believe the difference is being where God wants you and tithing what you have to the Lord no matter what your income level, including gifts and windfalls.

My dad was not very excited about me going to seminary. In fact, I think he was a little ashamed or embarrassed to tell his friends. My dad has not received most of the major choices I have made in my life very well. He always had aspirations of me being successful and making a lot of money. The ministry was not high on his list of successful occupations. The Lord is faithful though and got to him. At one of his Allstate Insurance Conferences he had to share a room with a senior executive in his company. They got to talking about what their children were doing. I think dad said his son was in graduate school. His roommate told him his son was at Fuller Seminary in Pasadena preparing for the ministry. Dad couldn't believe it. He said, "Why, that's where my son is going too." This successful executive then said, "No kidding. Aren't you proud of what they are doing? Isn't it wonderful." Dad said hesitantly, "Yeah, it is." From that day on he began to look at my career choice differently. I have tried to be supportive of my own children in whatever they have decided to do in life. Like my dad, I have often not been too enthusiastic about their choices. I understand how he felt now. You always want the best for your kids, but I want them also to find what God has for them to do and be happy.

I had another experience with my parents at seminary that was not so good. They were at Palm Springs for some kind of Allstate Conference. I missed seeing them and having them spend time with their first grandchild Briana. Gail and I packed up the little Mazda, took our last few dollars for gas and drove to Palm Springs to find them. We located them but they were less than enthusiastic that we had come. Dad was having some problem with one of his supervisors and they had pressing social engagements they felt they needed to attend. We sensed that we were imposing on their time. We quickly got back in the car and headed back to Pasadena. I remember Gail trying to comfort me while tears were streaming down my face on the ride home. I never felt closer to her. She couldn't understand my parents. We have always attempted to never let anything or anyone be more important in our lives than our children, except Jesus. I have found, once again, like my dad, there have been times when that has been really hard to do. The desire to succeed at your career can be a very powerful all consuming passion.

I was on a mission to finish seminary in record time. Don and the Lakewood Church were waiting. Every so often he would stop in on us to see how we were doing on one of his sporadic impulsive road trips. If you went full time, it would take you nine straight quarters to finish a Masters of Divinity (M. Div.) Degree that was required for full ordination in most denominations. I went straight through to keep the money coming from the government. I had heard horror stories of guys stopping their G. I. Bill in the summer quarter to work full time and then to return in the fall only to have it take months to restart. I wanted to get through quickly and I couldn't afford to have a lapse in support. I think I set the record for a M. Div. Degree.

One time when we were short on cash, I went to the seminary and asked for a scholarship based on my grades, which were almost straight A's, and the fact that I was a veteran of the Vietnam Era with a family. They considered it and turned me down because I was getting the G. I. Bill and my wife wasn't working. Here I was in a Christian center of higher learning preparing pastors for full time ministry and they were telling me that because my wife wasn't putting my child in day care and working outside the home, I didn't qualify for a scholarship. Something was wrong with this picture. For years after that, Fuller would send me or phone me with a request for funds to help struggling students. I never sent them a dime. Finally the Lord convicted me that I was wrong. I wrote the president and told him why I didn't give. He wrote me back and told me that their policies had changed. I have sent them money since, but it has always been hard. I actually did get a scholarship grant from them years later that I will recount in another chapter.

My senior year I did take a job at a United Methodist Church in LaHabra, California. I had to for my field education credits. It was a very wealthy quite liberal congregation that paid very well for a part time associate. The facility was outstanding but the leaders were far left from me theologically. It was a real struggle to try and share my faith with the youth there as I had at Lakewood. Often the leaders would counter everything I said. In my theology, the closer you are to the literal understanding of the Bible, the more conservative you are, and the further you get from that literal understanding, the more liberal you are. I find it intolerable to be at either end of that wide spectrum and find myself somewhere in the middle, everyone likes to think that, but I lean towards the conservative, which I also call evangelical. By evangelical I mean telling others of their need to personally ask Jesus to come into their lives, forgive their sins and give them eternal life. I also believe you can be too literal and conservative. I think that the Pharisees who condemned Jesus to death were the literal conservatives of their day. The problem was their literal understanding of the Bible was flawed. Jesus tried to correct it but they would have none of it. They finally had him put to death, mostly over issues concerning the proper practices on the Sabbath.

Once I had planned a youth retreat for the weekend at LaHabra. The pastor, Ed, was very similar to Pastor Don as a person but quit liberal in his beliefs.

He tolerated my beliefs because of my enthusiasm. This particular evening he was mad about something to do with the retreat. He called me into his office, made me stand in front of his desk and proceeded to speak to me angrily as if I was a child. I was shocked. I wanted to resign right there but the Lord wouldn't let me. I didn't need that kind of treatment. What a way to treat a fellow pastor and servant of God. I vowed never to treat people like that in my ministry. Throughout my life I have found that you may learn more from people you don't like than you do like. They teach you what not to do in life and they also show you something of yourself. All of us usually dislike in others what we subconsciously cannot stand in ourselves.

I also got involved in starting an evening service at First United Methodist Church in Pasadena. Though we weren't on the staff there, many of our friends were. Because of my guitar and preaching skills, they asked me to help them get started. It was a real challenge to try to get something new and contemporary going in that old traditional congregation. As I recall, I was overextending myself again and Gail was upset, but I did it anyway. It turned out to be a blessing. We would do the service at LaHabra on Sunday morning, where I was liturgist and taught a class, and attend or help lead the service that night at Pasadena First. After that service we would often go and get ice cream with those who attended.

One Sunday night I was the preacher. I decided to preach on the Old Testament. The senior pastor, George, was one of the most well-known and respected preachers in the United Methodist Church. He came that night and so did Dr. Bob, my professor from Fuller across the street. I was a little intimidated but got up there and preached to the best of my ability. Afterwards both of them came up to me separately.

Pastor George said that he felt that I should teach the Old Testament because I brought it alive for him. Dr. Bob told me that I had what few others had, the gift of preaching. These comments encouraged me greatly. I couldn't wait to get out there and try my preaching wings on a consistent basis. Pastor Ed let me preach only once the whole time that I worked at LaHabra. I have always tried to let new young preachers have the pulpit once in awhile.

Another incident that happened involved the Army Chaplaincy. The Army Chaplain recruiter came to Fuller trying to recruit new chaplains. Somehow we got together and I became very interested. He wined and dined me a little, even though I wasn't drinking wine at the time, a carryover from Don at Lakewood that I eventually discarded. The chaplain told me that if I would just sign the papers he had I would become a Second Lieutenant in the U. S. Army Chaplain Corps. That was pretty heady offer to a former Navy Third Class Petty Officer. I took all the papers home and talked to Gail. She wasn't impressed. She saw it as another distraction for me. I went up to my little study closet and spread the paperwork out before the Lord. As I was praying I sensed the Lord tell me, "No! Take all the paperwork and throw it into the garbage so it will not become a temptation." I immediately obeyed and I thought that was the end of the chaplaincy for me. As I have found so often, God has his time and place for everything, his no may not mean no forever. It can also mean wait for the right time and place. Twice I had looked at the chaplaincy and twice I had been turned away, once from the church and once from God. It seemed the chaplaincy was not for me.

I had a ministry with some of the students at Fuller during my time there. One such person was named Tony. He was Japanese from Hawaii and a

United Methodist. He was working as an associate at the Hollywood United Methodist Church just down the street from the famous actor and comedian Bob Hope's house. Tony was very interested in the gifts of the Holy Spirit and asked me many questions about my own experience. I shared with him my story. He asked me if I would pray with him to receive the baptism in the Holy Spirit and the gift of speaking in languages he had never learned, tongues. I prayed with him and he received both in a very beautiful way.

After that, he kept trying to get me to speak at his church. Finally an opportunity came. The senior pastor, who never let him speak, was gone on vacation. Tony could get whomever he wanted to preach. He asked me. Gail and I showed up with Briana expecting to see Bob Hope in the congregation. The church was crowded but, like most United Methodist Churches, the congregation was full of many gray heads. I preached a salvation message from John 3 about the need to be born again. President Jimmy Carter had made the phrase popular. I gave an invitation for people to come forward to receive Christ. Tony later told me that had never been done in that congregation. The communion rail filled up with people. I prayed with many to receive Christ into their lives. I learned later that some very famous Hollywood people were there, including the couple that wrote the music for 'Sound of Music'. Many of them received Christ that day. Praise be to God! You never know who is open to the Spirit of God, some of the most unlikely people. We must always be open to do what God would have us do when it comes to preaching and sharing his word. We must not be intimidated by the position people hold or how much wealth they have. Everyone needs the forgiveness of God.

Finally, I came to the end of my seminary training, nine straight quarters, two years and three months. It seemed like some kind of record. I had wanted to go through seminary as quickly as possible to get back to Pastor Don and the Lakewood United Methodist Church. At the beginning of the last quarter, Gail got a call from Dan, the District Superintendent of the Puget Sound District in Everett, Washington. He wanted me to call. I called and he told me the Cabinet, the Bishop and District Superintendents, wanted me to become the pastor of the Avon United Methodist Church in Mt. Vernon, Washington. I asked him about Lakewood. He told me they wanted me to go to Avon. He said it was a small country church with a few conservative charismatic leaders and that it would be a good match for them and me. I called Don and he was furious. Gail and I went to the Lord and felt his peace to say yes to Avon. We called Dan back and accepted.

I got in touch with the Lay Leader of the Avon Church. He sent me some pictures of the church, sanctuary and parsonage. We started to get excited about our first church. We pooled our pennies and hired an inexpensive moving company to take our stuff back to the Northwest. Barb and Charlie had moved the summer before and our good friends from Fuller, Marty and Elyse, had moved in with their new baby. Down below us were Mike and Patty who were also Fuller students, and, of course, grandma Alida. All of us were getting together one night a week for a community dinner. We had all grown very close. It was a sad day when the moving truck pulled up and loaded our furniture. More than a few tears were shed. After a big farewell party from all of our friends at Fuller and Pasadena First, we climbed into the orange Mazda with Briana now 2 ½, Bridgette and headed north to Washington State. There was the excitement of new adventures waiting ahead and the sadness of leaving such good and wonderful Christian friends. Those sentiments would be repeated many times in the years ahead. Fuller Seminary was a wonderful experience of Christian growth and community that we would never experience again this side of Heaven.

7
Avon Church

We got back to the Pacific Northwest in March of 1978. We drove up to Mt.Vernon to meet the movers on a typical cold wet gray Skagit Valley day. The church was almost 100 years old having been built by Nova Scotian pioneers of Avon in 1884. Avon was a river in Nova Scotia. It was built on the Avon bend in the Skagit River, the second largest river in Washington State, the first being the Columbia. Later the church was rolled over logs to its present location about two blocks away from the river on a parcel of ground at the intersection of Avon Street and Avon Allen Road. In the 1930's the parsonage was built next door and a basement was added to the church for a fellowship hall and kitchen. Only recently had indoor plumbing been added to the church facility. It was a beautiful white country church and parsonage in a New England style of architecture with a bell tower.

The original settlers to Avon were dry Methodists, they did not drink. To this day, Avon is a dry community. There are no taverns or restaurants that serve alcohol. Mt. Vernon was a wet community that did serve alcohol and so it grew and Avon died. Today the community of Avon is along the Avon Allen Road and is comprised of homes, a few small farms, a restaurant, car body shop and cleaners from time to time. Agriculture is the main business of the area. There is a huge Dutch community that grows tulips. Each spring people come from all over for the Tulip Festival in the Skagit Valley. At that time beautiful multi-colored tulip fields surround the church. The Cascade Mountains and the tip of Mt. Baker form the backdrop. Many photographers come from all over the country to take pictures of this beautiful rural scene.

We pulled up to the church that March morning. The first person we met was one of the long time leaders in the church and community. As I walked up to him, he asked, "Where is your Dad?" I said, "What?" He said again, "Your Dad, the new pastor." I said, "I am the new pastor." His mouth fell open and he just stared at me in shock. I was twenty-seven years old but God had sent me. I had to keep reminding myself of that and Paul's words to Timothy about not letting the people despise his youth.

We wound up at his house with some other leaders that night, waiting for our moving van to show up. They had a scanner on and we could hear people all over the valley talking about where the new pastor's moving van was. They got lost but finally found us. When they finally arrived about midnight, our furniture was a pile of rubble in the van. We unloaded it and there was much damage. The movers left after midnight. A few days later I got a call from the moving company asking when they had been there. Apparently, when they left us, they abandoned the truck and took off with the cash. Thank God they unloaded us first.

We then drove to Boise to see my folks. While we were there we blew the engine to our little Mazda. Mom and dad helped us get it fixed. I hurried back to preach my first Sunday service at Avon. It was April 2, 1978. I missed April Fool's by one day. About thirty people were present, a big Sunday. There was only one other family with children. Everyone else was retired or close to it. There was no nursery and when I asked why, they said they had no children. I tried my best to explain to them they had no children because they had no nursery. In the middle of the service, an elderly gentleman had a heart attack. My first sermon was my testimony, something I learned from Pastor Don, and I wondered if that was what triggered it. After the service we were in the Fellowship Hall in the basement having coffee with the people when suddenly we found ourselves all alone. They all simply went home leaving us standing there. I remember how alone we felt.

This church wanted a young pastor that would bring in the young people but they had no concept of what that would mean. They would soon find out. The church had almost closed its doors a few years before. They had shared a pastor with the United Methodist Church just a few miles away. The pastor and his family had lived in the other parsonage. A year or so before that, the church had a little revival with a Lay Witness Mission (LWM) that they held. In the LWM, lay people from all over the state come and give their testimonies in a weekend setting. Many of the Avon people, we later called them Avonites, had accepted Christ or recommitted their lives to Christ during that weekend. As a result, they decided to get their own pastor. They had not had one for many years. The first one they got was retired and in his 80's. Everyone loved him. He would go to meetings in the evening and when his favorite TV shows would come on, he would just get up and walk out. Finally, he went on a vacation. While on vacation he called and said he would not be coming back. When asked why, he said he had gotten married. That was when the Cabinet called me at Fuller.

The people had put a lot of work into the parsonage to get it ready for us. They were used to paying the pastor a minimal salary and taking care of them in other ways. That is the way it is in most rural communities. My yearly salary was $10,000 plus the parsonage and some denominational retirement. I had to pay all utilities out of that, including a very expensive oil burning furnace and all of my social security as pastors are considered self employed. We lived from paycheck to paycheck. When we moved in, the freezer was full of meat. They never did it again, but it was a nice first impression.

I wanted my office to be in the church away from my home so I could keep them separate. The church and the parsonage shared the same phone. We had a buzzer that went between them when the call was for Gail or me. We also had a big garden out back, which we all spent many therapeutic hours working in. Gail quickly learned how to can and put up preserves. One of the first things we asked them to do was to put up a fence for privacy and to keep the dog and baby safe from the highway. I remember one of our first nights laying in bed and listening to the whistle of the Burlington Northern train coming through the valley. It was out of a storybook.

I did not have a secretary and no one seemed to think I needed one. I told them I did. They hired a part time former schoolteacher, Joedy, to help out a few days a week. She was a Godsend. Her husband was a local school principal and she had raised a large Christian family. She kept me out of a lot of trouble helping me understand and communicate with the people in ways we could both appreciate. I also told the congregation I wanted to take two days off, Friday and Saturday, so I could have some quality family time with Gail and Briana. They reluctantly agreed. One parishioner thought I should have Sunday as my day off because it was his and he had to be in church. Why shouldn't I? All in all, they accepted this young pastor and his family pretty well considering how new it was for them

One thing Fuller Seminary had taught me was to preach biblical expository sermons. I would take a small passage of scripture, look at it in the context of the time it was written and what it meant then and apply it to our lives today. The people loved it. Soon the word started getting out about this young new preacher in the area. We started getting visitors every Sunday from the other churches in the valley. Most were just curious but some would decide to stay. I learned the hard way that this was a trait of many Christians in this community. They were always trying to find the latest move of God and head there. I later called them the people of the 'what's happening now' church.

We started growing. Our new nursery began to have other children. I started a program of visiting every member of the congregation and the new visitors. I tried to take Gail and Briana with me during the day but I still spent many nights out by myself. I found most of these people to be very warm and loving Christians. It was a joy to be their pastor. Some of them felt it was their job to help me grow and mature as a person. They were a little harder to deal with. I play the guitar and I started teaching them a few of the new contemporary songs in worship. Some liked them and some didn't.

That summer I had my first high school reunion in Yakima, the tenth. Gail and I borrowed her uncle's truck and camper and took Briana and Bridgette with us too. I had not seen many in my class since graduation. As I have already indicated in a previous chapter, I had been a wild and crazy guy in high school. When people found out that I was a Christian pastor, they could not believe it. Gail and I were not drinking at that time and we walked around all night and enjoyed meeting and talking to people without alcohol. We could not believe how some people made such asses out of themselves while under the influence. In the men's room I met one of my old friends all the way through childhood, high school and college. He had drunk too much alcohol. He was still single and living crazy. He looked at me and said, "Doug, you have everything and I have nothing." I thought it was a strange comment. On the way back we stopped at my favorite campground in the Mount Rainier National Park, Ohanapecosh, and camped. I started fishing in the little stream and was catching trout left and right. Later I found out it was a fly fish only stream. I was using bait.

By that first Christmas our Sunday services had more than doubled. Many were young families that Gail and I attracted. Money was never a problem to the church as a whole. We always had money in the bank. A lot of these young families were new Christians who believed in tithing and were giving a percentage of their incomes. We never had a pledge drive in those early years. I just preached and taught on tithing. I didn't want to know what other people gave. I did not want what they gave to influence how I treated them. Joedy did the money and kept track of who gave what. It was a great arrangement, as she did not attend our congregation. That first Christmas Eve following the service, one leader palmed me an envelope and said Merry Christmas. It was a love offering from the people. It really saved us. It was their way of saying thank you and of taking care of us. It was the last Christmas bonus I received from that church.

Often people would come over to the parsonage needing help. They would see the church and the house and just ring the doorbell. One time a young woman came to us. She was very suicidal. We took her in and tried to minister to her. She stayed with us for quite awhile. Her dad was a leader in one of the local towns south of us towards Seattle. We let them know she was with us. At one point her depression became so bad we had to have her admitted to an inpatient program in Seattle run by a friend of mine from Fuller. Joedy and I drove her down. Years later she found us and thanked us for loving her during that difficult time.

We got in the habit of opening our home and letting people stay there. One night I let a man stay downstairs. There was something very evil about him. The Lord woke me up telling me I was putting my whole family in danger having this man in the basement. I quickly locked the door to the downstairs. The next morning I asked him to leave. I never let anyone stay there again. God asks us to love our fellow man but he doesn't ask us to be foolish in doing so.

I also instituted the monthly Agape Feasts in those days. The early Christians used to have communion in the setting of a meal. We would have a good old fashion Sunday night Methodist potluck dinner and I would serve communion at the end of the meal. I always would have some special program, a singer, film or special speaker. I got the local paper to give us a lot of public relations on the events we were sponsoring. I tried to get us in the paper as often as possible. All of this started getting Avon the reputation as the church that was really growing and doing things for God or what I call the 'what's happening now church'. I also made sure I attended the local ministerial association and Methodist district pastors meetings. I met with a group of pastors from different denominations for prayer and fellowship. I was careful not to be seen as stealing other pastor's sheep or proselytizing.

My counseling load exploded. People started coming to me from all over. I would have Joedy screen them and ask if they had spoken to their own pastor first. I would also tell new visitors that we did not want to take them away from their own churches. I wanted to reach people who were not going to church. Two families like that came to us. One was a young family who had just lost a baby to SIDS. They had no faith and no pastor. One of our congregation lived next door and asked them if they could send me over. I went over and introduced myself. They let me in. I offered to do the service for their baby. They accepted. It was my first funeral, a little white coffin. It was heart breaking. I will never forget it. We were able to minister to this family in the service and reception that followed. They started coming to the church. We had a young couple's fellowship group by then like the group at Lakewood. We called them the "Under 35ers". They started coming. Before we knew it this couple had accepted Christ and I baptized them. They became members of the church. It was miracles like this that kept me going.

Soon the first service was full. We began to think about starting an early service. God was really moving among us. Part of it was the biblical preaching, the other was prayer. I had a prayer group that met at 6 AM in the morning during the week. It was only a few people but we poured our heart out to the Lord. The pastors group I met with ended with prayer each week too. We would all get on our knees and pray. It was profound. When God's people pray, things happen that are supernatural.

I found that if I didn't leave the parsonage on my days off I never quit working. The phone never stopped ringing. People were always having emergencies and the down and out would come to the door looking for a hand out. We bought an old fifteen-foot travel trailer and started camping on our days off. Gail and I love the outdoors, especially camping in the woods. She grew up camping and I just love it. We had a camper for a short time while I was enlisted in Lakewood and so this time we thought we would try the trailer. We found a lot of places around the area that would provide us sanctuary and protection from a demanding growing congregation. The church would often criticize us for this too. We decided we had to block some time out for the family or we would not get time away. I have never regretted that decision.

Gail started screening all incoming calls and was very tough about whom she would let me talk to on our weekends. Often the people would say it was an 'emergency'. That is one term that gets most pastors and their families. Once one of our girls was getting ready to have a birthday party. We got one of those emergency calls right in the middle of it. I took the phone from Gail. A woman in our congregation was in the hospital and wanted me to come and see her immediately. I turned to Gail. She said, "That woman may not die and no one will really care if you didn't see her, but your daughter will always remember that you didn't make her party." Gail was tough and she was right. I didn't go to the hospital. The woman was fine and I saw her the next day. I learned that not all emergency calls are really emergencies and that our families are at least as important as any emergency the congregation might have. Thank God for a wise wife.

Miracles became a regular occurrence among us. We had a young woman who came regularly to everything we did. She came from a big family who didn't go to church. She was on fire for God but came to me looking for more from God. Gail and I prayed with her one afternoon in our living room to be baptized in the Holy Spirit. She began to pray in a beautiful new language that God gave her. One by one her family all started coming to church. Finally her macho independent Dad showed up to see what all the fuss was about. On a Sunday not long after that, I preached a salvation message and gave an invitation. He was the first one to the communion rail to accept Christ. I was such a privilege to pray with him. I wound up baptizing his family, officiating at the weddings of all his daughters and baptizing the grandchildren. These are the great parts of being a parish pastor.

One leader was a man's man with a big family. He was suffering from chronic migraine headaches. These headaches were so bad that he would go into his garage and weep so no one would see him. The doctors could do nothing. He was struggling with suicidal thoughts to escape the pain. One night we showed the film 'Cross and the Switchblade' about Pastor David Wilkerson leading gang members to Christ in New York. When it got to the part where David led gang leader Nicki Cruse to accept Christ, the power of God came upon him and he was instantly healed. He never had another problem. Every week it seemed a miracle like this happened.

About this time Pastor Don from the Lakewood Church decided to split off from United Methodism and start his own church. He and the Bishop had a huge falling out over the charismatic renewal. The Bishop did not think this was a valid expression of Christian faith and attempted to stamp it out. He tried to move Don to another appointment, church, and wouldn't tell him where it was. He purposely did not send me to be Don's associate even though I had been promised to him. For these and many other reasons, Don took the majority of that great congregation and started his own church. It broke my heart. I remember parking our trailer at the old parsonage for Annual Conference and crying my eyes out over what had happened to that wonderful congregation. I believed Don was wrong and told him so. I learned in church history that schism has been the bane of the church over the centuries and is never the will of God.

Don's church went well for a while but then he had a heart attack. He almost died on the operating table. It left him permanently impaired. He couldn't write sermons any more. He could preach old ones but couldn't write new ones. Eventually, the people at the new church, his loyal supporters, gave him his severance pay and sent him and his wife off on their own. They wound up living with their children until their deaths. Don never recovered from the pain of their rejection. I always say that I would not be in the ministry today if it were not for Don's influence in my life. I eventually preached his memorial service and kept in touch with his widow Louise until she died.

That June I got a new denominational supervisor. He disliked evangelicals and charismatics and called himself a liberal. He came up to Burlington and took me out to lunch. I had the fastest growing church in his denominational area in those days. Within minutes of our meeting, he proceeded to tell me that we were in different worlds. I always wondered how someone could make those kinds of judgments about people without ever having taken the time to know them. He said that if I continued in the direction I was going, I might spend my entire career at Avon. I couldn't see anything wrong with that. At once I knew that he was going to be trouble. Some of the greatest opposition I have encountered in my ministry has come from clergy who were in authority.

The church had grown to the point where I needed help in ministry. I couldn't do it all myself. We started a new second service at 8:30 AM. My leaders tried to make that one a little more contemporary with guitars and new music. I didn't wear my robe at that service. At the 11 AM I wore my robe and we sang more hymns. I still tried to use my guitar for at least one song at 11 AM.

We interviewed many people for the part-time youth director position that we wanted to start. The position would be responsible for children's church through college age. None of the candidates seemed right. I sensed God telling me to wait. In God's time, Rick came to us. He was a godsend too. He did not have much formal education but he had some experience, contagious faith and a heart as big as could be. The church loved him and his wife Jan. Rick did wonders with those kids. Our children's church exploded, as did the youth group. Rick had a real gift with kids. All the young families coming to us brought many young children. At one point the largest age group in our church was under four.

Rick had a hundred children in children's church at his peak. He was also thinking about going into the ministry as a pastor so I had him do everything with me, like Don did to me. He was more like an associate pastor with a specialty in youth. We were a great team.

March 16, 1980 our second daughter, Lauren Beth, was born. Her name means 'victory' or 'victorious one'. We had tried since her sister was born in 1975 to have another child. We were married four years before our first child was born and four years before our second. I was sure she was a boy but Gail told me she was a girl. She has known the sex and names of all five of our children before they were born or came into our home. At one point Gail thought she was going to lose Lauren. She was bleeding. At the monthly Sunday communion service it was my tradition to serve the people at the communion rail. If they wanted to be anointed with oil and prayed for healing, they would lift their hand as I came by. That Sunday Gail raised her hand as I served her communion. It was very unlike her. She had to be worried. I laid hands and anointed her with oil. She told me later that immediately she could feel the bleeding stop. We have always called Lauren our miracle baby, although they are all miracles.

Lauren was born on a Sunday at 11 AM, right in the middle of the main morning worship service. Lauren has never wanted to be upstaged by anything. Rick was preaching that Sunday and I called the church so they could announce Lauren's birth in worship. We brought her home to a nursery we had put together in the parsonage. I could not get the church to put carpet in it so Gail and I carpeted it ourselves. I could never understand that congregation. It was little things like that which drove us crazy.

I have been playing guitar since I was about fourteen years old. I started with an electric. When I was living at the chicken coop I tried to take it up again. I never really got the hang of it until I was in the Navy. One summer I worked real hard while at sea trying to get better. While at Lakewood I even took a class. Little by little I got better. I was playing just about every Sunday at Avon teaching the church some of the new choruses. We called it contemporary Christian music. I had been praying for a new guitar for some time. Mine was an inexpensive nylon string guitar that Gail had gotten for me in college.

One Sunday a new member of our congregation was putting his Martin guitar in the back of his car. Martin is one of the most expensive guitars. By accident he backed his car over the then $1200 D-18 Martin. He was an insurance adjuster and he had it insured. He got a new one and the old broken Martin was just sitting in the insurance office. I asked if they would sell it to me. They agreed for $25. One week after I bought the guitar a new man started attending the church. He had been a television producer. He had a brother who specialized in repairing Martin guitars. He sent my guitar to his brother who repaired it for nothing using its own wood. It was scarred but it sounded just like a new one, maybe even better, a $1200 guitar for $25. Right after that the man quit coming. I have played that Martin almost every Sunday since. Thanks Lord. That guitar is like me, damaged but repaired and still going by the grace of God.

I was working in the garden that summer. We had a huge one. Suddenly I heard a commotion close by. I walked over to see two gophers fighting each other to the death. I had never seen such a thing before or since. I thought, "Ah ha, I can get two at once." They were always ruining my garden. I raised my hoe to strike them both. Just then the Lord spoke to me in my heart. He said, "That is just like my church. Christians are always fighting with one another and do not realize that the real enemy is standing right over them ready to strike a death blow." Some of my best illustrations for spiritual realities have come from the garden. Jesus used agriculture too in telling his proverbs.

Our annual Charge Conference that year with the District Superintendent (DS) was also eye opening. The Finance Committee had voted a salary increase for Rick but not for me. Gail and I were crushed. One of the really bad things about the United Methodist system is that yearly the church votes on your salary. I have tried to explain it to others as if your friends were voting on your salary. How would that make you feel? They want you to do well but never to make more than they do. One parishioner who did want me to make more was an old friend from the Navy who had moved to the Mt. Vernon area because of our friendship and gone to work for one of our leaders. My friend stood up at that meeting and said it was not right that Rick got an increase and I didn't. Someone made a motion to increase our salary and give us more housing allowance. It was voted on and passed but not after horrible things were said with Gail and I present and a close vote. My DS could not believe how cheap and unloving he felt the church was and told me so. Soon after that my friend lost his job. I know it was because he stood up for Gail and me. That year the leaders made sure that Gail and I did not get a Christmas bonus. These were more hurtful experiences from that church leadership.

Around this time we had our first church split. Some of the older members did not like the way the church was going. They did not like all the young people and the changes that were happening in leadership and worship. One of them said they wanted to hang a sign outside on the sanctuary door that said 'Full'. For decades these leaders had controlled that church and now they couldn't. I put new people in positions of leadership. I tried to make sure that new people joined the church before putting them in any these positions. We had one influential long time member who used to control everything with his pocket book. He did not like someone who I had teaching a class for new members. He came and told me to remove this teacher or he would leave. Before I came this man would always make the yearly budget with his contribution at the end of the year if the church ended in debt. For this payment each year he thought he could control the pastor. When he threatened to leave I told him I was not going to remove this teacher. He left that week and took a few folks with him. They began to criticize me in the community and wrote some letters to the Bishop.

During these days we had many miraculous things happen. One Sunday a woman drove by the Sunday service on her way back from an adulterous relationship. The Spirit of God told her to stop and go in. She sat in the back and stood up in the sharing time and admitted her sin to us all. Immediately I heard and saw myself point at her and say, "Woman go and sin no more". It seemed as if Jesus was speaking to her through me.

A woman came to me one day for prayer. She told me that she was in pain all the time as a hairdresser. She said she had curvature of the spine called scoliosis. I suddenly felt impressed to pray for her. As I prayed I could sense the presence of the Lord. Later she told me that the pain left immediately. Her back was healed.

Another parishioner called me and told me that she had a biker from the local motorcycle gang at her house. He was trying to escape the gang and she wanted to bring him over to talk about Jesus. I was scared but said yes. This was a bad group who had committed serious crimes. The biker was about 6' 5", 300 pounds and dressed in all this leather and colors. He was scary just to look at. I explained Christianity to him and he said he wanted to accept Christ. I called Rick and Joedy in and we prayed with him. Then he said he wanted to be baptized immediately. Rick and I took him into the sanctuary. When we laid our hands on him at the communion rail he began to sing the 'Alleluia Chorus" at the top of his lungs. The quilting club was meeting in the fellowship hall below and came up to see what was going on. You should have seen the look on their faces when they saw this huge biker singing the Alleluia Chorus. I sent him off to stay with a friend of mine in Southern California. He was afraid for his life. He knew too much and didn't think the bikers would let him go. He would call me from time to time to say that he was OK but they were after him. After a while the calls stopped. I never heard from him again. I hope to see him someday in glory.

I had a woman come to see me who had multiple personalities. The psychiatrists had tried to treat her and given up. She was a talented singer who had been on national television. When she would make an appointment and come in, I never knew what personality would show up. I sensed that she was demon possessed. I never make this call lightly. Usually it comes only after all other possibilities are exhausted. I also find it is very rare in our culture. Sometimes the demon personality would show up and openly expose itself. On one occasion she came into the reception area where Joedy and Rick were. The demon began to speak claiming it could blow all the books off the walls and the windows out if it wanted to. Rick and Joedy were frightened. Then it said, "If you think all these angels in here scare me, you are mistaken." As soon as she said that, everyone knew God had it under control.

There was a nurse in the congregation with the spiritual gift of discerning of spirits. Paul lists twelve of these gifts in the New Testament book of First Corinthians chapter twelve. No one manifests them all and that is why we need the entire body of Christ to do ministry. Some people seem to manifest one stronger than others and have a ministry in that area, such as healing. I try to find out who has these ministries and put them to work. I also never like to do spiritual ministry with a woman alone. I try to involve another woman if possible. When I did an exorcism, I called this gifted women. She often manifested discerning of spirits and was a nurse, perfect for this ministry.

We prayed together with this woman to be set free from demonic possession. It was strange as it always is. Dealing with the demonic is hard and unpleasant work. It is my least favorite thing to do as a pastor, but much needed at times. People have few places of integrity to go for this kind of ministry. Jesus and his disciples were always casting demons out of people. I often serve communion after prayer as a sign of God's grace and to insure that the demonic has left. The Lord's Prayer is also powerful. This woman seemed set free but we lost track of her. Such people need to follow up their deliverance with strong Christian commitment and discipleship or things can become worse. She also needed psychological healing from her multiple personalities.

The church needed more space so they gave Gail and I a $400 housing allowance told us to move out of the parsonage. They moved the church offices to the parsonage and made classrooms out of the basement. Many of the local United Methodist pastors did not want me to move too close to them and had phoned the Bishop. They were worried I would somehow attract their people to Avon by living close to them. The Bishop ordered me through the District Superintendent to stay on the west side of the freeway in the flats. I didn't want to live there because it was a flood plain. We eventually found a nice place but we couldn't afford it. Our parents helped us make the down payment and with the peace of God we moved in. To their credit, the church helped us paint and move in.

It seemed like everywhere we turned there was opposition. When God is using you in a powerful way, our spiritual enemy will always be there to attack at every opportunity. I was asked to speak at a Full

Gospel Businessmen's meeting in community about forty minutes away. There were some women from the local United Methodist Church in attendance that night. They heard my testimony and went back to their church fired up for Jesus. When they told their pastor about my talk, he was furious. He couldn't believe I had come into his community to speak and hadn't informed him beforehand. He called the District Superintendent and complained. The DS then took it upon himself to call all the other area United Methodist Churches and asked them if they had anything they could contribute negatively about me, several were willing. He solicited letters from them all. He then took these to the Board of Ordained Ministry where he held a seat. I was still in a probationary status in my work towards for Full Membership and Elder's Orders.

The summer of 1980 I was up for full ordination. By then I had one of the fastest growing United Methodist Churches in the Annual Conference, which included Washington and northern Idaho. All of this meant nothing to the DS who saw our growth as being non-United Methodist. He opposed my full ordination and his vote carried a lot of weight. The Board voted to postpone my ordination another year and have me fulfill certain requirements. They gave their report on me to the Executive Session, all Elders and the Cabinet, where I was not present. I was told later there was quite a discussion that ensued among the clergy. One Elder said that they did not know how to deal with success. This is from a Conference that has been losing members annually for decades.

I was devastated. I was a loyal United Methodist and we were experiencing tremendous growth at Avon because we were following the Lord and his word. Many of the charismatic/evangelicals at Avon wanted me to leave the denomination and start another church like Don had. The same thing was happening to me that happened to him. I had learned from Don's mistakes and did not have the Lord's peace to leave. If I did leave, I had too much integrity to start another church in the same community with people from Avon. That was anathema in my book. I never wanted to become a schismatic in my denomination or community. I do not believe that is ever God's will. There have been too many divisions already in the body of Christ through the centuries. God wants to bring his people together, not tear them apart. Gail told me, "Well, you still have a job and a church, just keeping doing what you are doing and leave the rest to God." It was good advice that I followed but it was hard to keep going.

Every so often we would load up the car with the kids and head for Boise, Idaho where my parents had moved. One summer it was very hot. We had just put new retread tires on the car, the best we could afford. It was so hot when we got to Eastern Washington that the tires separated. We had four flats on the way to Boise. The trip was a disaster and Gail was barely speaking to me. I would always go out and play golf with my dad, and sometimes my mom too, when we were there. Ever since their move to Bellevue years ago, they had been living on golf courses. Golf had become a huge part of their lives. They played all the time. I had been playing for years but always sporadically and without lessons. I was what they call a 'duffer'. I kept at it mostly so I could go out with my folks from time to time. On this trip dad and I were playing. Out in the middle of a fairway, dad turned to me and told me that he needed Jesus Christ in his life. That night at the dinner table I shared the Four Spiritual Laws with both them. Gail and I had the privilege to pray with both of my parents to receive Christ. I think they were Christians before, but now they really knew that Christ was in their lives.

Our growth at Avon just continued to increase. We would eventually reach over three hundred people and have four Sunday services per week. I would come home Sunday night and Gail would just pour me into bed. It was exhausting. I couldn't get out and visit everyone anymore; it was just not humanly possible. I had to depend on others to visit for me. My counseling load was overwhelming. I stopped seeing people who were going to other congregations. We needed more facility fast. Our building committee was working on many different plans, everything from a metal building to a new church in a new location. We had about $80,000 in the bank. The Building Committee settled on a plan that utilized the parsonage and original 1884 sanctuary, excavated a new basement under the entire structure and tied it all together in similar but new architecture. It was brilliant and from the Lord. We would eventually add 17,000 square feet to our facility including a new fellowship hall, parlor, nursery, classrooms and sanctuary seating. As of this first writing they use all that space every Sunday.

I started a home small group program to help me disciple and pastor this growing congregation. I began with six couples that I discipled for one year in a small group in our home to become leaders. Year two I teamed them up to start three more home groups and I started a new leader group. Within a couple of years we had over one hundred people in home small groups. Some of those groups are still going as of this first writing. They would sing, study the Bible, fellowship and pray for one another. I would go out and visit the groups and serve them communion. It was a concept I learned at Fuller. I believe this program aided our growth but also led to some problems later on.

About this time I had several women in the congregation who came to me in counseling saying that they were in love with me. This kind of thing is the curse of every pastor. Some people are drawn to those who are in authority and in the spotlight. In each case I told them to go home and tell their husbands. I went home immediately and told Gail. There is something about telling your spouse that someone is coming on to you that diffuses the whole thing. When it is a secret, it is tempting and dangerous. I can't tell you how many pastors, counselors, psychologists, doctors, lawyers and others whom I have known over the years who fell to this temptation. I loved my wife and family and had no desire for anything or anyone else to jeopardize what we had. When I told Gail, she was able to keep an eye on them and me. I don't think she ever really worried. She always trusted me and I have always tried to be worthy of that trust and never damage it.

There was a huge new church in Seattle that had built a school and had satellite congregations throughout the state. The son of one of our members was going there and attending their school. He would come by and tell me about it. I learned from him that they denied the Trinity and the divinity of Christ. It seems that all cults eventually come out here theologically. They had a large group meeting in neighboring city in the local youth ministry building. Their leaders drove up from Seattle. Somehow I got invited by the local youth ministry to a debate with the Seattle leaders and the Christian community. It took me all night but, by the grace of God, I finally got them to admit their denial of the Trinity and the divinity of Christ. As a result, many of the couples in that group started coming to Avon. I received death threats and was really afraid for my life. That Seattle church was huge and was praying for Doug Waite to die. Later, that congregation was exposed to the entire Pacific Northwest as a dangerous cult that abused authority and was involved in all kinds of deviant sexual activity, another common thing in cults.

One night two of my new parishioners came by to tell me that a local pastor and evangelist from their former church wanted to come in and say hello. I said, "Bring them in." I offered them coffee and we sat and chatted in my office. I thought it was really nice that they would stop by. I had few pastors do that. Without warning they proceeded to tell me that I was not saved because I wasn't baptized according to the true scriptural way that Jesus commanded and I wasn't going to heaven. I said, "Let me get this straight. You are sitting here in my office drinking my coffee and telling me that I am not saved because I haven't been baptized like you". They said, "Yes." I said, "I suggest you leave these premises right now before I throw you both out the window." They left in a hurry. I couldn't believe it. I saw this pastor after that in the community and he could not look me in the eyes. Being a Christian pastor is sometimes a lonely job and I think one of the hardest on earth.

We had some great victories too. I started a Conference on the Holy Spirit in a retreat setting at a local church camp each June. We would have a dynamic speaker come and teach on the baptism and gifts of the Holy Spirit. One year I got Fr. Dennis Bennett and his wife Rita to come like they did at Lakewood. Some people would drive down, others would stay in the lodge and still others would camp out. We had a special program for the kids too and baby-sitting. It was unbelievable. I had an African American fellow pastor, Rich, who would come and lead worship. Rich has the gift of praise. He could have anyone praising God in minutes. After a couple of years, people starting coming from all over the Northwest. On Saturday night we would have a huge healing service after the evening message. I would have pastors and Christian leaders and their spouses help me pray for the sick by laying hands and anointing with oil in teams of two. Sometimes the healing lines would go for an hour or more. God would give prophecy, word of knowledge and people would fall down in the presence of God. It was over whelming. People would get saved and filled with the Holy Spirit and begin to learn how to manifest the gifts of the Spirit. In those moments, I was caught up in glory. They were my best times at Avon. On Sunday I moved the entire morning worship service to the camp. We would come back to Avon truly revitalized and empowered.

Another successful program was our annual summer Sunday evening gathering at the amphitheater in Deception Pass State Park. We would have a potluck dinner followed with singing beside a huge bonfire with testimonies. It was a powerful evening. My favorite services were those where we would serve communion in the candle lit sanctuary one family at a time. We did this on Christmas Eve and also on Maundy Thursday. After I served the family communion, I would have a prayer. Often God would give me a prophecy or word of knowledge for them. I never felt closer to God's people and in awe of the Lord.

The summer of 1981 I was before the Board of Ordained Ministry once again. My DS still held a position on the Board. Once again he convinced the Board there was something wrong with me and that they should delay my full ordination. It was awful. Many of my evangelical/charismatic colleagues were incensed. I was deflated again. How could I have so much success and receive such rejection? It really hurt to be at Conference and know that everyone was judging Avon and I. Most of them knew nothing about either one of us. I was mystified. I asked, "God, what are you trying to tell me?" I went home again to face the angry people of Avon who also felt rejected. It was all I could do to keep them loyal to the denomination and paying their apportionments to the denomination. I was between a rock and a hard place. Gail told me to just keep going, and I did by the strength that only God supplied.

The summer of 1982 was a joy filled one. That year I had remembered that my mentor at Pasadena First, their pastor, was the attending Elder at my Bishop's consecration and one of his best friends. I called him and told him about the DS and the twice-postponed ordination. I found out later he called the Bishop and told him I was a brother and to ordain me soon, that the DS was bigoted and persecuting me. The next thing I knew, the DS was removed early and I was accepted by the Board for full ordination as Elder. My mentor was the Conference preacher that year and laid hands on me at my ordination ceremony. It was awesome. We were in Spokane and Gail was pregnant with our third child. It seemed that half of the Avon Church and my family came. What a wonderful evening it was. I really felt affirmed by the Church that night. The Bishop went out of his way to spend special time congratulating me in the service. It just goes to show that if God has called you to a ministry and you are patient and faithful, he will bring it to pass. He controls all things.

One of the other wonderful things that happened that summer was the birth of my first son, Jonathan Douglas, August 23, 1982. We have a family tradition of the first-born son taking this father's name as his middle name. Jonathan was a surprise to me from the beginning. I learned that Gail was pregnant with him

Christmas Eve 1981 around midnight after the evening services. As I was exhausted and getting ready to go to bed. I saw this little baby jumper on my pillow with a note. The note read, 'Merry Christmas from Jonathan'. Gail knew from day one that she was pregnant with a boy and that his name was Jonathan. I refused to believe that she was carrying a boy. I was sure that he was a girl. What are the chances of having a boy after two girls? The name Jonathan comes from the Old Testament name of the son of the first King of Israel, Saul. Jonathan was a faithful friend of David, the second King of Israel. Jonathan was the epitome of faithfulness. On several occasions in prayer I heard inside the Lord call me a Jonathan, that I was faithful. I loved that name and decided to name my first son Jonathan. It is my prayer that he will be faithful to the Lord all his life.

While I was in seminary I read the book 'Call to Commitment'. It was about a fellowship in Washington, D. C. called Church of the Savior that was started by a former Army Chaplain from WW II named Gordon. I was fascinated with the way this church married spiritual discipleship and mission, especially to the poor, in what they called mission groups. I felt led to move Avon in that direction. I took one of my leaders and went to their orientation retreat center called Wellspring in Maryland October of 1982. My good friend Charlie from seminary also joined me. At that weekend we learned about their theology, experienced silence and some of their mission groups. It was fascinating.

After an introduction, we went into about seventeen hours of silence. We were Christian leaders from all over the world who had never met and we spent the first seventeen hours together in silence. I had never had such an experience. It was profound. The next day we were all waiting upon the Lord in our own way. I was out in the beautiful Maryland countryside enjoying the turning leaves on the trees when the Lord spoke to me clearly in my heart and said, "I want you to become a Navy Chaplain." I learned that weekend, if get quiet enough for a period of time, occasionally his voice comes clear. This call came like my call to ordination while at Lakewood.

Prior to this trip, I had run into the senior chaplain at the local Whidbey Island Naval Air Station named Captain Jack. After getting to know each other, he had decided that I should become a Navy Chaplain. Everywhere I would go, he would be the speaker. I would go to the Gideon's pastor's dinner and he would be there speaking. I would go to pastor's day at the local Rotary Club and he would be there giving an address. At each event he would say in his talk, "And we need excited new young chaplains in the military like Doug Waite over there". Parishioners would look at me wondering what he was talking about. He had the Chaplain Corps detailer, who makes assignments, call me. He even sent the local senior Reserve Chaplain, a Captain, over to my house to meet with Gail and me. God was trying to get my attention. I would go to a social function and ask the person next to me what he did and he would say, "I am a Navy Chaplain". I couldn't get away from them. I no longer had a desire to become a chaplain. I was sure God had taken that away from me in seminary.

The call came to me at Wellspring to go into the Navy chaplaincy. God was very clear that it was Navy. He had said no to me years earlier at Fuller because it was Army chaplaincy and it was not the right time. Now was the right time and the Navy was the right place. My first response was to cry. I did not want to go into the Navy again. I detested separation from my wife. The last thing I wanted to do was leave my wife, two beautiful daughters, my new son and go out to sea on a ship. The Lord told me it would be OK for his yoke was easy and his burden was light. He said this yoke would fit like a glove. I told him that if this were really from him, he would have to convince my Bishop and my wife. I had gone to Wellspring to learn a new direction for Avon and came away with a new call for my life. While we were in D. C. near the Capitol, God spoke to me again in my heart and told me I would come back there and work some day. Little did I know this would come true 19 years later.

I flew home and took Gail out to dinner the first night. I told her what I thought I heard the Lord say to me about the Navy. She said, "Great, when do we go? I always wanted to be an officer's wife. No more church potlucks in the basement". I went down to Seattle and took my Bishop out to lunch. He had been arrested with the Catholic Archbishop at Naval Submarine Base Bangor protesting the arrival of the Trident missiles. I did not know how he would respond to my call. I told him what I felt the Lord calling me to do. He looked me square in the eyes and said, "If God is calling you to do something, then you had darn well better do it." He told me about how he almost became an Air Force Chaplain and how he didn't want to be a Bishop but his wife told him he had to answer God's call. He even offered me another appointment, church, if I was unhappy with Avon. I told him that was not why I was there. He then said for me to go, take three years and see if I liked the Navy. If I didn't like it and came back, he would give me a new church as good or better than the one I had. How could I lose? I felt these two people were God's confirmation to me that this call was from the Lord.

I still did not move on the call immediately. Avon was in the middle of a huge building program. We were close to breaking ground. How could I leave them now? When I asked God that he said, "I have the man picked out to take your place." Also, Church of the Savior had taught me to carry a call from God for at least a year before acting on it, looking for confirmation from God's people. I spent one day a month for a year at the Fir's Retreat Center in Bellingham in silence before the Lord asking him for clarification of the call to chaplaincy. It turned out the pastor at their Geneva Church there was also a retired Navy Chaplain, a Captain. We talked and he wound up writing me an endorsement.

I tried to get into the Reserves just to get my feet wet and see if I even qualified physically. I passed all the qualifications and was offered a commission as a Lieutenant Junior Grade in the United States Navy Reserve Chaplain Corps. I had come a long way from Electrician's Mate Third Class. I went to the church and asked them to support me in the Reserves. I thought it would be good for me, giving me some new friends, experiences, training, and income. They refused. They did not want to share me with the Navy. I went to the Lord and asked him why? He said inside my heart, "I never called you to the Reserves. I called you to active duty". Against the wishes of the church, I accepted my commission on August 17, 1983 and kept it secret from them. I started drilling one weekend a month on my own time off. I think many people knew what I was doing because my hair kept getting shorter. I loved the Reserves and had a great time. They assigned me to a U. S. Marine Landing Support Battalion, MAFREL 422, that drilled in Tacoma, Washington at the Reserve Center where the USS Orleck and USS Brinkley Bass had been tied up and where I had washed blinds years before. All the while I was making plans to go on active duty. Eventually I told the church on a Sunday morning after they turned me down for the Naval Reserve.

One night Gail and I attended a birthday dinner celebration of the Navy Chaplain Corps in Seattle. There were active, reserve and retired chaplains there of all ranks, many of them very senior. I was the most junior chaplain in the room. Gail and I did not know a soul and sat far back in the corner. The Deputy Chief of Chaplains was there from Washington, DC, a one star Navy Admiral and the most senior chaplain in the room. We were well into the dinner when I felt a hand on my shoulder. I turned around to see a broad gold stripe of a Rear Admiral (Lower Half), or one star. It was our Deputy Chief of Chaplains. He wanted to know who I was. We talked for a while and I introduced him to Gail. He had noticed me way back in the corner and sought me out to encourage me. This man, a Roman Catholic Priest, was a true pastor. He really impressed me as a leader and I never forgot what he taught me that night, to take the time to encourage those who are junior to you.

My parents came to visit us. We took them out to dinner one night at the Officer's Club at Naval Air Station Whidbey Island. During the dinner I told my mom and dad that we were planning to go on active duty in the United States Navy Chaplain Corps. My dad just looked at me and said, "You are going to take this big family of yours and leave them while you go wandering around the world on Navy ships?" Like many times before, he was not supportive of what I felt God was calling me to do. I always felt like I never pleased him in many of my major life choices. I have made them anyway. I know that the only two people that I really have to please in my life are God and myself. If I do that, I am sure to eventually please the rest of the important people I love. Today dad thinks my choice of the chaplaincy was a great one and he is glad I did it.

When I came back from my full ordination as Elder in June 1982, many were happy but many were not. When the denomination was holding up my ordination, I was a hero fighting the system. When I was finally fully accepted by the denomination, a group of these people felt that I had somehow sold out for my career. They began to fight me, grumble and complain about everything under the sun. One Sunday I could take it no more. I stood up in the pulpit and told the church we were United Methodist and would remain so. If they didn't like it, there was the door. The exodus began.

An early leader was one of the first in the exodus. He led one of the home groups. He started meeting with his home group and others about splitting from the denomination to start a new nondenominational church. Another new leader also wanted to leave. He had only come to our church recently from another church in the community where he had been a leader. He was also a friend and hunting and fishing buddy. He was an outstanding outdoorsman and had been a hunting and fishing guide on the Skagit River. For years he and I fished and hunted together for salmon, steelhead, duck, deer and elk. We had gotten very close. He was a dynamic Christian leader and I let him teach a class on the Holy Spirit at our church.

Every fall he and I would haul my trailer over to the Olympic Peninsula with his loaded pickup near the town of Forks. We would make camp and then begin to hunt elk. Often his airline's pilot buddy would join us. They were very good in the woods and taught me many things about hunting big game. It was great Christian fellowship and fun. We would stay out there almost a week. Hunting the Olympics is very hard work. The mountains go straight up and down. You are lucky if you can get a shot closer than about 400 yards. If you get one, it is five one hundred-pound packs out for miles. You have to field dress the 500 plus pound elk on site. It is an all day job but a rewarding one. One year I fed my family on nothing but elk and steelhead that I had gotten with this man. We became very close friends. Like my secretary Joedy, I was glad he was not in my congregation and did not encourage him when he left where he was and started coming to Avon.

My long time leader talked my hunting friend into meeting with his small group. Unbeknownst to me, they were planning to start a new church. My friend talked to me about becoming the pastor. I told him I would have none of it. They asked my friend if he would be the pastor. He accepted. This group decided they would begin meeting at my friend's place of business. They started meeting in his building in March of 1983. By the time the exodus was over, we lost over a hundred people, many who were tithers. It was a difficult time for me. I was really hurt by what my friend was doing. He did not seem to understand. We never went hunting or fishing again. We were friendly when we saw each other but it was never the same.

I was struggling to get the church to build the building they needed for the ministry God was calling them to. Rick had left to go to college and I had hired a new assistant pastor, Richard, from Fuller with another part-time secretary, Gerry, in the office. People in the community were saying that I was trying to build my own kingdom at Avon. I was in the middle of my second church split. First it was the old line

Methodists, now it was the new charismatics. I had made the mistake of building my ministry and finances on these new people. I should have known better. Many had come from other churches where they had been unhappy. It was just a matter of time before they would be unhappy with me too and leave.

The faithful who stayed felt led to combat the exodus with prayer. I felt that there was generational sin in that congregation from the sins of the community leaders who had gone before. Avon had always been plagued with gossip and division in its ranks. Some said Avon had a critical spirit. We held many evening prayer meetings in the sanctuary that were well attended. One night someone said they could see the eyes of Satan at the back door window looking in while we prayed. I believed it. On at least two occasions I had heard the voice of Satan laughing at me in my heart while I walked outside the church along the Avon Allen Road. We were locked in a spiritual battle that only the power of God could combat through prayer. Sometimes at night I would stay in the sanctuary alone by the communion table confessing the sins of the church to the Lord. I am sure it was these prayers of mine and others that enabled us to survive.

The exodus hurt us but we had a loyal core of about two hundred that banded together determined to build the new building. We broke ground that summer and were well into the first phase by fall. The church hired a contractor but provided much of the labor themselves. We had to meet in a school during those days. It was really tough going for me. I got depressed. Gail also couldn't stand all the negativity that was aimed at me from those who had left. I was working long hours and seldom home. By the New Year we were back in our facility but it was really torn up.

While this was all going on, I was preparing to leave on active duty the summer of 1984. I knew in my heart that this was what God wanted me to do. Gail agreed. I still felt a lot of guilt leaving these people in the middle of this whole mess. I stayed as long as I could, two years beyond receiving my call from the Lord. Leaving Avon was one of the hardest things I ever did. I was leaving a dream I had of pastoring a large charismatic congregation in the Skagit Valley. This whole great congregation had come together miraculously from the Lord. We had many wonderful memories as well as many painful ones.

In the middle of all this chaos, I discovered that my parent's former Episcopal priest who officiated at our wedding, Jack, was the rector of the Oak Harbor Episcopal Church close by. We got together and were amazed at how much we had in common. Our families and even our homes looked alike. We each had a daughter born on the same day and year. We would get together with Jack and Joan for fellowship and fun. Just before we left Avon, we had lunch. I was talking about how I lamented giving up my dream of the large charismatic church in Skagit Valley. His wife Joan prophetically spoke to me and said, "That was your dream, not God's". It really hit home.

Our farewell party was after the worship service June 10, 1984. I wore my Navy whites. The church played 'Anchor's Away' to my surprise for the recessional. They had a huge party for us in the new unfinished parlor and gave us a beautiful handmade quilt. A few days before, I had the movers come and pack up all our household goods. We rented our house to a member of the congregation. I was on my way first to Chaplain's School at Newport, Rhode Island for two months and then to my new assignment at First Force Service Support Group (1st FSSG) at Fleet Marine

Force (FMF) Camp Pendleton, California, the Marines. Gail would take the kids and move to Seattle, living with her grandmother for the summer. As we drove by the church for the last time, I wept. Avon had been a tremendous time of growth and maturity in our lives but it had exacted a huge price. The pastor who took my place was a builder who finished the new building. God knew what he was doing.

8

MILITARY CHAPLAIN

While Gail and the kids were at great-grandmas, I was in Newport, Rhode Island for two months of U. S. Navy Chaplain's School. I left on July 4th 1984, twelve years to the day since I left for boot camp in San Diego. I was in the largest group to ever go to Chaplain's School, about 120 men and women. Some were going to seminary, in the reserves and others were headed to active duty. We had four companies. I was one of the few going directly to active duty.

When I first became interested in the Chaplain's Corps, the detailer who made assignments would call me all the time about orders. Gail and I originally wanted to go to the East Coast to a ship. We had never lived on the East Coast and I thought a ship would be easy as I had been on two as an enlisted man. The detailer promised me I would be able to do that. When the orders finally came, it was to the West Coast and the U.S. Marine Corps. I tried to talk to the detailer after that and he would never return my calls. A year or so later I heard him speak to a group of chaplains. He began his talk with, "I am the detailer, and I ruin people's lives". It kind of reminded me of my chief in boot camp who told us that first morning that everything the recruiter told us was a lie.

I was thirty-four years old and had a desire to do my very best at Chaplain's School, especially in the area of physical fitness. The Navy Chaplain School was different from all other Staff Corps Schools in that we had a Marine Gunnery Sergeant whom oversaw our military drill, courtesy, and physical fitness. He saw that we were 'squared away' in the Marine sense of the word. It was not an easy job for this Marine warrior to take a bunch of civilian clergy, many who had never had any contact with the military, and turn them into military officers.

Since so many chaplains, about one fourth of the 1200 chaplains at that time, would serve with Marines, they had to meet Marine standards for physical fitness (PT). That included a three-mile run plus sit-ups and pull-ups in a timed test. I had been trying on my own to build up to the three-mile run. Many had not and struggled. I managed to get an 'outstanding', the highest overall score, on every PT test. I was very proud of that.

Since I had gotten out in 1975, the military had really changed for the better. When I left drugs were a real problem, morale was as low as it could get for a defeated force and there were race conflicts. When I came back in 1983, drugs had been eliminated due to the urinalysis, equal opportunity was going strong, and the Reagan Administration had restored pride and professionalism to the military. It was a complete metamorphosis, night and day.

I made some great friends at Chaplain School; some that I still stay in contact with today. My first roommate was a Roman Catholic priest from the Philippines who snored and kept me awake at night. I traded him for an Irish priest from the East Coast. Newport was a beautiful old seafaring town with lots of naval tradition. I loved it but I missed my family. I would call Gail and tell her about the new world I was experiencing and she would get frustrated because she couldn't experience it with me. The family was doing OK at great-grandmas but it was crowded and hard on everyone.

I learned many new things at Chaplain's School that I continue to use every day. My company commanders were great guys; one was a Jewish rabbi and the other a Roman Catholic priest from the Eastern Rite. The ecumenism was outstanding. I loved being exposed to all this diversity. Our motto was 'cooperation without compromise'. We learned to really appreciate and enjoy each other. None of us could have done this in our civilian settings. We would get up early each morning for exercise and run in formation with cadence for miles and miles. It was very motivating.

Sometimes at night and on weekends we would go out in town for dinner and fun. We had a particular piano bar that we would often congregate at. It was a great time. Every so often I would preach at the Newport Chapel or out in town at one of the local United Methodist churches. I also would borrow a car and occasionally drive to Boston to see Gail's sister Beth who was teaching there. I visited a former parishioner one weekend up in Connecticut. The Chaplain Corps would take us all over to visit submarines, aircraft carriers, the Merchant Marine Academy, and the Marines in the field.

One day I was in the uniform shop on base. I was getting fitted for my blues. As I left the shop, I ran into a Commander who I recognized. He had been a Lieutenant and my Department Head on the USS Orleck back in 1974. I asked him, "What are you doing with that silver oak leaf on your collar sir?" He said to me, "Petty Officer Waite, what are you doing with that cross on your collar?" It was good to see him again after all those years. He was attending the Naval War College at Newport. We ran into each other a few more times after that. He is retired now but still working for the Navy in Bremerton, Washington as of this first writing. Whenever I am there, I stop by and tell his secretary to tell him that Petty Officer Waite would like to see him. We always have a good laugh. Whenever I preach at the Bremerton Chapel, he comes. The Navy is really a very small community.

Finally, commencement day came. Like boot camp, I was in terrific shape and looking good in my choker whites. Gail flew in for the event along with my friends Barb and Charlie from Fuller who were pastoring nearby, and Gail's sister Beth. I borrowed a car and met Gail at a nearby hotel. We had a wonderful reunion. It was so good to be with her again. The commencement was spectacular, all 120 of us in our chokers. I graduated with distinction. I was very proud to be serving in the United States Navy as a member of the Chaplain Corps and looking forward to a new career.

Gail and I flew back to Seattle, loaded up the kids in two cars and started out for Camp Pendleton, California. Briana was almost nine, Lauren four and Jonathan just turned two. We got as far as Oregon when my little orange Mazda blew up. I was driving it with Jonathan. We spent the night in a motel; walked away from our little Mazda, loaded as much as possible into a U-Haul trailer and car top carrier and headed down the road. It was very depressing.

We arrived in Oceanside, California during the hottest time of the year. We were staying in the old Bachelor Officer's Quarters (BOQ) that had no air conditioning. It was sweltering. Tempers were raging. In the middle of all of this, we were driving around daily in the heat trying to find a place to live. I was also going to work each day. I worked for Captain Dan Finn; an older experienced Roman Catholic priest. He was the senior chaplain for First Force Service Support Group (1st FSSG) for Fleet Marine Force Pacific (FMFPAC). It was made up of many battalions who provided logistic support to the First Marine Division.

The First Marine Division waged the war in Vietnam and Desert Storm. I walked through the door and they promoted me to Lieutenant (LT) on the spot. The promotion had come in while we were on the road. This was very upsetting to the other Lieutenant Junior Grade (LTJG) who was looking forward for me to come so he wouldn't be the junior chaplain.

Each battalion had a chaplain. I was assigned to the Seventh Motors Battalion located then at the top of Rattlesnake Canyon near Mainside in the middle of the base. Camp Pendleton is one of the biggest military bases in the world in terms of square miles. At that time there was about 50,000 Marines there and 70 chaplains. Seventh Motors provided all the motor transport, trucks and jeeps, for the Group. It was a small battalion of about 500 men and women commanded by a Lieutenant Colonel (LTCOL).

The chaplain I was relieving was named Tom. He had gone to the Naval Academy and been a combat Marine Captain in Vietnam. Tom was a great big tough Marine who had become a Navy Chaplain. He had a terrific testimony of being healed from cancer and finding the Lord. He took me around and gave me an orientation to the battalion we call 'turn over'. We walked up to a Marine and Tom said in a rough commanding voice, "Were you in chapel this Sunday Marine?" The young man replied in a load voice, "No sir!" Tom continued eyeing him closely, "Are you going to be in church this week Marine?" Standing at attention he said, "Yes sir!" Tom turned to me, "That's how it's done chaplain." I thought to myself, "How am I going to survive?" Needless to say, I was just a little intimidated by Tom but he and I and our families became great friends.

We found an apartment in Oceanside at a place called Flower Hill Apartments. There were a lot of military families and chaplains living there. It was a total cultural change for Gail and I and the kids from Avon and Skagit Valley. We got Briana settled in school. She was in the fourth grade. We had come from an almost totally Caucasian community. Now my daughter was a minority in her classes. It was a little uncomfortable for Gail and I but Briana didn't seem to notice. The apartment had a pool and Jacuzzi and we made some wonderful friends there. We never really had any problems there except a few times, like when some girl pulled a knife on Briana by the garages. That was a little alarming.

About my second week in the battalion, my Commanding Officer (CO) came by the office and said, "Chaplain, I want a counseling appointment. Get your PT gear on and meet me by my office at twelve hundred." "Aye, aye sir", I replied. The adjutant, a Marine Captain, met me there too. Together the three of us took off on a little jog. Our battalion sat on the top of a ridge. We jogged down the ridge and into the valley along the river for the better part of an hour. Chaplain's School had gotten me used to jogging for three miles at one time but this was way over my endurance level. Eventually, we turned back and headed up Rattlesnake Canyon to the battalion. I was dying. About half way up the canyon I could go no further. I stopped expecting them to keep going. They stopped too. I told them to keep going. They told me that Marines never leave anyone behind. I felt like I had failed the test.

It was a good thing we had that Jacuzzi at the apartment. I would come home at night and Gail would drop me into it. I was a mess for the first few weeks. The next time the CO wanted a 'counseling appointment' I was a very anxious. Would I make it without stopping? We started out like last time down the hillside and along the river. At last we started up Rattlesnake Canyon. This time I decided that I would have a heart attack before I quit. To my astonishment, I made it all the way to the top. I was now in the club. The secret of winning the respect of Marines is to run with them and not quit, ever. On several occasions since that day, I have met challenges that I wanted to give up. Each time I remembered that day and determined I would die first. Every time I made it to the end. There must be a lesson here. The Marines taught me how to succeed through endurance and determination. If you are willing to go to the end of yourself, you can do a lot more than you think.

The first Christmas was the toughest for me. I missed my congregation and the decorated sanctuary with all the closeness of the people of God during the holidays. I was grieving the loss of the Avon Church. I clung to my family during that time. Gail tried to make the off time special with all kinds of great baking and cooking for all of us. It was a nice Christmas even though 70-degree sunny days seemed a little strange in December.

We went into the field right after Christmas on one of our first tactical exercises. I learned how to dive out of my jeep for cover in a firefight and how Marines live on the ground. I wanted to go for a helo, helicopter, ride. I asked the CO if he could arrange it. He told me, "No problem." As I was climbing into my first CH-46 Chinook helicopter, I saw that the CO wasn't going. I asked him why not. He said, "Chaplain, I never climb in those things unless I absolutely have to, too dangerous." That didn't make me feel good but I went anyway for a great ride. Every time I climb into a helo, I remember that CO's comment.

As I mentioned earlier, there were about 70 chaplains at Camp Pendleton. It was a great way to begin a career as it exposed you to so many chaplains both good and bad. I feel sorry for chaplains who get an isolated tour, such as a small ship, for their first tour where they are the only chaplains. I would counsel young chaplains against it. You need to be around other chaplains who are senior to you for fellowship and for mentoring to get started right. Somehow Gail became the president of the Chaplain Wives Club. We call it Spouses Club now. She was doing her best to get involved and help my career. They came up with some great social functions for all of us. We actually had fun when we got together. We became friends with chaplains and their wives there that we have kept up throughout my career.

I had an experience at Camp Pendleton that involved shooting badges. Marines are all riflemen. They are always qualifying on all kinds of weapons. They earn shooting badges for marksmanship that they wear on their dress uniforms. Some chaplains earn those too and wear them. I enjoy weapons and would often shoot too. I went to qualify one day and a Vietnam Marine Gunny stopped me. He asked me why I wanted to do that. He said, "Chaplain, we have all kind of things around us every day that remind us of war. We need something around us to remind us of peace." He continued, "If you wear those expert shooting badges and we get into a firefight, I am going to throw you an M-16. But if you do not wear those badges, I am going to give my life to protect you." That did it for me. I determined then and there I would never wear shooting badges or qualify again. I found out later that the Chief of Chaplains expressly forbade us to wear them too. We are noncombatants under the Geneva Convention and wearing such warfare devices jeopardizes that status. Some chaplains choose to ignore that direction but I do not, based on the words of that Marine Gunny and the Chief of Chaplains Directive. I want to always remind combatants of peace, not war.

One thing I started doing at Camp Pendleton was Inspirational Prayer Breakfasts. I would find motivational speakers such as war heroes, professional athletes, or other famous people who have a Christian testimony. I would host a big breakfast in a nice facility and ask a beautiful young woman to sing contemporary Christian music. The speaker would tell their story, sometimes with film or video, and give an invitation. Many would meet the Lord and be encouraged in their faith. At Camp Pendleton I had three of these, a famous Air Force Colonel, a pitcher from the San Diego Padres and a back from the San Diego Chargers as speakers. My singer also sang for Disneyland. Hundreds of Marines came and many lives were touched. I think it was one of the most important things I did spiritually while I was there. After a while they started calling me the 'Prayer Breakfast Chaplain'.

About this time Gail and I started our Preparing for Adolescence study with Briana. This is a book, tape series and workbook put out by Dr. James Dobson of the organization Focus on the Family in Colorado Springs, Colorado. This study, designed by a Christian psychologist, is an attempt to prepare preadolescents for that difficult time of life. Dr. Dobson recommends you do this study with your preteen prior to their thirteenth birthday. Gail and I and Briana would go on a date once a week to an ice cream shop, go over that week's chapter and fill out the workbook page. It led us into many discussions of various topics. We ended it with a weekend retreat with the same sex parent listening to and discussing the tapes. Gail took Briana to the armed forces hotel New Sanno in Tokyo. We have done this with all of our children. That weekend is a special time we all remember.

Something happened at Flower Hill Apartments that we would like to forget. Gail was babysitting the young daughter of one of our new chaplains who lived at the apartments also. The girl was playing with our children on the bunk bed in our second story bedroom. The bed was close to the window and the kids were all rough housing up on the top bunk. Somehow this little girl fell backwards off the bed and went through the window screen and fell to the ground below. The kids went and got Gail who ran down the stairs and found this little one in a heap on the ground, unconscious. Gail didn't know what to do so she ran upstairs and called 911 and then returned and held Carrie while praying in her prayer language for God to intervene. The aid cars finally came and took Carrie to the hospital. She was fine, just a few broken bones, thanks be to God. We were all very scared. The parents later received a settlement from our insurance company. I learned why it is important to have renters insurance with liability.

Eventually we moved into base housing. These were single-family units behind the hospital at the edge of a hillside. They were very spacious and nice. We also bought a little trailer and started doing some camping like we used to do in Mt. Vernon. We loved to pull the trailer to the beach at the recreation site on base. Once we stayed there for a week body surfing and laying in the sun. California beaches are the best.

We came back from one vacation to find out they wanted me to move to another battalion. It seems the chaplain who had been there was falling asleep at staff meetings and the CO had enough. Chaplain Finn assigned me as the new 7th Engineers Battalion chaplain. It was a much larger battalion, about 1200 men and women. I was sad to leave 7th Motors. It was my first active duty assignment and it had been a great experience. The new battalion was going to be a much greater challenge.

One of my CO's at 7th Engineers had been the All Marine Handball Champion. When I had been in seminary, I had learned handball and often played my giant buddy Charlie. I also played in a doctor's barn while at the church at Avon. I was out of practice but I let my new CO know that I played. Handball used to be a very popular sport until the advent of racquetball. People complained that it hurt their hands. As racquetball grew, handball diminished. I loved handball. It is one of the few ambidextrous sports and I do not like the danger of racquets. The game is the same. It is just the balls that are different, smaller and harder, and no racquets.

My CO and I started playing together. He was superb. I could keep the ball in play. We got in the base tournament. I was his doubles partner. We took first place. Then we went to the All Marine Championships. That year it was close to Camp Pendleton. It didn't take long for me to wash out in singles but I continued as the CO's doubles partner. We did not take first but we lasted quite awhile. I had a blast. The All
Service Racquetball Championships were also going on at the same time. Soon everyone found out I was a chaplain so they asked me to say the blessing at the final banquet dinner for all players. It was something to remember.

One of the new chaplains at 1st FSSG, Leroy, a Commander, asked me to help him start a lunchtime Bible study in the barracks of our two battalions. Leroy was a very impressive African American chaplain who preached like Martin Luther King and loved the Lord. He would lead gospel songs on the piano and I would lead contemporary praise on the guitar. We would trade off leading the singing and the study. After awhile, we had quite a large integrated group of Marines coming. It was special and we became friends.

I also got involved with David Wilkerson's band 'Praise' with Dallas Holm. It was the same band that played the night I went forward to dedicate myself to serve the Lord in full time ministry while at Lakewood. They wanted to do a concert on the base and have it televised. I worked like crazy and the Lord filled up the theater one night with all the television cameras and vans. My children got to go back stage and meet Dallas Holm and his band. It was a very special evening. Many people gave their lives to the Lord that night in the theater and on television.

I had my first experience with surgery during that time. I had a condition that was very painful. I tried unsuccessfully to live with it and correct it with natural means and prayer. It didn't work. The pain was starting to affect my work and my family. I went to see the surgeon and he recommended surgery. I was scared to death. Finally, I consented. There is an old saying that 'change comes when the pain is greater than the fear'. That was the case with me. As I was waiting in the hospital room the night before, I was reading every devotional book I had on trusting in God. I was really full of fear. The chaplain of the hospital, a Roman Catholic, came by and anointed me with oil and prayed for God's healing. He was a charismatic Catholic. That really meant a lot to me. I could not understand why God did not heal me without surgery. After a struggle, the peace of God finally came as I put myself squarely in his hands. If he wanted to use medical science to heal me, then so be it.

Surgery and hospital stays are such humbling adventures. You lose all your privacy and dignity. My surgeon had a terrible bedside manner. He was a Navy Captain and said to be one of the best. Why is it that the best surgeons are the ones with the worst bedside manner? Eventually they came and wheeled me into the operating room. Before I knew it, I was back in my room. After a while, the anesthesia wore off. I was amazed to find that I had no pain, I never did. It was a painless recovery. I was home the next day. It was a miracle. God used medical science to heal me with no pain. I thanked the doctor. His response, "I cut, God heals." I have not had that pain since. Praise God. Unbeknownst to me, this was God's way of preparing me for my next assignment as a hospital chaplain.

About this time I was asked to deploy overseas for six months with the Marines. There were a lot of young chaplains who wanted to go in hopes they would secure their careers. They thought that deployment would help them get extended beyond the initial three-year obligation and get promoted. They also thought it would get them out of sea duty on their next tour. My reasoning was that you never volunteer to deploy. As the senior Lieutenant, I passed. The guy behind me took it. He wound up getting a ship next and didn't get extended or promoted. I got shore duty, extended and promoted. Go figure.

After two years, we got orders to Japan. They wanted me to take the naval hospital at our base in Yokosuka, south of Tokyo on Tokyo Bay. Gail and I were really excited. We had always wanted to go overseas and see the world. On my last day at 7th Engineers, the CO asked me if I wanted to take the battalion on a run. Every Friday all 1200 of us would go on a run led by the CO. The executive officer (XO), number 2, would follow in the back with the chaplain.

The XO had never led the battalion. I felt very honored. I came up front and took the battalion on an hour run. What a thrill to lead that many men and women. At the end of the run, the CO put me up on a table and gathered everyone around me. He told me to tell them anything I wanted. I gave them all my testimony and invited them to accept Christ. It was really something.

Looking back, our time with the Marines was really special. I was always the only Naval officer in the battalion but they all treated me well. The Marines love their chaplains if they aren't afraid to run and go out in the field. They also want you to be genuine and can see right through you if you aren't. Gail always liked the way the young Marines treated her and the children with kindness and respect. We would consider another tour with the Marines anytime.

9
Japan

We packed up the green Cougar and headed back to the Pacific Northwest in the summer of 1986. Briana was almost 11, Lauren was 6 and Jonathan was 4. After visiting my parents in Boise, Idaho, we went to Annual Conference in Walla Walla, Washington where I celebrated my 36th birthday. Our next stop was Seattle where all the rest of our family was. We sold our Cougar and waited for our flight to Japan. Gail and I had a big party with all of our families at the old Naval Air Station Sand Point Officer's Club. It was a special night. We saw family we hadn't seen in years. They all went around the room and told stories about Gail and I.

We finally climbed on the big jet with our three children and headed for Narita International Airport in Tokyo, Japan. This was going to be a huge adventure for the Waite family. We were all really excited. When we finally landed, Jonathan and I went into the men's room. Everything in Japan is a little bit lower than it is in the United States. Jonathan's comment as he stood in front of the sinks was, "Look dad, I grew on the plane ride." The other thing that caught our attention was the tall thin Coke cans with Japanese writing on them.

A big bus from Naval Fleet Activities Yokosuka, Japan took us on a long ride through the crowded freeways and roads of Japan to our base in the south. We happened to arrive in August during a torrential rainstorm. It was very hot and humid. We stayed in the Navy Lodge as all families did who first came to the base. The rain was coming down in sheets.

We had to put towels under the doors to keep the water from coming into the room. We ate in the restaurant next door.

I went over to the Naval Hospital where I was assigned as the only chaplain. It was a nice modern hospital with many specialties. It serviced our US forces in all of Japan and even Korea. I had a nice office on the ground floor and a female enlisted Religious Program Specialist (RP) who assisted me from the office next door. She had my name already on the door. I was impressed. The XO was a Navy Captain, a psychiatrist. The CO was also a Captain, an osteopath, who had become a Naval Flight Surgeon. This was his second command. This was going to be a totally different experience. I think that is one thing I like about being a Navy chaplain. We have the opportunity to serve with every community in the Navy, Marine Corps and the Coast Guard. We even serve with the Merchant Marines in time of war. Every assignment is totally different.

The first order of business when you are living in the Navy Lodge in Japan with your family is to find a place to live, get your driver's license and buy a car. There is not enough housing on base so newcomers usually have to move out into the Japanese economy for the first year. We were fortunate in that the female chaplain I relieved had a wonderful townhouse in an area called Mobori Kaigan on the water by Tokyo Bay. We loved it. It was a three bedroom two level. Two of the bedrooms were tatami rooms with the woven cord floors. Briana got the one downstairs with the sliding shoji door. The Japanese use that room as a family shrine to their ancestors. Gail and I had one of the two upstairs rooms. Ours had a tatami floor and a big window looking out at Tokyo Bay. Both tatami rooms had sliding wooden and paper shoji doors. Ours also had storm blinds that were very unique. We would use them in the days ahead. Our place had air conditioning, uncommon in most places, and wall-to-wall carpeting in the living room. All Japanese homes are heated with kerosene space heaters in the winter. Like most of the world except the U.S., they only heat one room at a time.

We also had a big Japanese bathroom with an ofuro or big family bathtub separate from the tiled shower area. The Japanese shower before they bathe so they can keep the same water in the tub and reheat it. I used to love coming in from a jog along the water and soaking in that tub with a couple of the kids. Some of the appliances were US from the base. The only downside was the huge cockroaches that appeared from time to time.

While we were still in the lodge, Gail and I studied for and took our driver's test both written and driving. The Japanese drive on the left side of the road and their steering wheel is on the right. It takes some getting used to. You can always tell new American drivers because they turn their windshield washers on when making a turn. We also had to buy a car. The Japanese discard cars after just a few years, like many other things they own, because it is so expensive to get them reinspected and certified. The cars are called 'gomi' cars, translated 'garbage' cars, by the Americans and can be purchased relatively inexpensively as the Americans are subject to a different standard of inspections. We bought a low mileage seven passenger Nissan Vanette for about $1100. On about our seventh day in Japan we took our driver's test, bought a van and moved into our new Japanese home. We were more fortunate than many who languished in the Lodge for weeks.

Gail met a friend in the laundromat of the Lodge who has remained one of her best friends ever since. Her name is Jean and her husband was the XO on one of our cruisers there. She had two children close to the age of some of ours and we all became good friends. They also got a house out in the Japanese neighborhood close to ours. In future years we would also serve close to them in Europe and in Washington DC. I was with her husband when the plane hit the Pentagon in 9 11. We have been to each other's children's weddings. In retirement we have remained good friends.

When you move into a Japanese neighborhood, you are the ones who bring presents, called presentos, to your neighbors as a way of apologizing for the disruption your move has made to their tranquility. It helps you immediately get into the neighborhood. For us, the children became our passport to the neighbors. The Japanese love children and would invite ours in for food and to play. They liked to practice their English on them. Often we would not know where the children were and would have to go looking for them. Japan is a very safe place and we never worried. The children could walk to the local fast food place or even ride the train to Yokohama and never be bothered. Firearms are not allowed and there is little violent crime. Most of it comes from local mobsters called Yakuza. They have tattoos all over their bodies. Sometimes you can see them at the local bathhouses.

There are many things that bother Americans about Japan. One of them is the way they make all foreigners register with the local police. They say it is for your safety but I think it was so they could keep track of us. They even had a huge billboard in our neighborhood showing all the houses. The ones designated for foreigners were readily identifiable. All the Japanese knew where the foreigners lived.

I did not see a lot of overt racism but it existed. Sometimes when I was jogging along the sea wall I would get hissed at by the old men, a derogatory gesture. Every now and then you would see a sign on a restaurant or other establishment that said emphatically, "Japanese Only". I can honestly say that I did not really understand the insidiousness of racism until I lived in Japan. I had never been a minority until then. There is something unnerving about riding on a huge crowded train full of Japanese people who are all staring at you. You look around to see you are the only non-Japanese person there. I never sensed any real danger but felt hostility from time to time. The Japanese people may not like you, but they are very good at hiding it.

Japan is a patriarchal society. The men are the leaders in front and the women run everything behind the scenes. If you want to get anything done, it has to be man to man. American women would get so frustrated with this culture. They would try to be assertive with the Japanese men, like they are in the US, and get nowhere. Gail finally gave up and had me go to deal with the bank, phone company, salesmen, etc. She would ask a question and get stares. When I asked, I got action. It was a little disconcerting for both of us.

In a Japanese neighborhood everyone takes the responsibility for cleaning up after the garbage truck comes. The trucks are musical too. The first time we heard them we thought it was the ice cream man. Every once in awhile, this strange broom would appear at our door. We did not know what it was. Eventually we discovered that it was our turn to sweep up the garbage collection area. They must have been frustrated with these dumb 'gaigen', or foreigners, at first.

The stereotypical Japanese male gets up very early in the morning and rides the train to Tokyo where

149

he works for a large corporation. He works late in the evening and then goes out for a late dinner with his associates and young secretaries. They drink very heavy. He rides the train home late and sometimes very drunk. Alcoholism is a real problem in Japan for men and women. His family hardly ever sees him except for Sunday. Sunday is dad's day to take the young children and spell off mom. Japanese dads could often be seen on Sunday's taking their children to the park. Most families are made up of one, or at the most two, children. There are many beautiful parks throughout Japan. Sunday is also the one day of the week that you do not want to be on the highways. The Japanese have a car, one, which sits in their driveway all week long until Sunday. It is then that they take the car out for a ride. The highways are unbelievably crowded on that day. We would try not to drive around on Sundays. The rest of the time the Japanese people ride the trains. Trains are very efficient, safe and inexpensive.

One of our first Sundays we decided to attend the chapel on base, a very large religious program. After the service, one of the senior Protestant chaplains asked Gail and me out to lunch at the Officer's Club with his wife. We were having a nice time and thinking this couple was very nice. All of a sudden he started telling us about one of his young Lieutenant chaplains who was constantly getting in trouble. Finally he said, "Well, what do you expect from someone who went to Fuller Seminary?" I couldn't believe he made that comment to a chaplain he just met. I said, "Did you know that I went to Fuller?" Immediately, his face turned ashen and our lunch was over. I never got along with that chaplain, nor did I trust him.

The rest of the chapel was wonderful and we made many friends there. One couple was Frank and Sheila. Frank was one of the new chaplains assigned there. They were a little younger than we were but had a large family and were United Methodist. He had played football at Duke. Over at the hospital there was not much happening. The chaplain I relieved had been married to a pilot on the aircraft carrier USS Midway in Yokosuka. She also had a baby while she was there. The religious program really suffered. It was almost nonexistent when I got there. I had to start from scratch. There had not been services in the nice little chapel we had. I tried to get that going. I also tried to get a weekly Bible study going for the staff. Both were a struggle. I also helped out at the main chapel, one of the largest religious programs in the Navy. I would assist as liturgist and preach every month or so. I also tried to go to their chaplain staff meetings and fit into their duty rotation. I wanted to be a full player and not over in the corner doing my own thing.

Briana and Lauren attended the Department of Defense Schools (DODS) on the base. They are very good. Lauren started first grade there and Briana started sixth grade. The junior high and high school were in the same building. We didn't like that. Briana was also in gymnastics and eventually got on the cheer team in seventh grade. We even had a tackle football program. They played the other DODS schools in Japan.

After a short time, I became a very close friend of my Commanding Officer, Captain Jim. He was a Christian and had toyed with going into the ministry earlier in his life. He came to all my services and Bible studies. It is one of the only times that has happened in my Navy career. He even was my Lay Reader when I was gone. We started to jog together. I was still jogging about twenty minutes or so a day. Jim had not jogged for years and could go only about a block when we first started. I kept working with him and after awhile he could jog as long as I could. We also started traveling together with our wives. We made several trips to Korea shopping. One of those trips involved pheasant hunting.

We had a patient who was an Army Colonel from Korea. I made friends with him and he told me about some great pheasant hunting there on an island called Cheju off the southern coast. It was an Army rappelling school that was really a front for a flag/general officer pheasant-hunting club. For $75 a day you could get a license, shotgun, ammunition, guide, hunting dogs, Quonset hut stateroom, laundry, and an Army chow hall to eat in. They even cleaned, froze and stuffed your birds for you.

Jim and I planned a trip there with the base legal officer, Captain Winston. Winston was also a strong Christian. We took our wives to Seoul, Korea on the free military flight from Yakota Air Force Base (AFB). They landed at Osan AFB where you could take a bus to Seoul. We would then stay at retreat center the Army had there by the shopping district. We dropped the wives off to shop and flew to Cheju for $100 US round trip. The personnel at Cheju even met us at the airport.

Jim had never fired a shotgun in his life. I had to show him everything from scratch. Winston was an old pro. The hunting was the best I had ever seen in my life. We could shoot either sex; we only shot male cocks, and could get a limit of three in the morning, go to lunch, and shoot a limit in the afternoon. I can't tell you how many pheasants we shot. It was hard hunting though. The island was full of volcanic rock that poor labor intensive farmers had used to make huge stone fences around all their fields. All day long you would climb over these fences. At the end of the day you were exhausted.

We hunted for three full days. Even Jim, who had never hunted in his life, was shooting pheasants. The dogs hunted every day and were the best pointers I have ever seen. What a joy to hunt behind them. One night they took some of our pheasants to a local restaurant and fixed pheasant about four different ways. It was a wonderful evening. We all had one of our pheasants stuffed for $25.00 each. They would have cost much more in the US. We called them 'Cock on a Rock'. Each of us had one in our office after that. I still have mine.

Jim and Winston were both Captains, 0-6, so we put the frozen cleaned birds packed in dry ice in their luggage. We flew back to Seoul, picked up our wives who had a great time, and went back to Osan for the flight to Japan. At that time, the military did not check the contents of 0-6 luggage on their flights. We were able to successfully get all the frozen pheasants home. On New Year's we cooked a huge pheasant dinner at Winston's house for all our families. Each of us used a different recipe. During that trip we became good friends. It was like God had given me hunting friends like I had at Avon, thousands of miles from home. Thank you Lord for those special times.

Twice a year we got Environmental and Morale Leave (EML). This EML status allowed us to fly home high priority on military airlines. We decided to go to Hawaii. Gail and I gathered up the whole family and began the two hour plus drive to Yakota AFB. We got there just as a medical evacuation (medevac) flight was leaving to Hickum AFB in Hawaii. We got just enough seats for the five of us. The kids were really excited until we got on the aircraft. It was a C-141 Star Lifter carrying cargo, equipment and soldiers from the field in Korea. As we climbed into our web seating, seven-year-old Lauren said, "This is the worst day of my life."

They gave us box lunches with Twinkies though and suddenly she was in heaven.

We landed in Hawaii and went to the Holiday Inn for the first night. We laughed at the sign in our bathroom for the Japanese tourists to wash inside the tub. We could see Diamond Head out our window and the kids were really excited. First we slept and jet lagged. We went out to eat at an open air McDonald's. The kids thought this was paradise. So did Gail and me. It was so refreshing to be back in American culture after a year in Japan. The next day we moved to the Hale Koa military resort hotel at Ft. DeRussy where Gail and I had stayed in a little Quonset hut years before. It was really nice. The kids loved it. We lay by the pool and swam in the surf. At night we made all the shows at the hotel and walked along the beach of Waikiki. One of places I took the kids was the Arizona Memorial. It was really strange to watch the movies of the attack of Pearl Harbor. Most of the audience was Japanese. The Japanese come there to see the greatest military victory of their history. It makes them very proud. I look at it as one of the biggest terrorist attacks on our soil.

Towards the end of the week I started to worry about getting back to Japan. I started calling the Air Terminal at Hickum AFB. There were a lot of people trying to get out and not many flights. If we had to fly commercial it was going to cost us a fortune. This stress is the down side of flying military air on a standby status. I went out to the terminal a couple of times and could not get manifested. Finally, due to our EML priority, I was able to get us five seats back to Yakota AFB via Guam. Aside from the stress of getting back, it was a great vacation and one we will always remember.

I started a service in the hospital. I began in the small chapel on the third floor. The patient ward was on the fifth floor. Often patients and staff would come down but it was hard for them. I decided to take the service to the patients. I moved to the fifth floor in one of the training classrooms close to the nurse's station. It wasn't quite the same as the chapel but it worked. The CO and his wife came every week. The nurses were also very supportive. They started wheeling the patients down, some on IV's. They would even wheel beds down and put them by the door. I always had communion and offered prayer for healing after. Many asked to be anointed with oil. Soon we had a fairly large congregation of staff, their spouses and others from the base who saw us as an alternative from the chapel. There were not many Christian churches that spoke English outside the gate. We saw many miracles. God was at work. Our service got over in time for me to join my family at the main chapel and even help out there as preacher and liturgist.

I also started a weekly Bible study in our little chapel. Once again the CO came from the first day. It took some time but soon we had a nice group that joined us every Wednesday at noon. Some of the staff spouses even came. I have found that when the leadership is active in worship and Bible study, those they lead will follow them there also. The opposite is also true. I have had few CO's who were active in their faith. This CO would even have me pray with him when he had particularly tough Captain's Mast cases to pass judgment on. These are nonjudicial punishment cases under our military law called the Uniform Code of Military Justice (UCMJ). At Mast the CO determines guilt or innocence and hands out punishment. For most CO's, this is one part of the job they do not enjoy. The chaplain often attends. I spend

155

my time there quietly praying for all concerned, especially for wisdom for the CO.

One year I went to our chaplain's Professional Development Training Course (PDTC) in Okinawa. I was the only chaplain allowed to go because the base CO would not fund the other base chaplains to attend. My CO was separate as a tenant command and he funded me. I felt bad for the others but decided to go anyway. That year the Chief of Chaplains was there. He or she is the senior chaplain for all of the Navy, Coast Guard and Marines, a two star Rear Admiral. This was the same Admiral chaplain who put his hand on my shoulder that night at my first Chaplain Corps birthday dinner years before in Seattle. Then he was the Deputy Chief, a one star, who today is also Chaplain of the Marine Corps. He asked me where the other chaplains were from Yokosuka. I told him I didn't want to put anyone on report but the CO of the base wouldn't send them. When I left to fly back to mainland Japan, he was on my flight. He went straight from Narita Airport with me to the CO of Naval Activities Yokosuka, Japan (CFAY). The Admiral wanted to know why the CFAY CO didn't fund his chaplains to go to the PDTC in Okinawa. The CO denied that he did that. The next day the Admiral came over to the hospital to meet my CO and take a look at my religious program. Fortunately, I had just put together a slide presentation indoctrination class for new staff that I showed him. Afterwards, he asked me to write an article for our chaplain publication on being the only chaplain in an overseas Naval hospital, complete with photos. That article gained me some immediate recognition in the Chaplain Corps. He was a great Chief of Chaplains because he was a pastor first and cared more about people than his own prestige, a rare quality but one needed in a senior chaplain. One side note, the chaplains from CFAY went to the PDTC's each year after that. Our Chief was a true leader.

Every year we had a group of civilian Japanese doctors who would intern at our military hospital. One year we had a doctor who was the son of a Japanese pastor in Hawaii. He was a strong Christian and spoke excellent English and Japanese. We had many American retirees in Japan who were married to Japanese nationals or were estranged from their families in the US. As they got older, they would often come to our hospital to die. The staff would get close to many of them. I ministered to them and their families the love of Jesus. Upon their death, I would often be asked to do a Christian service for their Japanese families. Often these families did not speak much English. Less than one-percent of Japan is Christian. Most Japanese are a combination of nominal Buddhism and Shinto, the official religion of Japan. Monotheism was a completely foreign concept to them. For many it was the first Christian service they had ever come to. I would preach a Christian message and my doctor friend would translate. The Japanese idolize professionals like doctors. Buddhist and Shinto priests they fear. It was a unique experience I will always remember. For many this was the first time they were exposed to Christianity. As I would stand before them, often I would sense the overwhelming love that God has for the Japanese people. What a privilege it was to share the gospel of Jesus Christ with them. Japanese Christians are some of the most loving and happy people I have ever met.

During that time the Navy started testing for HIV positive military personnel. Many of these would develop full-blown AIDS within five years of diagnosis. Once identified as HIV positive, they would come immediately to the hospital. I would see them hours after they had been informed. They were young and terrified. Thoughts of death and how they were going to tell their loved ones consumed them. One night we got a young man whose dad was a pastor in the US. He did not know how he was going to tell his dad. He was so ashamed. I role-played with him. Then I helped him place the call. He was amazed at the compassion and love his dad had for him. Thank God his dad was truly in touch with Jesus. It could have gone the other way with more rejection and guilt.

After one year we moved into base housing. They were fourplexes that looked like flint stone houses. The houses were very nice inside. We had four bedrooms. The kids were in heaven. Everyone had their own room. It was convenient to work and school. Living on the Japanese economy was good but it was nice to be back on an American base. We have found that you always do better financially overseas when you live in base housing. Gail started teaching English to some Japanese women. Many of them were married to influential Japanese businessmen. They paid Gail in Japanese yen, which we used as our play money out in town. They would also bring presentos to the kids. Some of them were very expensive. Gail would fix these ladies a Japanese lunch and then teach them American customs and English conversation. She loved it. Some military spouses made six figure incomes teaching English. Another enterprise Gail got into was modeling. Lauren and Jonathan are blond haired and blue eyed like their mom. The Japanese are very attracted to blond hair. Many Americans find modeling lucrative too. The only problem is you have to go to Tokyo for shooting on a moment's notice. Little Jonathan, now about five, was so cute the

Japanese wanted to use him. Gail tried to take him up a few times but it got to be too difficult.

Gail also hired a cleaning lady and a man who brought us flower arrangements each week called 'iki bana'. We had a very comfortable lifestyle. One of our favorite things to do was get take out yakitori (chicken on a stick), yakisoba (fried noodles), kappa maki (cucumber roll sushi), hot sake and eat it at home. It was very inexpensive and tasted great. We still love Japanese food, especially kappa maki.

Gail and I were having some problems during these days. She says that they were some of the hardest for her. We were arguing a lot. One of the things we said to each other when we came into the military was that we would not let the Navy come between us. If it appeared that the Navy was destroying our family, we would leave. We always look at our family problems and ask ourselves if the Navy is the cause of our trouble. So far we have decided that they are normal problems that all couples and families experience. Many of our problems have come from my expectations. I have lots of them and when they go unmet I feel rejection. Gail says I then pout. I know that I withdraw when I am hurt. I remember one Christmas Gail and I were fighting. It seems many of our fights happen around the holidays. These are the times when my expectations are high. On this particular Christmas, Gail was so mad at me that she almost took the kids and went back to the US.

We had a lot of resources around us to help. An older couple that we called Mom and Pop had a Serviceman's Home off base for the sailors. The Assembly of God Church sponsored it. One year the couple was Augy and Dee. Augy was a retired Air Force chaplain. I got to be very good friends with him. He and Dee had a Marriage Enrichment retreat they put

159

on that was very good. Gail and I went to the first one at the home. I shed a lot of tears that weekend for reasons I still don't understand. I remember Dee asking me where those tears were coming from and I did not have a good answer for her. This weekend helped a lot of couples that were struggling. Later, Gail and I put one of these retreats on with Augy and Dee. Sheila and Frank also helped us from the chapel. A retired General and his wife who were teaching English, Buzz and Ruth, also helped us. We put it on at Tama, an armed forces resort area a couple of hours away. We did this a few times. My CO Jim and his wife Joann also went to one. It was great ministry.

My family and I also went to Tama to relax. It wasn't camping but it was close. We also would go to the armed forces hotel in Tokyo called the New Sanno. It was a wonderful place right in the heart of the city. When our families came to visit we would always take them to Tama and the New Sanno. We would also take the freedom flight, a free space available chartered airliner that flew new military families to Japan and Korea every week, over to Korea and back. Korea was a wonderful place to go and shop. We would stay at the Army religious retreat center in Seoul close to the shopping district. It was inexpensive and had a chow hall. One time we even visited the largest church in the world there, Pastor Choe's church, about one million members. Korea, unlike Japan, has many Christians and churches. The largest Christian churches in the world are in Korea.

One summer we took a vacation to our Marine Corps Air Station at Iwakuni south on the main Japanese island we lived on called Honshu. We drove there, stopping at the old capital of Kyoto and Hiroshima. In Hiroshima we went through the Peace Park museum. The presentation of the atomic bomb blast at Hiroshima was horrific. It gave Gail a migraine headache. Every government leader in the world should be required to go through that place. It convinces you that nuclear war is just not an option for our planet. At one point Jonathan turned to me and said, "Who did this daddy, the Russians?" I had to explain that it was our country that did it. This was the completion of a discussion we had started the summer before at the Pearl Harbor Memorial. When we came out of the museum, we found ourselves in the beautiful Peace Park. We decided to eat our packed lunch there. We felt kind of strange as Americans in that place. Jonathan started playing with a little Japanese boy in the sand, free from racism, nationalism and prejudice. They were soon friends communicating with no problems even though neither could speak the other's language. That scene gave us all hope.

During this time I was having some serious questions about staying in the Navy as a chaplain. I considered one of my gifts to be building churches. In the civilian parish I would preach to large groups on Sundays. I loved to preach. There is something about speaking to a large crowd who is hungry for God's word and to sense his anointing on your message. Suddenly it is no longer you speaking but God. There is no sensation like it. It is something I love to do. I had always hoped someday to be the preaching pastor of a large congregation like my friend George in Pasadena. The rest of parish ministry is not so special to me but I love to preach to God's people. I was sensing a loss of this as I took care of the spiritual needs of Marine battalions and hospitals.

One day I started talking to my friend the retired chaplain Augy. He listened for a while and then he started to speak. He told me of his own struggles as a military chaplain. He had gotten out as a Lieutenant

Colonel in the Air Force before he came in zone for Colonel. The reason was that he was the senior chaplain at a chapel and he had a Roman Catholic chaplain who worked for him. This priest was disrespectful, difficult and would listen to nothing Augy said. Augy finally quit and regretted it ever since. He agreed with me that I had the gift of building churches. He said, "Doug, that is the perfect gift for a military chaplain". He explained that everywhere we go in the military we are starting over from scratch. Either the chaplain before you did not do his or her job correctly or, even if they did, one third of the military moves every year. Invariably, you have to constantly build a new fellowship. A successful military chaplain is one that has the gift of building churches. Augy really turned my head around. I had never thought about it like that. Augy said, "Doug, stay in the chaplaincy. The military really needs your gifts". I started looking at what I was doing in a new light.

A job that I loved doing in the hospital was the Alcoholic Rehabilitation Service (ARS). The word 'Service' was later changed to 'Center' and it became ARC. As the chaplain, I would do the spirituality talks in their Twelve-Step program. The patients were from every rank, race and cultural background. Alcohol addiction is no respecter of persons. I would come in and talk about how human beings were not only physical and psychological but also spiritual. I told them the spiritual was the part of us that reached out to God. I would explain that Jesus was my higher power and that I would like to tell them the story of my healing from substance abuse. They would always agree, even the spiritually hostile ones. I would then tell them my testimony. They would really listen. I made the Four Spiritual Laws available and a New Testament to those who were interested. Many took them both. Sometimes they would make appointments to talk with me later. I witnessed to hundreds of our military members in that program. I met some of them later in my career, clean, sober and successful. Thanks be to God!

I decided to try one of my inspirational breakfasts in Japan. I did not know how to get a professional athlete to speak. I had heard that the Japanese baseball teams hired professional players from the US big leagues. I sent a letter to every professional Japanese team in English asking if there was a Christian player who would like to come and speak at a breakfast and give their testimony. To my amazement, one day an American player who was in Japan called me. He had gotten my letter and wanted to come and speak. Gail and I went up to Tokyo one night and watched him play. Japanese professional baseball is very different. The managers are constantly substituting players throughout the game. The crowds cheer more like a high school football game in the US. After the game he came back with us to Yokosuka and spent the night. In the morning we had a special breakfast at the hospital. Many came to hear him speak about his Christian faith. The Lord had helped me once again to do a breakfast, even in Japan.

One miracle that happened during that time I will never forget. There was a doctor in the hospital that was very senior. Like some physicians at his level, he was a great surgeon but had a lousy bedside manner. He acted like he was God's gift to the human race. He had no time for me, a mere Lieutenant chaplain. One day he got salmonella food poisoning from some chicken he ate in town. He was really in pain. He felt like he was going to die. The doctors could do nothing for him. I heard God tell me to go and pray for him as I was leaving to catch the train home. I said, "God, surely you don't want me to go to him. He acts like he wants nothing to do with you or me". God was insistent, "Go anyway". I walked into his room and asked if I could pray for him. He was all alone in his misery. Even the nurses were scared to be around him. He said to me, "Go ahead and pray chaplain. You might as well. Nothing else is working." So I said a simple prayer, "God please touch the doctor and heal him of this food poisoning. In Jesus name. Amen." Then I left for home quickly. The next morning when I came into the office the phone was ringing off the hook. It was the sick doctor. He said he wanted to see me right now. I walked into his room. He said, "The second you said that prayer, I felt the pain subside. I was brought up with the Lord but I got far away from him in college, medical school and the Navy. You have helped me renew my faith in God." All I could do was give praise to God. From that day on, the doctor would have me pray for all his difficult patients. He would say, "Has the chaplain prayed for you yet?" He changed from night to day.

The radiologist at the time had a big family of five. He and the local civilian representative of a Christian organization called Navigators did not believe it was God's will to ever try to prevent a pregnancy. Both of their wives were always pregnant. Though Gail and I thought their theology was strange, I liked them both. They would often come to my Bible studies and worship services. Once the radiologist asked our family to go fishing with his family. We loaded all our kids up in two vans and headed out to this little fishing lake by Mt. Fuji. The lake was stocked and you paid to fish. We paid our money, baited our hooks and started catching fish. Every cast we would get one. All the kids were catching fish like crazy. The Japanese were all staring at us. Later we learned that it was a fly fishing only lake. You were not supposed to use baited hooks. The Japanese never stopped us. We got a good laugh out of that.

I started handball at Yokosuka. I did not know any players so I put a sign up at the gym. After a long while, I got called from one of the local DODS teachers. He was a handball player too. He was a very good player. We played a couple of times a week. We decided to teach some others. I taught my friend Frank who was a natural athlete. I also taught my CO Jim. Before long we had quite a group of players. We decided to have a tournament. I wrote about it and sent the article to Handball magazine. I didn't know that the Japanese players read Handball magazine. One day I got a call from a Japanese man who worked for IBM in Tokyo. He belonged to a Japanese handball club there. They all wanted to meet us and to play. Before long we were playing at some of the fanciest clubs in the world. We would reciprocate and have them down to the American base. That was a real treat for them. We all became great friends. The next year we invited them to join our tournament. It suddenly became an international match. We had a blast and gave out trophies. My CO was the rookie of the year.

Gail and I were feeling led to adopt another child. We both felt that it was not good for Jonathan to be raised as the only boy. He would get too spoiled. He needed a brother. Gail, however, had no desire to bear another child. We decided that we would give a home to some child that did not have one. We didn't want an infant because they are easily placed. We wanted an older special needs child that no one else wanted. We had actually started the process in Southern California when we were at Camp Pendleton. At that time the county social welfare counselors had told us to adopt a child that was younger than our youngest so that child would look to our kids as the role model instead of the other way around. It made good sense to us. Military families get penalized in the adoption process because we move so much. You just get on the waiting list and you have to move and start all over somewhere else. It can take years.

When we got to Japan we continued the adoption process. There are two ways to adopt children in Japan. One is to go through the only official agency in Japan that works with foreigners, International Social Services (ISS) in Tokyo. The other is to find a child on your own in one of the private orphanages or through a local attorney. The danger with working on your own is you may not get a written release from the mother and won't be able to get a visa to go back to the US when your tour is over. We decided to go with ISS even though it was more costly. ISS met with us and did a home study with their bilingual Japanese social workers. This is a very healthy process because it really makes the whole family think and talk about adoption. As we got closer to making this a reality, I started to get cold feet. Did I really want to adopt another child? I was not so sure. Once again Gail was sure that God had a little boy for us and his name was David. The story of the friendship of David and Jonathan in the Bible is one of my favorites. Finally, after a little persuasion, I consented.

ISS matched us up with a Korean child after about a year of being in their program. We had to go to Korea to meet him. All we asked was that they would test him for AIDS, as we could not get a visa to take him to the US if he was positive. We were all at the Yokota airport getting ready to board the freedom flight to Osan when I got a call at the desk. It was ISS. They told me the little boy was no longer available. They were very apologetic. These Japanese social workers had lost face and were embarrassed. We never found out why the child was not available but we assumed it had something to do with the AIDS test. We went home devastated. It is really an emotional experience to adopt a child, almost like pregnancy.

The next week ISS called again. They had another little boy for us. This one was Japanese and he was very close to us in Yokohama at a baby home. We couldn't believe it. The Japanese do very little adoption. They do not even have a word for it. Japan has baby homes where their citizens can drop children off for the state to raise. Convicted criminals and merchant mariners often leave their children there. They can come back and get them at any time. Most of these children do not have a release to be adopted. Their parents can come and take them back at any time. Many do not and so these children spend their lives there. The Japanese government provides for them until they reach high school. At that time they are turned loose into society to do the most menial labor and often get sucked into crime and corruption. In the caste system of Japan, if you are fatherless your chances of success in life are almost nonexistent. This little boy was named Akira Yoshioka. His mother was fourteen when she got pregnant. The father was never mentioned except to say he was not a family member. Akira's grandfather had put him in the baby home when he was born and named him. His name means 'quick' or 'fast'. Gail and I prepared to go and see him without the children. We met the ISS social worker that would translate for us and headed for the baby home.

We started with a meeting of the baby home directors who told us about Akira. Eventually we got to see him. He was a cute little guy. We were the first non-Japanese to ever come to this home. The directors were worried that the children would be afraid of us. I had brought a Polaroid camera and started to take pictures of Akira to show him. He was very interested and before I knew it he was in my arms. The directors could not believe it. I think Akira knew somehow that we were his new family who had come to take him home. Later he told his caregivers that he wanted to see us again. The directors asked us if we would come back the next week with our other children and take Akira home. We did. That was August 1988. He was a little scared at first but before long our children had him feeling fine. He was as cute as could be and thoroughly Japanese.

We decided to name him David Akira. David's birthday was April 8, 1986, the same day as Gail's dad. He was two years old when we brought him home. He was very small and quiet. We all learned some baby Japanese to communicate with him. Before long he was learning English too from the kids and communication was never a problem. He did many things that were different from our culture. Gail would take him shopping and whenever she would stop to look at something, he would sit quietly until she was ready to go. It was refreshing. Gail says adoption is the only way to have children. You don't have to go through labor, they are potty trained, sleep through the night and feed themselves.

The day we brought David home was also the day I had picked to climb Mt. Fuji with a group of singles from the hospital. The CO Jim came along too. I brought Briana who was almost a teenager and one of her friends. We decided to climb at night because of the heat and humidity. I will have to say it was one of the toughest physical things I have ever done. When you got to a certain elevation, it was difficult to breathe. Mt. Fuji is almost as high as Mt. Rainier in Washington State, over 12,000 feet. Some people got altitude

sickness and could not go on. Briana, her friend, the
CO and I just kept climbing slowly toward the top.
Many times Briana and her friend wanted to stop and
would break down into tears. The CO and I encouraged
them to continue on. I was very proud of Briana that
day and discovered she was much tougher than I had
thought. She and her friend finally could go no further.
Jim and I finished the climb and made it to the top for
sunrise. It was spectacular. Briana and her friend were
very close but could not go on. We then started down
together and discovered that going down was just as
hard as going up. We were exhausted when we finally
got to our Japanese inn for the night.

Briana had her thirteenth birthday soon after
that. I will never forget that day. She had a dollhouse
that was specially built by a friend of my dad. It was in
her bedroom. The morning of her thirteenth birthday
she picked up the dollhouse and put it at the door of her
younger sister Lauren. It was her way of saying I am
no longer a little girl. I was amazed and saddened all at
the same time.

Somewhere during that time I started dating all
my kids. I would take them out individually for a
morning or afternoon. We would go out to lunch, a
movie or just go for a walk or drive. I would ask them
what they wanted to do. Gail seemed to get lots of
quality time with each one but I didn't. These dates
helped me to connect with each one. I especially
remember taking Lauren to a noodle shop close to our
Japanese house in Mabori. We would order noodle
soup and talk. Then we would go to the park that was
close by and play tag. It was a grand time. I have dated
my children into their their twenties. They were a little
more expensive in their twenties but I enjoyed them all
the same. They seemed to open up and talk to me about
what is going on in their lives. Often I would tell them

stories about my life such as I am relating here. I hope to continue these dates for the rest of my life with my grandchildren.

My CO Jim was the senior medical officer for all of Japan and Korea. The Navy medical clinics at all bases came under his command. He liked to visit them and he would take me and the senior enlisted man we call the Command Master Chief or CMC. We would arrive by air or bullet train, walk into the clinic, separate and spend the rest of the day wandering around and talking to the personnel. At night we would get together in the CO's room and compare notes. Between the three of us we could get a pretty good read on where a command was. Almost everyone would talk to one of us. It was brilliant plan.

On one of these trips we went to our Naval Station Sasebo near Nagasaki on the southern part of Honshu. Nagasaki is the most Christian part of Japan. It is where the early foreigners were first allowed to visit Japan. There in August of 1945, the US dropped their second atomic bomb on Japan. The epicenter of that blast was a Catholic Church at 11 AM on a Sunday morning. At the museum there is a whole floor dedicated to that Christian congregation. It clearly shows that the Christians of Nagasaki entered into the suffering of the Japanese people as a result of that single deadly blast. That museum was not as hostile to America as was the one in Hiroshima.

That winter we decided to go on a family skiing trip. North of Tokyo in Bandai was a Japanese ski resort called Nekoma. Neko means cat in Japanese. Bandai had a youth hostel. We would often stay at youth hostels because they were inexpensive, you ate family style and they had wonderful Japanese baths. The students who stayed there were usually college kids who spoke English. We learned a lot from them. The

170

directors put the five of us all together in a large tatami room and even gave us our own time in the big hot baths. Early the first morning there was an announcement that all would meet out in the front. We staggered out into the cold air to discover the whole place did exercises together. We just watched everyone and did what they did. It was fun.

They even had skis and equipment at the hostel. We fitted everyone up and headed for the slopes. Gail and I had been skiing since we were married but none of the kids knew how. We spent the weekend teaching Briana and Lauren. By the end of the time, they could traverse down the mountain on their own. Jonathan spent his time on the special sledding slope and lift they had set up. Little David did not like the snow and spent most of the time in the nursery. The Japanese resort had piped in music to the enclosed four person high-speed lifts and even heated toilet seats in the bathrooms. It was deluxe.

Sometime during these days Gail was gone for a weekend. I think she went to Korea with her friend Jean to shop. I was home with the four kids. One of those nights Briana was staying over with a friend. She and her friend went out the window in the middle of the night. The mother discovered them missing and called me. We called security and when the girls finally showed up we had them talked to by the base police. About the same time Briana got caught smoking in public. All of this behavior really upset me. I didn't want my daughter going the way of rebellion that I had gone. Gail says that I became very negative towards Briana from then on. She was not living up to my expectations. I only wanted the best for her. I still do. I think Briana and I are a lot alike. She is the oldest, wild and crazy like I was. I only hoped and prayed that she would find Jesus like I did. I prayed this for all my children. I even fasted one day a week and prayed for this miracle in their lives. It is a fact that most parents want to spare their children from going through what they went through. The truth is that they are just like you. They have your genes and most will turn out just like you did, for good and for bad.

My last big act of Christian ministry in Japan had to do with a program called Tres Dias, three days. This is a short course in Christianity that was started in Spain by the Roman Catholics. They call it Cursillo or rest. My denomination has their own version known as Walk to Emaus. The Tres Dias is a combination of Catholics and Protestants together. The Army chapel community in Korea had a huge Tres Dias program. They wanted to come to Japan and put it on for us. Frank, Jim, Winston and I all worked really hard to get it together. Finally the weekend came. We held it at a Catholic monastery by Tokyo. The men go the first weekend and the women the next. Winston was the only one who had been on one. It is really a weekend of being immersed in Christian love.

Tres Dias starts on Thursday night and runs through Sunday. On Friday night we were all sitting in a big circle listening to some worshipful music in silence and sensing the presence of the Lord. Suddenly, I could see the Lord standing in front of me in my mind's eye, some call it a vision, clothed like a king with royal robes. He had a large sword that he was carrying. He was asking me to stay in the Navy as a chaplain. I had just received orders to an aircraft carrier and was apprehensive about the prospect of spending long lengths of time away from my family. I said, "Lord, if you want me to stay in the Navy, I can do nothing but obey". The Lord then took this long sword and touched me on both shoulders; it felt like he was knighting me for the task ahead. It was a very moving moment for me. On several occasions since, I have had the Lord repeat this knighting in moments when I am having doubts about what I am doing in the Navy. Each time it has been a source of strength to know that I am in the military at his will doing his work.

We loved the Japanese public baths. They were very inexpensive. The women were on one side and the men on the other, totally separate. They had very hot baths and ice cold ones. It would almost make your heart stop to go from one to the other. They had one filled with special herbs for head colds and other ailments. My favorite was a hot bath were you laid on your back full length with this ice-cold pipe running through. You would rest the back of your neck on that pipe. It was fabulous. All of us would come out of there and feel so relaxed. We would take the whole family. Gail would take the girls and I would take the boys and we would meet about an hour or so later. It made a great evening. The Japanese really know how to do baths.

For our move back to the US, we call it Permanent Change of Station or PCS, we decided to go circuitous and stop in Hawaii. Our plan was to take a free MAC flight from Yakota and spend about ten days or so in Hawaii and MAC home to the West Coast. We thought we had a high priority on PCS like EML. It was August 1989 and very hot and humid. We got up to the air base to find out that we were not high priority and that there were no flights to Hawaii. Not only that, but there was no room in the Bachelor Officer's Quarters or BOQ. We wound up sleeping in the terminal with four kids for almost a week. Each day we would think we had a flight out only to be disappointed. At one point even the air conditioning went out in the terminal and it was hot and humid. One night I got the base chaplain to let us sleep in the air-conditioned chapel. The kids said they were staying in Jesus' house. Finally we could take it no longer. We took the first large transport, a C-5, back to the US. It landed at Elmendorf AFB in Alaska for the night and then on to McCord AFB near Tacoma, Washington. Our Hawaii vacation plans were a disaster.

While we were stuck at Yakota, I tried to make the effort to talk to Briana about what was waiting for her in Silverdale, Washington where we were going. She was moving just before her ninth grade year into a junior high just as I had done years before. I told her that it would be hard to make friends and the temptation would be to get into the wrong crowd. The crowd that will always take you in when you are new is the one that gets in all the trouble. The temptation is to go with that crowd to be accepted. Before you know it you've been swallowed up in their rebellion. I told her my story hoping that somehow she could avoid what happened to me. Most of what I said was to no avail. She was just like me.

10
USS Nimitz (CVN-68)

We finally arrived back in the United States in
August 1989 totally deflated from our journey. We had
lost the Hawaiian vacation we had been looking
forward to. I took my family to my mom and dad's
place near Bellingham, Washington to recuperate. My
folks had just retired and decided to settle closer to my
sister and me. We had not seen their new home. We
called their travel agent and asked about a vacation in
Eastern Washington on the water in the sun. They
suggested the Caravel Resort on Lake Chelan. We
called and they had one room left with a kitchen that
would accommodate us all. It was a beautiful spot right
on the end of the lake in walking distance of the town
of Chelan. There we tried to relax and recover from our
disappointment. We all swam and lay by the pool.
There was a little walkway around the end of the lake
that we took every day. We fell in love with the spot.
It was so good to be back in the United States. We
almost got over the travail of our PCS move.

We rented an apartment on the hill overlooking
the town of Silverdale close to the Naval Submarine
Base (NSB) at Bangor. It was about twenty minutes
north of the Naval Shipyards in Bremerton where the
nuclear aircraft carrier USS Nimitz (CVN-68) was
homeported. We wanted to get into housing at Bangor
but it was a wait. We were sleeping on the floor in
sleeping bags while we waited for our express and
household goods shipments to arrive.

My good friend and former CO Jim had gotten
me the orders to the Nimitz. He knew that we wanted
to be back in our home state and he also knew that I

needed to take the carrier in order to be promoted. Aircraft carriers are considered the premier operational ministry of the Navy. At that time there were only thirty-six chaplains in the entire Navy who had the privilege to serve on a carrier at any one time. Many chaplains never got that opportunity. Jim had gone to Washington DC on business and had paid a visit to the Chief of Chaplains, a two star Rear Admiral. Jim asked him to send me to one of the carriers in Washington State. When a CO goes out of his way to lobby for orders on behalf of a chaplain, it is not taken lightly. I owe much to Jim. He was one of the best CO's and friends of my career. Soon the orders came for the Nimitz. Many of my senior chaplains wondered how I had gotten the orders. No one knew who I was. I determined to do my best as the junior Protestant chaplain on the ship.

About a week after I checked in, I got a call from the Supply Officer at Bremerton. He said, "Are you Lieutenant Waite?" I said, "Yes." He continued, "I regret to inform you that your household goods shipment has been destroyed. It all burned up in a warehouse fire in Tacoma, Washington." I could not speak. I was in shock. I called Gail. She was speechless. She picked up all the kids at school while I headed home. I could not believe that the Lord would let this happen to us. In Japan we had put everything in three shipments. One was an express of one thousand pounds that we got. Another was stuff we couldn't fit in the apartment. Our main shipment was the one that was destroyed. It included family heirlooms, all our family videos, baby books, photo albums, Gail's sterling silver from her mother and all of our clothes, furniture, and athletic gear. It was everything a family of six collected over seventeen years of marriage. Most of what we collected for three years in Asia was gone.

I had contracted for a rosewood Ethan Allan bedroom set for Gail made in China. It was now ashes.

How could this happen? The U.S. military contracted truckers had loaded our shipment from Japan on the truck to be delivered the next day in Silverdale. It was getting late so they parked it in the lowest bidder storage lot next to the warehouse. An arson jumped the fence and started the fire on our truck. It burned so hot the truck melted. All we found later were ceramics that could survive that kind of intense heat. The warehouse burned down too with almost two hundred military family storage shipments inside. The only person who found anything was the one guy who had a fire safe. I bought one that night.

We drove the family to the site. Gail's dad met us and the chaplain I was relieving at the ship, Ed. We all balled our eyes out. We sifted through the ashes and found a few things but nothing much. Somehow all my annual fitness reports were in a heap on the ground. I have no explanation how they survived. We had insurance but it was only $20,000. The government had insurance too but it only amounted to $40,000 more. They can do whatever they want to your possessions and all they have to give you is $40,000. That seems like a lot of money but none of us knows just what our belongings are worth.

For months all we did was insurance forms. We had to itemize everything and get estimates for anything over $100. It was a nightmare. Every spare moment we were filling out forms and getting estimates. Fortunately I had taken a video of everything just before we left Japan and I had the video with us in the camera. It really helped us remember what we had. I would come home at night and find Gail pouring over paperwork. Often she was in tears. We were all sleeping on the floor. It was awful. We all went into a deep depression. Finally we got the total replacement value on our possessions. It came to $156,000 in 1989. Of that, we received $60,000 from our insurance and the government. Slowly we started to replace things but we had to go into debt for a lot of it. After that, I never carried anything less than $100,000 replacement value insurance on our household goods.

While this was all going on, I was trying to learn my new job as the Protestant chaplain on a Nimitz class nuclear aircraft carrier. It was crazy. I don't know how we survived those days. Christmas we moved into housing at Naval Submarine Base Bangor. Needless to say, Gail and I were having problems. We started going to counseling with a psychologist in the area. I think it was helpful. A third party can really help you see yourself. Most of us are blind to ourselves. Things seemed to improve. I also went to a Chaplain Corps retreat called CREDO during that time. I was sent with the Command Chaplain to learn how to do retreats, as if I needed to know. I was in some real emotional pain at the time and did not want to be there. The CREDO senior chaplain, a Roman Catholic, threatened to report me to the Chief of Chaplains if I didn't start participating more. I closed up more. I got nothing out of the weekend except one afternoon I realized that I was mad at God for the fire. It couldn't understand why God would call me into the Chaplain Corps, move me all over the world and then allow my possessions to be destroyed. It helped me to face and deal with that anger.

One good thing that came out of our disaster was that material things did not have the same importance they did before. We used to shop around and compare prices on everything to get the best deal on all purchases. We looked at all that effort as wasted time after the fire. Now, if we need something, we would just go in and get it. We also discovered that we hated to shop. Before shopping had been fun, especially for Gail. We couldn't stand to shop anymore.

Spring of 1990 the ship finally got out of the shipyards. We decided to have a baptism for David. I had waited to have my Bishop baptize him on the carrier Nimitz. Gail and I had it on a Sunday in the foc'sle, forward with the anchor chains, part of the ship. We invited about one hundred people. It was a great day. Many family and people from Avon came. Two of my fellow officers helped me give tours to everyone and feed them in the wardroom. We had a little reception later back at the house.

One of the things we decided to do with our insurance money was to buy a new twenty-four foot Wilderness travel trailer. We had always wanted one. The night we bought it home we sat inside of the trailer feeling sick for spending all that money. They call it buyer's remorse. We started to do a lot of camping. That summer we took a long camping trip with the trailer over to Eastern Washington camping at Lake Chelan and another big reservoir. On the way home we heard on the news that the leader of Iraq, a guy named Saddam Hussein, had invaded Kuwait. Little did we know how this would affect our lives for years to come.

On the way to Chelan we pulled our trailer over to our rental house in Burlington, Washington. Some tenants had moved out and it needed some work. We painted it inside and out with help from all our family. It looked so good we wanted to move back in ourselves. One reason we had kept that house was security for Gail in case something happened to me. It would give her someplace to go on short notice. While we were painting, I called back to Bangor to check our phone messages. There was one from the Naval Air Force

Pacific Chaplain in North Island, California who wanted me to call. I called and found out that I had been selected to the rank of Lieutenant Commander (LCDR). I was so excited to tell Gail and my folks. We celebrated that night. When I got back to the ship, the CO saw me one day and asked me if he had seen my name on the recent LCDR selection list. I said, "Yes sir!" He said, "I will have to do something about that." The next day I was frocked to LCDR. That meant I could wear the rank but I didn't get paid for it. It was great to have people call me Commander, a shortened version of that rank.

That Fall Gail and I had a chance to go to Pawling, New York for a pastor's seminar with the famous Norman Vincent Peale. Norman wrote the best seller "The Power of Positive Thinking". I was depressed and knew that Dr. Peale's message was something I needed. I asked the XO to send me and he agreed. I decided to take Gail and we also took Charlie and Barb from seminary days in Pasadena. Charlie was pastoring a Presbyterian Church in Texas. Barb was from New York. We met them in Manhattan and had a great evening touring the city with Barb as our guide. The next day we took a limousine to Pawling in upstate New York. We had a blast.

That evening the conference had a reception. There were pastors and religious leaders present from all over the world. Suddenly, they asked if there was a Chaplain Waite in the house and would he please come forward. I thought the ship was being deployed or something had happened to the kids. I rushed forward. The coordinator explained that Dr. Peale noticed I was on the nuclear carrier USS Nimitz and he wanted Gail and me to join him and his wife Ruth for dinner. I explained that we had guests with us and Norman invited them too. It was one of the most remarkable evenings of my life. Gail and I had Norman and Ruth to ourselves for the entire dinner. We told them all about the fire and how it had affected us all. We were having problems with Briana who was rebelling. Norman offered to put her on his personally prayer list. It really touched Gail and me.

Norman told us that one of his parishioners, a guy by the name of Dick Nixon, had once asked him to go to Vietnam and try to bolster the morale of the troops. He had spent a night on the carrier Kitty Hawk off the coast of Vietnam. He said it was one of the highlights of his life. He invited me to sit at his table because he wanted to be with a carrier chaplain. Barb and Charlie made a big impression on the Peale's and were later hired by their former parish in Manhattan known as Marble Collegiate Church. Norman preached there for over fifty years. He was in his nineties and writing another book, one of many. He gave a whole new meaning to the term 'retirement' for me.

The next day Norman preached a sermon on combating negative thinking with positive. He had special prayer for those who were suffering for depression. I felt a cloud leave me. God used that event to bring some healing that I desperately needed. I went home armed with all Norman's books that I would read in the coming months on the ship. Later his Peale Center sent me books, pamphlets, tapes and videos that I incorporated into the ministry on the ship. I have used them in every duty station since and they have touched many lives. The following year Norman's last book came out. On the back was a picture of him praying with the troops in Vietnam. I wrote him and asked him for an autographed copy of that picture. He sent it to me with a letter. It was dated two weeks before he died.

Norman's concepts have had a big impact on me ever since that special weekend. Gail had said for years that I tend to be a negative thinking person. If there is a knock under the hood of the car, I immediately think it is a thrown rod. At one point in the weekend Ruth spoke. She said that only Norman could have written the book "The Power of Positive Thinking" because he was the most negative man she had ever met. Her statement gave Gail and me great hope. Norman had written that book and kept it in a shoe box in the bedroom for years. Finally Ruth got it out and sent it to a publisher. They liked it but wanted to change the title. Norman had originally entitled it "The Power of Faith". The publisher said that it would never reach the unchurched with that title. They said he spoke of positive thinking often and should entitle it "The Power of Positive Thinking". Norman said that faith was positive thinking to him. His book has sold millions since the 1950's when it was first published.

When I returned to Bremerton, the operating tempo was rapidly increasing on the ship. We went back to sea doing our work ups to get ready to deploy on short notice to the Arabian Gulf region. It looked like the U.S. and her allies in the United Nations (UN) were going to war with Iraq over their invasion of Kuwait. The UN called it Operation Desert Storm. The Joint Chiefs of Staff wanted to have at least four carrier battle groups in the Gulf for air support. At that time a carrier battle group was a carrier and all the ships and submarines that went with it to war, about 10 total and 10,000 sailors and marines. We were the fifth and the next carrier to go. One week we were going and the next we weren't. It was like that for months and it drove us crazy. We all kept our stuff on board ready to leave at a moment's notice. Everyone expected a bad war with many causalities.

On New Year's Eve we got a call that our oldest Briana had been arrested and was at the juvenile detention center. She and another girl had stolen some goods at the mall, been apprehended and tried to make an escape. The other girl had assaulted an officer. We were just sick. I tried to get her out. They would not let her go. I called my lawyer and tried everything I knew to do, all to no avail. Finally I just went down and sat with her. I put my arms around her and she cried her eyes out. It was a moment I will never forget. The other father was yelling and screaming at his daughter. I remembered how supportive my dad had been when I had gotten in trouble with the police at about the same age. Briana wound up paying for the merchandise, giving it back, apologizing to the stores and doing some community service work. It left a deep impression on her and us.

Three days before we deployed to Desert Storm, our Command Chaplain, a Commander, was relieved from his position for cause. Our enlisted Religious Program Specialists (RP's) had caught him doing something he shouldn't have. They came to us, the other two chaplains, and asked us for help. The next senior chaplain, a Catholic priest named John, confronted him and he admitted it was true. He said it was over and he was getting counseling. He was coming in zone for Captain and asked us to keep it quiet. We all met with the RP's and decided to keep it in house as long as the chaplain was trying to get help.

I learned a great lesson on this one. Always tell the CO when the entire department knows. Later, one of the RP's got mad at this man and wrote a letter to the CO and the Air Force Pacific Chaplain telling them everything. Before we knew it, the CO, a screamer, was putting his finger in John and my chest telling us he was going to throw us off his ship. I saw my career floating away. The CO decided to take the Command Chaplain off the ship and replace him. He said it was because of his weight. No one would call it for what it really was. The CO also made sure the Captain's Board knew so he wouldn't get promoted. Three days before we left on deployment, a new Command Chaplain came, a Baptist named Al. He was a godly man and a breath of fresh air. He had just returned from another deployment. John and I had to spend every other night on board for duty before we deployed as our punishment. It was hard because we were just getting ready to leave for six months. I learned to always tell the CO what is going on when the RP's know. He or she will find out sooner or later and you will look disloyal.

We finally got our orders to deploy. It was so hard to say goodbye to my family for six months. I didn't know how I was going to do it. We left late February 1991 while the ground war was still going on. We were not sure where we were going or when we were coming back.

Late March we pulled into Subic Bay, Philippines. The U.S. Navy had maintained a shipyard and air base there for years. It was due to close soon. We had a wardroom party one night at Paradise Beach. The Philippine Islands are some of the most beautiful tropical islands in the world. The next day we went into Olongapo City by the base. There I saw some of the worst poverty I have ever seen. I saw people living in lounge chairs. Prostitution was one of the main businesses of that city. When the fleet was in, the young women came from all over to make money off the U.S. sailors through prostitution. Many are pushed into this work by their families. It is very sad. For about five dollars a sailor could get a young Filipino woman to do about anything. Sexually transmitted disease was rampant. Our sailors are young, weak and vulnerable. Combine that with loneliness, plus alcohol and many fall. I found out later that Thailand was very similar.

It was Holy Week and a huge group of marines were returning from Desert Storm where they had sat off the beach for a year as a decoy to Saddam Hussein's forces. They landed the same week we did in Subic. Sailors and marines were everywhere. Right in the middle of the whole place was a Christian Serviceman's Center. The center was playing Christian music and offering free pizza. Many sailors and marines stopped in for the free pizza and to take a break from the debauchery outside. The Center had a tremendous ministry going.

I had heard about a Philippine American orphanage in town run by a godly Christian woman. I walked around until I found it. It was an amazing place. These kids were the mixed children of prostitutes and U.S. military. They were outcasts. This woman took them in, cared for and loved them, educated and led them to Christ. Americans adopted some out. Many Navy chaplains sent support to this woman. I vowed to send money that weekend. I also stopped by the huge Methodist church close by. The church had a Christian school and broadcast devotions from their bell tower into the city every day. The pastor was educated in the U.S. and spent some time with me offering to let me preach some time. They had a great ministry to prostitutes and their children.

One night our Catholic priest John and I went out to an armed forces resort in a place called Grande Island. It had a hotel and things to do. John and I decided to go out and spend the night to get off the ship. On the way out we ran into one of the chaplains from the battle group ships. He was married and had an attractive Filipino woman he was taking out to the hotel. He was not expecting to see us. I never respected that chaplain again.

We decided to do a COMREL or Community Relations Project at the Christian Servicemen's Center in Olongapo. I took about twenty guys and we wound up building cement blocks by hand in the hot sun all day. It was hot and hard work. They were using the blocks to add a new addition to the Center. At the end of the day we had made hundreds of blocks for the new construction. We felt that we were doing something for the Lord in the heart of the enemy's territory.

Our next stop was Singapore. It is known in the Navy as one of the most romantic ports in the South China Sea. The CO let me fly in early on the Carrier Onboard Delivery (COD), a prop plane that lands on the carrier and takes mail, parts and about twenty-six passengers. I went with two other officers and stayed at the York Hotel where Gail and I were to stay. She flew out with some of the wives including the Gator's, navigator's, wife. We had a great time together. Singapore is very clean, modern, safe and expensive. The British presence there is still heavily felt. We visited Mt. Fabor and took a cable car to Sentosa Island where the British Surrender Chambers are from WWII. Gail and I took a Chinese junk for a special dinner one night from Clifford Pier. On a Sunday we attended Wesley Methodist Church. It was Communion Sunday and the place was packed. We couldn't believe the life and vitality in that Singapore church. They were really moving in the Spirit of God. The American Club was a favorite. The American businessmen have a club that U.S. officers can use. It had a pool, bowling alley and restaurant. It is very exclusive. After six wonderful days, Gail and I had to say goodbye again. It was really hard. I greatly missed my children.

Our Nimitz mission was to relieve the four carrier battle groups that were in the Arabian Gulf for this unprecedented projection of air power over Iraq. We arrived in the Gulf the 17th of April. Iraq was still attacking the Kurds in the north and many oil well fires were still burning. It was hot and going to get much hotter. Sea snakes were everywhere in the water. The first week in, we exploded a mine that was in our path. The allies wanted us to take over and fly Combat Air Patrol (CAP), over Iraq to keep them from attacking the Kurds.

Sometime during these days, a young sailor came to me and told me he thought his roommate was going to commit suicide. He showed me some pictures his friend had drawn. I agreed with him and called the sailor's Division Officer (Div O), who assured me he would get the young man to medical to be evaluated. Well, the Div O forgot and that night the young man almost succeeded in taking his life. The next morning his roommate went to the CO blaming me for what happened. The CO called the Div O and me into his cabin and proceeded to say that he held me 60% responsible, the Div O 30% and himself 10%. I should have followed through to make sure the sailor got seen. From that day on, whenever I thought someone was suicidal, I personally took them to medical and waited until they were seen.

I was using a lot of the concepts I had learned from Dr. Peale in my sermons. I read all his books and watched and listened to all his tapes. One Sunday I preached on how to deal with fear. I talked about visualizing Jesus there with you. One F-18 Hornet fighter pilot was sitting in the congregation. That night he flew a mission. He was low on fuel and was coming in for a landing on a dark night. He started to experience vertigo, a disorientation that often happens to pilots at night. He missed or 'boltered' on his first pass on the deck. He had one pass left before he had to eject. He was burning fumes in his jets. Remembering my sermon, he visualized Jesus there with him. He just relaxed and gave everything to Jesus. He came in for the last time, still in vertigo, and made a perfect landing. When he told me that story, I thanked God that he used my sermon to save this man's invaluable life and our nation a thirty million aircraft. These are the things that make you glad you are a chaplain. Thank you Lord!

One Sunday I decided to preach on healing and have a healing service at the end. My Southern Baptist Command Chaplain, Al, was a wonderful Christian man but he had never had a healing service. He finally agreed to help me. Al was worried that no one would come forward and we would look foolish. At the end of the service I gave the invitation and many came forward. Two squadron CO's were the first ones to get on their knees in front. Al's mind was blown. We prayed for them, anointing them with olive oil with the sign of the cross on the forehead using our thumb. The New Testament talks about this in James chapter five. One of those CO's told me later that he had been healed. God is awesome.

We anchored and went into Dubai, United Arab Emirates (UAE) four times in the three months we were in the Arabian Gulf. Each time I would stay with some of the ship dentists at the Hilton Hotel. The hotels were giving a special to U.S. forces in thanks for Desert Storm. I would lay by the pool, take a bath and call Gail. Combine that with a good meal in a restaurant and I was ready to go back to sea again. The Hilton even had a beach club on the shore. It was like the Riviera. I bought some carpets, gold jewelry and perfume for the family. The gold souks were unbelievable, blocks and blocks of nothing but gold stores. You could buy anything in 10, 12, 18 or 22 karat gold. You ordered it one day and picked it up the next. They sold it by the gram. The salesmen were open to negotiating the price. I had fun bartering and spent lots of money. In the Gulf you get special tax free money plus combat and family separation pay. The UAE merchants get most of it.

A number of officers were selected go do an officer exchange with the British infantry in Al Jubyl, Saudi Arabia, 300 miles south of Kuwait. It was the main U.S. port during Desert Storm. For some reason the CO picked me as one of them. We flew the COD in to meet the Royal Anglican Regiment, the last British armored infantry left in the area from the war. They had a chaplain named Chris. Saudi Arabia is the most oppressive place I have ever been. Religious police patrol in Land Rovers looking for infractions of their Islamic laws. Before we arrived some men had their hands cut off for smuggling alcohol. A woman had been beheaded for adultery. They do this in the public square and make foreigners watch. It is like going back thousands of years in time. Saudi Arabia seemed like nothing but sand, oil refineries and repressive Islam.

Since Saudi Arabia has some of the strictest Islam on the planet, I was told by my Command to take my Christian cross off my uniform as soon as I landed. They did not want my cross to offend the Saudi's. When we landed I started to take my cross off. The British Armored Infantry asked me what I was doing? I told them and they said that I was with them now and not to touch that cross. I walked all over Al Jubyl proudly wearing my cross. No one bothered me but I was surrounded by some tough looking Brits fresh from combat saving the Saudi's from Saddam Hussein and his Iraqi Army.

We went to the beach with the Brits and the religious police reprimanded us because we were showing our armpits and ankles. All the women there are veiled. I saw a herd of camels along the freeway. Chaplain Chris told me that after the war his troops found hundreds of dead Iraqi's all over the desert. No one would take responsibility for burying them. Chris and his troops took it upon themselves to bury these poor soldiers. Chris called it his ministry in the desert. We saw a huge cache of captured weapons from the Iraqi's. Many of them were made in the US. It was very ironic and sad. They had used our weapons bought with U.S. tax dollars to wage war against us. Something is wrong with this picture.

Our admiral landed once on the Australian ship HMAS Darwin. They had been in the Gulf for over a year. The admiral asked them if they needed anything. They said they would like to have a Protestant chaplain come and do communion for them. He came back to the ship and sent me over. They were in Bahrain, Manama. Our helo dropped me off at the airstrip with my guitar. I wandered around and eventually got someone to take me to the ship. The Aussie's were really glad to see me. We had a wonderful service up on the bridge. Most of the crew came. They had been out there a year and had not had communion or a chaplain. That afternoon the officers took me into Bahrain for lunch. We came back and had pizza and beer in their wardroom. Australians allow their enlisted to have two beers per day after they come off watch. The officers have an open bar in their wardroom but they only do this when they are inport. This system seems more reasonable than ours does, which never allows alcohol except for a beer day of two beers each after 45 continuous days at sea.

On July 12th I got one of the thrills of my life. It was our last day in the Gulf. Before we deployed I had gone to Naval Air Station Whidbey Island and gone through two days of ejection seat and water survival training. This is a requirement for anyone who wants to fly in a Navy jet off a carrier. Like my dad, I had always had a dream of becoming a Navy pilot. I couldn't do it because of my eyesight. Serving on the carrier, I at least wanted to get a ride, catapulting off (cat) and getting an arrested landing (trap). I got my back seat qualifications (quals) and kept bugging the squadron commanders to let me fly. Gail said I could fly anywhere but the Gulf. I figured if anyone let me fly, it would be Electronic Warfare Squadron VAQ-138 Yellowjackets from Whidbey Island flying their EA6B Prowler. They had four seats and that gave me more opportunity to fly.

The morning of the last day in the Gulf, I ate breakfast with the squadron CO of VAQ-138. I told him I had never gotten my ride and could I go when we left the Gulf. He said that I had to go that day or not at all. Knowing Gail would not be happy I said, "OK!" By 11:30 AM I was being briefed on a real mission. At 1 PM I suited up with full flight gear of flight suit, G-suit, harness, parachute, etc. I had passed my water survival test wearing all this stuff and almost drowned. At 1:30 PM I climbed aboard Prowler 622 on the flight deck in over 100 degree heat with the pilot Buckeye, Platt, Woody and me. I was strapped into seat #3 behind the pilot on the left side. We started engines for a 2:10 PM launch. Sweat was pouring off me as we waited for the cat. While waiting, I learned how to use the oxygen, radio, and arm the seat in case of ejection. We were on a real mission in the Arabian Gulf carrying a HARM anti-radiation missile.

The cat shot scared me to death. It is a sudden surge of piston steam power to throw that huge jet off the deck from zero to 120 mph in just a few feet and seconds. I was told if we dropped below 60 feet in altitude, I had to eject. When I asked if we were below 60, the guys said that was over a long time ago. We went to 25,000 feet and rendezvoused with another Prowler to do tactical maneuvers. We flew with another Prowler 50 miles north of Nimitz in the North Arabian Gulf (NAG), seven miles away from the Iranian coastline. I learned how to zero in a HARM missile on a target with radiated emission and how to jam radar installations. I didn't get sick but I came close. The whole time I kept quoting Isaiah 41:10 for strength.

Close to 4 PM we formed up (marshaled) at 12,000 feet (angels 12) and waited our turn to trap on the deck. Each jet waiting is marshaled at intervals of 1000 feet and they trap two minutes apart. It is an amazing ballet. The trap felt like my arms were going to rip out of the socket. The adrenaline rush was overwhelming. What an E ticket ride! I never again complained about how much extra money the aviators got than I did, flight pay. They were not paid enough for what they do every day. We should pay them like NFL players.

That night I was basking in the afterglow of successfully completing a lifelong goal when suddenly we went to General Quarters (GQ) or battle stations. An F-18 Hornet had hit the stern round down on approach at night and broken off the right strut or landing gear. The pilot went to full throttle after burner to get off the deck, caught the wire with his tail hook and ejected. The jet was sitting on the wire at a weird angle, on full power and no pilot. The pilot parachuted on the deck and we tackled him before he blew over. At GQ our young airmen rushed to the jet with AFFF foam to keep the temperature down while one of them climbed up in the jet and shut it off. I was the flight deck chaplain and first one to talk to the pilot in the flight deck battle dressing (first aid) station (BDS). We had a prayer of thanks for his life. I spent the rest of the evening in the BDS flushing out the eyes of young airmen with saline because they were stinging from the AFFF.

The next morning we left the Arabian Gulf for home passing our relief, the USS Abraham Lincoln (CVN-72). It was a brand new carrier on her maiden deployment. It was wonderful to see her come and us go. Little did I know then that I would be seeing her many more times in the future. July 20th we crossed the equator and had our Wog Day. Before a sailor is initiated into the mysteries of the crossing the line ceremony, he or she is called a slimy wog or pollywog. Once initiated in the daylong event that at times is disgusting, he or she then becomes what we call a shellback. It was Sunday and I had to preach. As soon as I finished my sermon, the shellbacks were waiting for me. I went on the flight deck crawling on all fours and blowing green slime out of pad eyes.

On July 25th we anchored at Phattaya Beach, Thailand. It was like a scene out of the movie South Pacific. The liberty boats would pick us up on the stern of the ship and take us to smaller boats that would take us close to the beach. We would then roll up our pants and walk the rest of the way with our shoes in our hands. Hundreds of young beautiful Thai women would be there waiting for us. It was a lot like the Philippines. The hotels and restaurants were nicer and inexpensive. I got a room and just relaxed by the pool.

It was so good to get off that ship. One day I went up to Bangkok. It was one of the most congested and polluted cities I ever saw. I just turned around and came right back to Phattaya.

On the 27th I took 80 sailors to a COMREL at the Phattaya Orphanage. It was an amazing place. The Catholic priest who ran it was from Chicago. The kids were mostly the children of prostitutes. They had a handicapped and a deaf and blind school with over 200 babies, children and teenagers. I brought enough food for a BBQ feeding 500, 25 gallons of paint and medical supplies. The priest told me to put all the stuff in a pile, grab a kid and love them all day. That was all he wanted us to do. It was an extraordinary day. I had a kid in both arms. We had been gone from our own kids for months. There were tears streaming down the sailor's faces. It was a joyous experience I will never forget. For many, this was the highlight of the entire deployment.

On July 31st I was selected once again to take the COD in early to Hong Kong. Gail was coming out to meet me as she had done in Singapore. I got our room at the Sheraton and waited for Gail to arrive the next day. The navigator's wife Ruth came too. After she arrived, we met our good friend Mr. Ho from the Chung Tai Furniture Company. Gail and I had gotten to know him in Japan and had helped him sell his rosewood furniture at the base bazaar. We had bought many pieces from him then that we later lost in the 1989 fire. We replaced some of them and took them to the ship to bring home. He later took us into Mainland China via Macao, a Portuguese territory.

From Macao we crossed into China past the People's Republic Army guards up to Cui Heng in Zhongshon Province. Mr. Ho wanted to take us there to meet his Chinese family who made the rosewood furniture we had bought. This town was also the hometown of the famous Dr. Sun Yat Sen, the Chinese version of George Washington. This part of China was one of the most labor-intensive places I had ever seen. We saw a group of men stripped naked building a road by hand and a farmer plowing his land with an ox. Just past the boarder were many nice buildings that were all storefront fakes to look like economic prosperity. As you keep going you see the real China. On the way home the Chinese guards tried to detain Mr. Ho but they saw he was with two Americans and let him pass. It was kind of scary but very interesting. We didn't know then that we would be back to China and it would become very dear to us.

Back in Hong Kong we spent a lot of time at the American Club again. They had a nice high rise downtown with a restaurant on the 49th floor. On the other side of the island they had a country club by the beach that was also very nice. One night the Sheraton threw the Nimitz Battle Group a big free party as the returning hero's of Desert Storm. It got so wild that one of the officer's wives got drunk and slid down the ice sculpture injuring herself. Once again, it was hard to say goodbye to Gail. The first few days of separation are always grief filled.

On the way home, one of our sailors kept bugging me about wanting to be baptized. I put him off wanting to wait until we got home. I thought it would be much more special and meaningful with family and friends. He would not give up. Eventually I gave in. We had a nice baptism for him on the foc'sle. I was really glad later that I did. Our first weekend home he was killed in a tragic car accident. That incident taught me to pay attention to the Holy Spirit in others who is trying to talk to you. I preached his funeral and was able to comfort his family with the knowledge that he was in heaven with his Lord and Savior.

We headed for Hawaii to pick up our Tigers. At that time we were an all male crew and Tigers were male members of your family over eight who rode the ship back to homeport from your last port before home. For us that was Pearl Harbor. On the way to Hawaii our supply ship USS Camden (AOE-2) lost one of their CH-46 helos with four crewmen. It was very tragic. Their families were all waiting for them in Hawaii. I wrote the words for the CO at their memorial service.

My dad, father-in-law and son Jonathan met me in Pearl. Jonathan was almost nine. He had his birthday on the way back. We had an air show and Jonathan even got to steer that gigantic carrier. It was a great time for us all. By the end of the week, Jonathan could find his way all over the ship, not an easy thing to do.

On August 24th we finally got home. It was a long six months. I hadn't seen the rest of my children for all that time. There were thousands of cheering family and friends on the pier. We were all in our whites. My mom, Gail, Lauren, Briana, David, my father-in-law's wife Millie and her son Dane were all there. It was so good to be home. I didn't know how I survived. It was only by the grace of God.

Coming home from deployment is always strange. On the ship you never make daily decisions like what you will wear, eat or do. You can go days and weeks without seeing the sun and human touch is limited to passing the peace at chapel services. Suddenly you are home. Your spouse has learned to do everything without you, bills, repairs, discipline and decisions of every kind. They have become very independent, if they were not so already. For example, Gail had hooked our 24-foot travel trailer and took four kids camping while I was gone. The Navy sailor who expects to come home from sea and just take over the reins of the family again has a rude awakening. I plan not to do any discipline of the children for the first two weeks. That gives me a chance to just ease back and enjoy them without being the bad guy. It is hard for the home front spouse to do because they want a break. We say the Navy spouse has the hardest job in the Navy.

My first night home Gail might say something like, "What do you want to eat". You find it hard to answer because you haven't thought about what you want to eat for six months. Your first morning home you just stare at your civilian clothes not knowing what to put on. All you have known is a uniform for the past 180 days. Driving is strange and takes some getting used to. You have not had any creature comforts, like a couch, or color either in most of that time. You go to the store and are overcome with sensory overload at all the products and colors.

The wise sailor takes everything slow and easy with no demands. Everyone has learned to live without you and they kind of like it. It is not easy for them all to adjust to having you back. It can make you feel left out and unwanted at first. Slowly, everyone lets you back into their lives and you become a family again. I have found that you never go back to the way it was before. The family has changed and you have to accept it. Most of the time, the changes are good.

Congress says you have to be home thirty days after a deployment before you go back to sea again. Carriers cost about a million dollars a day to maintain.

The government doesn't like to let them sit long. On the thirty-first day we were back at sea again qualifying new pilots down in San Diego. It is so hard to go back. We were gone for almost a month. During that time many of the crew told me that they had gone back to their churches and they seemed dead next to the fellowship we had during deployment. Some said Desert Storm was the most exciting church experience of their lives. I liked to describe it as taking a men's retreat to a combat zone for six months.

The Navy Tailhook debacle took place about this time. Tailhook was an annual gathering of all Navy aviators. Often it was characterized as alcohol infused debauchery. My CO had gone and taken a few of his officers. I had been invited because I was now a tailhooker after my Prowler flight. Gail told me she didn't want me to go and leave her so soon after getting back. I didn't and it was one of the best decisions of my career. Thank you Gail! Lots of sexual misconduct took place in Las Vegas that year and many careers were terminated or halted. The CO came back and said he was never going anywhere again without his wife.

I found out that the Navy had selected me for a fully funded year of postgraduate education in the area of homiletics, liturgy and church music. It was a dream come true. I started applying to civilian seminaries. Most of the seminaries were inflexible and would make me fit into their schedule. One influential liberal leaning Protestant seminary on the west coast said they did not want me because I was a military chaplain. So much for liberal open acceptance of others.

I really wanted to go to Princeton but I also wanted to turn this study into a Doctor of Ministry (D.Min.) Degree. The only institution that would allow me to do that was the one I already graduated from,

Fuller Theological Seminary in Pasadena, California. They had a program where you read 4500 pages of work and then come to the Pasadena campus for two weeks of all day classes. Afterwards you would write a fifty-page paper due in a couple of months. Most could finish their doctorate in five years taking one of those intensive classes a year.

I was determined to do all the course work in my one-year Navy program. To do so I would have to supplement my time at Pasadena with postgraduate classes in church music at Seattle Pacific University (SPU). We would stay in housing at Bangor and I would fly down to Fuller for the two-week classes. We did not want to move our family across country for one year. The Navy said I could stay in our Bangor house. I put my package together and submitted it to Fuller, SPU and the Navy. Everyone accepted it. It was a gift from God. He knew that I had always wanted to get my D. Min. at Fuller. I could never afford the money or time in the civilian parish. My chaplain friends called it the Doug Waite Good Deal.

After the first of the year 1992, the Nimitz began work-ups for another deployment that summer. Our Command Chaplain Al was diagnosed with Multiple Sclerosis (MS) and was medically retired from the Navy. I suddenly became the Command Chaplain as the next senior officer. A new young lieutenant had replaced the priest John. I had held every chaplain job on that ship in the three years that I was there. In July I left the ship and we began the 'vacation from hell', as the kids called it. I had always dreamed of taking my kids to the major national parks in the Western United States. While at sea I had planned the whole trip with AAA. Briana had just finished her junior year in high school and didn't really want to go with us. Somehow Gail got her to go.

Things had not been easy with Briana. She was still in a lot of rebellion towards us. We had some pretty big fights at the house. She was our first child to really get into her teens and like most parents we didn't have a clue what we were doing. I remember one fight we had that was especially bad. I had taken her car keys away from her. She just got furious. Somehow her brother and sister got them back for her and she took off, running away. I called the police thinking I would report the car stolen. The deputy who took the call said, "Are you really sure you want to do this Mr. Waite". He started explaining to me what would happen as a result. He talked me out of it. As it turned out, Briana had run away to her high school and was with one of her counselors. Eventually we all got calmed down. Gail and I were learning that raising teenagers you have to pick your battles and take your stand for the things that absolutely cannot be compromised. The rest is just not that important, let it go. It is not worth ruining your relationship to prove a point or assert your authority.

We loaded up the trailer with all the kids and headed off to spend a month together on the road sightseeing and camping. I was ready for some quality time with my family. We spent our first night in Spokane with my Uncle Bob and Aunt Joyce. The next morning we headed out to Butte, Idaho where we stayed at a KOA. Butte had the world's largest open pit mine. The kids weren't impressed. Eventually we got to Yellowstone, our first big national park in Wyoming. The drive across Montana was beautiful. It seemed like we were constantly going up and down mountain passes and our Dodge Van did it in style. Gail and I hadn't been at Yellowstone since we were kids. There were lots of fly fisherman around and I was impressed at how the park hired retired people in their concessions. One afternoon most of us went horseback riding. Another day I chartered us a boat to go out fishing on Yellowstone Lake. We really got into the fish, hook and release, and everyone caught them except David and I. We couldn't catch a thing.

Our trip continued down through Jackson Hole and Salt Lake City, Utah, past Lake Powell, where we wanted to come back with a houseboat, to the Grand Canyon. The canyon was spectacular. We stayed there for a few days. One of the best things we did was go to a midnight ranger talk about the summer sky, lying on our backs at the south rim looking at the stars. From there we continued west to Bullhead City in Laughlin, Nevada. We stayed across the Colorado River and took foot ferries over to the casinos. The kids had never been to anything like that. The girls thought they would come back for their honeymoons. Finally we arrived in Los Angeles camping at Disneyland Campground. The summer Olympics were on. We spent a couple of days at Disneyland. On Sunday we attended the Crystal Cathedral. It was about this point that we discovered we had picked up a mouse somewhere. It only made noise at night when we were trying to sleep. Briana had the couch and woke us all up one night yelling, "Get out of here stupid thing."

We started north from LA through Pasadena, past our old house and seminary, up to Sequoia National Park. Gail and I used to camp there with Briana and our dog Bridget when we were in seminary. It had been fifteen years. Those big old trees still impressed us, some of the oldest living things on earth. After Sequoia we went to Yosemite National Park, another one of our favorites. I had made reservations with the AAA books months before so we had a place to stay. Gail did not like our spot there. It was filthy and no hookups. We did have fun lying by the river with our rafts and riding the little trams around the park. On we continued up to Crater Lake National Park. I had never been there, only flown over it. It was beautiful and so was the campground.

We decided to visit our old friends Mark and Lynn in Portland. They had been with us enlisted in the Navy. Mark and Lynn had a bunch of kids like us about the same age. One of the boys had a crush on Briana. She was not impressed and it ended up not going well. Eventually we returned to Bangor in time for Gail's sister Beth's wedding. We had been on the road for almost thirty days. The kids called it the 'vacation from hell'. I can still hear Briana in the back seat teaching the kids to sing this song about calamine lotion over and over. I really miss those days of being together.

Beth had this huge traditional wedding as soon as we got home and everyone was in it. They had a wonderful reception at the Seattle Tennis Club, with Seattle socialites galore, that must have cost Gail's dad a fortune,. I was off the Nimitz and flew down to Fuller in Pasadena for my first two-week intensive Doctor of Ministry class. It was now almost three years since we had lost all our household goods. We were slowly recovering. I had spent much of that time at sea away from my family. It was time to stay home for awhile.

11
Dr. Doug in Spain

For my first two-week intensive Doctor of Ministry class at Fuller Theological Seminary in Pasadena, California, I took a Theology and Practice of Preaching class. I called my old friend George who was still the senior pastor of Pasadena First United Methodist Church to see if he could help with housing. To get the waiver for my academic program, I had to agree to fly myself to Pasadena and pay for my own room and board. The Navy paid for the tuition, which was significant. George found me the home of one of his parishioners to stay in for the whole two weeks. The owner was a doctor and had a beautiful home right by Rose Bowl Stadium. All he wanted me to do was feed the dogs and take them out.

That Spring I had attended our Professional Development and Training Class (PDTC) for the Chaplain Corps in San Diego. We were studying worship and touched on the Baby Buster Generation or what later became known as Generation X, the generation born beginning in 1965. At that time they made up the majority of the military. The average age of the U.S. military is 19. I became fascinated with this generation because it included most of my children. I decided to focus my Doctor of Ministry work on this generation. The title for my dissertation, which Fuller called a ministry focus paper, was "A Strategy for Increasing Baby Buster Worship Attendance in the Military". I started writing all my papers for my classes with this final project in mind.

While I was staying at the house in Pasadena, I had an exciting experience. Each night I would arm

203

their alarm system that was very sensitive to motion. One night I set the alarm off by accident and could not get it to shut off. One of the neighbors called and helped me turn it off. Not long after that, I could hear the police outside surrounding the house. I walked out the front door and showed them my military ID. Once they figured out who I was and what had happened, they left. I was very embarrassed.

The class was great. It was made up of pastors from all over Christendom and the world. Everyone had been in the ministry awhile and had much in common. We had everything from a Lutheran pastor in Sweden to a Colonel in the Salvation Army. I was the only military chaplain. The class would preach sermons we had brought with us, in front of each other and then critique ourselves. It was very humbling and affirming. The two professors would critique us theologically and exegetically, how we translate and understand the scriptures. Each of us also got time with a PHD in communication from USC who had reviewed a tape of our sermon. The entire process was very enlightening and I would encourage every pastor to take such a D.Min preaching class. They really pushed us to begin preaching without a manuscript. I had left mine long ago for a half page of notes. They challenged me to leave the notes too. It was stretching. As a result of that class, I haven't used notes for years. It is very freeing and allows room for the Spirit in my preaching I didn't have before.

During this time I made some phone calls for Gail. I really wanted her to go back to college and finish her degree. She almost had an Associate's Degree. I ordered all her manuscripts and got an appointment with a counselor at the local junior college. She was hesitant to go because of her age but she did. When I finished my Bachelor's Degree, I had offered to send her back to school. She said then that she wanted to raise a family first. For the past twenty or so years she had been a mom. Now her last child, David, was in school and she felt she could go back. She always wanted one of us to be there when the kids left for school and be home when they returned. Now I was home every day when I wasn't in Pasadena.

I offered to be Mr. Mom for the year. Gail took me up on it. I saw everyone off and then sat down to study all morning and most of the afternoon. Reading 4500 pages of material and writing 50 page papers between classes took every bit of spare time I had. My nose was in a book constantly, even waiting in traffic or riding the ferry. I was also taking one class a quarter at Seattle Pacific University (SPU) on Church Music that was part of my program. I was attached administratively to the Navy Reserve Officer Training Course (NROTC) at the University of Washington (UW). Twice a week I would take the ferry over to Seattle and stop at the UW on my way to SPU. It brought back a lot of memories to be back in that environment. I couldn't believe how young the college students looked and how old I felt.

We had someone in every level of education that year, grade school, junior high, high school, college and postgraduate. Gail was able to get government grants to help with the cost. All our entire family did was go to school. We were all students. I really enjoyed being around the family after so much time away. It gave me a little taste of what it might mean to be retired and around the house all the time. I loved it. It was great to wear civilian clothes, keep my own hours and wear my hair any way I wanted. I liked being involved in my family's life and seeing things the way Gail did all the time.

Gail was doing really well in school. She felt funny being so much older than all the other students. Gail discovered that there were many others just like her doing the same thing. Also, she is such a natural mother that the students all started gravitating to her for support and advice. Gail also discovered what I knew all along, that she was very intelligent. She was the top student in most of her classes.

That fall I put my name in a drawing for the Rose Bowl in the City of Pasadena. The UW Huskies were doing really well and I thought they might go to Pasadena. Sure enough, they won the Pacific Ten Title and my name got drawn for two tickets on New Year's Day in Pasadena. We called our old friends Tudor and Ceci from seminary days. They were pastoring in Pasadena. We flew down and spent a few days with them while attending the game. That was the year the Huskies were back for their third attempt in a row at becoming the Rose Bowl champs under Coach Don James. They lost that game to the Michigan Wolverines. It was a close and great game. We really enjoyed being with Tudor and Ceci again.

Our family was having problems with our new dog Hershey about that time. When we first came back from Japan we got another little Cocker Spaniel, blond like my boyhood dog Princess. We named her Yuki, Japanese for snow. She was cute but had a bad habit of biting people. While I was deployed overseas on Nimitz, Yuki had bitten the son of one of the Navy doctors across the street for no apparent reason. Gail had decided to have her put to sleep. It was really hard on everyone. When I came home from Desert Storm, I took all the kids to the dog pound to look for another dog. The dogs were all barking and jumping up like crazy except one. She looked like a hunting dog and just sat there quietly looking at us. Lauren said she had kind eyes. She was a Weimer Chocolate Lab mix and came from parents who were both field champions. Her name was Hershey. We took her home and she turned out to be the noisiest and most hyper dog I have ever known. She somehow fooled us that day in the pound.

I decided to start hunting again that fall. One of the guys on the ship had a grandpa who had a farm in Harrah on the Yakima Indian Reservation. It was close to where I used to hunt with my dad as a kid. I made contact with the grandpa and he said I could come over and hunt his property. I took Gail's dad Burdette, my oldest son Jonathan and Hershey with me. Burdette and I had tried to hunt near there with Bridget when Gail and I were first married. I had asked my dad to start hunting with me again but he turned me down saying he couldn't kill animals anymore. Burdette had been great about going and we always had a super time together. Jonathan was carrying a new BB gun about that time. He was ten years old. I hauled my trailer over. We had a wonderful time hunting the property in Harrah. I shot two pheasants on opening day. It was a great trip for all of us to do together. I came back in December with just Jonathan and hunted in the snow. That time we stayed at the Yakima Army Training Center, sneaking Hershey into our BOQ room. Jonathan and I had a super time. He shot his first shotgun on that trip, a bolt action 20 gauge I had shot my first time and my dad had too. It was wonderful to hang out with my son the way my dad and I had done years before in the same place.

The other thing we started doing that winter was taking the entire family on a ski vacation around the holidays. We were all skiing except David. The best ski resort that was close to us was called Crystal Mountain up near Mount Rainier. We called and got a condo for a few nights between Christmas and New

Years. It was fantastic. We put David and most of the others in ski classes. It didn't take long before all six of us were going down the slopes together. We really loved the night skiing at Crystal. The lighting and the slopes were so inviting. I loved going down the slopes single file and watching my family up ahead. We got so we could really fly down the mountain. Those are some of my favorite memories of my family. Every so often we would all stop together and just look around at the lights and the snow. When we skied back to the condo they had a heated outdoor pool in the center of the complex that the boys loved to sit in. Gail and I would take turns going with them. We would also walk over to the Snorting Elk Lodge and have hot toddy drinks. It was a great time.

We were negotiating orders during those days. We wanted to go overseas again, to Europe this time before the kids got any older. We really enjoyed our last overseas tour. Gail and I love to travel and see new things. We felt that our family was closer overseas too. The detailer offered us Rota, Spain. They wanted me to fill the chaplain billet for the Communications Station (Com Sta) there. I wanted to be at the chapel. I had never had a chapel since coming in and my new subspecialty was preaching, worship and music. The Com Sta was the next best thing. It got us all to Europe for three years of shore duty. Rota was also one duty station that everyone wanted.

I had a friend there named Mike who was also a United Methodist Chaplain. He had been my sponsor in my first duty station at Camp Pendleton and he had a big family like we did. They lived in a big Spanish house on the Atlantic Ocean next to a huge Spanish resort hotel, Hotel Playa de la Luz. Mike was leaving Spain at the same time that I was coming. I called him and asked if we could take over his house. To our amazement, the house became available. The chaplain relieving him did not want it.

Our dog Hershey was not an easy dog to control. She was very stubborn. I got books and tried and tried to train her to retrieve, sit, come, stay and heal. I wanted to make a hunting dog out of her. Like Yuki, she would bite strangers without warning. Once after she had bitten someone, I was going to have her put to sleep too. The kids begged for her life. About the same time, I was talking to Mike in Spain. He told me to make sure I brought a big guard dog with me to keep the gypsies away from the house. That suggestion saved Hershey's life. Soon Hershey would be on her way to Spain to become a full-time guard dog.

Briana was getting ready to graduate from high school and we wanted her to come with us to Spain. She was really torn. I remember taking Gail out for her traditional Chinese dinner on her birthday with the kids and talking about our move to Spain. When I asked Briana what she was going to do, she started crying. It broke my heart. She eventually said she would go if we would take her car, a Suzuki Samurai with a cloth top. We could only take one car so we decided to sacrifice ours and take hers if she would come.

One other thing requirement I had to get ready for Spain was have a Special Background Investigation (SBI) for Top Secret Clearance. I was going to a highly secure telecommunications station. I filled out forms forever. They asked me about everything in the last twenty years. People in black suits started visiting my family, friends, employers and neighbors. I had to do a personal interview too. He asked me everything under the sun. I asked him, "Does the President have to go through this?" He said, "No, we depend on the press to unearth everything about him." Wow, I gained a new appreciation for the role of the press in politics.

Finally June rolled around. We didn't have too much going on. Both Briana and Gail were graduating, one from high school and the other from junior college, I was finishing my course work for a Doctor of Ministry Degree and we were selling everything and moving to Spain. I was typing on my final project on the computer as the movers picked up everything around me. The computer was the last thing on and the first thing off our shipment. I got all my course work done for my doctorate but I had a long ways to go for my finished project. I had done half my research at the Bangor base and I was going to do the other half at the base in Spain. The Navy paid for all my tuition, about $5,000, except the last $1,000. I tried everything but could not come up with the money. One day a letter came from Fuller. They had decided to give me a grant for the balance. It really made up for the disappointment I had experienced years before when they denied me a scholarship because I was a veteran and my wife didn't work.

Finally we were on the plane to the East Coast. We flew through St. Louis to Philadelphia (Philly). Hershey was with us in cargo. Our plan was to take some leave in Philly, rent a car and drive down to Washington, DC (DC) for a little vacation. We had contacted a veterinarian in Philly whose receptionist offered to take Hershey for us while we were on vacation. We were hesitant but desperate. They met us at the airport and took her away. Briana had decided to stay back by herself for a couple of months and join us later.

We had a great time in DC. We visited just about everything you could see there in a week. One night we decided to see the Jurassic Park movie that had just come out. We found the theater in the paper and drove to it. It was in the heart of the black district of DC. We were the only non-blacks in the entire theater. One night we got lost driving around DC looking for the freeway back to our room. It was kind of scary walking into some of those gas stations late at night trying to figure out where we were. Many of the attendants could barely speak English and did not help us much. By the grace of God we found our way home.

We made it into the Capitol one day and watched the Senate take a vote on the Space Station. It passed. It was something seeing famous people such as Senator John Glen speak on the floor. We also went over to the Supreme Court and found out one of the Chief Justices had the last name Waite. One morning I got up early and took the Metro in to get tickets for a tour of the White House. While I was walking up Pennsylvania Avenue, President Clinton came by jogging with his daughter Chelsea and some of her friends. The Secret Service agents were jogging too in front and in back. I was about five feet away from the President and so shocked I didn't even say good morning. Later, we all got a good tour of the White House.

One other experience we had in DC was to go through the Holocaust Museum. Lauren had a fascination with the Nazi persecution of the Jews and others. It was an amazing experience to go through that entire complex. It is huge and very comprehensive. One of the displays was the shoes of thousands of Jewish people. There is also a room full of photos of an entire town that was exterminated by the Nazi's. It is hard to believe that this happened in our century. It was sad but very interesting to see. I think everyone should go to see what human beings are capable of doing without Christ in control.

From there we went back to the Navy Lodge near the Philadelphia International Airport. Barb and

Charlie joined us with their two boys from New York where they were working at Marble Collegiate Church in Manhattan. We had a good reunion and then prepared to get on the military charter jet for Spain. The receptionist from the veterinarian brought Hershey back to us just about an hour before we took off. We almost had a heart attack. They had gotten stuck in traffic. They said Hershey had been wonderful. We couldn't believe it. We loaded everyone up and took off for the long flight to Spain stopping once in the Azores to refuel.

When we finally landed at Naval Station Rota, Spain, we were amazed. Rota was a small town in the middle of nowhere. It was a hot dry agricultural area similar to southern California right on the Atlantic Ocean. My sponsor was the engineer at the communication station. He got my family and I settled at the large resort hotel in town on the ocean, Hotel Playa de la Luz, Beach of the Sun. It was a beautiful place with a big central pool and wonderful restaurants and buffets. The beach was outstanding. You could see Rota down the beach and the ancient town of Cadiz across the water. The house we were going to rent was a block away and the manager of the hotel lived next door to us.

One of the first things we all had to get used to were the topless women at the hotel and beach. Most of them were from northern Europe. It was nothing for these women to parade around all day with nothing covering their breasts, playing paddleball on the beach and rubbing themselves with oil. It was a little different for all of us to say the least. You could generally tell who the American men were because they stared at the women and took movies. I also saw the European men do the same thing. We stayed at the hotel for about a month while we waited for Mike and his family to move out and our household goods to arrive. Mike was gracious and allowed us to put Hershey in his big back yard with his dog to get her out of the pound on base.

While we were waiting to move in, something strange happened. We got a call at the hotel that there had been an accident out on the highway and those involved were asking for me specifically. I drove out to the scene where the duty chaplain, a Roman Catholic Captain, was waiting for me. The victim was a young American woman who was from Mt. Vernon, Washington. She was in Spain living with a civilian employee on the base. She was coming home from the commissary, the sun in her eyes and she had gone off the road straight into a cement wall. She died instantly. Apparently her family knew me and had attended the Avon United Methodist Church. Her boyfriend was there and wanted me to be there with him. I wound up doing a memorial service for her at the chapel on base. Who would have thought this would be my first ministry in Spain?

Eventually we moved into our new Spanish home. It was next to the resort hotel and we could see the ocean and beach from the second story deck. Spanish houses are white plaster on the outside and inside. High fences and massive gates surround them. Doors are very heavy with bars, they call gypsy bars, on all the windows. The heavy security is to keep roving gypsies from breaking in and stealing anything that is not anchored down. Everyone has a big dog too. Hershey was perfect and became an outside dog in her new Spanish doghouse. She has a ferocious bark and would charge the fence when people walked by. Gypsies would come to the fence occasionally looking for handouts. They would always point at Hershey and say, "Pero pelegro", or dog is dangerous. I would say, "Si, pero muy pelegro". They never bothered our house, not even when we went on vacation for two weeks.

The base was Spanish run. The U.S. had rented the space for the base from the Spanish government that also had a base there. We had to make many concessions such as Spanish guards on the gates, only flying the Spanish flag except on the fourth of July, senior chaplain has to be a Roman Catholic and hiring Spanish nationals exclusively for all the civilian jobs. At times it was very frustrating. Rota is not a very big Spanish town and the base was not very large either. There were only a few restaurants that served American food. Out in town the food took some getting used to. Everything was fried in olive oil. The people drank wine and sherry that was produced in the area. Seafood was very prevalent. Their hours were just the opposite of ours. The Spanish got to work late in the morning, took the afternoon off for siesta, worked later in the afternoon and didn't eat dinner until late in the evening. You could drive around after 10 PM at night and see entire Spanish families out together walking, socializing and eating together. We liked that part.

The entire country was one big bar. Everywhere you go in Spain there are bars, the supermarket, the car lot, the mall, everywhere. Anyone can buy alcohol at any time. Children are not prohibited from any of these areas. Our oldest children were constantly getting served alcohol without our knowledge. The good news was that you had to be 21 to get a license to drive so they were usually walking if they were drinking. It should be that way in the United States too. The Spanish people are brought up with alcohol so it is not a big deal to most of them as it is to American youth.

The other thing about Spain is tapas. Tapas are hors d'oeuvres. Every restaurant in Spain has their specialty tapas. Once you learned your favorites, you could make a meal out of eating them alone. Garlic potato salad and grilled or fried long green peppers are examples of tapas. Americans love to go tapa hopping. We would go out for an evening and just get the specialty tapas from every restaurant or bar in the area. One of our favorite areas to go tapa hopping was in Puerto de Santa Maria or Puerto as we called it. Puerto is another little town close to Rota. It is the spot where Columbus spent the night before he left for the New World. He named one of his ships after it, the Santa Maria. We loved to go there and take visitors. One bar was famous for flamingo dancing. The locals would dance flamingo and we would just gather around and watch them. Every midnight they would all sing a lament to Mary mother of Jesus that was very haunting and moving.

Not too long after we arrived, we were informed that my billet at the communication station was being cut due to the draw down in the military. Suddenly I was without a job. In one day they took my office, my vehicle and my enlisted RP. It was really depressing. They did not know what they were going to do with me. There was even talk of sending me back to the states. We had just bought a brand new seven passenger Spanish Nissan Serena that was made right there. It was only made in Spain and we loved it. The back seats folded up on the sides and both sides had sliding doors. We didn't know what we were going to do. There was talk that a new billet was going to open up at the hospital. The last thing I wanted to do was another overseas hospital. What I really wanted was to use my new expertise in preaching, worship and church music in a chapel setting.

Eventually, the hospital billet came through and I agreed to do it, but I didn't like it. I went over to see my new CO. He was another neat Christian doctor who was really glad I was coming. I also saw the XO that day. The XO told me that no one wanted me over there. That made me feel real good. One good thing was I had the experience and knew how to do the job. I didn't have an office or enlisted support. They found me a space on the second floor by the Alcohol Rehabilitation Service (ARS). I didn't like the location at first but I grew to love it. I got really close to every ARS class and they would wander down the hall to talk to me. God put me there. Once again the ARS became some of my greatest ministry opportunities. Alcoholics in trouble are wide open to hear about and receive Jesus, and many did. I still see some of these patients around the fleet. I continued to do additional duty (ADDU) to the communication station once a week because I had an expensive Top Secret Clearance.

One of the first things the hospital did was send me to Naval Hospital Bethesda, Maryland for a hospital chaplain conference. While I was there, I was able to do some Christmas shopping for the family. Hospitals always have lots of money to send people off to conferences and training we call TAD, Temporary Additional Duty. It is one of the benefits of the job. It was good to be back in the U.S. I also enjoyed spending some time in Madrid coming and going to the U.S. I was able to take a bus downtown and visit the world famous art gallery known as the Prado. It was estupendo and magnifico, stupendous and magnificent!

Briana finally came to Spain and started college at the University of Maryland with Gail, now a junior, at night. Briana was driving her Suzuki and I was riding my bike to the base and back every day, about a fifteen-minute ride. It was OK except for when it rained or the wind blew hard. The rain was rare but the wind came up in the afternoon almost every day. The rest of the kids were going to the DODS School on base. Lauren was 13, Jonathan 11 and David was 8. We traveled around the area visiting Gibraltar, just a couple of hours drive to the south. We liked Gib, as they called it, because of the British culture and exclusive use of English. It was an escape from Spanish culture every time we went. We liked to stay at the Rock Hotel, where John Lenin was married to Yoko Ono. High Tea in the ballroom was special.

The other trip we took that fall was to Morocco, North Africa. We crossed the Straits of Gibraltar by ferry and spent four days up in the Atlas Mountains in a little village that had been opened to non-Muslim foreigners for just a few years. It was called Chouen. The town was all white plaster with a bluish tinge to it, very beautiful. There was one hotel there. It was like going back in time 100 years. They still baked bread in a central wood fired oven for everyone in town. A passing stream turned the mill wheel where the grain was ground. The Muslim women were segregated and not allowed to go to the local café with the men and socialize. They washed all the clothes on the rocks at the river. Men's clothes were washed separate from women's up stream. Everything in Muslim countries puts men first and women second, even more than in Japan.

Our children were celebrities. They felt like movie stars. The local kids all followed them around and wanted autographs. One Muslim man wanted to give me a camel for one of my daughters. The local merchants all fought with one another for our business, even to the point of a fistfight one afternoon. Gail and I bartered for some carpets and a blanket and finally got them down to our price on the last day. The merchants were still trying to sell us goods as we walked on the bus. It was a very interesting weekend.

Gail and I also took a trip up to Germany. My denomination was getting together with all English speaking Methodist Chaplains and pastors at a place called Wustenrot. We flew on the medical evacuation (medevac) flight up to Ramstein Air Force Base in Kaiserslautern, Germany. At the BOQ there was a Hertz car rental agency. We rented a car and drove to Wustenrot and the Hotel Spatzenwald. We got lost in the country and found a little local German cafe. It was a Sunday afternoon and packed with families eating. I walked in and said loudly, "Does anyone here speak English?" I didn't know what else to do. Slowly, way in the back an old distinguished looking man got up and walked towards me. He spoke English and gave me directions to the hotel.

Spatzenwald was a very nice little hotel nestled in a rural area. Meals were family style as is often the case in European hotels. The German Methodist Church owned it. In America, Methodist's built colleges. In Europe, they built hotels for families, often with pastors assigned. The hotel was Methodist but had pornography on the TV at night, as happens in most of Europe. There are about one million Methodists in Germany. They have their own bishop and seminary. The bishop met with us. It was a very interesting couple of days. We met Methodist military chaplains, civilian American pastors and spouses stationed all over Europe. They told us about a special gathering of all English speaking Methodists at a Swiss ski chalet after the first of the year. We made plans to go.

That first Christmas Gail's sister Joan came to visit with her youngest two children, Drew and Jordan. It was very cold. We had a good time visiting Gibraltar. Then we drove to Portugal and stayed in the southern part known as the Algarve. We rented a neat cottage there close to the ocean. It was so cold we tried building fires in the fireplace. Portugal is about a day's drive from Rota through Seville. It is much like Spain and very inexpensive to eat and spend the night. Their pottery is fantastic. I also was able to get Joan out jogging with me on the beach by our house. We had a good visit. We just wish it had been warmer. Our van came in very handy

Right after the first of the year 1994, we drove as a family in our new Serena van all the way to Paris, France and Switzerland. The first night we stayed at one of our U.S. Air Force bases, Torrejone, near Madrid that was about to close. The chaplain met us and got us into the Bachelor Officer Quarters called BOQ. The Air Force calls them VOQ for some reason. We got up the next morning early and had a full breakfast in the chow hall that cost us about $10 total for six. Driving through Basque country in northern Spain, we spent the next night in Bordeaux, France. Everywhere we went, we tried to learn a little of the language like 'please', 'thank you', 'hello', 'good morning', 'toilet', 'coffee with cream' and 'good bye'. Usually the nationals would let us butcher the language and then say, "Why don't you just speak English?" It is very humbling at times to be a spoiled American.

Our night in Bordeaux we decided to try a French restaurant because we were hungry and there was no fast food we recognized. We didn't have a clue what we were ordering. Gail got something that sounded good. When it arrived we all almost gagged it was so gross. Later we learned it was some kind of intestines. The kids got burgers and fries and Gail and I tried to eat theirs with them. The next night we arrived at Camp Davie Crockett near Paris on the site of Euro Disney. The camp was wonderful. It is made up of full sized trailers that look like log cabins. They have a living room, kitchen, bedrooms, bath, washer and dryer. For a little extra you can rent a golf cart to drive around. The kids loved that. Walking distance away is a beautiful indoor pool with water slides. The kids really enjoyed it there.

The next day we did Euro Disneyland. We had done Disneyland in Anaheim, California, Tokyo, Japan and now Paris, France. The only Disney we haven't done is the one in Florida. They are all similar but this one was very expensive in U.S. dollars. It was a cold, windy and stormy day. The lines were very short and we went on almost every ride. We almost froze to death too. The next day we took the subway into downtown Paris. We got off at the Arc de Triumph where Napoleon is buried. We stopped first at the McDonalds there. Then we went up on top and looked at the Eiffel Tower and downtown Paris. We decided to try to walk to the tower. It was a long way and when we finally got there, the lines going up were very long. We took the subway to Notre Dame Cathedral and did the one thing Gail wanted to do, sit at a sidewalk café and have coffee and a pastry. From there we walked along the Seine River up to the Louvre museum that was closed due to a city strike. The girls loved the artists along the river painting. We got back to the camp exhausted but it was a great day.

The next morning we headed south past Lyon to Switzerland. From Lyon we drove through the tunnel to Geneva and Interlaken. Suisse as the Swiss call it, reminded us a lot of the Pacific Northwest. It is a beautiful snowy high wooded mountain country. We were headed for a Methodist ski chalet known as Hotel Viktoria near Meiringen and the Hasliberg-Reuti ski area. It was dark, getting late and snowing. We stopped for dinner, it cost us a fortune, and called ahead. They closed the hotel doors at 10 PM. We rushed up the mountain in the falling snow hoping we were following the right directions. Thank God it was dark or we would have been petrified. The next day we discovered we had been driving across a steep mountain slope. We made it to the hotel with five minutes to spare. Gail was a wreck.

The Hotel Viktoria was wonderful. It was built in the middle of the mountain by one of the ski lifts. Down below is a beautiful mountain valley and the Swiss town of Meiringen, made famous in the Sherlock Holmes stories. Meiringen even had a Sherlock Holmes museum. All the English speaking Methodists in Europe were invited to the Methodist gathering there that weekend. Most were US military chaplains and their families with some U.S. military Methodist lay persons from all over Europe. The United Methodist Church in the U.S. sent a Bishop to the gathering. The Bishop that year was Mary Ann, the Denver area Bishop who used to be my District Superintendent at Avon just before I went on active duty. It was good to see her and Jeff.

Hotel Viktoria was another one of those European Methodist hotels that was designed to be an outreach to European families on vacation. It had its own chapel and pastor named Peter. Many of the local Swiss came to the chapel on Sunday for services. The idea was to encourage unchurched European families to start attending worship in a beautiful relaxed environment. Peter was always available for them to talk. As I mentioned before, in America Methodists built colleges and universities. In Europe they built hotels and vacation spots, an interesting difference.

We loved the hotel. It was very modern, warm, cozy and European. Meals were served family style in a dining room looking out over the valley on the mountain range directly across. The food was great. Gail and I especially like the European espresso and hot

221

milk. You could see the Eger glacier and a beautiful blue lake way below. The chapel had a whole wall that was glass looking out at that beautiful mountain scene. It was one of the most gorgeous places I had ever seen. We would gather in the chapel for meetings and hymn singing at night. The children were in classes or preparing for Confirmation that took place at the end of the week. Jonathan was in the Confirmation class.

In the afternoon we were free to go skiing. It was some of the best skiing in the world. We rented our skis and headed out to the slopes each day. Prices were not that bad. It was beautiful snow and lots of skiers. We had a blast. We skied and skied together just enjoying one another's company as a family. As I have said before, some of our best times as a family have been on the ski slopes playing follow the leader. At night we would eat like horses and sing in the chapel. It was a great time.

One of the more interesting meetings we had was one morning with the German bishop. The meeting was made up of mostly pastors. The bishop talked to us about the church in the former Soviet Union. He had responsibility for the Methodists there too. There are Methodist pastors there who meet in shacks and live on less than $5 a week. The bishop had diplomatic permission to travel and bring money to these pastors. The stories he told us were amazing.

We drove all the way back to Rota through Switzerland and France across Spain. We spent the night in an abandoned U.S. base near Barcelona run by the Spanish military. The next day we made it through Madrid back to Rota. We would drive the whole way, once we reached the freeways, at about 90-mph. Gas was about $5 a gallon but we had coupons from the base that reduced the price in some places. Food prices were astronomical. Lunch at McDonald's near Lyon cost me $50 U.S. The freeways also had very expensive toll stops all along the way. It was not cheap to travel in Europe as an American in those days. Spain was about the least expensive country there.

Once home I continued working on my Doctor of Ministry final ministry focus paper. I had been taking every Saturday at home to continue writing this paper. I was doing research with a questionnaire on the base at Rota as I had done at Bangor. I would go to my office, lock the door and bury myself in the project. It was the only way to finish the 192-page work.

Eventually I got the first draft done and sent it to my mentor Rob at Fuller in Pasadena. Rob had it read by a PHD for theological content and a PHD for literary content. The paper then came back for my changes and additions. I would phone Rob and discuss the challenges over the phone. It was not easy but at last my final project was accepted. I couldn't have been happier. Gail and I went out to the local Spanish bar for a drink. I had always wanted to do a Doctor of Ministry Degree but had thought I would never have the time or money to do it. God had made it possible. The research and work really taught me how to write and organize my thoughts. The idea for this book came out of it too. Now I could add Doctor to my many titles such as Reverend, Chaplain, Pastor, and Lieutenant Commander. I kind of liked that Dr. and started putting it on some of my correspondence. Gail thought I was silly and soon I got over it. I still like to respond to people who introduce themselves as, "I am Dr. So and So" with "And I am Dr. Doug". It always takes them back but sometimes I forget to do it until it is too late.

At the hospital I was up to my eyeballs trying to get a new small chapel built. I finally got a Religious Program Specialist (RP) in another office next to mine. The Pastoral Care Directorate was growing. We still had no place to pray or worship. There was a nice big space on the second floor near the hospital nursery and operating room wards that I thought would be perfect for a little chapel. I would often see people there crying in distress with nowhere to go. We just needed to wall it in and decorate. All that stood in my way was the Clinical Director, a physician who was a full Captain. He did not really I belonged in the hospital and didn't want to give that much hospital space away for spiritual things. It was a battle and I didn't have much horsepower. Fortunately, the Lord and the Command were behind me. We had a new CO and XO who were spiritual men that thought the chaplain and spirituality was an important part of healing.

The Lord made a way for me to build a small chapel despite powerful opposition. When God wants something to happen, nothing on earth can stop it. You just have to be persistent and not give up. Eventually the way opens up. The senior base chaplain, a Roman Catholic Captain named Rock, was dying of cancer. He was well known in the Navy medical community and was an honorary Navy Nurse. They sent him back to Bethesda Naval Hospital to die. After his death I got the idea to name the new room, The Rock Prayer and Meditation Room. Everyone, except the Captain physician, was enthusiastically supportive. The hospital budgeted the money and the plans were drawn. I got to pick out everything. We don't usually name rooms or buildings after chaplains so I had to go all the way to the Chief of Naval Operations (CNO) for permission. The name was granted and the prayer room became a reality. It was beautiful when completed and much used next to the ward, nursery and operating room.

I tried doing a Sunday service at the hospital as I had done in Yokosuka, Japan but it just didn't seem to have God's blessing on it. I was helping out over at the large Rota chapel, assisting in worship and occasionally preaching as I had done in Japan. Gary was leading the large Protestant service and we really hit it off. He played the guitar, preached and had ministry styles and goals very similar to mine, just like Frank in Yokosuka. I finally stopped the hospital service and just helped out at the main chapel with Gary and the other Protestant chaplains. It was a great program and very successful. We even started a youth group there.

Back in the hospital the ministry was going strong too. I would ride my bike back and forth to work each day and shower at the hospital in the morning. They had water hours in Rota and you couldn't get a good shower off base until later in the morning. I would arrive early enough to visit and pray for all the pre-ops. People are really open to prayer when they are getting ready to go into the operating room. Often the staff would be administering anesthesia while I prayed with the patient. They would bow their heads too and I would include prayer for them as well. Tears would come to many eyes. I also spoke to the ARS Program once a week and was always available for counseling. I had a weekly lunchtime Bible study for the staff that was well attended. Every day I would visit the new patients and offer prayer. Most took me up on it.

One patient got to me. He was a fairly young man, retired from the service, who was dying of cancer. As a young man he had been abused by some religious figure and he could never get over it. He believed in God but wanted nothing to do with him. He would tell me to get out of his room and leave him alone. He even told the nurses to not let me in. I prayed hard for him. Every night they would wheel him down by the back loading dock and let him smoke. He was dying of lung cancer. I would walk past him and get on my bike and ride away. A couple of times I had the opportunity to talk with him and I urged him to give his heart to Christ. He recoiled from me and from Christ. It broke my heart. One day he died. Ministry is not always stories of victory and miracles. Human beings are all free to accept or reject the Lord.

We loved our summers in Rota. The beach was fantastic. All the Spanish people spend their off time down at the beach. On weekends entire extended families would gather to swim, eat, socialize and play cards. Our neighbors would invite us over sometimes and loved to try their English on us. We would also try our Spanish. We spent many wonderful hours on the beach next to the hotel just a short walk from our house.

That summer Briana Euro-railed all over Europe with her friends from high school. I came home from work one afternoon to find them all sitting in our house. They had drunk all the beer and were starting on the food. They stayed for awhile. Both of the girls also got a job at the hospital that summer in a special program. Briana worked in radiology and Lauren worked for the operating room. Briana started dating one of the radiology techs there. Later she started going out with the son of a Guardia Civil Spanish national policeman. Her Spanish really began to get good. She was attending the University of Maryland with her mom on the base. They would go to classes together at night.

Briana also went Euro-railing with her cousin Justine. They went everywhere. The rest of us had planned a trip to Germany using the AMAC military air system. There was a C-9 medevac flight two times a week to Ramstein Air Force Base in Germany from Rota. Gail and I had done it once before. We flew up and rented a Nissan Serena van at the BOQ just like the one we had in Rota. We drove it south to Garmisch south of Munich. It is a ski resort in the winter and a Bavarian get-a-way in the winter run by the military. Garmisch has former Nazi officer-housing areas that are now refurbished and rented out to U.S. military on vacation. Now you have to be stationed in Europe to stay there. The U.S. also built some new hotels there. It is a wonderful place and very beautiful. The apartment we had was huge with very high ceilings. We made it our headquarters for exploring the area.

On our way to Garmisch, we stopped at the former Dachau Nazi Concentration Camp. It was an unbelievable experience to go through. All that is left standing from the original buildings is the main dining hall. The foundations of the rest of the camp are still there and they have reconstructed one of the barracks that the prisoners were housed in. We walked through the exhibit and looked at all the pictures, such inhumanity to man. At the very end is the liberation of the camp by U.S. forces. If there was ever a time that I was proud to be a U.S. service member, it was there. The joy on the faces of the prisoners, as the U.S. forces rolled into camp to liberate them, is overpowering.

We walked out back by the ovens that are still standing. They were never used. Most of the hundreds of thousands who were murdered at Dachau were shot or gassed. Many were captured Russian soldiers. No one knows how many Russians are buried there. Most of the thousands of clergy Hitler imprisoned, Protestant, Catholic and Jewish, were sent to Dachau. Many were murdered there. There was an old man sitting by the firing squad wall under a tree the day we were there. He was from Poland and had been a prisoner. He came every day. He spoke excellent English and Lauren and I started asking him questions. He said that the original German guards were not really that bad and would even play volleyball with them. It was only when the SS guards came in at the end of the war that things got sadistic and ugly. It was very interesting to talk to this survivor of such horror.

From our apartment in Garmisch, we met Briana and Justine who had been Euro-railing in Greece, the Riviera and northern Europe. They had stopped at Heidelberg, Germany to call us. While Briana was on the pay phone someone stole her purse, passport, traveler checks and Euro-rail pass. She was a basket case. Fortunately, the German security put her back on the train to us. When we met them they were living on peanut butter, jam and crackers. They were really glad to see us. We took them back to the apartment where they ate for hours. I asked Briana how she liked Munich. She said, "I don't know, we only stopped in Munchen." Munchen is German for Munich. Sometimes she really makes me laugh.

The next few days we visited Innsbruck, Austria and the Olympic museum, Oberammergau site of the every ten year passion play, the castles of Ludwig the mad prince who built magnificent Newschwanstein and the beautiful Bavarian mountains. Gail and I will never forget driving in those mountains with all the kids along the border of Austria singing at the top of our lungs popular singer Whitney Houston's hit single, "I Will Always Love You" that was playing on the radio. We hiked up in the mountains one day and saw a German shrine built to the war dead with pictures of young German men who were killed. We felt strange standing there as Americans. We also visited a lake where the German people changed into their bathing suits right in front of everyone. The Germans have no sense of modesty when it comes to nudity as Americans do. It was pretty strange for us. We had a great time and brought Briana back with us. Justine continued on by herself against our strong advice.

That fall we felt that we really needed to get Briana back to the United States to continue her education. She had a marine propose marriage to her. One night she was partying in a Spanish bar when a new senior chaplain tried to pick her up. He did not know who she was. When he found out, he took off like a shot. We never discussed it but Briana told me right away. I lost respect for that chaplain after that. There were some other things he did too that turned Gail and me off. Briana applied to some universities and was accepted at Washington State University (WSU) in Pullman, Washington where my mother had attended at one time.

The other thing that happened that fall was our trip to Israel. Gary and I had put together a tour of the Holy Land from the Rota chapel. We used Ami Lloyd out of Haifa who does all the tours for the U.S. Navy in the 6th Fleet. We had about 24 people including our wives and Gary's two daughters. Gail and I decided to leave our kids at home. We flew to Madrid from Rota and then to Tel Aviv on El Al Airlines. It was a trip of a lifetime for me. The Israeli's always clap when they have a safe landing.

We spent the first night in Tel Aviv. It was a little tense as a suicide bomber had blown up a busload of people just that week close to the hotel and Palestinians had kidnapped an Israeli soldier. The first day we drove up to Haifa via Caesarea and Aco. We held a Sunday service on Mt. Carmel where Elijah had dealt with the prophets of Baal. I preached using that passage. We then drove up to the border of Lebanon and spent the night in a Kibbutz called Gesher Haziv. It was really interesting.

The next day we visited Tel Meggido where the famous author James Michener wrote "The Source" and the Plain of Meggido where one of the last battles on earth will be fought between God and the forces of evil called Armageddon. The tels are mounds or small hills all over Israel that are ancient cities that have not been excavated. Excavations are going on all over the country. We were traveling in a nice air-conditioned bus with a Jewish guide and driver who knew more about the Jewish and Christian Bible than I did. We stopped at Cana where Jesus performed his first miracle and we saw a marriage procession close to the chapel there. That night we stayed at the St. Gabriel Hotel in Nazareth. The hotel was a former monastery. It was something to spend the night in the city that Jesus grew up in. That night after dinner, we all gathered to share how we had been blessed that day.

The following day we took a boat out into the middle of the Sea of Galilee. The sea is just a good size lake surrounded by hills. We ate St. Peter's fish for lunch in Capernaum and visited the site of the Sermon on the Mount and the town where Peter's house was. The foundation of the Capernaum Synagogue from Jesus' day had been excavated. At every site Gary and I would read scripture that pertained. We also would sing praise songs on the bus accompanied by an old guitar Gary brought.

We went to a site on the Jordan River and had a baptism of those who desired it. Gary and I did it together. Then we baptized each other. It was great. The Jewish guides watched curiously. After the baptism we went up into the Golan Heights to Caesarea Philippi. Caesarea Philippi is a beautiful remote spot at the base of snow capped Mt. Herman by Lebanon. It was there on retreat that Jesus' disciples first realized he was the Christ. The Jordan River also starts there.

After another night in Nazareth, we headed to Mt. Transfiguration. We had to ride crazy taxies up to the top and back. On from there we went to Beit Shean, one of the ten cities of the Decapolis and the largest excavation in Israel at that time. Here was a huge stadium and streets with Roman columns that Jesus had walked by. It was amazing to think about. Israeli soldiers were all around watching with machine guns at the ready. We didn't worry much because we were not the targets and the guides knew when it was safe. Later that day we drove up the steep pass from Jericho to the Mt. of Olives. We could see the Jewish Temple Mount across the Kidron Valley with the sun setting in the west. It was breathtaking. That night we stayed at Hotel Shalom in Jerusalem.

Thursday we visited the old city of Jerusalem and the Western or Wailing Wall. It is the remains of Solomon and Herod's Temples and Israel's most sacred site. The men and women go separately to write prayers and put them into the cracks of the wall. The men have to be covered. Our Jewish guides said the Jews believe the Kingdom of God is somehow located directly above the Temple Mount or Mt. Zion. Gary and I both went and said prayers. We miraculously got up on the Temple Mount just as Israeli soldiers were closing the area off because of some disturbance. Our guides knew the soldiers and they let us go through. We walked past the Muslim Dome of the Rock to the site where the Jewish Holy of Holies probably had been. The Jews told me that they did not have to tear down the Dome of the Rock to rebuild the Jewish Temple as some suppose. We walked the Via Dolorosa, Way of Sorrows, and saw streets that Jesus must have walked. It was an amazing experience.

At the end of that day we visited Gordon's Garden Tomb and had communion. It is one of the few really beautiful historic sites in Jerusalem. Most of the others have huge old Roman Catholic or Orthodox churches built over them. The authenticity of some of the sites is questioned as the Roman Emperor Constantine's mother named them in a vision she claimed to have during the Fourth Century. The British General Gordon said in 1883 that he believed his was the place where Jesus was crucified and buried. General Gordon's followers maintain it as a garden and there you can celebrate communion with your group. It is very moving.

Friday we headed to Bethlehem. It is very close to Jerusalem, only a few miles. The Orthodox Church of the Nativity is there dating from the 4th Century. The door is constructed so you have to bow to enter. Palestinian machine gun emplacements surrounded us as we left the buses. I needed film and the Jewish guides were very afraid to let me out of their sight. later active duty U.S. military were forbidden to go there. Below the main sanctuary is the cave they believe Jesus was born in. Who can say? We bought a nativity, some crosses and a camel all made out of olivewood there in the town. I looked out at the hills and envisioned shepherds watching their sheep at night. Every Christian should visit the Holy Land.

Our last full day we drove to the Dead Sea and spent some time at a spa close to En Gedi. The Dead Sea is one of the lowest places on earth. The mud of the sea is said to be medicinal. The Israeli's also use it for cosmetics. People come there to recuperate. We all swam, or rather floated, in the Dead Sea and coated each other with mud. It was a blast. Afterward we continued on to Masada. There Herod had built his last holdout high on a mountain in the middle of the desert. Huge cisterns built into the rock collected the little rainfall that came there. It was an amazing and ingenious fortress. Historians say that after Jerusalem fell to the Romans in 70 A. D., the last Jewish Zealots gathered at Masada. The Romans laid siege to the fortress and built a mountain of their own to conquer it. Their work can still be seen there. I figured it took tens of thousands of slaves to accomplish with a supply line going hundreds of miles. When the Romans finally got to the top, all the Jews had committed suicide. Today the Jewish special forces come to Masada and take their military oath of commitment to 'never again' let there be another holocaust. I rode the cable car up and Gail hiked to the top. The view was breathtaking.

We left Masada and headed back stopping at Qumran. This is the place where the Dead Sea Scrolls were found early in the 20th Century. The Qumran fringe religious community lived in the desert during the First Century. They collected and stored many manuscripts in clay pots in the caves there. One that was found had the complete scroll of Isaiah from the Jewish scriptures dated hundreds of years B.C. It is on display in the museum in Jerusalem. It is almost word for word the same Isaiah we have in our Bibles today. This speaks to the accuracy of our scriptures. They haven't been tampered with as much as we might think. Our last night we visited the Biblical Resources Institute and had an authentic Last Supper together much as Jesus might have had with his disciples. It was a moving experience.

Saturday we spent a little time in Jerusalem before heading to Jaffa and Tel Aviv. Gail visited the Jerusalem Holocaust Museum and I visited the Jerusalem Museum. I also visited Arthur Schindler's grave, the man who was credited with saving many Jewish lives in WWII depicted in the film Schindler's List. Jaffa is the place where it is believed that Jonah left for Spain. Everyone wanted to have lunch at the Hard Rock Café in Tel Aviv on the way to the airport. We got off the bus and headed in while our guides drove off. Suddenly we noticed that one of Gary's young daughters, Lauren, was missing. We didn't know if she got off the bus or not. We hunted high and low for her. Gary's wife Karen was beside herself. We even called the Embassy, not knowing if she had been abducted. Eventually we were able to locate the bus drivers who were having lunch. They checked the bus and found Lauren sound asleep in the back. Our relief was indescribable.

We got to Ben Gurion Airport with no time to spare. Going through customs on the way out of Israel is one of the tightest security systems I have ever experienced. It takes hours to go through all the lines, checks and interrogations to get on the plane. It must work because Israel has one of the safest terrorism records in aviation.

That fall I taught a class for the University of Maryland on Philosophy of Religion. It was my first attempt at teaching a secular subject. I taught night classes. Briana and Gail were taking classes while I was teaching. I had some of Briana's friends in my class. It was a very hard assignment. I struggled to stay ahead of the class, prepare meaningful lectures, give assignments, do my regular job and spend time with the family. It did it for the experience and the tax-free money. I decided that teaching secular subjects was not something I wanted to do for a living. Since I was a chaplain, I held back on sharing my own theological views in the class unless the students asked.

One night the dean came and sat in the back listening to me. He asked me afterwards why I wasn't putting more of myself into the class. I told him that as a chaplain I felt I shouldn't. He told me to do it. I wish he had said that at the first of the quarter. It was kind of fun being Dr. Waite for a change. I might be willing to try teaching again but only in a seminary setting where I can share my theology and experiences freely.

Right after the first of the year, Briana left for school in the U.S.. It was really hard to let her go. We felt we were doing the right thing at the time but looking back we are not so sure. There is nothing like the grief of your first child leaving home for the first time. It stays with you for weeks. Briana has always been amazing. She got on the plane and headed off to the United States to check herself into a university and dorm she had never even seen. She has always been so independent. I think that maybe it has come from growing up traveling around the world. She also has our genes and maybe that has something to do with it. We all missed her greatly that year.

We went back to Switzerland again the next year for the second European English Speaking Methodist Conference. We drove up this time to spend the night at our former base at Zaragoza. The second night we stayed at a French motel in Lyon, France. The conference met again at the Hotel Viktoria in Hasliberg-Reuti. This time the bishop was Cal, our bishop from the Pacific Northwest Conference. We couldn't believe that both years we went the bishops were friends of ours who we knew well. Two couples came with us from the chapel at Rota. It was a great time once again. We did a lot of skiing.

One afternoon I was skiing the top of the mountain by myself. It was a beautiful run. That afternoon I decided to take the whole family back up, including David who was almost nine. While we were getting on the lift, the Swiss attendant tried to stop us but we could not understand him. We thought he was just concerned about young David who we thought was good enough to go. When we got to the top we found out what he was trying to say. The wind had come up on the powder snow and it was a total white out on the top of mountain. There were some very steep drop offs and we could not see five feet in front of us. We were all terrified. Thank God I had made one run down when it was clear and I thought I knew which way to get down. We got very close to each other, single file with Gail in front and me in back, praying all the way. I believe at one point we really didn't think we would make it. It was very serious. Somehow, by the grace of God, we made it down. We collapsed at the hotel when we got back. Our family became much more careful after that.

On the way home we drove through a country I never knew existed called Andorra. It is a very modern winter skiing and summer fishing resort country for many British citizens and other wealthy Europeans. We liked it. We kept driving and eventually came back to the former U.S. base at Zaragoza near Barcelona where we had stayed the week before.

That spring I took Jonathan on the same sex parent retreat that is part of Dr. James Dobson's Preparing for Adolescence program. Gail took both the girls just before they turned thirteen. Now it was my turn. We had already gone through the book and workbook with Gail. On the weekend we listen to the audiotapes and just hang out and talk. Jonathan and I decided to go down to Gibraltar for our weekend. The preteen gets to choose where they want to go. Jonathan wanted to go there. We loaded our bikes and stayed at a place called La Linea in Spain next to the boarder of Gibraltar. It was a great weekend. We would ride our bikes through the little Spanish town across the border and go out to eat. We went to a movie one night. We talked about growing up and everything under the sun including sex. It was the kind of weekend I always wished my dad would have taken me on but never did. I later wrote in my journal that I would miss my first little boy. He was growing up.

Gail and I would get away every so often for a weekend. It is something we have always tried to do and I think it is one of the secrets of the longevity of our marriage. That summer we went to the Costa del Sol on the Mediterranean side of Spain. It is a very famous vacation spot, especially for the British. Many Brits retire there. We stayed in the La DuQuesa Hotel near Marbella. We had a great time just being together and experiencing new things. One evening we tried to get a banana split at an ice cream shop. They didn't know what we were talking about so we got some bananas and taught them how to make one.

In August we took the boys to England. It is one country I didn't want to miss. The two girls were in the United States. We caught the C-9 medevac flight to Ramstein AFB in Germany via Pisa, Italy. From there it flew on to RAF Mildenhall in England. As we were landing, I could not help but think of the Wait's, it is said my grandfather put the 'e' on the end, who left Wales in the 17th Century for America. One of their own was coming home almost four centuries later. An Air Force Chaplain family named Henry we met in Switzerland met us and took us to RAF Alconberry to spend the night. In the morning we caught the bus to Heathrow Airport in London where we bought seven-day Travelcards on the London subway they call 'the tube'. We took the tube to Hillingdon, close to U. S.

Naval Activities United Kingdom at RAF West Ruislip on the outskirts of London. We stayed at the Master Brewer Hotel there. The next day we did the rounds in London visiting the free Imperial War Museum and Piccadilly Circus. The following day we visited Madame Tussad's Wax Museum and Leicester Square where we got tickets for the musical "Five Guys Named Moe". It was a great evening, as good as Manhattan. Other highlights were the London Dungeon, the Tower of London, a boat ride up the Thames to Westminster Cathedral, and the Changing of the Guard at Buckingham Palace.

At Buckingham Palace an American gave me his last day of a Britrail card. I left Gail and the boys and headed up to Oxford, a place I had often wanted to go. Once I had considered going there for a PHD. I seriously looked into it but felt that God was not calling me to be a professor. I visited the John Wesley sites at Lincoln College including John's study. John started the Methodist Movement, it became a church later in America during the Revolutionary War, in the 18th Century with his brother Charles. That Sunday Gail and I took the boys to the Wesley Chapel in London that John Wesley built. They have a museum dedicated to him and his old house restored. He is buried there. Across the street his mother and brother are buried with many other famous people such as Isaac Watts, Defoe, and Bunyan. The next day we reversed our travel plan and headed back to Spain via a night's stay at RAF Mildenhall in England and Sembach Air Force Base in Germany. It was a great trip.

In September my folks came to stay for a couple of weeks. We took them all over playing golf, eating Spanish tapas, and lying out at the topless beaches. Gail's folks had made a similar trip. We took them to Gibraltar and even to Portugal. In Portugal we stayed at the Hotel Dom Pedro Marina in Vilamoura. Portugal is a very nice and inexpensive country. One of the favorite things we did was watch the Seattle Mariners in the American League Playoff games in the BOQ. It was great fun. We had a good visit.

In the fall, Gail got word that her sister Joan had cancer again. This time it was in her hip. Joan was about the same age as her mother,50, when she died of that terrible disease. I was trying to get orders back Washington State. The detailer was telling me that there was nothing close. The closest they could come was Kodiak, Alaska. We considered Kodiak but felt it was just too hard to do with the kids after Spain, besides, it didn't have a mall. One night I was jogging on the beach and pouring my heart out to God about orders. I heard him say to me clearly not to worry about it because it was all taken care of.

Gail went on Emergency Leave back to be with her sister who was going to have a bone marrow transplant. At the same time, I was at another hospital chaplain conference in Bethesda, Maryland. We met in Bethesda with our old Japan friends now Admiral Jim and his wife Joann. I had an appointment to talk to the detailer on Friday and took Gail on the Metro in the rain. I was in my blues. When we arrived, the detailer had gone home early for the weekend and stood us up. Gail and I were both furious. Suddenly the Deputy Chief of Chaplains, a one star Admiral, walked out and asked me what I was doing there. I told him what happened. He took Gail and I back into his office and started talking to us. His wife had just gone through cancer treatment too. He took out a notepad and started writing. He asked me where I wanted to go. I told him Washington State. He said he would see what he could do. By the time I got home I had orders to Whidbey Island Naval Station in Oak Harbor,

Washington about forty minutes away from our rental home and Avon Church. Once again, God had everything under control. I had to keep telling myself that constantly in the tough days ahead at Whidbey. Sometimes getting what you want can be hard to live with.

12

Back to the Pacific Northwest

We had orders back to the Pacific Northwest but all was not joyous. I had some email and phone contact with my new Command Chaplain at Whidbey Island Naval Air Station (NAS). These emails and phone calls were very strange. Immediately he asked me where we planned to live. I told him we owned a home forty minutes from the base and we planned to move back into it. He became very irate and told me that I could not do that. When I told him I was anyway, he told me that I would not be the Protestant Chaplain, he would give it to my junior and that I would be standing the duty every third week staying in the BOQ on base. I couldn't believe this guy. By this time I had my orders and there was no way I could get out of them. I learned a big lesson from this. Before you ever accept orders anywhere, find out some information from a few reliable sources on the senior you will be working for. I didn't and regretted it.

We prepared to leave Spain on short notice. Lauren had a boy friend who was heartbroken she was leaving. We were able to get a new chaplain coming in to take the Spanish house and most of the items that went with it. That was a real blessing. The hardest thing we had to do was to sell our new Nissan Serena. I tried everything. We were getting closer and closer to our departure and no bites. I became desperate and started going to car dealers and asking them. Eventually I found one who made me an offer. It was less than it was worth but he knew he had me in a bind.

I took it. It had been a great family vehicle. We wanted to take it home but the customs people would not let us. They were not made to U.S. safety standards.

We bought a new Ford Aerostar through the military overseas buying service. We had to pick it up in Norfolk, Virginia. Our friends Admiral Jim and Joann lived there. We would fly from Spain to Philadelphia and then to Norfolk where we would pick up the van and drive it to our home in Burlington, Washington. The only problem was our watchdog Hershey. We considered leaving her in Spain but the kids wouldn't do it. On Wednesday January 10, 1996 we left Spain for the US. It was hard to say goodbye to Spain and our wonderful Spanish home on the beach. The last few nights we stayed at the Hotel Playa del la Luz and the manager put us in a suite. He lived next door to us. Lauren was balling her eyes out. Those are always some of the toughest times to be in the service.

While we were getting ready to leave Spain, Gail's sister Beth was having our home in Burlington remodeled. She had it repainted, new carpet throughout, new bathroom fixtures and accents, new drapery, new counter tops and linoleum. It was like a new house. Just before we left, our neighbor Jim at the end of our cul-de-sac in Burlington was killed in a tragic trucking accident. He had just called us about putting in natural gas in the neighborhood and we were able to tell him we were coming home. It really hit us all hard. Jim and his wife Peggy had been good friends who always helped us with the house.

When we landed in Philadelphia it was snowing. We were worried that we wouldn't get Hershey off to Seattle on the plane. We elected to fly her ahead and have Beth pick her up. The airlines will not fly pets when it is too cold or hot. We all stayed at the Holiday

Inn that night and took Hershey with us. In the morning we were able to get her out early. We then flew to Norfolk but we were the last plane they deiced and let go before a new storm hit. Jim and Joann met us at the airport. They took us over to pick up our new van. That evening we were ready to head west. We spent the night in Flag Quarters and left early the next morning.

The first day we drove to Hickory, North Carolina and then on to Nashville, Tennessee. Other night stops included Little Rock, Arkansas, Elk City, Oklahoma, Albuquerque, New Mexico and finally Gail's folks in Mesa, Arizona. We stopped in Nashville to see our endorsing agent and visit the headquarters of the United Methodist Church and Vanderbilt University. We also stopped in Memphis, Tennessee to visit Graceland, the home of the king of Rock and Roll Elvis Presley. We spent two nights in Mesa with Gail's folks and then two nights with my folks in Sun City West, Arizona. Heading north we stopped at Edwards Air Force Base, California, Redding, California, Portland, Oregon and finally Seattle, Washington. Coming through northern California we had to chain up the van twice and were often stopped dead in snowy winter traffic. We put about 4,000 miles on our new van. When we were at Edwards, we called Whidbey and found out the chapel there had just been destroyed by fire. We couldn't believe it. I had been a Navy chaplain for twelve years and had never been stationed at a chapel. Now the chapel I had finally received orders to just burned up. I was not thrilled.

We stayed in Seattle for four nights before heading up to Burlington. I checked in at Whidbey, got Gail and the kids settled and immediately flew to Denver, Colorado to go through training for Preventive Relationship Enhancement Program (PREP). The senior chaplain just had to have me go right away for this training so I could help them put on marriage seminars. I was really angry. In my first meeting with him, he asked me once again if I was going to live in Oak Harbor. When I said no, he said I would not be the Protestant Chaplain though I was senior. I would be the Division Officer in charge of the chapel rebuild. I would also stand duty on the base every third week and I would immediately go to Denver for this training. It was a great start. I thought I had walked into the twilight zone.

Lauren was starting in the middle of her sophomore year in a brand new high school. I don't think people understand the kind of stress the children of military professionals live under all the time. She was petrified to go to her first day of school alone. Her biggest fear was that she would have to eat lunch all by herself? We called old friends from Avon who had a daughter who promised to sit with Lauren for lunch. Lauren was known as the Spanish exchange student. For a long time the high school kids thought she really was Spanish. Moving around the world also has it rewards for military kids. They make friends fast and become very outgoing and self-sufficient. Whenever their teachers ask if anyone has been to a particular country, our kids can usually raise their hands to most of them. The military lifestyle has many pros and cons for children. I think it is good in the long run though I grew up that way and said I would never put my kids through constant moves. If God calls you to the military, what can you do? You have to depend on him to take care of your family and he does.

While this was all going on, I was in zone for promotion to Commander or 0-5. One of those who sat on the board was my old friend Chaplain Leroy, now a Captain. We had worked together at Camp Pendleton years before. He was now the U.S. Navy Air Force Pacific Chaplain and the immediate senior of my chaplain boss. He called me one day to see how I was doing. When I told him I was not running the Protestant program he couldn't believe it. He called the senior chaplain up on the phone asking him what he was thinking. I had a doctorate in homiletics, liturgy and church music. To not let me run the program was like putting your first string quarterback on the bench. The chaplain stuck to his guns and would not relent. The next thing I knew Leroy was flying up to pay us all a visit. There were two other Protestant chaplains with me who were new Lieutenant Commanders and years junior to me. One of them had already put his papers in to get out because of the senior chaplain. The other one was named the Protestant Chaplain in my place.

Leroy went out to dinner with all of us and some of our wives. Gail was there and it was one of the first times she had met the senior chaplain. He kept interrupting Gail all evening whenever she tried to talk to our old friend Leroy. When I happened to mention that I was just in zone for Commander, Leroy pretended that he did not know. I bought it hook, line and sinker. I thought, "If Leroy didn't even know I was in zone and he sat on the board, there is no way I made it." Later, when he called me to tell me I was selected for Commander, we had a good laugh about his acting that night.

Leroy wanted to meet with the Protestant chaplains separately in the BOQ after dinner and he didn't tell the senior chaplain. We all gathered and told Leroy our side of what was going on. He listened and gave us some ideas about how to work with our senior. The next day the senior chaplain called my two other fellow chaplains to his house and started asking them everything they knew about Gail and I. The designated

Protestant chaplain spilled the beans about our meeting with Leroy. The senior chaplain later asked him to write what had transpired down in a report. He did. When I heard that he was trying to dig up dirt on Gail, I decided to declare war. I have learned through the years that whenever I am cornered and backed up against the wall, I attack. You can do lots of things to me and get away with it, but when you drag my family into the battle, be prepared for a war.

From that point on, the senior chaplain was totally belligerent towards me. He was sure I had invited Leroy up to Whidbey. He would give me every crappy job he could think of. It felt like he would stay up all night thinking of ways to make my life miserable. I consulted with my friend Admiral Jim who told me to just keep my mouth shut and bite the bullet. I couldn't do it. This man, I could not bring myself to call him a chaplain, would yell at people on the phone and hang up on them. Our Leading Petty Officer (LPO) and the civilian secretary all wanted to put in their papers because of him. The chaplain I relieved had put his papers in to retire before he came in zone for Commander. It was the unhappiest staff I had ever seen. In my opinion this senior chaplain was abusive to everyone. I was the next senior to him and felt a responsibility for everyone else. Someone had to confront him with his abuse and it looked like I was it. I couldn't keep my mouth shut and look myself in the mirror. I prayed about it and felt the Lord tell me to speak up.

One day after the senior chaplain had thrown me out of his office with very abusive speech, a routine experience, I decided to go to the CO and tell him what was going on. I first went to the XO and then to the CO. They listened to me but were not convinced I was telling the truth. I found out later that the senior chaplain was bad mouthing me to them and every 0-6 Captain chaplain he knew. I learned one thing about the Navy through all of this. Never take on a Navy Captain unless he or she has done something illegal and you have witnesses that will talk. A Navy Captain will always win in any war you try to wage. They have a lot of power and authority and some abuse it. The senior chaplain told me that I would probably make Commander because Leroy sat on my board, but I would not go any further if he had anything to do with it. He told me privately, "I will make sure you never make Captain". This from a fellow chaplain.

Eventually the Commander list came out and my name was on it. I was ecstatic. My goal for the Navy had always been to make Commander and retire with at least twenty years. At that time a chaplain had to make Commander to retire. The senior chaplain called me to tell me, something traditionally done, and it took every ounce of strength he had to do it. I could tell he was talking through clinched teeth. Leroy called right after him and told me to get in this chaplain's face and not back down. He said, "Doug, you are the only one who is not afraid of him".

The very next day I made an appointment to see the civilian psychologist on base. I had become very depressed over all of this. I dreaded coming to work each day. Up to that point I was afraid to seek help because I felt if senior chaplain found out, he would use it against me. Now I felt I was bullet proof. I had made Commander and would retire. He could not stop that. I decided to continue to meet him head on but it was taking a toll on me psychologically and affecting my family. I met with that good civilian psychologist for the next six months. She helped me see that I was often busy helping everyone else but not myself. She said I needed to do something for me every week. If I didn't take care of me, I would not be able to take care of anyone else. It made a lot of sense. I started calling my old friend Jack who had married Gail and me. He was my confidant and prayer partner.

I was staying in the BOQ for a week at a time every third week. It was ridiculous. Here I was on shore duty and spending every third week away from my family. The senior chaplain's rationale was that I needed to be close to the base if an emergency happened. I took the duty chaplain book and did research on the number of times a chaplain had to respond to an incident in less than 40 minutes, the time it would take me to drive from Burlington. They were almost nonexistent. I wrote a point paper and gave it to the CO asking him to rescind the senior chaplain's directive. The CO responded by making me stay on the base only half the week. It was his compromise and, I felt, an example of his poor leadership. What point did it make for me to stay on the base half of my duty week and not the other? He did it only to appease the senior chaplain and he let me go home half my duty week to acknowledge my point.

The senior chaplain was furious at me for going over his head. He found new ways to make my life miserable and to make me look bad to others. Eventually he got me hammered on a Fitness Report, our yearly evaluation. It was the first bad Fitness Report I had gotten in all my years in the Navy. I figured it would probably cost me Captain at some point but I could not be silent while this man continued to ruin people's lives. If it cost me Captain then so be it. I told that to the CO too. I told him I was the only one who had the guts to tell him the truth about what was going on. He listened but the chaplain had poisoned him towards me. I wrote my first rebuttal for the record on my Fitness Report and the CO forwarded it. Part of the reason I had been so vocal to the CO was that XO made me believe that he would protect me. When the XO didn't protect me, I felt betrayed and alone. In retrospect I wish that I had told the CO and XO once what I thought was going on and then kept my mouth shut and waited for the senior chaplain's retirement. Live and learn, I should have listened to Admiral Jim's advice.

About this time it was discovered that one of our enlisted Religious Program Specialists (RP's) had embezzled money from the Religious Offering Fund and set the fire in the chapel to cover his tracks. He was both making the deposits and writing the checks, a bad practice. The cash was going in his pocket, about $17,000 from the Catholic account, while the checks he wrote to Catholic charities were not being mailed. When an audit was about to happen, he lit a fire on his desk and it spread to the entire structure, resulting in about $880,000 in damage. Once the senior chaplain walked him to the post office box to watch him mail the checks. When the bank called saying we were overdrawn, the RP ran. He was later picked up in Las Vegas, court marshaled and sent to prison.

Over at the Avon United Methodist Church I had once pastored was the pastor who had relieved me at Lakewood years before. His name was Len and his wife was Barbara. This was the last pastorate of his career and he had not really wanted to go there. Avon is a tough church for any pastor and especially so for one near retirement. Len and I renewed our friendship and he had me preach every so often. Gail attended that church with the children while I was at the chapel on base. I attended whenever I could. It was good to be back in that church after twelve years. They had completed all the construction and even burned the mortgage I had gotten them into. The facility was great. I wished I had it when I was there. Len and I also met monthly for breakfast, prayer and fellowship.

About at this time we were having problems with David and Jonathan at school. They had both been diagnosed with learning disabilities while we were in Spain and were on Independent Education Programs or IEP's. The support we were getting for them was substandard and Gail and I had to stay on the school all the time. We also had Jonathan diagnosed as Attention Deficit Disorder or ADD. The school saw him as a troublemaker and he could not seem to shake it. Gail and I always tried to be their advocates.

It was good and strange to be back in Skagit County after all these years. Skagit is a wonderful agricultural valley with four definite seasons. Each season has its special sense there. It was great to experience them again. We had a few friends from the years before but not many. I think some of those from Avon were still mad at us for leaving to go into the Navy all those years before.

That summer I went to my first Promise Keepers (PK) event at the King Dome in Seattle. Former Colorado football coach Bill McCartney started PK. For a few years they had been having huge gatherings of Christian men at major stadiums all over the U.S. I had been overseas and unable to attend even though we started a PK group that met weekly at the hospital in Spain. I took Jonathan, my brother-in-law Harold, nephew Ben and father-in-law Burdette. We also took a group of men from the chapel at Whidbey. There were about 60,000 Christian men at the Dome all weekend praising the Lord. It was an awesome experience. At one point they called all the pastors to come forward. As I made my way through the thousands of people who were cheering us on, I had the sense this was the way it would be when we arrived in heaven. There would be thousands and thousands welcoming us home. At one point Jonathan went forward. It was very moving. I joined another PK group at Avon as soon as I got back.

Gail threw a big party for me for my selection to Commander. We had it in our back yard on a beautiful sunny August day. Many of our friends from Avon and the Navy came. It was a time to celebrate. It is a great honor to get those gold scrambled eggs on the brim of your combination cover. In the Navy his happens at Commander. Very few ever get that far in their Navy careers. Many of my chaplain friends did not make it. The day I was selected I was jogging around the loop near our home. As I got to the stretch near the wetlands where no houses are, I had a sense of God's angels applauding me as I ran under the trees. It was like I was ending a great race at the finish line. It gave me assurance sensing that my life was pleasing to God.

We went back to Lake Chelan that August and stayed at the Caravel again. We hadn't been there since we lived in Bangor. Gail's dad Burdette and his wife Millie stayed at the City Park. We had a great time as always. I took a boat from the base and we tried to do some water skiing. We also rented a Sea-Doo for the day. The kids had a ball. I did a lot of fishing too with the boys. Briana's boyfriend came for a few days.

That August 28th Gail and I celebrated our 25th wedding anniversary. We decided to go to Hawaii. I got us the best room in the new wing of the Hale Koa Hotel at Fort DeRussy next to the Hilton. We stayed a week. Briana stayed with the kids. I gave Gail a new diamond ring. I bought it from a jeweler in Oak Harbor who had sold us a small travel trailer. Part of the deal was a discount on a ring for Gail. We had a wonderful time. All we did was lie by the pool and eat. We did manage to take tennis lessons together for the first time every morning. God has blessed our union over and over.

Gail went back to school again that fall at Western Washington University in Bellingham, Washington. She had been to many institutions from Central Washington in Ellensburg, North Seattle Community, Olympic College Bremerton, University of Maryland in Spain and now Western. It had been a long haul for her but she kept at it. It was not easy having her in school again. She was finishing up in history to receive a Bachelor of Arts from the University of Maryland. She was at the top of her class. She is a very intelligent woman. Now she was thinking of doing a Masters Degree. I think the education helped to reinforce her already good self-esteem. Gail could do and be anything she wanted. I am glad she wanted to be my wife and the mother of our children.

One day I was sitting in a staff meeting at the chapel when a call came in for me. It was the emergency room in Sedro Woolley. Lauren had been in an accident and put her head through a car window. She was OK. I was at Whidbey and Gail was up at Western in Bellingham and the nurse could not get in touch with either of us. The next day I made sure we all had cell phones. We initially got beepers for the kids and then cell phones. It is always good to know that you can get in touch with your family or them with you when an emergency comes up.

Another chaplain came during that time to replace Kim. His name was Sonny. Kim was going to resign but Leroy and I talked him out of it and Leroy got him another set of orders. Sonny was a hunter and fisherman par excellance. He had been the South Carolina duck-calling champion. He was amazing on that duck call. NAS Whidbey had some great duck blinds on government wetlands. I started going out hunting with Sonny for ducks, especially when I had to stay on base for duty. I had never seriously hunted ducks before. I bought chest waders and decoys and started taking Jonathan too. Our dog Hershey was a retriever but did not know what she was doing. Sonny was used to hunting with well-trained dogs that his dad raised. Hershey only disgusted him and he would ask me to leave her home.

Once Sonny's dad, a retired Army Colonel, came to visit. He wanted to do some duck hunting. I knew about a place over in Skagit County in a barley field planted by the state that Sonny wanted to hunt. I met them one weekday morning in a driving rainstorm with Hershey. Sonny's dad immediately liked Hershey and saw her potential. That morning the hunting was great in the barley field. Sonny and I both had our limits before 8 AM, very unusual. We finally ran out of shells and had to go into town to dry out and get more ammunition. We came back and resumed hunting. That morning we shot 28 ducks. Hershey retrieved every one, some twice as they would crawl away. Sonny's dad said that many of those ducks would have been lost without Hershey. This was the day Hershey became a duck dog. From that day on she knew what duck hunting was all about and loved it. Often I would catch her eyes watching the ducks come in when I missed seeing them. Sonny's dad said she wouldn't be great but she would be useable. Her only downfall was she liked to go the other way and chew on the ducks and you had to get them away from her right away.

I also took the boys pheasant hunting that season in Yakima where I grew up. We went back to the Hendren farm we used to hunt in Harrah when we lived at Bangor. Mr. Hendren was still there though his wife had died. I went the first year with my father-in-law Burdette and my boys. We got a few ducks and missed some pheasants. It is always good to get out with the male members of the family and hunt together. We stayed at the Yakima Training Center.

That year right after Christmas the family went back to Crystal Mountain where we had skied while living at Bangor. We left in a severe snowstorm, stopping in Puyallup to visit my Aunt, Uncle and Grandma Chubby. Grandma and I had always been close. She now had Alzheimer's and was in a nursing home near my Aunt and Uncle. I would stop to see her whenever I could. She didn't know me but still had her sense of humor and laugh. We stayed at the Silver Skis Chalet at Crystal. All of us skied a little the first day. The second day the power went out. The third day we got snowed in. It was not a great ski retreat. Still it was good to be back with my family.

The senior chaplain put in his papers to retire that spring. I was overjoyed. Even though I was a Commander select and could have fleeted up to Command Chaplain, the Navy detailed another Commander in to take the senior chaplain's place. He was a friend of mine. The senior chaplain tried to turn him against me but the new chaplain already knew what kind of chaplain I was because we had worked together at Camp Pendleton. He called me to tell me I would be the Protestant Chaplain as soon as he took control. By that time I didn't want it.

That summer we had a tragedy happen. Briana was living in Bremerton, working and going to the junior college there. She had a serious boyfriend . He came from a big family and had a brother who was separated from his wife. The brother came over to his house one night to find his wife with a new boyfriend. He came back with a gun and killed them both, with his two children in the house. He then killed himself.

Briana's boyfriend went crazy when he got the news and took a big sword and hacked everything in Briana's apartment to pieces including many family heirlooms. Briana ran for her life and hid with friends. She called us and I called the police. The police went over to her apartment and found her boyfriends mom who was inside cleaning up. When Briana's boss found out what was going on he fired her. He was afraid that her boyfriend might come to work and do something. The slain wife worked with Briana. Gail and I went to get Briana and bring her home. She was hysterical. We filled out a restraining order on her boyfriend. The whole thing was awful. Against our advice, Briana eventually went back to him and later regretted it. It seemed she did what she wanted and seldom listened to us; often it costs her dearly. I remember when I was the same way.

Ron and I were getting along well at the chapel. We were very compatible. It was a tremendous change from what we had all been living under. I was now the Protestant Chaplain running the chapel and standing duty from my home on a cell phone and beeper. Still, the former senior chaplain had done a lot of damage to my career and psyche. My Fitness Reports improved with Ron's help but they were still not the high marks I was used to. I was exhausted and weary of Whidbey even though the retired community there was wonderful and supportive.

Two members stood out. One was a retired Navy Chaplain named Fred. Fred became a very close friend of both Ron and I. He would do weddings, counseling and fill in preaching for both of us. He was like another member of the staff. The other was a retired Navy Captain. He would take me out fishing in the Puget Sound. One day the Silver Salmon were really running. We took his boat out through Deception

Pass to a bar in the middle of the Straits of Juan de Fuca. The silvers were hitting the downriggers as soon as we could get them in. Before we knew it we had limited. We came back to his place to fillet the fish. He gave all of them to me. It was an outstanding day.

The first of August 1997 I put on the rank of Commander. My mom and dad, Burdette and Millie and my four children all came. I took the oath at the chapel from the CO and we went to the Officer's Club for a lunch reception. I was very proud to wear those new scrambled eggs on my cover. Later that month we went to Lake Chelan again. I tried once again to take the MWR boat from the base at Whidbey. It became more of a hindrance than help. Gail is always afraid of breaking down in boats. I finally talked Gail and her sister Joan to go out with me. We left all the kids with a Sea-Doo and went for a spin. All I had on was my bathing suit. The engine sucked up a black plastic bag and blew overheated. We were stopped dead in the water. Another boat finally towed us to the beach. None of us had any ID or money. A nice older couple gave us a ride to the Casino. From there we took the bus back the Caravel. I later picked up the boat. After that it was even harder to get Gail our in a boat. It is a shame because I love boating.

In early October the chapel at Whidbey took a group of men to the "Stand in the Gap" Promise Keepers Conference in Washington, DC. It was one of the most amazing things I had ever been to. Estimates were that a million Christian men were coming. All the way there on every plane Christian men were headed to DC. The flight attendants would ask us to sing and we would all start singing praise choruses. The pilots would welcome us and tell us they would see us there. The morning of the event we took the Metro to the center of town. It was standing room only. Hundreds of thousands of Christian men from all over the U.S. were on those trains and everyone was smiling and singing Christian songs. We all gathered in the center of town. There were so many men there was hardly a place to sit down. Most of us spent the entire day on our knees and faces repenting our sins and the sins of our fathers. The Spirit of God was present in an awesome way. I was deeply touched.

That fall I took my boys back hunting in Yakima with my brother-in-law Harold and nephew Ben. We stayed at the Training Center and hunted at the Hendren place again in Harrah. Jonathan was packing a shotgun for the first time. He had the little 20 gauge I had bought him. Five minutes before the season opened, Harold's dog came over and bit Hershey in the nose. She was bleeding and snorting and couldn't smell the rest of the weekend. At one point she got lost in the corn and couldn't smell her way back to us. It was very windy and you couldn't hear very far. I walked around the cornfield shooting every so often in the air. I thought I had lost her. Eventually she came running to me. We didn't do very well with pheasants that trip but we shot a lot of ducks. Again it was great to be out with the boys. David came for the first time carrying the BB gun that had been Jonathans. Gail was worried that something was going to happen to her boys.

That Christmas vacation we decided to go skiing at Whistler in British Columbia, Canada. Briana had moved into a house on the water in Bremerton with her boyfriend and some other guy. We didn't like it but couldn't do much about it. She was still going to school at Olympic. Somehow we got her to go with us up to Whistler. It was great having all my children there skiing together again. We got a special three-day rate by sitting through a time-share talk. Our condo was very nice, two bedrooms with two baths and a kitchen, and was built over a mall with underground parking. We loved it and the skiing was great. Briana and Lauren would go out clubbing at night. On one gondola ride to the top, a German family like ours was riding with us. The father spoke good English and we started talking. It turned out their favorite place to ski was Hasliberg-Reuti in Switzerland, the same place we had skied twice when we were living in Spain. Here we were, a German and American family, skiing in Canada and both had the same favorite spot in Switzerland. The world is becoming a very small place.

Admiral Jim retired that spring. He had his ceremony in Norfolk, Virginia and asked me to come and do the prayers and offered to pay my way. It was a great honor and I accepted. I took Gail with me too. At the ceremony I think Jim had every Flag and General Officer on the East Coast there. The room was full of military brass. He was the Atlantic Fleet Surgeon and spent a lot of his time with NATO in Brussels. As is often my custom, I wrote a new verse of the Navy Hymn for his benediction. We had a grand party afterwards. Later that evening we went over to their quarters and stayed up late talking to all their family. It was a very special time. Friends like Jim and Joann are one of the great blessings of a military career.

Both boys were playing soccer at this time. They started playing baseball when we first came back from Spain but neither one of them liked it. They also played basketball. Soccer seemed to be the favorite and they both did quite well at it making the select league teams. We have always felt that if we kept the boys in sports we could keep them out of trouble. Gail and I spent many weekends going all over the Puget Sound area watching both of them play. She is the true screaming soccer mom.

I feel like I should say something about the spiritual disciplines I was keeping at that time. I am a very type A personality who is extremely organized and methodical most of the time, a true Methodist. Gail is always teasing me about it. I have devotions every morning. I get up early enough to spend about thirty minutes with the Lord. I read at least a chapter or two from the scriptures, usually going through the Old or New Testament each year. I have done this since I made that commitment at Basic Youth Conflicts Conference with Bill Gothard in the spring of 1971 when I first became a Christian. It has taken me through the Bible many times. Gail was joining me then and we read the Upper Room together. We would then join hands and each of us say a short prayer. I believe these prayers are very powerful. I also keep a daily journal. I have done this since about 1979. Each day I write the date and a short paragraph about what happened the day before. Gail started doing this too. I keep track of my scripture reading and a brief note about what the Lord spoke to me about in it. Periodically I read back one, five and ten years or more in my journals. I would be able to read back twenty or more years but many journals were destroyed in the 1989 fire.

After writing in my journal, I would spend time in prayer using the Lord's Prayer as a model I would go through each day: praise of God, petition, and confession. I use my prayer language every morning for a few minutes at the beginning of prayer. I keep prayer lists each week from the worship service, PK meetings and other needs that come up. If I have a long commute, I will use my driving time for prayer. On Friday mornings I was fasting until lunch from the night before. Those mornings I would spend extra time with the Lord later in the morning, often in the chapel, praying for my children, their future spouses and my grandchildren to give their lives to him.

I have been praying for my children's future spouses since they were very little. Every night when they were small I would go in and lay hands on their heads and pray for them. They all accepted Christ as young children and made various commitments to the Lord at camp, youth groups and retreats through the years. As of this writing none of them were really walking with the Lord but they have him in their hearts and he continues to draw and protect them. I believed some day they would give themselves totally to him and that my prayers and fasting had something to do with that.

I also was taking time on the fast days to try to listen to the Lord. Often I visualize him there with me and I can hear him speak words of encouragement to my heart. Sometimes I will write them down in my journal. At the end of the day I try to read something positive before I go to bed such as an article from Guidepost Magazine. I believe that whatever your mind has on it at the end of the day is what it ponders throughout the night while we sleep. I want that something to be positive and faith filled. At Whidbey usually taught a weekly Bible study and most often preached and lead a service on Sunday. I like to take communion as often as possible. Gail and I have tried to also give a tithe of our income to the Lord. The percentage has varied over the years. I am always after Gail to give more. I see ten percent as a goal to reach. She considers our adopted children as part of our tithe to God. I agree with her. Sometimes when I am on shore duty I will also take a day of prayer to God and go away to a retreat center for an entire day spending time in silence and reflection with God.

These are my spiritual disciplines that keep me

going with God and the Holy Spirit. They vary with the assignment I have and what is going on in my life at the time. I recognize that I am a sinner and that I am constantly in need of God's forgiveness and grace. He loves me more than I could ever know and is always ready and willing to receive me. His patience is beyond comprehension.

I also have some physical disciplines. I believe they all go together: body, psyche and spirit. At Whidbey I was jogging about thirty minutes three days a week. I sensed that jogging for thirty minutes released natural antidepressants in my brain. The other days I tried to go to the gym and do weight training. I usually do not exercise on Sundays and reduce my devotions on those days because of corporate worship. I seem to always be dieting to check my weight.

My Command Chaplain Ron at Whidbey was retiring and he asked me if I would like to fleet up and take his place at Whidbey for three more years. I said yes and he called the detailer who said it could happen. I was doing my taxes one afternoon at home not long after that when I got a call from my old friend Leroy, the Navy Air Force Pacific Chaplain. He was responsible for all chaplains on all the carriers and air wings in the Pacific Fleet. He said to me, "Do you want to be a permanent Commander?" I said, "What?" He repeated it. Leroy continued saying, "If you take that job at Whidbey for three more years, you will probably not make Captain and will be a permanent Commander." He then asked me to become the Command Chaplain on the nuclear aircraft carrier USS Abraham Lincoln (CVN-72) in Everett, Washington close by. I told him I wanted to have some time to pray about it because I already had a carrier. Carriers are hard duty and much time away from family.

I spent the next few days talking to God, Gail

and my good friend retired chaplain Fred at the base. The consensus seemed to be that for my career and psyche, I should take the job. I really didn't want the carrier because I knew it meant going back to sea for months away from everything I love. I agreed the benefits were real. Also, like the Whidbey tour, it would leave my family in Burlington for another thirty months. I decided to take the job.

It was Lauren's senior year at Burlington High School. When Gail and I were pastoring at the Avon Church in the late 70's and early 80's, we had always dreamed of our children going to that high school. Now our dream came true with Lauren. Lauren has always been a singer and Gail had her in private voice lessons. She was also in the choir at school. She is very good and has lots of stage presence with no fear, exactly what you need to become a professional. For her high school graduation she sang a solo for everybody and brought down the house. Her sister Briana cried through the whole song.

That summer we went to Chelan again to the same apartment at Caravel. Gail's sister Beth and her husband Steve came this time. We had our usual wonderful time laying in the sun, taking walks around the end of the lake, golfing, water skiing, Sea-Dooing, eating, drinking and enjoying each other. Gail and I keep coming because our children come with us. We feel that it is worth whatever the cost may be to have this quality time together as a family.

That fall I heard about a great pheasant hunting guide and spot in Montana. He was a friend of my hunting buddy Sonny. I put together a trip for my boys, Burdette and Steve. We drove to Choteau, Montana straight from Burlington via Seattle. It is a long drive. Choteau is close to Great Falls. It is the town where they shot the Robert Redford film "Horse Whisperer".

We stayed in the Best Western motel. Early the next morning we went out to the farm. Our host had a great dog named Shadow who was a pointer. That dog was a hunting fool. It was the first time Steve had ever hunted. We hunted hard, saw lots of pheasants and had a great day. David was packing a shotgun for the first time. I wanted my boys to experience really good pheasant hunting the way it is supposed to be done, with great dogs. We all had a ball. At night we would go over to the local restaurant and eat steak. Our guide even cleaned and froze our birds for us. We hunted one more day and then headed home. Later we had a big pheasant dinner with all the family at our house.

Gail and I had been working on another adoption since Spain. We had seen the plight of the Chinese girls when First Lady Hillary Clinton visited China. China's one child per family policy left many girls abandoned in the orphanages. When we saw the taped footage we felt God was calling us to go and get one of those girls. We started the process then and continued when we got to Burlington. I began to have my doubts when Gail got serious. Most of my male friends and family thought I was crazy to take in another child in my late forties. Gail said that this was her ministry, raising children. She also said that if she had to follow me around the world in the Navy doing my ministry, I should go with her to China to continue hers. That sold me.

Somehow we heard about an agency in Seattle called Americans Adopting Orphans or AAO. A couple that had adopted two children from China ran it. They were wonderful and got us started putting in the paperwork. With the Chinese government everything is a mountain of bureaucratic red tape. If you cross all your tees and dot all your eyes with the paperwork, you get in line for adoption and wait. It took us about a year. In our home study we said we would take a healthy little girl aged two to seven. We always leave the babies for those with no children. Besides, we like our adopted kids to be potty trained and sleep through the night when they come home. That is the only way to have children.

The first child they tried to match us up with was beautiful but had visible physical handicaps that we didn't think we could handle. We asked Beijing to try again. The second child was healthy but when we checked the paperwork she appeared to be older, about nine. We asked them to try a third time. Our agency told us no one had ever done that with Beijing. Finally we were matched with a third healthy little girl named Wu Ying. The Chinese put the last name first. Ying was her first name and Wu was the district she was abandoned in next to a police station. She was almost three and looked very sad in her photo. We called this her orphanage face. The other kids said this was the one when they saw her picture. The report said she had no upper body strength but there was no physical evidence of problems in the photo. Our agency said this was a code that she was healthy and they were trying to make her a special needs case to get her out of the country. The agency sent a Chinese doctor to check her out. He said she was perfect. We accepted her and made our plans to travel to China to bring her home.

Gail and I flew from Seattle to Guangzhou, old Canton north of Hong Kong, via Los Angeles (LA). From LA we flew sixteen straight hours in a Chinese Boeing 777. The U.S. Consulate is there. We rested at the White Swan Hotel and then flew to Kunming in central southern China above Laos. We stayed there at the Green Lake Hotel. The four star hotels were very nice but surrounded by working class neighborhoods that were crowded and Spartan. We only had a few days to pick up Wu Ying and get back to the Consulate before our visa for her ran out. Our travel agency, Lotus Travel, had transportation and translators waiting for us everywhere we went. We went to the auditor's office the next morning and saw Wu Ying for the first time. She was with the orphanage director and eating crackers. Ying let me pick her up right away as David had done ten years before in Japan. We think both of our adopted children knew whom we were before we met them. The Lord had this all planned from the beginning of time. We started our paperwork immediately and got it done in record time. In China the price they tell you for the adoption never varies. Nothing is done under the table as it is in some countries. They let us go to the orphanage that afternoon and see where Ying had spent the last year. She was abandoned there at eighteen months and was now almost three. They let us take movies, which was unheard of. It was very sad. The facility was nice and clean but there were so many little children abandoned. Most were girls. There was even a set of twins. We wanted to take them all home.

Gail and I decided to name our new little girl Mae Ying after Gail's mom Shirley Mae. Like David, we desired to let her keep her Chinese name as her middle name. The Chinese workers were calling her 'mei mei'. We thought it was nice they were using the name we had for her. Later we learned that 'mei mei' is 'little sister' in Chinese. She has been Mae Mae ever since. She only cried when we first took her from the orphanage director. She had never really been out of the orphanage. She did not utter a peep on the plane ride from Kunming to Guangzhou and the beautiful White Swan Hotel on the river. We met up with an older couple that had no children and were adopting a nine-year-old girl. They had really studied Chinese and were able to communicate with her. We were able to communicate with Mae through all of them. Mae was very quiet and serious until she started playing with the other girl. Then her vibrant personality came out.

The next day we got our girls physicals and took both to the U.S. Consulate to get visas for home. It was our last day to get it done and the Lord worked it out. What a miracle! God wanted us to have Mae. That afternoon Gail and I visited the Christian Church that was just across from the Consulate. They gave us a tour and introduced us to the seminary they had there. We met with the head of the seminary and he blessed little Mae. The next day we flew home. Mae never uttered a sound the whole way. The other family traveled with us all the way to Seattle. Many of our family met us at the airport. We had traveled over 32,000 miles and on the last leg to Seattle from LA, Alaska Airlines lost our luggage. The luggage showed up later.

We drove home and introduced Mae to our children. Briana was home and Mae immediately attached herself to her and Lauren. Our five children were finally all together. Mae is as smart as they come. We think her parents must have been rocket scientists. She learned English in only three months, most of it from our other children. That December we went back to Whistler and took Mae. My cousin Craig came with his family too. It was so cold we couldn't ski. We celebrated Mae's third birthday there on December 19th. That is the date the orphanage gave her. A year or so before Gail had clipped a picture out of the Seattle paper of a group of young Chinese girls in a ballet recital and put it on the refrigerator. Gail had said she was praying to have a little girl who looked just like them. There is tremendous power in faith filled prayers with visualization. Mae looks exactly like those little girls. She is a gift from God like all of our children.

Chaplain Ron retired that fall and suddenly I was the Command Chaplain of the base. Once again I had gone full circle. I had a two-year window for the CO to write a new Fitness Report to replace the one he had written when the former senior chaplain influenced him negatively towards me. I had been with the same CO for almost three years and he had seen me under two Command Chaplains. I decided to ask him to change that report. The two-year window came and went and he didn't do anything. However, for my detaching Fitness Report as Command Chaplain he wrote a very strong report calling me his most trusted advisor. He told me in my outbrief interview that he decided to do that rather than write a new Fitness Report to replace the old one. I only hoped the promotion board would see that they were all from the same CO.

Just before I left Whidbey, I bought a new car. When I made Commander I said that I was going to buy a sports car. Gail loves Ford Mustang's. Her dad had a 1966 yellow Mustang when she was in high school that he gave to us as a wedding present. The choice came down to a white Mustang or a black Camero. I decided to go with the Mustang because of Gail and I just liked it better. I bought it and brought it home to Gail. I had been driving Briana's old Suzuki Samurai that we had taken to Spain and brought back. It was cheap transportation but was dangerous on the freeway. We felt the Mustang would be safer on my daily drive to the ship in Everett on the freeway each day. Besides, the Mustang looked cool. Now it was time to go back to sea once again.

13
USS Abraham Lincoln (CVN-72)

I detached from NAS Whidbey Island December 1998. It was a happy day to finally drive away from that place. I don't think I realized just how deeply those years had affected me. I went to fire fighting school at Bangor. I was the most senior officer there and they made me the 'on scene leader'. As we were getting ready to go and fight the fire, I gathered my entire team and had prayer. Everyone thought it was hilarious. It only seemed natural to me. Two of my officers in the fire team were also assigned to the Lincoln with me. I reported to the USS Abraham Lincoln (CVN-72) on December 23rd, 1998.

The Abraham Lincoln (Abe) had just returned from a six-month deployment two weeks before I reported aboard. In early December I had received a phone call from one of the chaplains. He wanted to inform me that the Command Chaplain had been relieved for cause and taken off the ship in Hawaii. The Command Chaplain had apparently gotten himself in trouble when they were in Hobart, Tasmania while visiting Australia. He had gone to Captain's Mast and been reprimanded and confined to his stateroom on the transit to Hawaii. This was the man I would follow on Lincoln. It seems almost everywhere I have gone, senior chaplains have gotten themselves in trouble. The Chaplain Corps appears to have trouble growing senior leaders who maintain their integrity once they reach the rank of Captain. It is almost as if the rank goes to their heads. My first week aboard Abe, the Weapon's

268

Officer, an old friend from Whidbey, came to my office and told me he hoped I never became a Captain. He said every chaplain Captain he had known had serious problems.

The staff I inherited had been very beat up. They were really hurting, especially the chaplains. I knew that some serious healing had to take place with this team before they could function well together again. This was my assignment. It was Christmas and they had not even decorated their religious spaces.

I met with the XO as soon as I reported aboard. He told me that what happened with the former Command Chaplain had been the most painful fifteen minutes of his entire career. Even the senior officers onboard were hurting from what had happened. He said to me, "All I know about you is that you are a Methodist and have a lot of experience." Someone told me that when you follow a person who has gotten in trouble, you could do no wrong. You are 'golden' as they say in the Navy. I hoped and prayed that I could keep myself out of trouble. "But for the grace of God go I."

The ship was still in the post-deployment standdown. No one was around. The Protestant and Catholic Chaplains both came in to meet me. After Christmas I started moving in. I sensed a spiritual heaviness around my office and stateroom, the same office and stateroom I inherited from the chaplain who had been relieved. I called up my old friend Father Jack who was the rector of one of the largest charismatic Episcopal churches in the Pacific Northwest. He came up and met me for lunch on the ship. We went to each space and had prayer and anointed the spaces with oil. I sensed a release in these areas. I believe that sometimes, spiritual oppression can linger in a physical setting and can only be removed by special prayer like Jack and I did.

It was awhile before I met the CO. He was a tall man who was very sure of himself. He had signs around that read, "It is good to be King" and other things like that. The XO told all the Department Heads to just treat him as a three star Admiral and we would be OK. In my intake interview with him, he asked me what the crew was saying about him. I thought that maybe this was an examination. Was he testing me to see if I was a 'yes' man who would tell him what I thought he wanted to hear, or was I someone he could rely on to tell him the truth no matter what? I opted for the second choice. I said, "They say you are vain sir". He looked at me for a moment and then changed the subject. I must have passed the test because he always seemed to respect what I had to say from that day on. It could have gone the other way and backfired in my face. I guess life is like that. You take chances, go with your guts and live with the results. My hunch was right that time. I can't say that is always the case.

Congress says that ships returning from deployment have to stay in their homeport for thirty days after they return. Almost a month from our return, we went back to sea. It was the same way on the Nimitz. These nuclear carriers cost about one million dollars a day to maintain and the Navy does not like to let them sit for long. It was strange to go back to sea again after over six years of shore duty. Everything seemed familiar to me. These Nimitz class carriers are all almost identical. When I first came aboard I forgot in my conscious mind where Religious Ministries Department was. Then I just quit thinking about it and went wherever my legs took me, relying on my unconscious mind. I went right to it, funny how the unconscious mind works.

My team was a Catholic Priest who was a prior marine, and Brian, a solid Nazarene family man who reminded me of myself as a Lieutenant. I also had an air wing chaplain who was a single Full Gospel minister. My RP chief was a seasoned Senior Chief who was a strong Christian and had been managing a large group of RP's. It was a large staff for a chaplain to lead. Our congregation was over 2500 sailors from the ship's company and another 2500 air wing personnel. My first night back at sea I did the evening prayer for the entire crew from the bridge at the usual time of 2155. Though it was hard to leave my family, it was also good to be back in that operational setting.

Our carrier is part of what we used to call a battle group made up of six other ships and two submarines, about 10,000 sailors total, 20% at that time were female. This was my first of four ships in the Navy that had females. The XO said I would love it as the male sailors were not as crazy when they went ashore in foreign ports.

There were also four other Protestant chaplains out on the other ships. The carrier has the only Catholic chaplain who is supposed to travel around the battle group on the helicopters or 'holy helo' as we call it. The Command Chaplain on the carrier is supposed to be the Battle Group Chaplain and relate to the Battle Group Commander who is the Admiral on the carrier. The Captain I relieved had called himself the Battle Group Chaplain but had not officially been designated that title by the Admiral. The Admiral's XO is called the Chief of Staff or COS.

One of the first things I wanted to do was see the Admiral and ask him to designate me the Battle Group Chaplain. When I went up to meet the COS and Admiral, I was received warmly. The Admiral sat me down, looked me in the eyes, and said, "Your job is spirituality. If anyone interferes with that, I want to know about it". He told me to consider myself the Battle Group Chaplain and to stop by anytime I wanted. He was an amazing man. I was really encouraged.

The carrier has an air wing made up of about eight squadrons of aircraft, all the way from F-18 Hornet fighter-bombers to C-2 prop jets called COD's plus four other kinds of aircraft. COD's carry passengers and mail back and forth to the beach. Our carrier alone could put on a pretty good war. Each squadron has its own CO and XO who are Commanders. Right off the bat some of the squadron CO's met me at lunch and asked if I could do something about flying on Sundays. They wanted to have one day off a week on Sundays. Most of the time we fly seven days a week when the wing is aboard. I took that information to the Air Wing Commander or CAG, a Captain. He was a Christian man too. He told me that one day off a week was an idea good enough for God so it should be good enough for us. He supported it. I asked our CO and he supported it too. Later I brought it up with the Admiral who said he also supported no fly Sundays. The reality was that we still flew most Sundays and no one would take responsibility for trying to change it. I made my feelings known on the subject constantly.

Our first trip out we stopped at Santa Barbara, California for a port call. Our CO had been an aide to Presidents Reagan and Bush and spent a lot of time in Santa Barbara while at the Reagan Ranch. He knew all the movers and shakers in town. We were one of the first carriers to ever stop in Santa Barbara. I had a good friend from seminary who pastored a church there, Marty and his wife Elyse who were our neighbors. Marty was at the Vineyard Church. I stayed with them and Marty asked me to preach that Sunday. I gave a personal tour of the ship to a large group of his family and friends. It was a great visit.

I was one of seventeen department heads on the ship. We call them DH's. We are like squadron CO's in our responsibilities. Some of the DH's are former CO's of squadrons or ships. A few of these departments have 500 or more sailors in them. We meet 1800 (6 PM) every night at sea with the ship's XO we call 'Big XO'. This nightly meeting is called Eight O'clock Reports. Most of us are Commanders and we socialize and often become very close friends. This camaraderie is one of the best parts of being in the Navy.

Jimmy was the senior dental officer and a DH. He was Japanese and a non-practicing Buddhist. We became jogging partners and friends. His Japanese wife was pregnant full term with their second child. One night we got a call saying their child was still born. Jimmy was with his wife at the time. I called him and told him he was in my prayers. Later he called back and asked me to do the service for their son. They lived at Whidbey Island. I said I could do a Christian service if that was OK with them. They agreed. The service was held at the NAS Whidbey Chapel, which was packed with sailors from Whidbey and the ship. I added a Buddhist prayer for Jimmy and his wife's comfort. Funerals like that are tough, but they give me the opportunity to preach the gospel to a largely unchurched audience. Jimmy and I became very close after that.

While at sea with the air wing aboard, we have a huge congregation. On a good week we have over 500 people attending services and studies for nine different faith groups. The other two Protestant chaplains and I only do the three Protestant services on Sunday. Lay readers do the other services. We have a nice chapel that can seat about forty people. Only one of the Protestant services, 0800 Communion, can fit in the chapel. The other two services meet in the bow anchor chain area known as the forecastle or foc'sle. We can seat well over a hundred there. It gets very noisy however, when jets are launching from the forward catapults. Sometimes we all wear ear plugs. The other two services in the foc'sle are Free Church in style and have a praise band that leads worship. The average age on the ship is nineteen so we are trying to target what we called then a younger Generation X audience in those services. It is the best Christian ministry in the Navy and the closest you will have to a real congregation, minus family members and retirees.

That March I was able to get the CO of the first new F-18 Super Hornet squadron to be the speaker at our prayer breakfast. He was then a Captain and a hero in naval aviation that had shot down the first Mig jet in Desert Storm. He had video coverage of his aerial combat he wanted to use in his talk. Some objected to this but most didn't. It was very well attended. The CO and senior enlisted man, Command Master Chief or CMC, attended. This Navy hero said his talk was about answered prayer. He told an amazing story of how his sister in the Midwest had awakened in the middle of the night impressed to pray for her brother. Later they compared times and it was the same exact time he had been in combat over Iraq. It was a powerful talk that moved many. He was not even supposed to fly that day and was put in his jet at the last minute.

We then went to Victoria, British Columbia (BC) in Canada at the end of that sea period. Victoria was another favorite of our CO. My son David joined me there. We stayed in a motel and rode the ship back to Everett on a six-hour Family Day Cruise. We launch

274

jets and let our families see what we do for a living on those cruises. One night I went to a black tie dinner at the Empress Hotel in downtown Victoria. Many Canadian and American dignitaries were there. I said the prayer and sat with our new XO. Victoria is always a great visit for the ship. We pulled into Everett and ran to Lauren's 19th birthday at the Keg in Seattle. It was a crazy homecoming.

The Generation X brief that I made from my Doctor of Ministry paper was still being requested, especially by the Coast Guard. I gave the brief to all the Coast Guard in San Diego on one of our trips down there. When we got back to Seattle they had me come to the Seattle Coast Guard headquarters and give it there. All the Coast Guard CO's were there with their Admiral. It was a very interesting day and got me thinking of doing duty with them. No other branch of service has the diversity of opportunity that Navy chaplains have.

The end of March we took the ship to the Bremerton shipyard for a six-month periodic incremental availability or PIA. We do this about every eighteen months. During that time the crew has to commute from Everett leaving at 0400 and returning after 1800. They are very long days. Many opt to stay over in Bremerton during the week in the barracks or BOQ. That is what I did. It was just too much to drive to Everett every morning from Burlington and catch the 0500 bus to Bremerton getting home about 1900 at night. Many did do that and you could tell whom they were, the ones yawning all day. They tried to sleep on the bus and ferries. I would come down on Sunday nights and stay in the BOQ through Friday noon when I headed home. Once again I was spending time away from my family while in the area. As I always say, there is no good time to be on a Nimitz class carrier, especially the Lincoln. You are always gone, even when you are home.

While in the yards we moved half of our department to a barge next to the ship. The ship was really torn up and many of our spaces were unusable. We put one chaplain and some of the library and the chapel over on the barge. We also ate on the barge and the duty rooms were over there. While in Bremerton we tried to do some marriage and single retreats along with community relation's projects such as repair and painting. I made contact with a men's Bible study that I once belonged to and attended once a week. It was good to see those brothers. I also attended the Bremerton Ministerial Association. Some of the same people were there from my Nimitz days. I would occasionally reflect on the times the Lord had brought me to Bremerton, on the Brinkley Bass, the Nimitz and now the Lincoln.

For the first time in my career I was able to attend the yearly chaplain's Professional Development Training Course (PDTC) in Hawaii. I took Gail with me and we stayed at the Pearl Harbor Submarine Base BOQ that had an outdoor pool. Many of the Chaplain Corps brass come to that PDTC because it is in Hawaii. At the end of the week Gail and I moved to the Hale Koa armed forces hotel near the Hilton on Waikiki. It always brings back a lot of memories to go there. The new Naval Air Force Pacific Chaplain was talking to me about taking the Submarine Force Pacific Chaplain job there. It sounded like a good deal to me. Gail and I wanted to be stationed in Hawaii.

On May 21st Gail and I officially adopted both Mae and David in a Washington State court. David and Mae were adopted in their own homeland too. It was legal and we never thought to adopt David in the U.S. Since then, some had decided to take that extra legal step in the U.S. One advantage was that it gave both children a U.S. birth and adoption certificate in English. Because of David's age, the judge allowed him to answer for himself when asked if he wanted to be adopted by us. All our family came to the courtroom. It was a great experience. We had a nice lunch afterwards in Mt. Vernon.

We have an organization in the Chaplain Corps called CREDO that does nothing but run retreats. The Bremerton CREDO put a retreat together just for the chaplains in the Pacific Northwest. TJ, Brian and I went. In fact, we did the music for the whole retreat. They called us the three amigos. During the sessions we got in small groups. I heard that both TJ and Brian were sharing how my coming to Lincoln had really been a blessing. It was great to hear the affirmation. The healing was beginning.

Half way through the summer I got a new RP chief and a new Catholic chaplain. Personnel are always coming and going on a carrier. I also started an all hands lunchtime Bible study and a new officer's fellowship we called Wardroom Christian Fellowship or WCF. Both were well attended. I invited everyone in the department to come up to our house in Burlington with their families for a barbecue party. The chaplain before me made these times mandatory so I made it optional. Some chose not to come but most attended.

That summer the CO decided to see what I was made of. He gave me the assignment of giving suicide prevention training to the entire crew and making sure that everyone attended. I worked with the senior medical officer (SMO) and put together a video with him for the crew. We then showed it continuously and made everyone fill out a statement to their record that the XO, SMO or I had to sign to say they had seen it.

The CO was impressed with how I handled it and told me so. Once again I passed his test.

During this time our oldest son Jonathan was getting into trouble with the law. Most of his friends had become school dropouts and were using drugs. Gail and I were beside ourselves trying to figure out what to do. We knew Jonathan was struggling with drug use and we had him in counseling and even put him in an inpatient treatment program in Bellingham. Nothing seemed to help because of his friends. They had more influence over him than we did. The marijuana was much stronger and addictive than it was when I was his age. Many of the valley farmers were growing it in their basements to supplement their incomes. It was readily available and potent.

While we were in Santa Barbara, Marty and Elyse had told us about the miracle of their son. They almost lost him to hate groups. Finally they shipped him off to an offshore program that changed his life. He found Christ and was transformed. We started looking at these programs too. We knew we had to get Jonathan away from his friends. All the programs we looked at were very expensive.

I came back to Bremerton to discover that Briana and her boyfriend were having a huge fight. Briana called me to come over to their house right away. I had been trying to spend time with her while I was in Bremerton, taking her out to dinner and a movie once in awhile. I did not like to go to their place if her boyfriend was there. I didn't approve of their relationship. Briana had finished junior college and was working full time for a radiologist and going to Western Washington University full time at night. She and her boyfriend were breaking up. I could tell Briana was scared and mad. I got right over there. His parents were there too. It was the first time I had met them.

His parents were trying to talk them into working it out with counseling. I wanted her out of there. They both were making accusations about the other. The end result was Gail's 76-year-old dad and I packed Briana up in one night and put all her furniture in storage. She then left for South Lake Tahoe to spend the summer with some friends. Gail and I thought that was the best thing for her; get her away from her boyfriend and out of town where he couldn't reach her.

The new pastor at Avon was Edd and his wife Pam. When I was just starting out at Avon, Edd and his wife came to the parsonage to talk to Gail and I about going into the ministry. Edd and his family later joined Avon and he began the long journey of college and seminary on his way to ordination. He quit his job, sold his home and went back to school with a bunch of kids. Eventually Edd finished seminary and was ordained serving churches in Eastern Washington. When Len and Barb retired, I put in a good word to the District Superintendent telling them Edd would do well at Avon. Low and behold, he got the job. He had gone full circle. It was great having a pastor there whom I had helped bring into the ministry. Every so often he would ask me to preach. It is always nostalgic and good to preach at Avon. Many of the traditions they take for granted are things that I started years ago. It makes you feel good knowing these traditions are still continuing on and you had something to do with it.

I went to Annual Conference for the United Methodist Church that year in Moscow, Idaho and learned from Pastor Edd at Avon about a program in Eastern Washington called Jubilee Youth Ranch. A wealthy Christian apple grower who wanted to help kids started it. It was a Christian behavior modification program out in the middle of nowhere near the Tri-Cities on the Snake River.

My last living grandma, Chubby or Alice Gilliam, died at the age of 95. She had been in a nursing home in Puyallup with Alzheimer's. My Uncle Stan decided to have services at Sumner and in Pomeroy where my mom had grown up. The whole family came to Sumner. I preached and Lauren sang. My folks were there. Then some of us followed Stan as he took the body to Pomeroy. Jonathan came with me while Gail and the rest of the family stayed back. We all stayed in Pomeroy. My grandfather, Ransom L. or 'Dick" as he was called, was the sheriff there of Garfield County. He died when my mom was fourteen from wounds received in France with the Army in WWI. Stan buried grandma right next to him. I did the service. Many family members were there.

On the way back home, I drove Jonathan to Jubilee Ranch and didn't tell him until we were almost there. It is close to Pomeroy. We met with the counselors and toured the facility. They had a tackle football team that was practicing. Jonathan wasn't very impressed. When we got home Gail initiated the paperwork and Jonathan was accepted. It is very expensive to send kids to these schools. We were able to get a scholarship to pay for some of it. The rest came out of his college money we had saved. We figured his college money wasn't going to be worth anything if he was in jail.

One night about that time, Jonathan broke into a truck in Sedro Woolley and got arrested. The police put him in the juvenile detention center in Mt. Vernon. We had to talk to him through the glass window. He would ball his eyes out and plead with us to get him out. It broke our hearts. I was going to get a lawyer and get him out but everyone, the prosecutor and the guards, tried to talk me out of it. They said to leave him there for a while to teach him a lesson. Though it was extremely hard, I listened to them. When his court hearing came they brought him into the courtroom wearing orange coveralls and in handcuffs and shackles. I wore my uniform and stood behind him. We had let the prosecutor and judge know that we had a program lined up for him at Jubilee. They made it part of his sentencing. If he finished a year at Jubilee successfully, they would drop all charges. If he didn't, he would be coming back to face them again. They were super and wanted to support Gail and I by taking some of the heat off of us.

The week Jonathan was in detention, I took David on his same parent Dr. James Dobson 'Preparing for Adolescence' weekend. He wanted to go to a Mariner's game at their new Safeco Stadium. We went to the game and then went over to spend the night at the Bangor BOQ, as there were no hotel rooms in the entire city of Seattle. There was heat lightening and rain on the ferry as we rode it in the dark after midnight from Seattle to Bremerton. The next couple of days we listened to Dobson tapes, ate, watched movies and talked. Jonathan's situation was a great illustration of what not to do. One afternoon we jogged up to our old house at Bangor. We had a good time together.

We got permission to take Jonathan to Chelan with us for a family vacation before we took him to Jubilee. Beth and Steve came again and brought their girls. We had been in the same unit for quite a few years. Beth and Steve decided to upgrade to a room like ours too. Steve and I played a lot of golf. I would begin the day jogging with Mae in her jogging stroller or alone around the end of the lake. A couple of days Gail's high school friends Marilee and Ray took Steve, David and I water-skiing early before the wind kicked up. Every evening we would all barbecue together on the lawn by the lake. It is a wonderful spot. One day we rented a Wave Runner all day. I had always taken my older kids on a date to lunch and try to find out what was going on in their lives. Briana flew in from Tahoe one night. We usually celebrate Jonathan's birthday there.

During all those years we had become friends with many other families who picked the same week as we did. Our kids had become friends with theirs. Jonathan was supposed to stay close to us but took off with these kids at a party one night. I found him at 0130 and we had sharp words. We had ceased to have the authority in his life to check his behavior. He needed to go to Jubilee soon. We prayed we would make it in time.

Gail and I sent Briana back to Tahoe and went home. On August 26th Gail and I drove Jonathan to Jubilee Ranch. It was very hard to leave him out there with people we didn't even know. He was not a happy camper but resigned to his fate thanks to the courts. We drove back to Richland and spent a couple of days trying to celebrate our 28th wedding anniversary by the pool in that Eastern Washington heat. I remember the full moons each night over the Columbia River as we walked along the river walk. I love Eastern Washington, especially on a warm summer night with a full moon and a light breeze. I spent many years growing up like that in close by Yakima.

That September I attended a mandatory clergy sexual misconduct workshop for my denomination. They talked about the sexual predator, someone who preys on hurting weak people who come to them for help. Sex is not the issue with the sexual predator; it is power over the opposite sex, usually men over women. Sexual misconduct is a real problem with anyone who meets confidentially with clients or patients such as pastors, psychologists, psychiatrists, physicians and lawyers. I have seen people I have known in all these professions, some professing Christians, lose their careers and families over sexual misconduct and even go to jail. I talked in Chapter 7 about what I do when women have come on to me in the ministry. I tell Gail immediately. That procedure has been very effective for me and kept me out of trouble.

Later that month we went back to sea from the shipyards. The work-ups after the yards are always taxing and difficult. Many have been on the ship for months and never been to sea. We went to San Francisco for their Fleet Week. It had been years since I had been there. The Nimitz used to go all the time to Alameda. Now all the military is gone from the Bay area. I used the opportunity to rent a car and drive to South Lake Tahoe to see Briana. She was living with a group of girls in a condo on the lake. It was a nice place. I liked it. She was a waitress and hoping to go to work for one of the ski areas. The weather was nice and she showed me all around that beautiful area. She had no steady boyfriend and was still healing from boyfriend. Thank God he had left her alone. I couldn't believe the numbers of people in that community who were members of her generation. I could see why she liked it there.

I drove back to the ship stopping to see a good friend of mine named Reed and his wife Cindy in Hayward. Reed and I went to Navy boot camp together in July of 1972. I wrote about him in Chapter 5. I hadn't seen him for years, since the Nimitz was in Alameda. He was an engineer teaching at a university. We have both come a long way since boot camp. The next day Briana drove to meet me with her girl friend. They joined me and some other officers at a reception held on the USS Essex (LHD 2). We call these ships 'gator freighters' because they are amphibious transports for marines. It was good to have Briana around my Navy environment. The girls didn't meet any exciting young officers.

When we got back to Everett, I had a small window to go hunting in Montana again. I knew that I was going to be deployed for the 2000 season and then moving. It might be my last chance to hunt with the boys for years. We had to get special permission for Jonathan to join us from Jubilee. He had a few problems but in general was doing well there. He had even joined the football team. We drove to Seattle and picked up Burdette and Steve for our long twelve-hour drive to Choteau. That evening, as we entered Montana, we experienced the Aurora Borealis in the sky. I had never seen it before. It looked like a meteor shower coming down in curtains over the mountains. We watched it for what seemed like hours. It was fascinating.

There were a lot of birds in the field that year and we did well. Both of my sons were now hunting with 12 gauge shotguns. They were becoming men. Jonathan was carrying my old Winchester shotgun my dad bought me when I was his age. David was carrying my dad's old Ithaca lightweight. I was using the short Spanish over and under that I had bought at the gun club in Spain. Everyone shot pheasants both days. I limited the first day, three roosters. David limited the second. He was very proud. Once again we came home with many pounds of frozen pheasant. We had another big family barbecue pheasant dinner. I made the rest of the meat into smoked pepperoni sticks. It was another successful hunt. Those times were some of the best in my life, hunting with my dads and my sons.

I had to report to the ship the night I got back from hunting to get underway. It was a very tight window but we made it. On the way back we put Jonathan on the bus to Jubilee at Ritzville near Spokane. It was hard to send him back. We had a good time. Later I learned that he somehow brought some marijuana back to Jubilee with him. He said he got it on the bus but I think he brought it from Skagit Valley. He was bragging to the other Jubilee kids and someone turned him in. He denied it at first and they hammered him. They did not tolerate lying. He was restricted to his room for a long time. It was really hard on him as a seventeen-year-old but he got through it. Behavior modification is designed to teach the kids to take responsibility for their actions. They learn that the decisions we make have repercussions you must live with. They also teach them to tell the truth no matter what the first time. These are important life skills everyone needs to learn.

The Lincoln headed back to sea. We went down to San Diego where we spend a lot of time. On the way I got my first Fitness Report (Fitrep) from the CO. It was very high. These reports would determine if I would make Captain. I bring my bike and golf clubs on the ship. I try to play golf and stay off the ship at one of the BOQ's whenever we hit port. My favorite BOQ is the amphibious base at Coronado but is a longer bike ride to the ship. The Navy Air Force Pacific Chaplain had our whole department over for dinner one night with some of the other Battle Group Chaplains. He was still talking to me about taking the Submarine Force Pacific (SUBPAC) job. He said he was going to be the Pacific Fleet (CINCPACFLT) Chaplain and would try to get the SUBPAC job for me. It sounded like Hawaii was sowed up.

That December when the ship returned, the department had a holiday open office. It is something that I try to do wherever I go. I invite the crew up to the office for goodies and refreshments in the atmosphere of holiday cheer. Gail and I also had the department over to the house again. Mae had her second birthday with us, her 4th. She loves butterflies. We had a butterfly theme party with all available relatives at the house. Everyone bought her something to do with butterflies. Even her cake was a butterfly.

Jonathan was allowed to come home for the holidays, by the skin of his teeth, for a home visit only with no friends. Briana came home too. It is always good to have all our children under the same roof. Lauren would get on my case each Christmas to decorate the exterior of the house so I did. The family got a nice big tree and trimmed it together. We also went skiing up at Steven's Pass. Mae even went skiing. I took the wrong lift with her and wound up bringing her down from the top at night. It took us forever. I had visions of the white out in Switzerland. Jonathan did OK until Christmas Day. He wanted to go with friends and I said no. He took off anyway after an ugly scene at dinner. It was not pretty. We sent him back to Jubilee early. He hadn't learned much.

Y2K came and went without incident. I knew this was going to be a tough year for me. We were scheduled to spend nine of the next twelve months at sea. In August we were to deploy to the Arabian Gulf for six months. Before that we were slated to go to the Rim of the Pacific (RIMPAC) exercise in Hawaii for two months. Duty on a nuclear aircraft carrier is arduous.

We headed back to sea in January doing carrier qualifications off the coast of Southern California, our second home. We got a new Admiral who was active in the Protestant service and loved to talk to me about hunting ducks. I started taking the 'holy helo' over to the other Battle Group ships to meet the other chaplains and CO's. We started our ecumenical 'Praise Nights' again where we get music, skits, dance, and testimonies from all the Christian congregations in one gathering of praise to God. It is a great time.

Guidepost Magazine, associated with the Peale Foundation, has kept in touch with me ever since I got to know Norman and Ruth Peale. They were having an Advisory Board meeting in February near Palm Springs. They invited me to come and speak about military outreach. I use Peale material all the time. President Ford was at one of the dinners. Guidepost offered to pay all my expenses. I was able to talk the XO into letting me fly off the ship to San Diego and attend. I rented a car and drove to Rancho Mirage. It was a great couple of days in a beautiful setting. Gail was invited but couldn't come.

Right after that the ship went to Santa Barbara again. This time Gail flew down and stayed with me at Marty and Elyse's place. We had a great reunion with them. I took them to a Lincoln reception at the Yacht Club one night and a $100,000 Navy League reception at the Fess Parker Double Tree the next. The owner of the LA Lakers was at the table next to us. It was a high roller evening. Elyse brought a bunch of her single girlfriends who danced with all our guys. It was very stormy and our liberty boats couldn't get back out to the ship. Our sailors were stuck on the beach at the armory. Eventually we had to bring them by helo back to the ship.

When we got home again, a big church down in Seattle asked me to come and speak. They were a nondenominational church in Edmonds. One of the members of their staff was a Reserve Navy chaplain. They wanted to adopt our ship for prayer during the deployment. I spoke at their main worship services and many of their Bible studies. It took all day. Gail and

Mae came with me. Hundreds of their people signed up to support us in prayer by email. I knew we would need it.

Harrison Hot Springs in British Columbia is a place I always wanted to visit. My folks used to go there when dad was with Allstate Insurance. I got some reservations and took Gail for a weekend. It is fun just to go across the border into that British culture. Harrison is a remote spot on a mountain lake built on some hot springs. We had a good time lying in the pools and eating. One night we drove to the closest little town to see a movie. We decided to take the kids there sometime in the future.

I had signed up for a men's retreat with my boys. Jubilee was going to let Jonathan go. It got canceled at the last minute. I decided to take David and go spend the weekend with Jonathan in Richland near the ranch. When we got there we had to find Jonathan at a huge Christian concert in Richland. He was there as part of the set up crew from Jubilee. The three of us stayed at a hotel. The next day we toured and went to a movie. That night we attended a semi-pro hockey game. I met all of Jonathan's counselors and leaders. That Sunday we attended the church that they took the Jubilee boys to. They were made to sit in a group and not interact with the church. I introduced myself to the pastor and told him about Jonathan. I was disappointed that the church didn't reach out more to the boys but kept them isolated. They missed a great opportunity.

That time at home didn't last long. The ship left the end of March for San Diego again. I heard that Briana had sprained her ankle right after she had gotten a new job and was really depressed. I wanted to help her but felt powerless. I called her and said a prayer for her ankle. She told Gail later that the pain left as I prayed and she was able to stand on it immediately. Thank you Lord for continuing to care for my daughter Briana. On this trip I was able to get my friend Marty from Santa Barbara to come out to the ship as a CO's distinguished visitor or DV. He flew out on the COD and stayed with me a couple of nights. I was great showing him the carrier and flight operations. On the way back we stopped at Victoria, BC again. This time Gail came and brought Mae, David and Jonathan from Jubilee. We stayed in the hotel and toured around that fun city. I also got a new female chaplain that came aboard in Victoria. The weekend ended with everyone coming aboard for another Family Day Cruise back to Everett with jets doing cats and traps.

While we were back in Everett, the department decided to do a community Easter Sunrise Service on the ship and invite the public. This had been a dream of Brian, one of my chaplains. I let him run with the idea. He did a wonderful job of coordination. We all worked very hard on it. I asked my buddy the Navy Air Force Pacific Chaplain to be the speaker and he accepted. We got a praise band from the church my old NAS Whidbey boss was serving up in Lyman on the Skagit River. They named themselves 'Shipmates' after the event. A local Christian recording artist also joined the festivities. All the Everett churches got invitations and it was advertised on Christian radio and in the papers.

I didn't know how many people would come to the service. The logistics of parking everyone and getting them down on the pier to the ship was enormous. That morning as I drove up to the wharf with my family, I couldn't believe it. There was a steady stream of people going to the brow. We completely filled up the hangar bay. It was amazing. Some guessed we had almost 2,000 people. I was so rattled I wore my blues and forgot my ribbons, all the while standing right in front of the Admiral who came that morning. If he noticed, he never said anything. I was mortified. My AIRPAC chaplain boss noticed immediately and laughed at me. All in all, it was a glorious day. The XO couldn't believe what my department had accomplished. We were able to feed everyone afterwards too by the miraculous grace of God. The food we set out was only for about 400 but it fed almost 2,000 with some left over. I was reminded of Jesus and the loaves and fishes.

One afternoon Gail and I were taking a walk around the loop by our house. Suddenly her cell phone rang. It was Lauren's boyfriend. He and Lauren had been going out for a while. He was a welder who worked construction. He asked to speak to me. Gail thought it was strange but handed me the phone. He asked me if he could marry my daughter Lauren. I was surprised. I had always hoped some young man would do that. My estimate of him went up considerably. I told him that the decision was Lauren's but if she said yes he had my blessing. I only asked that he never hurt her. Lauren did say yes and they were engaged. The plan was for her to finish college before they got married.

The ship left in May to do a Change of Command in San Diego for a new CO. I talked my former CO into sending a formal invitation for my parents to attend. My folks drove from Phoenix and stayed with me at the Coronado BOQ. We attended a special reception at the Hotel Del Coronado hosted by the Navy League from Santa Barbara. The ceremony was held on the flight deck in beautiful weather and was very impressive. The old CO was frocked as a Rear Admiral. He and the new CO were roommates at the Naval Academy and flew in F-14's together. At the reception my parents and I sat across the table from retired Vice Admiral James Stockdale, the senior officer POW in the Hanoi Hilton in North Vietnam. Our nation awarded him our highest honor, the Medal of Honor. He also ran at one time for Vice President. He was a real character.

Lincoln headed right out to sea from there for two months of Rim of the Pacific 2000, or RIMPAC, in the Hawaiian Island. Many of our allies participate with us in this important naval exercise. The carrier spent four days at Pearl Harbor for liberty. I went over and stayed at the BOQ at Sub Base and rode my bike. It was a good exercise but not the kind of trip you want to make right before you are deploying for six months. Thanks to the XO, I got off the ship when she headed back to sea and flew home for Jonathan's high school graduation.

In spite of everything, Jonathan had a successful year at Jubilee. He finally learned to tell the truth, shut his mouth and do what he was supposed to. In addition, he finished his junior and senior year in high school. He was eligible to graduate. Many of his friends there could graduate too. We all came home for the festivities, even Briana. We took the van and all drove to Richland for the ceremony, which was out by the ranch. It was all very moving and I was glad I went through the hassle and expense to try and come home. Jonathan also got a scholarship to North Seattle Community College where he planned to study Culinary Arts. We brought him home with us. It was good to be together again as a family. After a day home I flew back to Oahu and the ship.

The ship pulled back into Everett on the 1st of July and began our leave period known as Prepare for Overseas Movement or POM. One day the Admiral asked me if there was anything we could do to spruce up the chapel, it looked so military and Spartan. I told him I knew an interior decorator. He asked me to come up with some plans and he would come up with some money. I talked to my old friend Don in Mt. Vernon who had drawn up the plans for the Avon Church remodel with me years before. Don came down to the ship, met the Admiral and drew up some plans. We came up with about a $13,000 face-lift. The Admiral pushed everyone and it happened. It was a real answer to prayer. Also during our POM we did several Predeployment Seminars for the crew and their families. These are evening meetings where we bring in subject matter experts to talk about all the problems of separation and how to prepare for and survive it. These meetings were very successful.

Gail and I had decided we needed to get Jonathan away from his friends if he was going to be successful. Miraculously, some Navy housing came open at Discovery Park in Seattle. It is an area known as Ft. Lawton and used to be an Army Fort. The senior officer housing was built at the turn of the Twentieth Century overlooking Puget Sound. The three story Victorian homes were beautiful. Our CO and XO lived there. One opened for us and we took it. We put our house in Burlington that we had bought in 1981, up for sale with our old friend Al. He let his daughter Holly sell it. It came down to the end of July but we finally got a sale for more money than we were asking. It was hard to let that house go but it was time. We needed to move and the house was getting to be too hard to maintain. We took the profit and put it into mutual funds hoping to leave it there for a while.

The first week of August we moved into our new quarters at Ft. Lawton. The housing sits in the middle of about 500 acres of park. We scurried around and got moved in so we could go on our summer vacation to Lake Chelan. This time, my entire family came and Gail's sister Beth and her family. Briana, Burdette and Joan didn't make it. It was the week before our normal week so we didn't know anyone. It was kind of nice. This was the first time my sister, mom and dad came. Sue and Harold brought their boat and we did some water skiing. At the end of the week we drove back to our new quarters. I was able to spend a couple of nights in the house before the ship left on deployment.

Abe Lincoln deployed on August 17th. The week before, I found out that my new female chaplain would not be able to make it. She needed surgery. The chaplain they wanted to take her place was one from Whidbey I had trouble with. I couldn't believe it. How could this happen, deploy with someone I did not want to work with again? I was up front with him about my feelings and I prayed for the grace to make it. It was hard for me but we did quite well together. I think the Lord wanted to do some healing in both of us. He left mid-cruise and my female chaplain returned from surgery.

We picked up our air wing in San Diego and headed west. The plan was to stop in Hong Kong and Thailand on the way to the Arabian Gulf. We were flying support there for the UN sanctioned Operation Southern Watch. It was designed to stop Iraq from harming its neighbor's north and south and kept them from smuggling oil to pay for weapons of mass destruction. Our seven ships and two submarines with 10,000 sailors headed out to do that mission for our nation and its allies.

On the way we ran into a typhoon and had to head south to avoid it. I had just flown over to one of our frigates to do services the night the storm hit. The seas were heavy and they were not able to fly me back for a few days. That little ship was rocking and rolling.

I took my Meclizine and hung on. I didn't get sick. While we skirted the storm we overshot Hong Kong. Many had their spouses joining them there. Everyone scrambled to reschedule. We had already been there so Gail didn't plan to come. The Navy decided to substitute the Singapore port call for Hong Kong. Gail had already been there too. Just as we were getting close to Singapore, the Joint Chiefs of Staff decided they needed us in the Arabian Gulf to relieve the other carrier there. They wanted that battle group to go off the coast of the Balkans for the former Yugoslavian elections. Off we went to the Arabian Sea bypassing Thailand too. Gail had planned to come to Thailand and we were very disappointed. We lost some money on the tickets, as did many others. We should have gotten fully refundable tickets.

Abe pulled into the Arabian Gulf two weeks early in mid September without ever having a port call. Everyone was really disappointed. Young men and women come into the Navy to see the world. No one was happy. Immediately one of our F-18 Hornets crashed in the sea with no explanation. The pilot, single and very popular, was never found. The crew was depressed for days. All the chaplains tried to spend time with everyone in that squadron. We had a huge memorial service on one of the elevators with a Hornet 'missing man' fly by. The Admiral called me up to his office. He was hoping to return with every sailor we started with. It was very hard on him, the CAG and the squadron CO and XO.

About this time I got an unexpected email from my old friend Leroy. He was now the Chaplain of the Coast Guard in Washington, DC. He wanted me to come to DC and be his deputy when I got off Lincoln in June. My friend at CINCPAC Fleet had told me that I was in line to become the Submarine Force Pacific

(SUBPAC) Chaplain. When I contacted him and told him about the DC offer, he said that the SUBPAC job had become a 0-6 Captain position and I couldn't take it. He then started talking to me about becoming the regional chaplain in Guam. I was emailing Gail all this time and trying to decide what I should do. Leroy really wanted me in DC to introduce me to all the heavies there and to help me understand the 'big picture'. After much agonizing, I accepted the new job as Deputy Chaplain of the Coast Guard in Washington, DC. Gail and I knew that this meant we would be leaving Lauren and Jonathan on the West Coast to finish college. It would be a tough move for us in many ways.

I had been emailing the 5th Fleet Chaplain in Bahrain, Manama. He invited me to take the COD into Bahrain and spend a couple of days with him getting the lay of the land. I had visited our Navy facility in Bahrain during Desert Storm almost ten years before. At that time it was very small. When I got to the base I could not believe how it had grown. The terrorist threat was high and armed Marines patrolled the compound carrying automatic weapons and wearing desert camouflage utilities.

Bahrain is a fairly modern Arabian city. It is liberal by Saudi Arabian standards, the strictest of the Islamic countries. Many Saudi's come there on the weekends like Americans go to Las Vegas. The 5th Fleet Chaplain and his wife had a huge home out in town. They invited me to stay a couple of nights with them. It was heaven to have my own room in quiet with a bathtub. They even had a small swimming pool. George's wife took me out to the Gold Souk in town where I was able to buy a few gifts for the family. She was able to talk the merchants down in price. Most of the gold is 18 and 22 karate. We all went out to dinner.

Surprisingly, Bahrain had about every fast food restaurant in America represented. I flew back to the ship a little refreshed.

In October we finally were able to get off the ship in Jebel Ali, United Arab Emirates (UAE) near the city of Dubai. We had been at sea almost two months. I went into town and got a hotel with the senior medical officer (SMO), a psychiatrist named Lou.

The dentist Jimmy, and other DH's I was friends with, had gotten off the ship before we left on deployment. I had been praying for a good Christian friend. The Lord sent me Lou. We were close to the same age. He had a heart attack a couple of years before and had really committed his life to God. His dad had been a Lutheran pastor and Navy chaplain in WWII. Lou had gone through a painful divorce and had recently remarried. We really hit it off. The hotel we shared in Dubai was a blast. We did a little shopping and even went to the beach. I took him to the same Persian carpet shop that I had visited and bought carpets during Desert Storm. It was just great to be away from that ship.

As soon as we left Jebel Ali, the USS Cole was hit by a terrorist bomb in Yemen not very far from us. Seventeen U.S. sailors were killed. The Admiral called me up to tell me. I got a team ready to go there. The 5th Fleet Chaplain wound up going instead. After that attack, we went to the highest alert, Threatcon Delta. What that meant for us was we would not go into port again the entire time we were in the Gulf. For the next three months we just floated around in a little box like area. Our jets continued to fly over Iraq almost every day, often coming under fire. They returned it too. It was a miserable time for the crew. After 45 straight days at sea we are eligible for a beer day where everyone can have two beers. We had one beer day and almost two.

The Christian ministry was super during this trying time. All our services and studies were at maximum attendance. We were running over 550 per week in attendance for nine different faith groups. I had more than one service where I gave an invitation and saw many accept Christ as their savior. In conjunction with all of this, I had an email prayer network of hundreds on and off the ship who were lifting us up to the Lord constantly. I believe those prayers really made a difference.

There was a lot of debate from the command about pulling into Jebel Ali at the pierside 'sandbox' or staying out at sea for the Christmas holidays. I lobbied with the Admiral to go in. The CO didn't want to. He said it was like passing on a curve. I knew the troops needed it. The SMO agreed with me and had gone to the Admiral too. Eventually we won out. We pulled into the 'sandbox' over Christmas. It was Islamic holiday of Ramadan so we could not drink or play loud or live music until after 7 PM in the evening. Still it was a needed break from the daily grind at sea. At sea we work seven days a week for sixteen hours or more a day. After a few months of that kind of stress, it begins to wear on the toughest sailor. Everyone needed to relax and blow off some steam before we headed to Australia, even the CO.

On New Year's Day we transited the Straits of Hormuz out of the Arabian Gulf into the Arabian Sea on our way to Australia. It was so good to leave the Gulf behind. I do not want to ever see it again. We took our time going down to Australia arriving at Fremantle and Perth mid January. Once again Dr. Lou and I shared a room at the Hyatt in Perth. It was like paradise to lie by the pool and drink a couple of beers.

We were in aesthetic overload after months on that drab gray steel warship. The first night we wore our whites to the Royal Perth Yacht Club for a reception. Later we came back to the hotel and had a drink in the lobby. The Admiral and his COS came and sat with us for a while. After they left, the waiter spilled red balsamic vinaigrette all over my white uniform. It also splattered on the Operations Officer who had just joined us. I looked like I had been shot with a shotgun. The hotel manager had both our uniforms cleaned by the time we woke up the next morning.

The next day we went up the river on a wine tasting tour. It was a great trip, about eighty of us from the ship. We took a nice flat bottom jet boat up the Swan River to Mulberry farms. We also stopped at the Houghton Winery. I bought some of their wine to bring home. The trip back down the river was great too. It was just an all around good time and we were all ready to blow off some steam from the months at sea. The next day Lou and I played in a ship golf tournament at the Vines Golf Club. That course is the site of the famous Heineken Classic with all the big names. Joining our foursome was the new Gator, and Mini Boss (assistant Air Boss). Gator actually hit a kangaroo with a ball. There were so many roos, as they call them, on the course. Perth was a great stop and much needed.

From there we headed to Hobart, Tasmania arriving on January 20th. Tasmania is the most southern state in Australia, an island. Originally it was a British penal colony in the 19th Century. Gail traveled with the CO's wife to meet me there. I got to the pier on the first liberty boat. We were all in our whites. I saw Lou's wife Lisa who came from Florida and the CO's wife, but no Gail. The CO's wife said Gail was shopping so I waited patiently at a huge flea market for her to come out. She never did. I finally gave up and walked to the hotel, the Grand Chancellor, at the head of the pier. Gail walked out as I walked up. We had a great reunion. The first night there was a reception by the city of Hobart that we attended. We then went out to dinner with Lou and Lisa. There was no outside pool so we went to the beach the next day hoping to catch some sun. The temperatures there were like Seattle in June. Though it was January, it was summer down under.

The second night we went to a reception on the ship attended by many Australian dignitaries. Gail and I spent a good part of the evening talking to a young woman and her husband. She sat on the Australian Parliament and was representing the Prime Minister. Australia is a very interesting place. It is the physical size of the United States with the population of Los Angeles. Most everyone lives on the coasts, as the interior is not very habitable. The people are very open, warm and friendly to Americans. One young woman asked me if we had Coca-Cola in the United States. She couldn't fathom that it came from anywhere other than Australia. The culture was a cross between Britain and Canada. Hobart reminded us of Victoria, BC and Gibraltar. Gail and I only had four nights and five days together. It was really hard to leave her at the hotel and walk back to the liberty boat for the ship. I hope I never have to do that again.

January 26th we were underway again, this time for San Diego and home. I had a team of three female social workers from the Family Service Centers on the West Coast who were doing a Return and Reunion Seminar for all first time deployers, a few thousand sailors. On February 7th the air wing flew off for their bases all over the United States. It was sad to see these friends and parishioners go. We had gotten very close, especially the Christians. We had all grown close to God and each other to survive the demanding deployment. Most of us would never see each other again this side of heaven.

On February 8th we arrived in San Diego. There the rest of the air wing got off to be flown to their home bases. Many family and friends were waiting for them. The wing makes up about half of the ship or over 2500 personnel. It always brings tears to my eyes to see these reunions after so many months. That night I went out to dinner with the former wing chaplain who left the ship in December, his mother and some old Chaplain Corps friends Frank and Sheila from Yokosuka, Japan. Frank and Sheila drove down from Camp Pendleton to see me. It was a good reunion. The next day my son David showed up with his friend Ryan to ride the ship back to Everett on the Tiger Cruise. It was great to see them. We got underway about 3 PM for home.

I took David and Ryan jogging on the flight deck as we were pulling out of San Diego. It was a beautiful day. I said goodbye to Naval Air Station, North Island. For many years it had been a home away from home. I did not know when I would see it again. The seas were very rough when we got out to open waters. I think the seas off the West Coast of the United States are the roughest in the world, especially in the winter months. I took David and Ryan up to the bridge while I did the evening prayer. David almost threw up there but made it to the head. I found out later he was not only seasick, he also had the flu. Ryan was seasick too. I put them both on medication and sent them to bed. They stayed there most of the next day coming out only to see an air power demonstration by the new F-18 Super Hornets. That Sunday I preached what I believed to be my last Sunday at sea. I could not imagine a scenario short of a full-scale war that would put me back to sea again.

We pulled into Everett, Washington at 10 AM on Monday February 12th, Abe Lincoln's birthday. Our sailors were in their blues and manning the rails as we came into view of over 5,000 of our family and friends waiting on the pier. Gail was there with Lauren and Mae plus Ryan's mom. It was a joyous reunion. I was so glad to be home. We all had to leave in our blues. It was so great to walk into the beautiful house I had left six months before. We went out to lunch at Denny's in Ballard and Jonathan met us. Later his girlfriend came by the house with her baby son. Briana called to welcome me home. It was so great to finally sleep in my own bed and take a bath. I thanked God for bringing me home safe again and for watching over my family while I was gone.

The next thirty days I spent mostly with the family. During that time I helped both Lauren and Jonathan buy used Hondas. I also was able to get Mae naturalized as a U.S. citizen at INS, finish everyone's taxes and get fitted for my new Coast Guard uniforms. Gail and I also attended a conference of more conservative United Methodist pastors in Eastern Washington. It felt so good to be home. I took all the kids out on dates and got caught up on their lives. Lauren even took me with her one day while she was registering for classes at the UW. It was very nostalgic to be back at my alma mater with my daughter.

On March 20th we went back to sea. This would be my last time underway on Lincoln in the open seas. It was hard to go back to the ship. We ended the trip with another Family Day Cruise from Victoria, BC. It was my third trip there on Lincoln. Gail and the kids decided not to come with me. Lou and I got a room together, made all the receptions, dinners and golfed in the Saturday tournament. It would be our last time hanging out together in a foreign port. We had done Dubai, Perth and now Victoria. We had hung out all over the world. He had become a good and trusted friend.

In April the ship went back to Bremerton and into the shipyards. It was the fourth time I was in the yards there on three different ships. I got a room in the BOQ again but tried to commute every day on my bike and the ferry. It worked out pretty well. Briana came to visit us for a week. Gail and I went to Hawaii again for a chaplain's conference. We figured it would be a while before we came back again. I also went to my first Coast Guard chaplain conference in Petaluma, CA.

All the while we were getting ready to move again. We sold Lauren's car and started looking for apartments for her and Jonathan. Gail finally found something she felt would work on Greenwood Avenue. We moved them in June. The movers came for us the week of June 25th. June 29th was my last day on the ship. We had a big Chinese dinner with the kids that night. We left for Washington, DC the next day. Gail was driving the van with Mae and I was driving the Mustang with David. We were off to another adventure with the military but this time we were very sad to be leaving three of our five children behind.

14
WASHINGTON, D. C.

We started driving across the United States in our two cars on June 30, 2001. The first night we stopped at my Uncle Bob and Aunt Joyce's house in Spokane, WA. From there we kept heading east on Interstate 90. The second night we stayed at the home of Buzz and Ruth Wagner's in Hamilton, MT. Buzz is a retired Army Brigadier General. We had spent time together during our tour in Japan years before. Ruth had been battling cancer for years. It was good to see them again and get reacquainted. Within weeks of our visit, Ruth died. We were so glad we had taken the time to see them.

Next we stopped at Yellowstone National Park. It was our first visit back since our "vacation from hell" in the summer of 1992. David had some vague memories of that trip. We stayed in the cabins at Yellowstone Lake and went on a guided fishing trip the next day like we had done in 1992. Once again we caught a lot of big brown speckled trout and released them. Everyone caught fish this time. Yellowstone is always a treat to visit. It is such an unusual place.

As we continued our journey east we kept in touch with each other with walkie-talkies. Most of the time Mae rode with Gail in the Aerostar minivan and David rode with me in the Mustang. I usually would lead. My speedometer registered a slower speed than Gail's and I had cruise control and she didn't. She would drop back behind me and then would speed up to catch us. Sometimes she would be going pretty fast. One evening in Wyoming, while she was speeding up to catch me, a Wyoming State trooper stopped her. I pulled over too, waiting for her. He said she was going 90. She explained what happened. He looked up the road at me and said, "Is that your husband?" She said, "Yes" and he came over to talk to me. When he saw my Naval Air Station Whidbey Island sticker and military ID, he said he had been stationed with the Navy at Whidbey. He and I got to talking and before we knew it he let Gail off with a warning. That military ID often works wonders with the police.

We spent a couple of nights at an Air Force Base in South Dakota close to Mt. Rushmore. I had to check the ammunition I was carrying, the movers wouldn't ship it, at the base armory. Gail found some great Black Hills gold jewelry at the exchange there. We visited the Mt. Rushmore cave and a strange site where everything seemed out of proportion. Mt. Rushmore was very impressive and interesting. It is hard to imagine what those early engineers and craftsmen had to do in creating that national treasure. As we left that area, we had to stop at Wall Drugstore and have a lunch of buffalo burgers. Gail found more jewelry there.

We had planned to visit my old Command Chaplain on the Nimitz who was in the advanced stages of MS. Looking closer at the map we realized that his place was too far south. Instead, we decided to visit Gail's Aunt Geneva and cousins in Glenwood, Iowa. Geneva is Gail's dad's sister-in-law. Burdette originally came from Ulysses, Nebraska close to Glenwood, Iowa. After a nice lunch and visit we continued on to Iowa City. David had been doing pretty well up to that point, but as we loaded up the cars, he refused to get in. He didn't know what he was going to do but he was not going with us another mile. Gail and I pleaded with him in the hot sun to please change his mind. I threatened to report him as a runaway and Gail just cried. Finally, by the grace of God, he got back into the car but with Gail and Mae. I rode by myself that day and the crisis passed.

On eastward we continued. Both of our cars had some mechanical difficulties that cost us some time and several hundred dollars but they were minor problems that were easily corrected. We were so thankful that we had Ford cars. No matter where you are in the United States, there is a Ford Motor Company garage close by. We decided then and there to continue buying American automobiles.

Our next stop took us to the home of Tudor and Ceci and their daughter Elizabeth in Ft. Wayne, Indiana. They were old friends from our seminary days in Pasadena, CA. Both of them had graduated from seminary and were ordained. They were taking a sabbatical from fulltime ministry and doing other forms of employment. We really enjoyed spending a night with them and catching up on all that had happened to us since we last were together.

From Ft. Wayne we went to the theme park at Cedar Point, Ohio on the Great Lakes. It boasted the most and largest roller coasters in the U.S. David rode on them all. He has no fear when it comes to those kinds of things. Mae and Gail spent most of their time at the hotel pool. It was a good stop.

After Cedar Point we started our final approach down to Washington, DC through Pittsburgh, PA. Most of the nights on the road we stayed at Hampton Inns. They always had a pool and included a breakfast buffet with the room. We arrived in Arlington, Virginia on July 13th, two weeks and about 3,000 miles from when we started in Seattle. We stopped by our new home at 6400 26th St North. It was really a nice brick ranch with a full basement but no garage. It also had a fenced backyard. Our good Navy friends Lenny and Jean had found and secured it for us.

Originally we were going to take the rental home of the chaplain I was relieving, Jim, in Burke, VA outside the beltway. The Capello's visited the Burke place and said it was too far to commute and they would not live there. They found a nice ranch inside the beltway a block from their house but it was more money. Gail and I decided to take the Arlington house site unseen because it was closer in, nicer, next to the Metro and close to our friends. We also valued the opinion of Jean and Lenny. It proved to be a good decision.

Our first couple of nights we stayed with Lenny and Jean at their home. We were also reunited with our dog Hershey. We had sent her ahead on the plane to their home before we started our trip east. Lenny and Jean also had a large hunting dog named Star that Hershey got along with great. They planned to have us dog sit for them sometime in the near future.

On Monday the 16th we took possession of our new rental and our household goods shipment arrived. Though we have had worse moves, this one was not one of our best. The movers broke some things and lost a few items including our antique piano bench. Moving is always so hard. Still it was good to be back in our own beds and to begin to set up house again.

I checked in at my new office, on July 19th at Coast Guard Headquarters on Buzzard Point. It was next to Ft. McNair on the Anacostia River just south of the Capitol. Chaplain Jim and I began about a two-week turnover. The job was fairly complex. I wore about three hats. On one hat I was the Deputy Chaplain of the Coast Guard working directly for the Chaplain of the Coast Guard, Captain Leroy. With another hat I was the Headquarters Chaplain who works directly for

Coast Guard Chief of Staff, then a Vice Admiral. The Vice Admiral signed my Fitness Report. I also related to the Headquarters Support Command Commanding Officer, a Captain. Coast Guard Headquarters has a population of close to three thousand active duty and civilians. My third hat was the supervisor of all the Headquarters Training Command Chaplains, thirteen total. They are located at the Coast Guard and Merchant Marine Academies, the boot camp in Cape May, NJ, the Baltimore shipyard and training schools at Yorktown, VA, Mobile, AL and Petaluma, CA. It is a huge position. Every one of those hats could employ a chaplain fulltime. Jim had done a pretty good job managing it all. I listened carefully as he quickly showed me the ropes.

I was the fourth chaplain to hold this position. One of those had been passed over for Captain and one had been selected. Jim and I were both in zone for Captain so we wondered how we would do. I figured with a 55% selection rate one of us would make it and one of us wouldn't. We agreed that the one selected would buy the other a steak dinner.

A previous chaplain had managed to scrape together a little chapel on the ground floor. It was actually very nice. A group of about 20 Christians meet there every morning for 15 minutes to read the Daily Bread devotional and have a word of prayer to start the day. The group had been meeting for several years and was very close. The majority were very conservative evangelical Christians. The devotional was lay led every day but Thursday. That was my day to do whatever I wanted. I started with a guitar song, presented a favorite verse for the group and ended with a prayer circle. It was a good way to start the day.

One of my first Sunday's on the job we had our Third Annual Ecumenical Worship Service at Ft. Meyer

Memorial Chapel near Arlington Cemetery. The keynote speaker was none other than the President's Chief of Staff, Mr. Andrew Card. He told us that President George W. Bush was a very spiritual man who read his Bible every day, even when he was traveling. Andrew's wife is an ordained United Methodist minister who was serving a church in the Arlington District. One of my jobs was to plan this service every August and to also do two Prayer Breakfasts for the building in the fall and spring. I was going to be busy.

Jim finally left and I began to try to get into a routine. It was very hot out and humid. I tried coming in early and running before devotions. Coast Guard Headquarters is close to a low-income housing area we called 'the hood'. We all try to avoid it as much as possible though we had to drive through it every day. I stayed away from it by jogging over at nearby Ft. McNair along the river. It was beautiful to watch the sun come up by the river. If you waited to run, the heat and humidity became unbearable.

Lenny started taking me out in his duck boat on the Chesapeake Bay near Annapolis to catch blue crabs. He would tie bait, cured eels, onto a long rope line, drop it on the bottom and pick it up from the bow netting the crabs as the line came to the surface. The crabs would hold onto the eel bait right up to the boat and then try to swim off. You had to be quick with that net and it took me awhile to get the hang of it. The crabs were smaller, quicker and a light bluish color. They tasted very good. We would take the two dogs and spend the morning on Saturdays.

About that time Leroy wanted me to go on a trip with him to Alaska to visit our chaplains there and go salmon fishing. He said it would be a bonding trip for he and I. It sounded like fun except for one problem; the trip fell on our 30th wedding anniversary. I talked to Leroy about it and he said that Gail would just have to try and understand. I objected. The next day he relented and said I didn't have to go. I think he told his wife Sharon and she told him there was no way he was taking me away from Gail on our 30th. It was also their 30th that year. Gail and I wound up staying at Ft. McNair and going on an expensive dinner cruise on the Odyssey up the Potomac River. We did not spend the night at McNair but came home about midnight. It was a good celebration.

Right after that, Lauren came and visited us with her fiancé Tyler. He had never been out east. I took leave and we had a good time touring the monuments, eating out and going to movies. One thing Tyler wanted to do was go crabbing on the Chesapeake. The morning of September 11th we were supposed to go on a tour of the FBI Headquarters in downtown DC. Lenny offered to take Tyler and I crabbing that morning. We crabbed and got a few, returning to the dock about 10 AM. During that time we heard a huge explosion on the water. We did not know until later that it was an airliner hitting the Pentagon all the way in DC. Suddenly Lenny got a call on his cell phone as we were loading his boat. It was his daughter asking if he was all right. He didn't understand her question. She said that terrorist airline highjackers had hit the Pentagon and World Trade Center Towers. We turned on the radio and raced home, about 50 minutes. We arrived at my house just in time to see the second World Trade Center Tower collapse. It was horrible. The television kept showing the airliners crashing into the towers and people jumping off of the burning buildings. We were all in shock.

I called Leroy and asked what I should do. He was on his way over to the Pentagon and he told me he would call as soon as he knew what we could do. He called a little later and told me to report off of leave to the Navy Annex and the Chief of Chaplains Office close to the Pentagon. All the chaplains were taking shifts down at Ground Zero about 50 yards from where the airliner had impacted the building. We had erected a large tent close to the burning building with a cross and Star of David on it. It was our headquarters. I drew the late night shift and came to the Annex after midnight. You could see the Pentagon still burning and all lit up with eerie spotlights. People and equipment were everywhere.

I parked at the Annex and walked down with some chaplains and enlisted Religious Program Specialists (RP's). Leroy was in charge as the senior chaplain at the chaplain tent. They were pairing up chaplains and RP's and sending us out in twos to minister to whomever we came in contact with. I was matched up with a very tall chief. We walked around everywhere talking to FBI agents, FEMA personnel, rescue workers and firefighters. Everyone was frustrated because the building was still on fire, about 2000 degrees, and too dangerous to look for survivors. We were taking turns going into the Pentagon courtyard. On my shift it was so smokey and acrid smelling you had to wear a mask. I came upon two men in different military uniforms leaning against a tree. One was an officer and the other one was enlisted. The officer was Army and the enlisted man was a Marine. Both men had lost everyone in their office areas. They were standing there grieving their colleagues and friends horrible deaths. I stayed with them for a while staring at the flames and saying little. Both told me my presence brought them a measure of peace and comfort. A family member with a government ID was at the tent when I returned. His son in law was in the building and missing. He waited expectantly with us. I ran into chaplains I knew whom I hadn't seen for years in all branches of service.

The next day I went into Headquarters. Leroy was still at the Pentagon. He told me that they were pulling out the first 38 bodies. They were taking them south to Ft. Belvoir in refrigerated trucks to be loaded onto helicopters and flown to Dover Air Force Base in Delaware for identification. Leroy wanted me to hurry and get there to meet the bodies. I went as fast as I could and arrived in time to see the first truck unloading into the first helicopter. An Army chaplain was there with many enlisted soldiers moving the body bags. FBI agents and state police were all around. None of the body bags had flags draped over them. I asked why and was told that was because they didn't know which bodies were the terrorists. Once the helicopters were loaded, the Army chaplain and I would take turns leading in prayer with those who were present. All the bodies were badly burned. The rank of only one person was identifiable. It was an awful scene. I felt very humbled to be there praying for these people.

My next assignment was to spend another day down at the Pentagon. The Army Chaplains had taken over since the Pentagon belonged to them. The chaplain Colonel in charge didn't really seem to want non-Army chaplains around and would send us off away from the main action. He kept saying that I was Air Force because Coast Guard uniforms look similar to the Air Force. I kept correcting him but he seemed not to care.

They were still finding bodies inside the burned out wreckage. As I was waiting for the shift turnover brief in the chaplain tent, I noticed a young Army chaplain in the back of the tent with his head in his hands. I told the Colonel I thought something was wrong with the young chaplain but the Colonel ignored him and me. I went back and started talking to him. He had just debriefed some FEMA personnel and the stories were ghastly. He was overcome with the horror of it all. I just listened to him and let him deescalate. Often senior people, even chaplains, forget to take care of the caregivers. They need ministry sometimes too. I had prayer with this young man and he seemed better. Later he gave a full-page interview of this experience to the Washington Post. He talked about the mysterious Coast Guard Chaplain who ministered to his needs that morning.

The chaplain Colonel assigned me over to the main food area. The other areas of ministry were the morgue, chaplain tent and escorting the recovery personnel into the dangerous building. At the food area people would come to take a break from the exhausting and grueling recovery efforts. MacDonald's had set up a free food stand there, as had the Red Cross and North Carolina Men's Ministry. There was a huge white tent we all sat under with many tables and chairs. Everyone was really tired and depressed. I would walk around the tables and sit and talk with everyone. It was a form of Critical Incident Stress Debrief to short circuit posttraumatic stress syndrome. They all talked openly about their experiences.

In one burned out office room they found everyone still at their desks in position frozen as if they had been watching the World Trade Center on the television. It was horrific. One group of soldiers found one of their own that had obviously bled to death from his wounds before anyone could get to him. I did a 12-hour shift and headed home. As I was leaving, a group of family members of those missing came down to the site in buses. Their visit coincided with a decision to go ahead and start knocking down the fractured building, as there was no longer any hope of finding survivors. As the family members watched the wrecking ball work, many collapsed on the ground. It was the worst thing I had witnessed so far, those poor people.

A man at Headquarters had lost his wife in the attack. She was a civilian who worked as a secretary for the Army at the Pentagon. We also lost some Coast Guard reservists on the flights and in the World Trade Center. The President called for a Day of Prayer and Remembrance and we had one at Headquarters. Leroy had been living at the Pentagon for days. He wanted to come and speak at the service. We held the service in one of the big conference rooms. It was standing room only. Gail came and brought Lauren and Tyler. They were stuck in DC and could not get out. They were scared to fly and considered renting a car to drive back to Washington State. We sat right behind the Vice Commandant of the Coast Guard who later would become the Commandant. Leroy preached an anointed message that received a standing ovation from us all.

Eventually Lauren and Tyler got up the courage to try and fly home. They made it back with no problems. Our Coast Guard Chaplains had formed an Emergency Response Team in New York to help with the recovery efforts at the World Trade Center. Chaplain Doug was heading it up. Leroy ordered me to take over coordination of scheduling chaplains, active and reserve, to go to New York for about 10-14 days at a time. He also wanted me to relieve Doug there as the chaplain in charge. Doug was getting burned out. I drove up to New York the end of September for ten days.

Our chaplains were staying at the Coast Guard base at Staten Island underneath the Verrazano Bridge. They were sleeping two to a room in the Navy Lodge there and eating in the enlisted dining facility. The chaplains would go into Manhattan each morning, in a van or on the ferry, and walk around ministering to all at the morgue, Family Support Center and Ground Zero where the World Trade Center once stood. They went in twos and would gather together in the evening to debrief together. No one was allowed to say they were doing 'fine' as we went around the room.

I arrived in time for the evening debrief. These chaplains were doing superhuman ministry to the people of New York. They were the only uniformed military chaplains seen at Ground Zero. The New York police and firefighters treated them like one of their own. We had about ten chaplains but we could have used every chaplain in the Navy. The next morning they took me down to get our badges, which took hours. Then we went to the Trade Center site. As I stood in the middle of all that devastation, I was overwhelmed with the immensity and utter revulsion of it all. I can honestly say it was the worst thing I have ever experienced. As bad as the Pentagon attack was, the World Trade Center attack was a hundred times worse. I stood there and all I could think to do was call Gail. I tried to describe to her on the cell phone what I was experiencing.

We made all our chaplains go to Ground Zero first before they started ministering to others. If you didn't, the first time you went down there you were unable to focus on anyone else. My roommate at the Navy Lodge was Dr. Endel, a seminary professor and reserve Navy Chaplain. That second night we went back to our room in shock. I had nightmares for many nights after that.

My main job in New York was to coordinate the ministry of the other chaplains and provide for their logistical needs. I also debriefed them in the evening. I arranged for Internet support, got a reserve Religious

Program Specialist and secured the use of a van and driver for the team. The driver was a reserve enlisted Coast Guardsmen who was also a New York City Police Sergeant. He could get us anywhere expeditiously. I went back to Manhattan once more. This time I went to the Defense Morgue first. Just as I arrived they were bringing in the remains of a firefighter. Everyone came out and stood at attention lining the street and saluting. A police motorcycle escorted ambulance pulled up and a flag draped stretcher was taken off. We saluted together. It was evident the flag only covered a partially filled body bag.

After that I went to the Family Support Center. There the families of those missing in the Trade Center rubble gathered daily for support and news. The police were beginning to escort the families down to the site by ferry three times a day, 50 at a time. They asked our chaplains to accompany the families. We were well trained and the people felt safe with us in uniform.

That day I accompanied a young woman whose twin brother had died in the Trade Center. He had just gotten the job. The family was from England. It was the twins' birthday. The whole family was there from England. Another man was escorting the widows of some of his personnel from his office in the Trade Center. He had not been in the building at the time. He told me I should be escorting his widow. A large group of United Airlines flight attendants came. We accompanied them. Many had lost friends and were being laid off. One chaplain said that going on those trips was an experience like doing one hundred funerals at once.

Eventually my ten days came to a close. Between the Pentagon and the World Trade Center, I was an emotional and spiritual wreck. I needed some down time to recuperate. I drove home in a daze. All of us who served in New York formed a close bond. It was like a battlefield experience. The only people who could understand it were those who had been there. I was glad it was over for me.

When I got back, my wife Gail took one look at me and told me to go see someone to talk about what I had been through. She is a very wise woman. One of the first things I did was make an appointment with a counselor to discuss my experience. It is not good to come back from a traumatic experience like 9 11 and use your spouse to debrief. Leroy and I were the only two military chaplains to serve at both terrorist sites and we were both messed up. I encouraged him to seek out someone to talk to as well.

It took weeks for me to get over my experiences at the Pentagon and World Trade Center. It seemed like everything else had been on hold. One of the first things I had to tackle was the Headquarters Fall Prayer Breakfast. The fall breakfast was supposed to be a non-Christian speaker, and the spring was supposed to be Christian. The fall before a Jewish Navy Chaplain had spoken. This year the Muslims wanted one of theirs to speak. I looked all over for a good Muslim to speak. I could find no Muslims in Congress. Others wanted too much money and were unknown by most at Headquarters.

One day Leroy asked me what I was going to do for a Prayer Breakfast speaker. I told him that I was looking for a Muslim but I was not excited about it. He asked me what I would be excited about. I told him who I really wanted to ask was the Chief of Naval Personnel (CNO), Admiral Vern Clark. He had just taken over leadership of the Navy and was the son of an Assembly of God pastor, a PK or 'preachers kid'. Leroy told me to do what excited me. That day I asked Admiral Clark and he accepted.

We had the breakfast on October 11th, one month after the terrorist attacks. The place was packed and I sat at the head table with Leroy, the Commandant of the Coast Guard and the CNO. Someone took a picture of us all together. I had it signed by all of them. Here I was sitting next to two of the five Joint Chiefs of Staff of the armed forces, both four star Admirals. It was heady stuff.

Slowly life started getting back to a new normal. Lenny asked me to go hunting in the duck boat with Star and Hershey. He did most of his hunting at Marine Corps Base Quantico, Virginia where they train Marine Officer Candidates, Special Forces and have the FBI Academy. It is a huge base with lots of water and woods. David and I both got our Virginia and Quantico hunting licenses. We would go out on Saturdays with the dogs and the duck boat, which also made into a blind. We tried to duck and goose hunt. We did much better with the geese. Star and Hershey would take turns retrieving. Hershey did pretty well unless it was a long retrieve. Then we would have to get Star to retrieve with commands from Lenny. Star was very well trained. We had a great time. It was good therapy after the draining ministry following September 11th. One snowy day we got our limit on the Potomac River near Alexandria. We later made most of the geese into smoked goose sausage. It was delicious.

The next big event in the Waite household was Christmas. We invited all the kids and offered to pay their way home. We wanted to be together as a family again for Christmas. The last time we had done that was 1999. Briana and I had both been gone in 2000. I decorated the house in Arlington with all my outdoor lights which had been stored in boxes for two years. Lauren was the one who would get the most disappointed if I didn't do it. We cut a tree and decorated it before the kids arrived. They came in two planes to Baltimore. Baltimore tends to be the least expensive place to fly into or out of but it was an hour from our house. Dulles and Reagan National are much closer but expensive. Everyone had been to the DC area before except Briana. We took her to all the usual tourist places such as the monuments and the Smithsonian. The White House and Capitol buildings were still closed since September 11th.

We enjoyed a wonderful celebration together Christmas morning. It was just like old times. Gail and I love it when the kids are all together with us. Soon we had to put our three oldest back on planes for their homes on the West Coast. It is always so hard to say goodbye. We are a close family. I think it is because of all the moves and the time together overseas. Those experiences drew us together and we learned to count on each other for support.

January 2002 brought up all the anxiety about my selection to Navy Captain. The zones were out. There were about 24 chaplains in the zone and I was near the top at number six. We are listed in the order of our seniority. It was a tough zone. Many of these chaplains were stellar performers with terrific reputations. I was not sure I was going to make it. I thought the Fitness Reports I got at Whidbey Island would disqualify me. My chaplain boss there had told me he would see to it I never made Captain. I could still hear his voice.

In spite of all this, I had a strange peace about the whole thing. In January I also became eligible to retire with 20 years of active duty service, 50% of my base pay for life plus medical, commissary and exchange privileges. In June I would turn 52. My plan was that if I somehow managed to get selected, I would stay ten more years and retire at 62 with 30 active years

and 75% of my base pay. Age 62 is mandatory
retirement unless you are selected for Admiral. If I
was not selected, I planned to retire in June 2003 and go
back to the Pacific Northwest to pastor United
Methodist churches again. I felt both options were
good ones. God was also supplying his supernatural
peace to me as I put all this in his hands. I truly
believed that he would guide my future through the
promotion board. I told all this to the Chief of
Chaplains before the board met.

The board was supposed to meet in late January
but did not meet until February 4th. The Navy Chaplain
Corps had been plagued with many lawsuits from
chaplains over the last several years that had not been
selected. These chaplains had been claiming religious
discrimination; especially against non-liturgical
Protestant free church type denominations. Usually the
boards were made up of six chaplains, two being line
officers, not chaplains. As a result of the chaplain
lawsuits, the CNO decided that the majority of the
chaplain boards would be made up of line officers with
only two chaplains, one being the President of the
board. The President of the board was one of our two
Admirals, as is the custom. The other chaplain was an
old friend of mine. I hoped it would help. Leroy kept
trying to find reasons to get me over to the Chief of
Chaplains office at the Navy Annex so the flags could
get to

know me before the board met. I owe much of my
success in the Chaplain Corps to my friend Leroy.

The board convened and adjourned and the
waiting began. It usually takes three months for the
results to be released. The slate of selectees has to go
before many different offices for approval such as legal,
the CNO and the Secretary of Defense before it can be

released. We would all follow the progress on the Navy Bureau of Personnel website. Some of us in zone would call each other offering support as we waited together.

At the same time I was working feverishly on the Annual Coast Guard Chaplain Conference and Leroy's Change of Watch and Retirement. Every year all 50 Reserve and Active Duty Coast Guard Chaplains meet together for a week of instruction. This year it was to be held in DC. I was put in charge of the conference. We decided that the topic would be "Disaster Ministry". I lined up speakers from all the disaster agencies that we had worked with at the Pentagon and in New York. It was a huge undertaking. In addition, Leroy was retiring after thirty years of service as a chaplain.

The Commandant Admiral James Loy was retiring too so it was the perfect time to choose a new Chaplain of the Coast Guard. I might have been considered if I had been selected for promotion to Captain the year before. Commander Doug, our Atlantic Area Coast Guard Chaplain, had been selected for Captain the year before and was a prime candidate, especially since his work after September 11th. The other two candidates were CAPT Ron, Pacific Area Chaplain, and CAPT Bill, former Coast Guard Academy Chaplain. The new Commandant nominee, Vice Admiral Collins, looked at all three packages and selected Doug to relieve Leroy at a ceremony during our Annual Conference. I was put in charge of that too. The work became so overwhelming that I had to bring down Chaplain Stephen from Baltimore once a week to help me.

Just before the Conference, my wife Gail got involved in a three day cancer walk from Baltimore to DC, 60 miles, sponsored by Avon cosmetics. Avon had them all over the country. Each person who walked had to secure financial pledges of $1900.00. Gail secured $4500.00. Over 4500 walkers were involved and raised almost 7 million dollars. I was very proud of Gail for her accomplishment in this project. She trained for the walk and completed it successfully, even coming into DC in the front of the pack. The closing ceremony was very emotional. I took the kids to meet her half way and offer her encouragement. On the way home, I was called by my daughter Lauren that my son Jonathan had been arrested for possession in Wenatchee, WA. The drug task force had also confiscated his car. I decided not to tell Gail until she got home. I secured the services of a lawyer and got him out of jail at the end of the weekend. He was facing felony charges with intent to distribute. His story was that the drugs were not his but a friend's that he had taken over the mountains. Gail and I were just sick about the whole thing.

The Chaplain's Conference finally came and was a huge success. The Change of Watch was on that Thursday at Fort McNair and was a full blown military ceremony with tents, cannons, color guard and almost 400 guests including many civilian and military dignitaries. It was a logistical nightmare for me but Stephen and I somehow pulled it off with God's help. Doug was a good choice for me, as we both knew each other from the past. He had relieved me in Japan at the hospital in 1989 and we were still friends. It was sad to see Leroy leave the military. He had been a good mentor and friend to me and had furthered my career on more than one occasion. I vowed to be the same kind of caring chaplain to other young chaplains as he had been to me.

Eventually the results of the Staff Chaplain Captain Board came in on May 21st. The day before I had been called by a chaplain on the West Coast telling me a carrier chaplain he knew had already gotten the results. Gail was away with her friend Jean visiting our daughter Briana in Monterey, California and calling me often asking about the board results. I had decided I wanted Leroy to give me the news, good or bad, even though he was now retired. I called him and he went to work with his sources.

Early on the next morning I went for a jog. After I came back Leroy called. I had gotten to know his style and knew that when he spoke real slow and deliberate he had good news. He began to talk slow. I knew I had it. It was a complete shock to me. I was sure I would not be selected because of the declining Fitness Report that I had gotten from Whidbey Island. I wanted to call Gail at Briana's but it was too early. She told me the night before not to call too early and get her up. I drove into work in a daze. On my chair was a set of Captain's eagles with the note, "From the Captain fairy". They were from Doug. I couldn't wait to tell Gail. I don't think she really thought I would get it either.

I kept getting calls and emails of congratulations all morning and over the next several days. Twenty-four of us were in zone. Only ten of those were selected and two were above the zone. It was very humbling. At 10 AM Commandant Loy walked in with Wilbur to congratulate me. I could not believe that the Commandant of the Coast Guard, one of the five Joint Chiefs of Staff, would take time out of his busy day to come down to my office and congratulate me. He is a true leader that I also wanted to emulate as a senior officer. I asked him if he would stay while I called Gail to tell her on speakerphone. He agreed and I called. He asked to talk to her too. All Gail wanted to know was yes or no. I quickly told her yes and introduced the

Commandant who also gave her words of congratulation. It was a grand moment for us that I will never forget.

I called my dad and mom to let them know. Dad cried when I told him. It was an emotional moment for us both. How did this former Navy enlisted recruit from Yakima, WA become a Captain select in Washington, DC? God works in mysterious ways by his grace.

The next day there was a quarterly silent retreat out at the Church of the Savior Dayspring Retreat Center in Germantown, Maryland. It was at this retreat center that I had first heard my call to chaplaincy almost twenty years before. I had started going back out there periodically since we were living so close. In February I had been out there for some hours of silent retreat and had asked the Lord if I had made Captain. I thought I heard him say yes and I told it to Gail but no one else. So it seemed that God wanted me to become a Navy Captain in the Chaplain Corps. I was very grateful to the Lord. What would this mean for us in the future? Now I would probably stay for thirty years and retire at 75% of basic pay at age 62 unless I made Admiral. I suddenly became aware that I would become eligible for promotion to the rank of Admiral, what a miracle!

The summer continued with my getting used to a new Chaplain of the Coast Guard. I had signed on to support my friend Leroy and now he was gone. I began immediately to negotiate with the Detailer for my next set of orders as a Navy Captain. I wanted to leave as soon as possible. I did not want to stay in DC as a Captain and Deputy Chaplain of the Coast Guard. The Detailer, a friend, talked to me about working for the Chief of Chaplains. I did not want to do that. We wanted to get back to the West Coast to be closer to our children and parents. We looked at many different jobs including the Pacific Area Coast Guard Chaplain job in Alameda, CA and the Naval Forces Japan Chaplain job in Yokosuka, Japan. He was going to become the new Pacific Forces Chaplain in Hawaii in 2003. He asked the Chief of Chaplains if I could become the Naval Surface Forces and Naval Air Forces Pacific Chaplain in Coronado, CA. I was ecstatic. It was a dream job for me. I would have supervision of all the Naval chaplains in the Pacific on all ships including aircraft carriers, about 70 chaplains. I would be able to travel the West Coast, Hawaii, Guam and Japan. I couldn't ask for a better job. It was one I had always aspired to. The family was excited too but reluctant to believe that it was really going to happen.

We had a family vacation in June visiting the largest Naval recreation area in the Solomon Island area south of DC. We also spent some time at the Atlantic Ocean in Ocean City. I was doing some traveling with the new Chaplain of the Coast Guard to Mobile, AL, New Orleans, LA, Alaska, Seattle and Cape May, NJ. It seemed I was always traveling or on leave.

Late August Briana and Lauren came for a couple of weeks to visit. They brought home their significant others, Tyler and Justin. I had never met Justin before. We took them to New York and to the beach at Solomon Island. It rained most of the time they were with us. Still we had a good visit. I liked both of their young men. They ate and drank me out of house and home though.

The end of September was Jonathan's trial. I flew back for it. I wanted to do everything in my power to keep him from getting a felony conviction. The lawyer was not very confident we could win. It was going to a jury trial. The state had three policemen. We had Jonathan's former girlfriend and her sister as witnesses that the drugs had not belonged to him. I had people praying everywhere that the felony would be dropped. The prosecutor offered us a deal but it did not drop the felony. We held our ground and the day before the trial was to begin the prosecutor offered to reduce the charges to a misdemeanor if Jonathan waived his right to a trial and successfully completed an outpatient treatment program for his cannabis addiction. We agreed and it was over before it started. Jonathan also got his car back after four months. We were all overjoyed that the felony charges had been reduced. God is so good!

October I was scrambling to find a speaker for the next Coast Guard Headquarters Fall Ecumenical Prayer Breakfast. I had been trying to get President Bush to speak a couple of times. Each time the request would get hung up on some administrative assistants desk in the bureaucratic chain and never reach the President's Scheduler until it was too late. I tried one more time and got the same result. I decided that the President was just too hard. One night while I was praying I felt led to ask the Secretary of Transportation, Norman Mineta, to be our speaker. I had lunch with him once and he told me that he was a United Methodist layman from California. I asked Norman with Chaplain Douglass' help and he accepted. Norman was interred in a Japanese camp in California during WWII. From there he went on to become a councilman, mayor, Congressman and first Japanese member of the Cabinet in two Presidential Administrations. He is a very mild, kind, humble Christian man.

Secretary Mineta gave an excellent talk on the power of prayer in his life to overcome pain and disappointment. He spoke to us in great detail about the events of 9-11 and what led to his decision to ground more than 4,500 American airliners in a two-hour period that day. It was the first time in American history that our air space had been closed. Prayer got him through that day. It was a powerful talk.

I went over to the Navy Chief of Chaplain's office one day for a meeting. I was met by his Executive Assistant (EA) who told me we had to talk. The Deputy Chief of Chaplains, a Catholic one star Admiral and Chaplain of the Marine Corps, had called from California while on a business trip. He had decided he wanted another chaplain, a Catholic, to take the Naval Surface and Air Force Pacific Chaplain job in Coronado, CA. I was really disappointed. Gail had warned me not to bet on that job. I was actually too junior for it. They offered me the same job in the Atlantic Fleet in Norfolk, VA. I did not want to stay on the east coast I felt we had to get closer to our children and family on the west coast.

I called the Detailer and asked him what Captain job was open on the west coast for summer 2003. He said there was only one, the Pacific Coast Guard Chaplain job in Alameda, CA. I did not want another job with the Coast Guard. They were a great organization and had treated me well but I was a sailor. I wanted to get back to the Navy. I felt like God had me boxed in. My only choice to move west and back closer to our family was the Coast Guard in Alameda. Reluctantly I came to the conclusion that this was what God wanted. My last three assignments were all ones I did not want to take but felt the Lord leading me to take: Lincoln, DC and now Alameda. So far the first two had not been so bad. In fact, they had helped further my career and given us opportunities we would never have had. They had also been hard but God had gotten us through. The only thing harder than doing the will of God is not doing the will of God. He always knows best.

The night of the Pentagon attack I ran into the only other United Methodist military chaplain from the Pacific Northwest Annual Conference that covers Washington State and northern Idaho. His name is Lindsey and he is an Army chaplain. He was working at the Pentagon and preaching on Sunday's at a community church called Westmoreland close to our house. In May 2002 he asked me to fill in for him at the church. The church was made up of members of a former Baptist congregation and a group from a Presbyterian church close by that had closed. Most of the members were elderly and the numbers were small. I had a good time preaching that May Sunday. Little did I know Lindsey was setting me up. He had orders to Germany and he was looking for a replacement preaching every Sunday. The church liked my preaching and asked me to take his place. In August I started preaching every week. It was good for me to get back into that discipline. I had missed it since returning from deployment on Lincoln.

Gail and I had also been helping start a Bible study at the Clarendon United Methodist Church. When we first arrived in Arlington we had looked for a good United Methodist Church to attend. One Saturday I called all the United Methodist Churches in the area listed in the Yellow Pages. Most either did not answer or had answering machines. Only one had a live person on the other end, Clarendon United Methodist. They were getting ready for Vacation Bible School. We visited that first Sunday and continued attending the remainder of our tour. Their pastor Glen and wife Karen became good friends. We had been attending the 8:30 AM contemporary service at Clarendon and then going to the 9:45 AM Bible study made up mostly of couples with children still at home. We always try to keep our children, in this case Mae, in Sunday school and support the local United Methodist Church and pastor. We decided to keep both going. We attend the early service and Bible study at Clarendon and then head over to Westmoreland to preach. It is a full Sunday morning but a blessing. We really enjoy both groups. One of the highlights at Westmoreland was going out to lunch after service with some of the members that we have grown to love.

My next big adventure was with The Duck Boat (TDB). The year before I had done all my hunting with Lenny in his Duck Boat. They were moving and he had taken the boat north. I could not figure out how to go hunting with David, and later Jonathan when he came for Christmas. Hunting is one thing that my son's and I loved to do together with our dog Hershey. It is a real bonding and adventure time for us. Gail encouraged me to go out and buy a boat to hunt with. At first I just brushed it off, we couldn't afford it, but I knew that if I didn't, my boys and I would not be able to have that time together. David was almost 17 and I knew that I only had him around for another couple of years.

I started looking for a used Duck Boat like Lenny's. They have a very different unusual construction. They are camouflaged and made especially for waterfowl hunting. The TDB Company says they are made by duck hunters for duck hunters. One mariner said they looked like a bullet. Lenny had a 17 footer that would hold three men and two dogs, perfect for us. Used ones were hard to find but I decided to try. I located two within driving distance. Gail encouraged me and even went looking with me. I wouldn't have done it without her encouragement. We found a good one across the Chesapeake in Preston, MD. It was exactly what I wanted and in great shape with many upgrades. We bought it and took it home.

Lenny took it out with me for the first run. David also came. Lenny had to leave early so David and I continued hunting without him. We had a successful first hunt and even shot a duck. Hershey retrieved it. On the next trip Lenny and I went out alone to Marine Corps Base Quantico just before dark. I had checked everything before we left and Lenny did too. As I was pulling out of the driveway the trailer came off the hitch and ran into the back of our new 2002 Chevy Trailblazer putting great big dents in the bumper and the back door. I was just sick. I thought I had done something wrong. Lenny said it all looked good to him. We were mystified.

David and I started taking the boat out by ourselves. We were hunting on the Potomac River south of Alexandria at a place called Belle Haven. One morning we got down there at 5:30 AM ready to launch the boat in plenty of time to put out our decoys and set up the blind on the boat before shooting time began. As I got out of the SUV to unstrap the boat, I noticed that one side of the blind had come unsnapped from the side of the boat and fallen off. David and I hurried back retracing our route that morning looking for the other half of our blind with the spotlight and praying like crazy. We got almost home and found it on the side of the road by the onramp to the freeway we had traveled down. Thank you Lord!

Trip four was also a fiasco. David and I were going out alone for the second time. We had taken the blind off the sides and double-checked the hitch. Everything looked fine. Just before we got on the freeway, the boat came off the hitch again and slammed into the back of the SUV causing even more damage. I couldn't believe it. What was going on? We decided to keep going anyway. We got out in time to put up our blind and set the decoys before shooting time began.

We had some great shots at ducks and geese and missed. The excitement came when we started to leave. I was bringing in the stern anchor and it seemed to be stuck on something. I pulled harder and it popped loose. Suddenly I noticed water coming in the back of the boat and filling up the stern.

Immediately I knew that I had somehow hooked the boat plug with the stern anchor and pulled it out. I quickly turned on the automatic bilge pump, God bless the person who installed it, and jumped in the river to find the plug. David and Hershey didn't know what was going on but they knew I was in a panic. Hershey started to whine and cry. The tide had gone out and the water was shallow but I still could not find that plug. As I leaned over searching the bottom, the bilge pump icy discharge went right down into my chest waders. David charged to the beach looking for a stick to put in the hole. I was worried he would trip over a submerged log and go down. I grabbed a rubber glove and shoved it up there to almost stop the water and give the pump time to catch up. Our damage control measures saved the boat.

We picked up our decoys and looked one more time for the plug, praying hard. I stepped on something and, sure enough, it was the plug. We made it home alive and in one piece but we had our doubts a couple of times that morning. Gail was having second thoughts about the whole project and wondering if she had done the right thing encouraging us to get the boat.

Gail and I tried to prepare our little family for the move to California. I made a trip there to check out the housing. The Pacific Area Coast Guard Headquarters on Coast Guard Island in Alameda, CA has a housing area north of San Francisco in Novato. It is an old Air Force base called Hamilton Field in Marin County. Everything but the housing has gone back to civilian control. The housing is old, elegant and quite large. It is Spanish style with wood beam ceilings, enclosed sunrooms, sweeping staircases, butler's pantries and maid quarters worth well over a million dollars each. I visited one and both local schools. The Novato High School football team was playing that Saturday for the district title. It was undefeated and stayed that way for the year. I left my card with some stats on David and the coach called me the next day. He was very interested in having David on his team the next season.

David and I continued to hunt every Saturday and as many weekdays as we could both get off until mid February. The snow continued, at one point reaching two feet. The Potomac even froze over. David and I took one of the Fridays it was snowing and headed for the Potomac by Belle Haven. We were the only hunters out and had to break ice to put the boat in, breaking both tale lights. It was extremely cold and we had the roof up on the blind and the heater Gail got me for Christmas going full blast. Twice geese flew or swam into our decoys. David got the first one, I got the second and David got the third. We also missed a few good shots. It was a grand morning, making our whole season seem successful. Hershey went in the freezing water wearing her new neoprene camouflage jacket to retrieve the geese. Each time they proved too heavy for her and she had to swim back without them.

Preparing for a Permanent Change of Station (PCS) move is not easy. Most of the time it is three years between them. This time it was only two. These moves are really exhausting and one of the main reasons people retire early from military service. You just get too worn out and the moves are expensive. No matter how the government tries to reimburse us, we always lose money. The only plus is you are always cleaning your house of unused and unwanted items.

After looking at all the options, we decided to pack out the house after I returned from a three-week school in Newport, RI that started the middle of May. Gail and the kids would stay in the house while I was gone. The kids would finish school and Gail would substitute teach at Mae's school. When I returned the end of May, we would pack out and fly the kids to Seattle with the dog. Gail and I would then ship the Mustang and drive the SUV and boat to Novato via Seattle for Lauren's graduation from the University of Washington, my alma mater. I would leave for Alameda, CA the day after my birthday and Gail would come later with the kids, dog and Mustang when our house and household goods were ready. All of these military moves are very expensive and exhausting but few civilians understand that unless they have done it. These frequent moves across countries and continents really take a toll and few can stand more than about 20 years of it.

My promotion to Navy Captain would be Monday June 2nd 11 AM at Coast Guard Headquarters. I asked my former Commanding Officer and friend RADM Jim Black, MC, USN (Ret) to do the honors and read me the oath of office. My Coast Guard boss VADM Thad Allen would give a welcome and Rev. Leroy Gilbert would say a few words. The Protestant community at Headquarters would give me a farewell potluck luncheon. The new Chaplain of the Coast Guard, CAPT Doug, would be my MC. I invited all the local Navy chaplains and the two congregations where I worshipped. I got permission to bring champagne. I hoped it would be a grand celebration. I really looked forward to wearing those silver eagles and four gold stripes.

The end of February I took Gail to Monterey,

CA for another conference and to see Briana, my new base and the housing at Novato. We had a great time visiting with Briana, Justin and my cousin Craig Waite and his wife Shawn. After the conference we spent a few nights in San Francisco with the kids. We all visited Novato housing and hung out in the city. It was a lot of fun.

Back at Headquarters I was trying to put another prayer breakfast and annual conference together, my last ones I hoped, before I left. These things were really exhausting. We made the mistake of asking another Cabinet member, National Security Advisor Dr. Condoleezza Rice. All of these important political figures have layers of receptionists, schedulers and administrative assistants that make them almost impossible to communicate with. I am convinced that administrative assistants run Washington, DC and maybe the whole country. We had asked the President in the past and I am not sure that he ever even knew that we had. The only reason we asked Dr. Rice was that she is the daughter and granddaughter of Presbyterian pastors and her family attends the church in Norfolk, VA that Chaplain Doug preaches at. We tried sending the request formally from the Commandant of the Coast Guard, faxing it to her scheduler and even giving it to her aunt. Eventually her scheduler called to say she couldn't do it. They usually wait until it is too late to ask someone else.

Once again Doug and I were scrambling to get a good speaker. We tried the Attorney General and the Army Chief of Staff next. Everyone was tied up with preparations for the war with Iraq. We thought of asking Admiral Collins, Leroy and even Chaplain Doug. Finally Doug asked me. He said, "Doug, it is too soon for the Commandant, Leroy has had his time, I have three years left but you are leaving soon. Why not do the breakfast as your swan song." I prayed about it, ran it by the Chief of Staff who agreed and decided to do it. With the war in Iraq looming we felt that we needed the breakfast no matter who was speaking.

The end of March 2002 I made what I thought would be my last trip with Doug as his Deputy Chaplain of the Coast Guard. We had two chaplains in Puerto Rico who needed a visit and we decided to take our wives and go. We flew into old San Juan on Friday March 14th and stayed at the Wyndam Old San Juan Hotel. It was nice and close to Coast Guard Station San Juan and across from the cruise ship piers. On Monday we visited with the command at Borinquen and headed back to San Juan. Tuesday we visited with the San Juan command and moved to the Marriott in Condado just east of old San Juan. We got a beautiful room on the pool level looking out at the beach. It was gorgeous and we really enjoyed it. That day I also decided that I would quit drinking alcohol. I felt it was what God wanted me to do. I had quit before but after a while I always came back. This time I wanted to quit for good. It was expensive, I drank too much, it wasn't good for me and it kept me from losing weight. March 18, 2003 in old San Juan, Puerto Rico while jogging along the old ancient wall of Ft. Morro, I gave it up. I would go back to alcohol and give it up many times over the years.

Wednesday night we drove over an hour east to Fajarda and the Wyndam El Conquistador Resort and Country Club. My parents stayed there years ago at an Allstate Insurance gathering and had asked us to visit. We met the Doug and his wife at the huge isolated sprawling luxury hotel for dinner. They were visiting our Navy base at Roosevelt Roads, the largest in the world. On the late night full moon drive back to San Juan, the first American offensive of the Iraq war began. President Bush addressed the nation late in the evening. Our country was at war with Iraq and we were in Puerto Rico. David was worried about our flight home.

That evening I had gotten an email from a pastor in the Pacific Northwest Annual Conference of the United Methodist Church in Seattle. He was sponsoring anti-war demonstrations and marches at the Federal Courthouse there all week and encouraging clergy to wear vestments and lead the marches. I sent him an email back telling him I would only wear my vestments to a march in support of the war. I told him that if he were to try the same thing in Baghdad they would arrest, torture and have him executed. I asked him to use his rallies to pray for all the brave Americans and their families fighting the war and for the chaplains, many who were United Methodist, who were ministering to them in the vestments of camouflage desert utilities. I signed it "in bed with the government", a phrase he had used to describe all military chaplains once at Annual Conference and in reference to me that day.

The next day I got a response from the pastor in Seattle. He basically said I was going to hell for my position. He emailed it to everyone on the original email minus the Bishop and District Superintendents he had copied before. I copied his response and sent it to his list plus the original one, as many I knew would be interested. I wanted the clergy in Seattle to see who was leading them. Comments started coming in from all over. The experience once again reminded me of how different I was from the majority of clergy in my home conference and the abuse they had been giving me for decades. I tried to forgive them. Once we were back in Virginia, the war went quickly for the U.S. with minimal casualties. Iraq would become an extension of the U.S. for years to come. We all joked about having bases there and sailors and marines coming home with Iraqi wives soon. It wouldn't take them long.

April 3rd I spoke at the Headquarters Spring Ecumenical Prayer Breakfast. VADM Allen called it the Asymmetrical Prayer Breakfast as a Navy Captain was MC and a Coast Guard Vice Admiral was introducing a Commander who would speak. Attendance was lower than when Secretary Mineta spoke but still respectable. I spoke on Philippians 4:6-7, my favorite verse on prayer, and gave examples from this autobiography on answered prayer in my 20's, 30's, 40's and 50's. It seemed to touch many hearts. I had never spoken at Headquarters before as a spiritual speaker. The next day my folks came to pay us a visit. They stayed with us for about five days. The weather cooperated for only a couple of them. The rest were cold and rainy. We visited the DC sites and even made it to the Naval Academy one cold rainy day. It was a good time.

The Chief of Staff for the Chaplain of Senate, Dr. Lloyd Ogilvie, called me. I had known Dr. Ogilvie from Fuller Seminary and had visited him in DC. Dr. Ogilvie's wife had just died and he had to resign from the Senate. They were looking for clergy to open the Senate in prayer and asked me to do two days, April 3rd and 4th. I was speaking at the prayer breakfast on the 3rd so I asked if Doug could do it that day. They agreed and I was to do the 4th. On the 2nd they canceled Doug and on the night of the 3rd the Senate adjourned until the following Monday. I was pretty upset, as I had put a lot of work into the prayer during my parents visit. Monday they called and asked Doug to do Wednesday the 9th and for me to do the 10th and 11th.

Gail and David decided to join me on the 10th. It was a very special honor and experience. The two things I wanted to do while in DC were to pray at the Senate and shake the hand of the President. I was very excited. Gail and David sat in the gallery and I was put on the floor of the Senate. The junior Senator from Alaska, Lisa Murkowski who was appointed after her dad was elected governor, introduced me. She was acting for the President of the Senate, the senior majority Senator, also from Alaska, who was gone. We walked to the podium together and after she rapped the gavel and introduced me, "Rev. Dr. Douglas John Waite, Deputy Chaplain of the Coast Guard", I gave a short 90-second prayer broadcast all over the world on C-Span 2. Then I stepped back down with Lisa and we all said the pledge of allegiance to the flag.

After the prayer I decided to stay around and be available to the Senator's for a while. They have a chair on the floor of the Senate just for the chaplain. I noticed two things while sitting there. First, the Bible was on the President of the Senate's desk. Second, the words "In God We Trust" were inscribed over the main door way. A belief and trust in a divine higher power has always been a part of the government of our country. I felt privileged and blessed to be sitting in that special chair. Once again I heard the Lord remind me that twenty years before he had told me I would come back to the DC area. I never would have expected this. I knew I had really arrived when they let me use the 'Senator's Only' restroom.

That Friday, April 11th, I came back by myself and said the prayer again. This time the junior Senator from Minnesota, Jewish Senator Coleman, introduced me. Family and friends from all over the U. S. were watching me on C-Span 2. This time I spent quite a bit of time with the Senate Pages. They were high school kids from all over the country doing a semester at the Senate. Many of them were interested in the Coast

Guard and the military academies. Both days the Senators were telling stories of bravery and valor by our military forces in Iraq. It was very moving.

The following Sunday Gail, David Mae and I went down to the Outer Banks in North Carolina. The keyboardist at Westmoreland Church, Susan, offered us their house at Colington Harbor near Nag's Head. It was right on the water and had a dock. I took the Duck Boat. We put out crab pots, spent a day at the Atlantic Ocean beach, and even went out fishing for striped bass in the sound. Mae was the only one who caught a bass. She caught two at once. It was a good time but I was missing our other children. When we are on a resort area vacation, Gail and I often think about having a place on the water where our family could gather together. We would like to do that at Lake Chelan in Eastern Washington. God willing someday we will.

The end of my time in Washington, DC was spent preparing my last Annual Coast Guard Chaplain's Conference with 53 active and reserve chaplains attending, getting ready for the packers at home, the office and preparing to detach on May 9th. In preparing for the conference we included a tour of the White House with a man named Dan who worked for the President. We hoped to work it into a picture of us all in uniform with the President. I wasn't sure Dan could make the picture happen so I decided to fax over a personal letter on Coast Guard letterhead to the President's Chief of Staff, Secretary Andrew Card. He was a former Secretary of Transportation, had spoken at our Annual Worship Service and had a wife who was a United Methodist minister. I hoped he could help us.

The night before the White House tour, I got a call from Secretary Card's office that we would get to have a picture with the President. The morning of the tour we were all very excited. About 15 spouses went too. In the middle of our tour the secret service took the chaplains outside on the staircase on the south lawn. We filled the staircase for a picture leaving space between Doug and myself directly in front. It was Doug's 50th birthday. Suddenly the President appeared and began to talk to us all about how important our ministry as chaplain's was to our military service members and their families, especially in time of war. He stood next to Doug and I for our photo. Doug asked him if we could pray for him. He turned around and grabbed us, putting his right arm around me. I laid my left hand on his shoulder. Doug said a powerful prayer lifting President Bush up to the Lord. All the chaplains extended their hands towards him. It was a very special moment I will never forget. As Doug said, "Amen", we all lifted our heads and I saw tears in the President's eyes. He is truly a humble servant of God.

Two of my goals for our tour in DC were to pray in the U.S. Senate and to meet and shake hands with the President. I accomplished the first one and instead of shaking the President's hand, I got to lay hands on and pray for him. This was even better than shaking his hand. Coast Guard Headquarters and DC had been a job and area we really didn't want. We came kicking and screaming to pay back Leroy, hopefully make Captain, and in Leroy's words, "see the big picture". We accomplished our goals and then some. It was a hard tour in many ways but we found that we really did enjoy that part of the world in spite of all the difficulties. We would have considered staying in the DC area if our family was not so far away.

15
Captain Douglas J. Waite

I detached from Coast Guard Headquarters on 9 May 2003 and headed north on the 10th to Newport, Rhode Island via a night at West Point. I was being sent to our Navy Chaplain School at Newport to attend a class entitled "Strategic Leadership and Ministry" or SLAM. It was designed for Captains or Captain selects, like me, to prepare us for ministry on flag officer staffs. I had not really had a course since attending the basic chaplain course in 1984, so I was kind of excited and honored to attend. It was a small class made up of Captains who had been around for a while. I knew most of them. I was the only Captain select.

I had pulled my duck boat to Newport hoping I would have some time to go fishing. The class started out OK but went downhill from there. Newport is close to our Coast Guard Academy at New London, Connecticut and I had a chaplain there who was retiring on a Friday. I asked to attend but was met with some resistance from a junior officer who was in charge of the course. I attended the retirement and found out that the President would be at the Academy the following week for graduation. I was able to secure tickets for all the chaplains at the school to come with me.

When I returned to the school the following Monday and made mention that I had tickets for all of us to go and hear the President at the Coast Guard Academy graduation, I was met with silence. Later I was told that the class would not be going. I planned to go anyway. When word of my plans reached the ears of the junior officer, he informed a senior member of the schools staff, a friend of mine, to tell me not to bother to come back to class if I went. When I heard this I was furious. What was his problem? I checked the schedule for the day of the graduation and the speakers were all locals, junior officers, whose topics I did not feel were more important than hearing the President of the United States. How often do you get that opportunity? I was dumbfounded.

I called the junior officer that night at home and confronted him on his comments to my friend. He admitted to them and then said, "Are you still going to attend?" I did not respond but told him I was going to call his boss, which I did. His boss, a Captain Chaplain, had not heard about any of this and said he would talk to the junior officer. The next morning they all called me into the senior chaplain's office and the junior officer apologized. They told me I could go to the graduation but it was that morning and I felt it would be too rushed. I never went. The rest of the time there was strained since the junior officer was in charge of the class.

All of this just spoke volumes to me about how short sighted and inflexible the Navy Chaplain Corps could sometimes be. Most of what was presented during those three weeks I felt was superfluous to what we needed as senior chaplains. What was a junior officer doing heading up a course for Captains? I did get some good things out of the course such as a Philosophy of Leadership paper and a Strategic Plan of Ministry on PowerPoint plus some good dialogue with the other chaplains on problems we all might face. The fellowship was also good but the rest of it you could keep. I wrote a critique to the senior chaplain but doubt any of my comments were given much attention or thought.

One morning at the school I was jogging and praying about my dog of twelve years, Hershey. We were planning to fly her ahead to Lauren in Seattle. Her health had been deteriorating and I knew sometime soon I was going to have to put her to sleep. I got back from my run and Gail called. Something had happened to Hershey. She was paralyzed at the hindquarters. Gail and David took her to the vet who said she had an aneurism and she would not recover. Gail and David made the decision to put her to sleep. It broke all of our hearts. I felt terrible that I was not there to help them. Gail had put our last dog Yuki to sleep twelve years before while I was deployed to Desert Storm. Military families get called upon to do things that other families do not. They are a special breed and our armed forces would not be able to function without their support and labor of love on our behalf.

After three weeks of SLAM, I came back to DC for my promotion and to pack out our household goods. Gail flew my son Jonathan in for the festivities. My new date of rank as a Captain was 1 June 2003. June 1st fell on a Sunday so the promotion was planned for the following Monday June 2nd at Coast Guard Headquarters. My former boss and Chaplain of the Coast Guard, CAPT Doug, was to be the MC and I had speakers such as my old chaplain boss CAPT Leroy Gilbert and former Commanding Officer (CO) RADM Jim Black, MC, USN (Ret). Both of these men had played a huge role in my selection as Captain. Jim had been my CO and friend in Japan and had personally gone to the Chief of Navy Chaplains to have me assigned to the USS NIMITZ (CVN-68) where I was deployed to Desert Storm. Leroy had stood beside me during my dark days at Whidbey Island under the oppressive senior chaplain and given me jobs on the USS ABRAHAM LINCOLN (CVN-72) and Deputy

Chaplain of the Coast Guard. I would never have made Captain without them both. I felt greatly honored that both could attend and speak.

The ceremony was planned for 1100. It was to be both a promotion and hail and farewell for me and my relief. The promotion went great but too long. I told stories about Jim and Leroy and thanked everyone, especially my family who brought tears to my eyes. My two sons David and Jonathan put on my new shoulder boards. I also received the Meritorious Service Medal, my second one, and we had a potluck from all of the faith group communities. Many of the other chaplain Captains in the area attended. It was a real head sweller. I had a great time and bought champagne for everyone, even though I had quit drinking.

We went right from that high to the low of packing out the house. It took the movers three days to pack up and one day to load in the van. I was on leave the entire time. We flew David and Mae ahead to Seattle. Gail and I did not want to make that 3,000-mile drive with them again. Saturday June 7th Gail and I started across the U.S. pulling the duck boat and taking the northern I-90 route. We drove about 400 miles a day and spent the nights in motels. Things went pretty good until we got to North Dakota. Coming off a freeway exit ramp, I ran into the back end of an elderly gentlemen, cutting his nose with his glasses in the impact. Both cars had little damage and the elderly man was OK but the police cited me. The whole thing made me sick.

We also found out about the same time that we would not be moving into one of the big four bedroom Coast Guard senior officer houses at Novato, California. I was the most junior Captain reporting in of four. There were four four-bedroom houses. One of the Captains living in the houses was retiring but he was getting rehired as a civilian and would be allowed to stay in his house. This moved me to the three-bedroom list. Gail was crushed.

We arrived in Seattle on Thursday June 11th in time for Lauren's graduation from my alma mater, the University of Washington, on Friday June 12th. All of our family was there including my mom and dad who flew in from Phoenix. Gail's sister Beth and her husband Steve threw a big party at their house for Lauren afterwards. I was very proud of her achievement. She told me she did it for me, that I had to have one child who graduated from the U of W. She made me very happy and proud but I told her all along she had to do it for her and not for me.

Gail and I stayed at Beth and Steve's and helped both Lauren and Jonathan move. Lauren was moving to Vancouver, Washington and Jonathan was moving to South Lake Tahoe, California with this sister Briana. The Doug Waite family was leaving the Seattle area. I stayed for a week and then went ahead to my new duty station as the Coast Guard Pacific Area Chaplain in Alameda, California. First we all went to Lake Chelan in Eastern Washington. We stayed at the Caravel Resort there, as it is a favorite gathering place of my family. I put the duck boat in the water and we had a grand old time together. After a few short days by the lake, I headed to Alameda with Briana, Justin and Jonathan following on their way back to South Lake Tahoe. Gail and I hoped to have a retirement place on that lake some day.

I arrived in Alameda on Tuesday June 24th. I stayed at the Homewood Suites by the chaplain I was relieving. I would be working for a three star Admiral, VADM, who was over the entire Pacific area for the Coast Guard. I would directly supervise eight active and three reserve chaplains in four districts covering ten states and 27,000 military and civilian personnel. Two things I wanted to do right away were to start going to the operational briefs, my predecessor didn't attend, and secondly to move my office to the command suite as it was hidden away from the rest of the staff. When I met with the Admiral's Chief of Staff, RADM (Select), he told me that he wanted me to start going to the operational briefs and to move my office up to the command suite. I couldn't believe it. The good Lord sure made that one happen fast.

The housing in Novato north of San Francisco on Highway 101 was about 30 miles away and a good hour in traffic. Novato housing is on an old Air Force Base called Hamilton Field. The housing was built in the 1920's and is Spanish style stucco with maid's quarters and butler's pantries. They had assigned us to the three-bedroom house at 220 Sunset Drive that was to be remodeled by the end of August. Gail, David and Mae joined me after the fourth of July and we moved into a furnished temporary two-bedroom apartment at Novato as we waited for our house to be finished.

Gail had her eye on a beautiful huge four-bedroom home at 222 Sunset Drive that was assigned to the Pacific Area Operations Officer. It was also being remodeled. After some unfortunate experiences with the Lieutenant housing officer, where Gail and I were both disrespected by her, I had to put her on report. Gail was ready to pack up and go anywhere else. She hated it there. Suddenly, the Operations Officer decided not to wait for his house and we were the next in line for 222. We couldn't have been happier. There was just one problem; the remodel was now not going to be completed until the first of October. This move was turning into a disaster. Thankfully, we were able to move into a three-bedroom apartment to wait it out.

While I waited for the family to move down I had been looking for a new hunting dog. This time I wanted a German Shorthair Pointer that was trained like Lenny and Jean's dog Star. Star could hunt ducks or pheasants and was remarkably well trained. I started looking. After much research I decided to get a new eight-week-old pup and start from scratch. We finally found one in Santa Rosa north of Novato. I took Gail and the kids and we ran the whole litter through a series of tests. Only one dog passed them all, the biggest male who was kind of chubby but mellow. Gail liked him immediately. He was the only one who would point at seven weeks. We decided to get him and picked him up at eight weeks.

We tried lots of names. One of them was the name Otis after a friend of ours who named his son Otis like the elevator company. I was also looking at a pheasant club to join and I took the pup out there to have them look at him. The trainer looked at the pup and said, "He looks like an Otis." The name stuck after that. Gail and the kids started calling him Otie. I decided to train Otis myself with the pheasant clubs help. Otis would probably grow to a large 65 pounds. He had huge paws. He grew rapidly and was a constant source of fun and frustration chewing on everything, digging in the yard and playing this annoying game of chase with anything valuable he could get his mouth on. Otie drove Gail nuts but he was very cute, a characteristic that always seemed to earn him her forgiveness.

I joined the Black Point Game Bird Club and started taking Otis out there for my own training program. I was following a book I had found but soon learned the technique was contrary to that of the trainer at the club. I decided to give it up, stick to the basics, and let the trainer have Otis for a couple of months when he got to be about one year old. The club had an opening pheasant hunt bash that looked like fun. For $100 each, you could get a field for three with seven birds planted per hunter. I wanted to take David and Jonathan but Jonathan just couldn't make it from Tahoe. I invited my cousin Craig Waite to take his place from Aptos. I asked the trainer if I should bring Otis. We were also renting a trained hunting dog. Otis was then about 3 months old. The trainer was reluctant and thought the heat and pace would be too much for Otis.

I left Otis home and we started a great day of hunting with the old veteran pointer Parker. He was marvelously pointing and retrieving the birds we shot. I knew Otis could do this. I ran back to the apartment and got him. The club is only about 10 miles from Hamilton Field. Parker was not happy with Otis and kept growling at him. Otis followed right on his backside. Suddenly Parker was on point. It was David's turn to flush the bird and shoot. As I stepped back, Otis flushed another pheasant at the same time Parker's flew. I shot that one and David shot his. Parker retrieved David's and Otis retrieved mine. It was terrific and worth a million dollars to see my new pointer in action at just 3 months. I had made the right decision to get him. A couple of weeks later, David and I took him out and he flushed another pheasant we shot over him. Otis retrieved it like a champ. He was going to be a great hunting partner.

In August I started to visit my chaplains in the Pacific Area. Since the salmon were running in Alaska I decided to start there. I took David with me to Kodiak. The pink or humpy salmon were really thick in the rivers. The Chaplains there met us and took us fly-fishing on All Terrain Vehicles (ATV's). We had a blast and limited every day. At one point David asked if he could quit fishing because he was getting blisters from catching salmon. We brought back two coolers full of salmon and halibut. It was a great trip

David was trying to make the varsity football team at his new high school in Novato. He made all the camps and workouts prior to the season starting. His coach in Virginia had said that he would probably start David at full back on varsity this year if he weren't moving. The coach at Novato had heard of David's abilities from me and was very interested. We hoped he would be able to play.

As the season progressed, David was playing full back but on the third string. He got little playing time at practice and almost nothing at the games. I tried to talk to the coach but he did not answer my phone calls or emails. Eventually he put David on some special teams and David was able to get a little playing time. If the team were far ahead in points, he would sometimes put David in for a few plays at full back. It was discouraging to David but to his credit, he hung in there and didn't quit. He seemed to be enjoying his new surroundings and teammates even if he didn't get the playing time he craved. This was an answer to prayer.

Mae got settled in her new second grade class and Gail took the state test to start substitute teaching in California like she did in Virginia. Our house at 222 Sunset Drive was not finished until the middle of October. It was over four months since we had seen our household goods. Just before the move in day, Gail fractured her ankle picking black berries with Mae. I had to take a day from work to help her get around. That ankle plagued her for weeks and made the move in that much more difficult.

The house was beautiful and one of the nicest we had ever lived in. It was built in stucco Spanish style with a tile roof, much like our house in Spain. It sat on a hill overlooking San Pablo Bay towards Mare Island and Vallejo. It had four huge bedrooms and two full baths upstairs and gigantic dining and living rooms downstairs with maid's quarters and a finished sunroom. The kitchen with butler's pantry had been remodeled and rewired. Most all the floors were refinished wood. It had been painted inside and out. The basement became the laundry, freezer and tool room with tons of space for storage. We had our own driveway, a luxury on Sunset Drive, with a garage. Over the garage was an outside patio area. Deer, owls, hawks and coyotes could be seen and heard daily. Some said it was the nicest house on the base. We felt sure it was and maybe the nicest in the military. Gail had asked God to give her that house and he had answered her. It had just taken some patience and time. I used to say Gail had the spiritual gift of 'house'.

I began to look for duck hunting spots to use my duck boat. When we arrived I had noticed the large duck blinds out in San Pablo Bay just below our new home. I had trouble finding anyone who knew anything about the duck hunting in the area. I had taken the duck boat out several times in the Bay trying to figure the hunting out. The bay was very shallow and one had to pay strict attention to the tides. One day while jogging at the old airfield with Otie, I noticed some men in boats working on the blinds. I could see they were coming from the opposite direction of the boat launch I used. I searched and found a dirt launch close that they were using. I ran into these hunters at the launch and tried to get some information from them. They were not happy that I wanted to hunt in their little domain. One told me that they had hunted there for 45 years and did not welcome any newcomers. I could not help but think about how I had been traveling all over the world most of my life in the military protecting the very freedom they enjoyed and wanted to keep to themselves. I continued to search for a place to hunt.

The weekend before Veteran's Day, the Capello's came to visit from Hawaii. Jean spent time with Gail helping her decorate the house. Lenny and I spent four solid days hunting with Otis. We would hunt the mornings in the duck boat in a different location each time searching for the ducks. In the afternoons we would hunt the pheasant club. Our first afternoon out, Otis made a beautiful point on a rooster, better known as a ring neck pheasant. It was his first real point and Lenny was very impressed. We flushed and shot the pheasant and Otis went to the bird but then tried to run off and play chase with it. He pointed for us each day after that. He was acting like a real pointer at five months. Lenny and I also found a spot close to the house where the other duck hunters hung out. I went there many times after he left and found mallards almost every time. I missed hitting most of them. I tell people I don't really shoot ducks, I just scare them.

My two big projects at work were: 1. trying to get a chaplain to ride the two polar icebreakers in Antarctica for the winter. 2. Planning a conference in Hawaii for January 2004 with all the Pacific Area Coast Guard chaplains focusing on ministry in a 9 11 type disaster scenario. Both projects had their obstacles but seemed to come together with God's help. I was also able to start a daily fifteen-minute devotional group using the Our Daily Bread booklet like we did at headquarters in Washington, DC.

We moved to the West Coast to be closer to our children. At Thanksgiving Briana and Jonathan came. It was great to have them there but we missed Lauren. Lauren went to Tyler's in Bow, Washington. Right after that, Lauren and Tyler decided to relocate down by us. They both moved into our guest and maid's quarter's rooms and started looking for jobs. They also brought Jake the Doberman Pincher and Lola the three-legged cat. Tyler helped me make the backyard fence bigger for the dogs. Gail and also threw a party about then for all the active, reserve and retired Navy chaplains in the area. Lauren and Tyler helped. It was a huge success. Both Admirals and all three Chiefs of Staff at Novato housing dropped by too and we sang Christmas carols.

Just before Christmas I was able to deploy my District 11 South Chaplain to Australia to ride one of the polar icebreakers, Polar Sea, into the ice of Antarctica. We had two breakers deployed there for about three months, both with crews of about 150 Coasties. Both of their commanding officers had asked me to send a chaplain with them this year. Sung Hee volunteered and I was able to get him reserve coverage to go. He missed his wedding anniversary and Christmas. I was able to get him selected as the Coast Guard Chaplain of the year for his efforts. He started sending us pictures of himself doing services and Bible studies, walking the ice with penguins around, and baptizing some Coasties out on the ice. His ministry was terrific. It was the first time the Coast Guard had ever deployed with a chaplain to the ice. His ministry gave me a great sense of accomplishment and got the interest of the Commandant.

We had another great Christmas that year. All the kids were home again for Christmas plus Tyler and my mom and dad. My folks stayed up at the Temporary Quarters (TQ) at Novato housing. They like to have their privacy and their own bathroom. We had some great family dinners and a wonderful Christmas morning. I think Christmas morning with all the kids is just about the best morning of the whole year. As usual my folks left early the day after Christmas. They never liked to stay anywhere very long. My dad always quotes Poor Richards Almanac, "Fish and relatives start stinking after three days".

I took Jonathan and Tyler duck hunting the day after Christmas. We didn't see anything. Jonathan had to go back to Tahoe and so Tyler and I started hunting ducks together over the Christmas holidays. He was not working until after the New Year. Several days we went out in absolutely terrible weather, driving rain and wind. We got a few and really got soaked. Tyler and I enjoyed each other's company in the blind. We even got invited out to my neighbor Mike's duck hunting club at Honker Bay near Pittsburg and the Delta. Their floating blind had been blown to shore in one of the storms and we helped them get it back in place with the decoys.

I used my new GPS Gail gave me for Christmas to find my way around the bay in the dark and fog. The only thing I don't have on the boat now is radar. I can cross a bay in the fog and dark but I cannot keep from hitting another vessel. David still goes out with me occasionally but usually I didn't see any game when he was with me. We also took Otis out to the pheasant club, he went in the boat too, and one day he pointed four roosters in about 90 minutes. He had an amazing nose and instinct plus enthusiasm for hunting upland game birds. I kept trying to get him out in the water too but he didn't like it very much.

After the first of the year 2004, I started doing a lot of traveling. First we went to Hawaii and I took Gail, David and Mae. David and Mae had never been there before. We stayed at the armed forces hotel at Waikiki called the Hale Koa, a long time favorite spot of Gail and me. I was organizing a conference for all my Pacific Area chaplains and Gail and the kids were on holiday. The District 14 Commander, RADM Charlie Wurster, and his wife had us over for dinner one night with the Chaplain of the Coast Guard, District 14 Chaplain, their pastor and all our spouses and some children. His house is at the lighthouse at Diamond Head. It was a special evening.

My conference was on disaster ministry like we had at the Pentagon and New York after the terrorist bombings of September 11th, 2001. The scenario was a terrorist bombing of a cruise ship in the harbor in Oahu with mass casualties. The Coast Guard was in charge and all the Pacific Area chaplains were mobilized. It went for two days and ended with a luncheon of all Oahu Navy and Marine Corps chaplains plus representatives from many civilian agencies such as the Red Cross and the FBI. Chaplain Doug spoke on 9 11 and the District RADM plus my VADM boss. I wanted my chaplains to be ready in case we had another terrorist attack on the West Coast like 9 11. After the conference we were able to stay another couple of days and visit with friends such as the Capello's, Johnson's and we even ran into United Methodist Bishop Mary Ann Swenson and her husband Jeff. We attended the Polynesian Revue at the hotel one night and David was selected by the dancing girls to go up on the stage and dance with them. They all gave him kisses afterwards. It was a highlight for him.

Gail and I flew back from the conference to San Francisco, dropped off the kids, and flew out the next morning to St. Petersburg, Florida for a Navy Chaplain 0-6 Captain conference with our two flag officers called Senior Leadership Symposium or SLS. About 130 chaplains were there from all three sea services. Many of their spouses came too. It was a strange experience being with these senior chaplain leaders, many who I had called sir most of my career. I decided that they were all just the same people they had always been but now they wore eagles and four stripes. I felt honored to be in their company. Many changes were coming for the Chaplain Corps. I saw some of them unfold before I retired. We ended with a worship service where the Chaplain of the Coast Guard told me that the Navy Chief of Chaplains was talking to him about having me take Doug's place when he leaves. I was not sure that I wanted it.

We were home just a short time before we started our next big adventure. Gail and I decided to take a military hop to Japan with Mae and David in mid-February while the kids were out of school. We had always wanted to take David back to his homeland and let him experience his culture, visit the orphanage he came from and maybe see some of his birth family. Gail had kept up with our social worker in Yokohama who had helped us adopt David in 1988. She had helped David make contact with his Japanese grandfather who had named him Akira. They had exchanged letters and pictures. Now we told her we were planning to come over and we would like to visit the orphanage (baby home) and hopefully meet his grandfather. She said it was good we were coming now as she was retiring soon. She would try to make the arrangements and help us with translation.

We started to try to get out of Travis Air Force Base on a military flight to Japan on a Thursday night. Saturday we moved to the temporary family quarters on the base. Sunday morning at 0500 we were manifested on a KC-10 straight through to Yakota Air Force Base on the island of Honshu near Tokyo. It was a 12-hour flight. Japan is 16 hours ahead of the west coast and we landed on a Monday about noon.

The last time Gail and I had been at Yokota was in August 1989 when we were stranded there trying to get to Hawaii with four kids on our return to the United States after living three years at Yokosuka. We never did get to Hawaii and had to take a flight to McCord Air Force Base near Tacoma, WA. David was just three at the time. He remembered nothing from those years.

We pulled our suitcases a few blocks out to the Japanese train station and got on the wrong train to Yokosuka. We had to get off and backtrack and it was all very exhausting. David's first impression of Japan was that it was very crowded and concentrated. Eventually we made it to our old Navy base at Yokosuka and checked into the Navy Lodge there. We could not believe how Yokosuka and the base had changed since we were there. There were new structures everywhere. Chaplain Karl, Naval Forces Japan Chaplain, had us over to his beautiful home for a terrific Chinese dinner. We could hardly stay awake to make conversation.

The next day we toured the base, saw our old street, haunts and I got a chance to see Chaplain Gary, the Command Chaplain on the aircraft carrier USS KITTY HAWK. It was supposed to deploy that day but was delayed. Gary and I had a great time catching up on our lives. After that we all got our bags and headed up to the baby home on the train. We had lunch at a noodle (udon) shop in the Gumoji Train Station and ran into our old social worker and her sister who was an English teacher. They loaded us in two taxis and took us up the hill to the Kuriachi Baby Home. Everyone was waiting for us. The director was still there and looked the same. The nurse who had been there when David was a baby was now retired but came back to see him. His old caregiver, then a young girl of about 16 who had often taken David home for the weekend as a baby, also came back, now a wife and mother of two.

It was a grand reunion and they fawned over David, took pictures with him and exchanged presents with us. David walked around and looked at everything asking questions. It was a super time. Afterward we headed up to Tokyo by train to spend a few days at the New Sanno Armed Forces Hotel there. The following day we did some site seeing and went to the Buddhist Temple at Asakasa Kannon. David and Mae found it all very interesting. We enjoyed a tempura lunch there together.

Wednesday was the day we had all been waiting for. David's grandfather had agreed to come to the hotel, visit with us and have lunch. The social worker would also come with her sister and translate for us. I came down to the lobby early just in case and saw a man about my age sitting alone who looked like David. Sure enough, it was his grandfather. He wanted to know where Akira was. David soon showed up and we had a very good visit. We ate Mexican food that David's grandfather had never had before. We learned many things about his birth family. His biological grandmother was dying of cancer. The rest of the family seemed to be estranged from the grandfather. David's mother is married with two children. His uncles do not know that he exists.

Too soon the visit was over. We got many pictures and movies. We learned a great deal. David had a positive experience that will stay with him the rest of his life. At the end his grandfather gave him a great big hug that was priceless. We all shed a few tears.

The next night we took the shuttle bus from the New Sanno to Yokota. The Coast Guard there got us into temporary quarters while we waited for a flight home. We were there three nights and we did some site seeing in the town of Fussa, bought some woodblock prints and ate terrific sushi and yakitori. I had forgotten how good it all tasted there. Saturday morning we caught a DC-8 commercial flight back to Travis via Guam and Hawaii. It took us about 24 hours. At each stop we relaxed in the Distinguished Visitors (DV) lounges for 0-6's and above. We were always the first on and off and vans usually met us on the tarmac to take us to the lounges. The Air Force knows how to treat senior officer's right. Many retirees were also in these lounges waiting for flights. We got back home exhausted but very grateful for such a wonderful experience with our two Asian kids. We planned to do the same trip with Mae to China when she is in high school.

During the middle of the trip to Japan we learned that Lauren had broken her engagement to Tyler and canceled the wedding. Now we came home to face the fallout. They had many fights since they had moved in with us and after one, where Gail was present, she had told them she did not think they should get married. Lauren finally took her mother's words to heart and called it off. We had already reserved a place in Tahoe and bought a $600 dress. Still we wanted her to make the right decision and agreed with her reasoning. If it were this hard before they were married, what would it be like after? The real problem was that Tyler was still living in our maid's quarter's guest room with Jake the Doberman Pincher. It was all very awkward. He and Lauren were trying to relocate from Washington State to Northern California. They had jobs but not enough money to move out and get apartments yet. We all spent the next few weeks in the same house. It was trying at times.

Gail's dad came down for a visit while his wife Millie was in the hospital. He had just had surgery too and was very worn out. Briana and Jonathan came over from Tahoe to see their granddad. At the end of the visit they decided to take Jake back with them. Tyler could not afford a place where he could also take such a big dog.   We all felt sorry for Tyler. He was far away from home and had lost his fiancé and his dog. It was hard for him. He was not treating Lauren well though and that sobered us up. He needed to go and soon.

Eventually Tyler found a place and moved out. To their credit, Tyler and Lauren remained friends. Actually neither of them knew anyone else and so all they had for a social life was each other.   The only thing that changed was that Lauren no longer wanted to marry him. It took her a lot of courage to make that decision and I was very proud of her. I also believed it was the right decision and so did her mom. She was frustrated being now 24 years old, a college graduate and still living at home. Marin County was one of the most expensive counties in the country, $779,000 for the median home at that time and Lauren could not afford to live there on a vet clinic receptionist's salary. She began to think about relocating to a less expensive area and a better paying job.

Gail and I began to think about retirement. I had achieved most of my goals in the Chaplain Corps and now qualified for about a 55% of base pay retirement for life. I had often thought that I might go back to parish ministry after I retired. I enjoyed preaching, teaching, counseling and leading God's people. However, I could not stand the low salary, housing, petty squabbles, evening and weekend meetings and the minority of vicious, evil and bigoted people who often ran the church.

A pastor has all of the responsibility and none of the authority. I tell my military leaders it is like being the commanding officer of a ship and having the crew vote on your salary every year. Pastoring God's people is one of the toughest jobs in the world and one of the most important and undervalued. I had been good at it though I chaffed under its yoke. God had wisely taken me out of it to do military chaplaincy that I also enjoyed and excelled at. I missed the preaching and teaching though and was willing to return with my retirement check if that was God's will. I also needed to do it soon if I was going as my mid-fifties were approaching. As always, Gail was ready to do whatever would make me happy.

As we started to consider the options, it seemed that God was silent, or was he? He had me selected for Captain. Would he have let that happen if he wanted me to leave the Corps? I didn't think so. I had eight more years to go to receive the maximum 75% of base pay retirement at 30 years of total active service and mandatory Captain retirement of age 62. Those two fell on the same year for me, 2012.

I began to crunch the numbers and decided that a lifetime retirement check of 57.5% of my base pay a year at 23 years or 75% at 30 was a huge incentive to say a little longer, not to mention the great paychecks over the next 8 years. I figured I would have to find a church paying me more than the average to break even. I figured that probably wasn't going to happen. Financially it would be economic suicide for me to leave the Navy early, even though the moves every two to three years were killing us.

I made the decision with Gail to stick it out to age 62 in the Navy unless the Lord really intervened and told me to leave or my health failed. I would probably never go back to the local church as a full time pastor but I could volunteer to help out in the church with economic stability for the rest of my life. I could continue to provide leadership to the Chaplain Corps and especially the young chaplains coming up the ranks. I was developing a heart for helping the young chaplains with their careers. I also would have the opportunity to see if God wanted me to wear stars. I always said, "Someone has to be an admiral, why not me?"

Gail and I had started to invest for our children's college and retirement in 1992. My friend and former navigator of the USS NIMITZ, Mike, had gotten us started with financial counselors USPA&IRA who were all former military members targeting active military members. They had a program based on savings, insurance and monthly allotment investing in mutual funds they called dollar cost averaging. Later this group became known as First Command Financial Planning. We had a different agent wherever we moved and most were very good.

When I was promoted to Captain I put almost all of my significant salary increase into insurance and mutual funds. From this program we were able to send all of our children to junior college and a four-year state university if they so desired. When we sold our home in Burlington we put that profit into mutual funds too. By 2004 we had sent three to college and had money in mutual funds, including two Roth IRAs, and significant whole life insurance for future protection. It was a good program and growing even though stocks had been through a rough few years.

Our financial retirement plan was sound but it had two weaknesses. First, the military retirement was good for the life of the retiree but upon their death it ended unless you paid into an expensive program called the Survivor Benefit Plan or SBP. If you paid into this monthly program, at your death, your spouse could receive a maximum of 35% of your retirement for life if after age 62. Later they changed this to 55%. Through lack of planning, many military members had no choice but to take the expensive SBP unless they had offsetting insurance and investments to take care of their widowed spouse. I hoped I would not have to take the SBP at retirement, though it was Gail's final choice to accept or reject. I needed more life insurance to make that happen. I would need to buy it soon or it would become too expensive.

Second, Gail and I had no real estate investments. We had sold our house in 2000 and put the profits into mutual funds on the advice of First Command and others. Those funds lost a third of their value the next three years. Our dads told us they had been through this many times and to just leave it alone and it would come back. If we took it out our paper loss would become a real loss.

During the downturn in the markets interest rates had fallen to their lowest levels in forty years. The housing market was going off the charts and we were being left out. If rates were going to start back up due to the improving economy, we would not be able to enjoy those low interest rates when the time came to leave the service in 8 years and buy a home. Our financial advisor told us to get more insurance and if we really believed rates would go up, to buy something now while they were low and rent it out until we could move in. We decided that was good advice and began to look for property. Since we were pretty strapped financially with one still in college and three still at home, I would buy more insurance each year when I received a salary cost of living increase.

Gail and I decided that we would like to spend our retirement winters in a warm climate by the water and our summers back in the Pacific Northwest. We loved Waikiki Beach on Oahu in Hawaii and we loved Lake Chelan in eastern Washington State. Why not try to secure something in those two locations for retirement? The problem was that both were very expensive places to buy property. We started our search with Hawaii. We had some military friends who had retired there.

In May of 2004 Gail and I spent 8 days on Oahu. I was attending a conference and Gail was on vacation. We stayed at the armed forces hotel Hale Koa at Fort DeRussy in Waikiki. Immediately we began to look at property. We wanted a two bedroom two bath condominium (condo) with some kind of view, a pool, something we could rent out for a senior officer's basic allowance for quarters (BAQ) of about $2300 a month and within walking distance to the Hale Koa, not too much to ask for.

The realtors could find very little in our maximum price range of close to $300,000. We did find one however. It fit the description except for one thing, it needed to be gutted and completely redone. A Vietnamese family of six had been living in it for nine years and it was a complete mess inside. They were asking $318,000 and we made them an offer of $260,000. They countered with an offer of $285,000. We accepted it. We then got down to the paperwork for financing when they decided that they had changed their mind and now wanted $308,000. We could not believe it. We walked away. It was very depressing. Maybe we couldn't retire half the year in Hawaii. We asked God to close the door if he didn't want us there and it seemed he had done just that. How did he want us to spend our retirement? We would have to spend more time in prayer and meditation asking him.

The next week I had a United Methodist minister's conference in my hometown of Yakima, Washington. I flew in, checked into the hotel and started going through the phone book looking for old high school friends. One I found was my old friend

Steve. He was still selling used cars. I went over and spent some quality time with him in his office. He was really glad to see me.

I also called Steve's former wife Kathy who was a good friend of Gail and I. She came down to the hotel the next morning and had coffee with me. We had a nice visit and she encouraged me to call my old high school girlfriend Corey who lived in town. I took her up on it and called Corey at work. I had not talked to her or seen her in almost 35 years. She could not believe I was calling her and asked if I would like to meet her for coffee the next day. That night I told Gail what I was doing. We met at a local Starbucks the next day. I knew who she was immediately but she did not recognize me in uniform. She was looking for an older heavy balding man with glasses, her idea of what I looked like. She said she thought she would recognize me though by my distinctive `swagger'. In my uniform she did not know who I was but she did say I had the same walk.

We had a nice visit and decided to go to lunch. On the way she told me that another old friend named Steve lived across the street from her but they had never talked. After lunch I went over to her house to see Steve. It had been twenty years since I had seen him. We had a good visit. He could not believe that my old girlfriend Corey lived across the street from him for over ten years and he did not even know it. We both went over to Corey's and he apologized to her profusely. Together the three of us went to go through my old house two blocks away that was for sale. It was a real déjà vu experience of being with these two old acquaintances in my former childhood home. It could not believe it was happening. We all left vowing to try to stay in touch and get together in the future.

One night Tyler called us wanting to talk to Gail

and me. We had him come over for dinner. He began to cry and tell us that he really loved Lauren; he felt he had blown it and he wanted to try it again with Lauren. Lauren was there listening. He apologized to us all. He said he felt he needed to win us over to win Lauren back. We told him that it was all Lauren's decision, we did not dislike him and that we forgave him. We also suggested that he get into counseling and start going to church. He agreed and started immediately. Soon he and Lauren were dating again. Tyler really appeared to change. We all saw a difference in him after the counseling started.

I started the summer of 2004 determined to train Otis into a good hunting dog. The club owner Mike Sutsos was a nationally known trainer. Mike started training after the hunting season ended and he had a month or so break. He liked dogs to be close to one year to begin. Otis would be one year June 22nd. We had two choices. I could leave him at the club for a month at a time for $600 or I could bring him out for short sessions at $50 each. Because of lack of funds I opted to do the training with Otis. I also wanted to be trained myself. Otis was a natural pointer but he was not holding on point and was unpredictable on his retrieve. At one point he quit retrieving all together even though I had shot many birds over him the season before and he retrieved most of them.

Mike had me begin a force retrieve on him pinching his ear to get him to take a retrieve dummy or bird when I told him to "fetch". It was hard for me to do but eventually Otis began to retrieve on command. Next we began to steady him up to "wing and shot". Once on point he was expected to stand still until the bird was flushed and shot. Then he was to go for the retrieve only when told to "fetch". Mike used a combination of stern voice and shock collar with live birds for this training. He said that Otis was very smart, learned quickly, but was testy and always pushing the boundaries, especially with me. He had to learn to do what I told him when I told him and do it immediately. I took him for a lesson at least once a week and slowly we made progress.

The new Commander was a one star that was picked below his senior two stars to wear three stars, VADM, by the Commandant. He seemed to be a spiritual man who valued chaplains. On the previous VADM 's suggestion, I asked him if he considered me a part of his immediate staff. He said he did and we soon hit it off. The climate in the office completely changed for the better with his new personnel. It was fun to come to work even though I was gone a lot of the summer.

In July I took Jonathan and David with me to Kodiak, Alaska. I had taken David the year before and we had so much fun I wanted Jonathan to experience it. I was traveling so much I had enough air miles to take them with me at no cost. We spent the first night in Anchorage. The weather was super, over 70 degrees and sunny. We flew to Kodiak the next morning. This year I was hoping to catch the Sockeye Salmon run. They are called "Reds" because of their deep red delicious flesh. We started out fly-fishing the first night late and discovered that Sockeye were really hard to catch. They didn't bite like the pink fleshed Humpies we caught the summer before. You had to snag them in the mouth. If you caught them anywhere else you had to release them. It took us three days to figure out how to do it.

One day an aviation chief offered to take us out on his boat. It was very windy and we wound up making a long transit around the backside of Kodiak to a place called Whale Island. We saw whales and other wildlife on the trip around. We caught six large 30 pound Halibut. We had a blast. That night we were cleaning fish late into the evening. We also got to ATV over to the place we had fished the year before. It was not as good as the last summer but we had a great time over and back. After we cleaned all the fish we had 100 pounds of filleted Sockeye and Halibut. The end of the trip we were fogged in for two extra days and could not fly out. That is how it is in Alaska. It was really terrific to share my love of Alaska with my two sons.

One night our real estate agent in Hawaii, Eve Shere, called Gail and I. She had the perfect condo for us with everything we wanted. The only problem was that it cost a lot more than we wanted to spend, $419K. It was three blocks from the Hale Koa with a magnificent view of the mountains and the ocean from the 27th floor. It was over 1000 square feet with a beautiful lanai, two bedroom and two baths completely furnished with upscale furniture. The building had security access and sat on the Ala Wai Canal across from the convention center. It was perfect. It had originally been owned by the Sony Corporation who decorated it but never used it. An elderly Jewish Rabbi Eve knew now had it but he had died and his family wanted to sell. Gail's friend Jean sent us pictures and we fell in love. She went over and looked at it and told us to buy it immediately. Eve said she would hold it for us until the first showing.

The next two weeks we tried to figure out how to do financing. We finally came up with the money by taking out all that was left of our Andis Place house mutual funds and a mortgage from USAA. One day we fasted and prayed together asking the Lord to give us direction as to whether or not we should take this risky financial step. We both felt him tell us to proceed. The devotion the next day was on taking risks in life. We offered Eve her price but we asked her to remodel the bathrooms. She accepted. We took a military hop over on the 4th of July weekend to see it. It was all we hoped for.

The condo closed in late August while we were on vacation camping at Lake Tahoe. We now owned a condo on Waikiki Beach. The only problem was we didn't have the money to make the payments. We would have to rent it out until retirement in 2012. We hired a property manager named Yan and started to pray. Jean thought she had a couple of visiting nurses but they fell through. Gail was not sleeping worrying about it. One night I asked her to fast and pray with me again asking God to send us some renters. She agreed and within a day of our fast Yan had three college girls willing to sign a lease for 9 months at $2150.00 a month. We were overjoyed at the grace of God once again. When Gail and I fast and pray together, God makes things happen.

The summer of 2004 I also did a lot of preaching. I preached at the chapel up in Kodiak. The following week I rode the cutter BOUTWELL to San Diego and preached out at sea. My old congregation in Mt. Vernon, Washington, Avon, asked me to come back and preach. I attended the Methodist Annual Conference in Moscow, Idaho and another United Methodist congregation in my birthplace of Puyallup, Washington asked me to preach. I was inundated with preaching and I loved it. One of the biggest congregations in Novato, Marin Covenant, called and asked me to preach. Preaching is something I love to do, it is my passion and I do not get to do it enough as a Captain.

On my trip to Puyallup I was called one night that my Uncle Stan Gilliam had died there. I had the privilege of praying with him over the phone just a few weeks before. I could not believe that his funeral was scheduled for the Saturday before the Sunday I was scheduled to preach there. The Gilliam family asked me to do the eulogy at the service. I did not have to change one of my travel plans. God knows everything before it ever happens. His timing is perfect. He is never early and never late but always on time. Our job is to get ourselves on his schedule and not our own.

Two weeks after Stan's funeral my Uncle Gene Waldher died in Tucson, Arizona. He had been a great hero of World War II, Korea, Vietnam and the Cold War. As a young aviator he was shot down over Germany piloting a B-17 and spent 18 months in a Nazi prison camp, Stalag Luft III. The Germans, as the Russians advanced, turned him loose. Just before the Russians arrived, the Americans evacuated the POW's by air with many tears of joy and relief. He went on to fly B-29's in Korea, B-52's in Vietnam and U-2 spy planes in the Cold War. He retired as a full Colonel with 28 active years. Strangely, he never seemed interested in my career though I achieved the same rank. His family called and asked me to do his service. I was honored to do it and did.

We also changed churches about this time. For over a year we had been attending the Novato United Methodist Church. It was an old church where the average age was probably seventy. We tried all the United Methodist churches in the area and this was the one that we felt we could try and get involved in. It had a new pastor, a female, who was more liberal theologically than we were but who was a pretty good preacher. Her daughter and ours were about the only children in the church. The people were very loving and saw in us a way to reach the military at the old Hamilton Air Force Base Housing. This church had reached its hay day when Hamilton was still open prior to 1975.

One week I got the pastor's email newsletter informing us that they had found a new organist and he would be starting the following Sunday and would also be bringing his partner, a man. We attended that service and the organist and his partner sat in the front pew. The congregation gave them a standing ovation. On my way out I asked the pastor if his partner was his lover. She said he was. I went home and sent her an email that we would no longer be attending. Our General Conference had just gone through a tough couple of weeks emphatically stating once again that homosexuality is not considered an acceptable Christian lifestyle in the United Methodist Church. This pastor chose to ignore this fact in picking a very important staff position and parading them before the congregation. Gail and I could no longer support them. Quietly we left. We began to attend the Marin Covenant Church where we had sent Lauren and Tyler. I hated to leave the United Methodist Church but the spiritual needs of myself and my family came first.

Right after this I had quite a shake up. I had been pruning the trees around our house to improve the view of San Pablo Bay. I was doing some dangerous things high above the ground. I tried to be safe but eventually I fell two stories to the ground, landing on my butt, back and elbows. One elbow was sliced to the bone cutting a tendon almost all the way through. I hit so hard that I lost feeling in my arms. At first I thought I was paralyzed. As I was going down I remember saying more than once, "Help me Jesus". Dazed and confused I scrambled out of the woods covered with wood chips, dirt and blood. Gail and Lauren were in the front yard and saw me coming. I told them over and over that I had an accident and that I thought I had a concussion. I could not make my brain think clearly.

Lauren thought I had a cardiac arrest and wanted to call 911. Gail wisely took me to the shower and then to the emergency room. I was there for hours. Eventually my mind cleared up though my elbows were a mess. I was so scared of paralysis that I vowed never to go on ladders again. I would only trim as high as I could reach for the rest of my life. Gail would never forgive me if I paralyzed myself.

Eventually Tyler proposed again to Lauren on the Deception Pass Bridge in Washington State. She accepted for the second time and they even bought a new ring. Plans started for the 2005 wedding. She wanted me to do the service and to have it outside by the water with a nice reception and dancing. We started looking at facilities at the old Presidio in San Francisco and a very nice restaurant in Sausalito overlooking the bay. Prices were astronomical as is everything in that area.

One day at work my Vice Admiral boss overheard me talking to the Master Chief about looking for a spot on the water to have the wedding. The VADM said, "I have a place on the water". He lives in a huge Coast Guard home on beautiful gated grounds by a lighthouse on Yuerba Buena Island between the Oakland and San Francisco Bay Bridge. His house looks at the bay, the bridge and San Francisco. Underneath the lighthouse are sea lions. It is a beautiful idyllic spot; exactly what Lauren was looking for. We all went to look at it and fell in love with the site. We began to talk to caterers and set the date for May 21st, 2005. Invitations would go out to about 160 of our family and friends, most from out of state. We expected about 120 to attend at the most.

During this time I was searching for new chaplains to work with me in Alameda, California and Kodiak, Alaska. I thought I had the Navy chaplain stationed with the President at Camp David coming to Alameda. He said he wanted the job and then resigned his commission six months out. I was disappointed but managed to get myself invited to preach for him at Camp David on Thanksgiving Sunday. Gail could come too. I had always wanted to preach there.

We arrived at Camp David Sunday morning November 26th. It was the tightest security I had ever experienced. The President was not there and at his ranch in Crawford, Texas. The active duty stationed there were my congregation for the morning. They often worship with the President and his family. It was a good experience and afterwards we got to have lunch with the Navy Commanding Officer and get a tour of the compound. It was very interesting. Many historic decisions have been made there over the years of the Presidential Retreat's existence. I was really impressed with the lengths the American people will go to insure that their Commander in Chief has a safe place for recreation and retreat. If quality time for retreat and recreation are important to him in his decision-making, it should be important to all leaders at every level.

About this time I received an unexpected invitation to be the keynote speaker at a Promise Keeper sponsored men's retreat in the Santa Cruz Mountains February 2005. They wanted a military chaplain to speak on the topic of spiritual warfare. The text that immediately came to my mind was Ephesians 6:10f. There the Apostle Paul says that we do not wrestle against flesh and blood (human beings) but against the spiritual forces of evil in the heavenly realms (demonic spiritual beings). After prayer I felt led and honored to accept this invitation. I also knew that it would be a battle with the forces of darkness.

I was at a conference in Tennessee when I got a call from Gail that Lauren was having trouble seeing in her left eye. She went in for an exam and they rushed her to emergency cold laser surgery in San Francisco for suspected histoplasmosis. Histo is fungus common to the Ohio River Valley, a place we have never been. It can get into your lungs and eyes. Once in the eyes it starts microscopic bleeding in the retina that takes away vision. The cold laser can stop the bleeding but the damage, once done, is irreversible apart from God's intervention or new technology. We were all devastated as of course were Lauren and Tyler. I sensed this was a spiritual attack.

Next I began to experience a strange tingling and numbness in my left arm and chest area. I felt exactly like the sensation I had when I was injured falling out of the tree in September. After an MRI, the doctors could find nothing. One night my mom suddenly collapsed in her kitchen. Fortunately, my sister Sue and her husband were visiting and were able to catch her and take her to the emergency room. Then Gail and I got a call from Lauren while we were at a conference in Florida that our eighteen-year-old son David had been arrested for stealing CD's at the local Target store. Finally my pointer Otis turned up with a leg he could not stand on caused by a tick bite infection. All of these added up to what I thought were attacks from the enemy for the work I was doing preparing for the spiritual warfare retreat. This men's retreat must be something special that would do great damage to the kingdom of darkness.

I responded by fasting and praying and asking everyone I knew to pray as well. I went on the longest fast I have ever attempted, over four days. On the advice of my good friend and mentor Fr. Jack Tench, I asked the church at Marin to come over and pray through the house and anoint us all, calling on the Lord to protect us from the enemy. They came over and we prayed through the entire place anointing everything. I felt we had the enemy on the run again.

Finally the weekend of the retreat came. I had asked Jonathan, David, Tyler and Justin to go with me. They agreed, a miraculous event given our schedules and how spread out we were. Over a hundred men came, mostly from two churches in San Jose. Many worked in Silicon Valley. The first night I gave an invitation and about a third of the men asked Jesus in their hearts. One of my young son's was among them. The next morning I gave another invitation for the Baptism in the Holy Spirit and half of the men responded including one of mine again. That night I asked the men to make a commitment to read the Bible for five minutes a day. Three quarters of them responded positively.

On the last morning I asked the men to commit themselves as spiritual warriors. Every man stood up. I could not believe it. I was awe struck and humbled at what God had done. As I had suspected, much damage had been done to the enemy's plans for these men. Praise be to God! My tingling eventually stopped, Otis' leg healed, my mom was OK, David got a fine and community service but Lauren's left eye continued to be damaged. There is a spiritual war raging and sometimes there are casualties. I continue to hope for a miraculous healing for her with or without improvements in technology and medical science

Spring Break I took Gail and Mae with me for a visit to District 14 in Hawaii. The chaplain there and I paid a visit on the senior Navy chaplain in the Pacific, a job that I only dreamed about having some day, Pacific Fleet and Pacific Command or PACFLT and PACOM Chaplain. A few months before I had talked to our one star Rear Admiral Chaplain, also Chaplain of the Marine Corps, asking him about jobs that I might take next. I really wanted to go to Hawaii my entire career and had never been able to pull it off. I mentioned a job there and asked him for his input. He told me that he knew I would do well at any job the Navy Chaplain Corps had. He said that his philosophy was always to ask the senior leadership for the hardest jobs and see where they wanted him. I decided to take him up on his advice and asked him for the PACFLT and PACOM Chaplain billet in Pearl Harbor or the Chaplain Corps Detailer job, assignment officer, in Tennessee.

In the summer of 2006, the summer I would be up for a new assignment, the Chaplain of the Marine Corps would probably fleet up to become the two star Chaplain of the Navy controlling all three sea service chaplains, at that time about 870 representing 150 faith traditions. He would have the power to give me one of those jobs if he wanted to and thought I could handle it. Detailer and PACFLT/PACOM Chaplain were high-level jobs that also made you very competitive for selection to flag rank Rear Admiral, one star. We elect one Rear Admiral every three years. These two jobs are much sought after by chaplains for that reason. I was very competitive to become the next Chaplain of Coast Guard but it was not a flag rank competitive job. No chaplain had ever been selected to Rear Admiral, Chaplain of the Marine Corps, from the Chaplain of the Coast Guard position. Also, Gail and I did not want to go back to DC.

I would only have six more years left in the Chaplain Corps in June 2006. In June 2012 I would reach the maximum retirement age for Captains and below, 62, and would be eligible for the maximum 30-year retirement, 75% of base pay for life. Six years left equates to two more three-year tours. I felt now was the time to make my move and maneuver myself into a competitive flag rank Rear Admiral job. After prayer and fasting I felt that God wanted me to make myself available to be selected to the rank of Rear Admiral. I let my good friend and mentor Chaplain of the Marine Corps, soon to become Chaplain of the Navy, know my intentions. If he didn't make it happen now, I doubted it would ever happen. He said he would seriously consider me when the time came.

I had been waiting for his answer when I stopped into the PACFLT/PACOM Chaplain's office at Makalapa in Pearl Harbor, Hawaii for a friendly visit. I had never been there and was curious. As I was taking my chair he informed me that he had heard through the Chaplain Corps grapevine that I was going to relieve the Chaplain of Naval Forces Japan, CNFJ, in Yokosuka soon. The CNFJ Chaplain had to leave the job early and they needed me to take his place. I was shocked and called the Chaplain of the Coast Guard asking him to find out if it was true. He investigated and said there was something to it and to stand by for more to follow. My hopes for the PACFLT/PACOM Chaplain job seemed to go down the drain. Gail was not going to be happy.

The next week I was at Marine Corps Base Camp Lejeune, North Carolina for a conference and ran into the Chaplain of the Marine Corps. He took me aside and told me that the information about the Japan job was to just be a conversation between him and me and not to get out to the Corps. He had a leak in his office. The CNFJ Chaplain needed to be relieved soon and the Chaplain of the Marine Corps was interested in me taking the CNFJ job for about a year and then stepping up to take the PACFLT/PACOM Chaplain job sometime in 2006. I was excited and saddened all at the same time.

Gail was working on her Master's in Education at Dominican University and needed another year to finish. David needed to get his feet on the ground in junior college. If I left for Japan in summer 2005, I would have to go by myself as a geographical bachelor. That did not sound like fun. I could try to leave Gail, Mae and David in housing in Novato. What was I going to do with Otis and the Duck Boat, sell them? I was really looking forward to another summer not moving and another hunting season close to my sons and new son-in-law. I would have to give all that up to go to Japan. Gail was not happy but willing to consider it if we could get the PACFLT/PACOM job in Hawaii. After prayer and consultation with Gail, I told the Chaplain of the Marine Corps I would do whatever he wanted me to do. He said he would be in touch.

I was trying to get to the Arabian Gulf and the 'War on Terror' in Iraq. We had seven Coast Guard cutters over there and about 400 personnel. Some of those Coasties were from the Pacific Area. I made plans to travel around the 1st of June to Bahrain and from there to Kuwait and our forces in the area. I hoped to visit some of our other Navy and Marine Corps chaplains too. Just a few weeks before I was to leave, my Vice Admiral boss said he did not want me to go.

I was depressed about not going to Iraq but another opportunity came up for ministry. One of our high endurance 378-foot cutters named MUNRO had gone to the Arabian Gulf with a Marine Expeditionary Strike Group of six other warships. On its way home MUNRO went around the world through the Suez and Panama Canals. The CO and I decided a chaplain would be desired to go from Aruba through the Panama Canal and then to San Diego, about a two week trip, to address Return and Reunion issues with the crew after a six month deployment. I sent this exciting opportunity out to all my chaplains and no one responded. After sending out a second notice, I decided to take the job myself.

Just before I left, Saturday May 21st and Lauren and Tyler's wedding finally arrived. Over 110 family and friends gathered in the Bay Area from all over the United States. Celebrations started as early as the Wednesday night before when Gail and I hosted Tyler's family at our house for a BBQ. They brought hard liquor and some hard drinking young men and the party began with a bang. People were staying at the Hamilton Field Temporary Quarters by our house and the Marriott Courtyard Hotel close by in south Novato. Thursday night some of our family and friends started arriving. Gail's friend Jean was staying with us and helping Gail as was her sister Beth.

On Friday the 20th we had the rehearsal at the Vice Admiral's quarters about 4 PM. It was so windy that I gathered everyone on the side of the house rather than where we would probably be the following afternoon in front. Following that, Tyler's family hosted all of us at a beautiful restaurant on Pier 39 at Fisherman's Warf in San Francisco. Gail and I's parents were there as were RADM Black and his wife from Florida. It was a great evening.

Saturday the 21st all the women left early to get their nails done. Then they all went down to the Vice Admiral's house to dress and have their hair done about noon. I stayed back and contracted the airporter bus to take the rest of us down about 2:30 PM for a 4:30 PM wedding.

I asked some of my Coast Guard cutter and helicopter friends to see if they could come by the Vice Admiral's house about 4:30 PM and take some pictures. At 4:30 we were almost ready to start when the cutter and helo showed up. They made a big hit. I had the Marin Covenant pastor, Art, do Lauren and Tyler's premarital counseling and start the service so I could walk Lauren down the aisle. About 4:40 PM we finally started down. The weather was absolutely gorgeous with no wind. God really showed Lauren and Tyler his favor giving them a warm, clear and beautiful day. Thank you Lord!

After a long period of pictures following a reception line, we gathered in a tent for a sit down dinner. Our caterer was Elegant Occasions who we met while looking for places to have the wedding at the Presidio. They were expensive, I could have bought a new car, but they did a superior job. We also had a Master of Ceremonies/Disc Jockey that did a great job. Gail and Lauren had decorated all the tables in themes representing many of the places we loved and lived such as Skagit Valley, Japan, Spain and Lake Chelan. Toasts and speeches followed dinner and included a song that Lauren and I sang as a surprise to Tyler.

After dinner we all gathered in the front lawn terrace to dance, dance and dance some more. It was a spectacular evening with a full moon shining on the water. The city of San Francisco helped us out with a full fireworks display right across the water in honor of Armed Forces Day. The celebrations continued until about 11 PM when we hiked everything up the hill to the airporter, loaded our vehicles and headed home arriving after midnight. Pastor Art's son Josh was missing with Lauren's friend Nicole. We looked all over for them and left without them. They eventually turned up after midnight at the Vice Admiral's house. They had been down at the lighthouse. Josh's unhappy mom had to come back and pick them up.

The next morning we all gathered again at our house for a brunch about 11 AM. Lauren and Tyler arrived and opened gifts. Many of our family and friends came over. It was another great time of being with family and friends that we love and enjoy. The weather was warm and beautiful. People started leaving and going back to their lives. Gail's sister Beth and her family plus her Dad Burdette and RADM Jim and his wife came back for one more dinner. It was a fabulous wedding and weekend we would all remember for the rest of our lives.

The following morning I was up at 3 AM to catch a ride to the airport with Lauren and Tyler. They were going on their honeymoon south of Cancun in Mexico and I was flying to Aruba to ride the cutter MUNRO through the Panama Canal to San Diego. I arrived late Monday night in time for a wetting down celebration at one of the local outside pubs. Many of the Lieutenant Junior Grade Officers had recently been promoted and were throwing a party to celebrate. I stayed there until about 10 PM and then got a ride to the cutter at the cruise ship pier.

Aruba reminded me of Rota, Spain, small, warm, sunny, nice beaches and arid unlike Hawaii. The following morning the Commanding Officer and Executive Officer, invited me to play a round of golf with them at the Tierra Del Sol Resort and Country Club. We had a really great time together.

The following morning we got underway for the transit to San Diego through the Panama Canal. I immediately started a weekly evening Bible study. They had Catholic and Protestant Lay Readers that did services on Sunday but little else of a spiritual nature. I was hoping that by supporting the Lay Readers and starting a few other programs, they might continue them for future deployments. From the idea of one of the crewmembers, I also started a daily fifteen minute devotion using the Our Daily Bread devotion like I did in Alameda. I also participated in both Catholic and Protestant services. They had been gone for six months without a chaplain and many wanted to talk to someone who was not in their chain of command.

The CO had me stay in his guest stateroom and take my meals with him in his cabin. We really enjoyed our time together. I also tried to take a few meals with the Wardroom, Chief's Mess, First Class Mess and the rest of the crew. We went through the Canal in eight hours, leaving the Atlantic for the Pacific. I had never gone through it before. The weather cooperated and the sea state was mostly calm. I would jog in the morning on the weather decks and give the evening prayer every night before taps. Most had never been around a chaplain before. It was a great two weeks for me. I am just glad it was for only two weeks and not six months.

The summer went on and no word about orders. Once the Detailer called to say that the Japan jobs were taken care of, the Chaplain of the Marine Corps liked me and I was going to get a good job. I tried to be patient. Finally the Chaplain of the Marine Corps called me. I was in Anchorage, Alaska involved in an exercise called Northern Edge with my District 17 Chaplain. Chaplain Bob said that he wanted me to take the Pacific Fleet job in 2007 when the present chaplain retired after extending for one year. In the mean time he wanted me to take the Navy Surface and Air Force Chaplain job in Coronado, CA for about 18 months before going to Hawaii. He also wanted to keep my name on the list for Chaplain of the Coast Guard.

I was a little disappointed about having to wait for the PACFLT/PACOM job but glad to be headed that way. The Navy Surface and Air Force Chaplain job was one I had always wanted and thought I was going to get two years ago. I would be the supervisory chaplain for all the surface warships and carriers in the Pacific plus the air wings, over 100 chaplains and enlisted Religious Program Specialists (RPs). It would be a good preparation for the PACFLT/PACOM job. I was honored but not excited about moving the family to Coronado for just 18 months.

Awhile before, Gail and I fasted and prayed together about a couple of things including her continued education efforts. After fasting Gail felt called to quit the Masters in Education she was working on. It was expensive and taking up too much of her valuable time plus very stressful. She had no intention of becoming a teacher so she decided to stop. When she heard the news of the Navy Surface and Air Force Chaplain job she said she was willing to go wherever with Mae.

Late August Hurricane Katrina hit and demolished the Gulf States. We set up a Chaplain's Emergency Response Team (CERT) and deployed about 10 chaplains there to help with the disaster. About three weeks into the CERT I was asked to go down and relieve the leader who needed a break. I arrived in Alexandria, Louisiana on 18 September for 10 days at the Incident Command Post (ICP). About the third day I went down to New Orleans. It was absolutely awful. People who could get into their homes had appliances, furniture, carpeting, plaster board and everything they owned out on the street. Areas that could not get into their homes looked like something out of a science fiction movie. Entire neighborhoods were completely empty with cars sitting where they had been parked. The water line from flooding was over the door ways. Trunks were open on cars where people had been loading up to evacuate when the water came and they had to flee on foot for their lives. Beautiful boats were stacked by the sides of the road where people abandoned them once on high ground. I had never seen anything like it.

One of my chaplains was from Biloxi, Mississippi. When he got there it had been totally destroyed. He did not recognize anything. He called me in tears. The Coast Guard Station at Gulfport, Mississippi had been completely wiped off its foundation. The station mascot dog had been inside and perished. At the ICP many of our Coasties had lost everything. Some had insurance and some did not. Though devastated they continued to work helping others. The Coast Guard saved over 34,000 lives in three weeks. That is the same number they save nation wide in eight years of search and rescue. People were exhausted.

While I was at Alexandria Hurricane Rita came roaring in and hit the U.S. right at the Texas and Louisiana border. I was in the hotel that night. Wind gusts hit about 65 mph plus with torrential rain and we were over 100 miles away. The hotel lost power and water as did the entire town. Rita slowed us down and added to the devastation and frustration. We set up a second CERT where Rita hit. There was a sense of sadness that permeated everything. I was continually reminded of how we felt when all of our household goods were destroyed in 1989. At day 10 I was ready to come home.

I got back just in time to take all my boys, Jonathan, Tyler, David and Tyler's Dad Tom, to Kodiak, Alaska for some work and Silver Salmon, Coho, fishing. We had been planning it for months. It was just what I needed after Katrina and Rita. We flew in on a Saturday and immediately started fishing. As usual, it took us a couple of days to get organized with the right bait in the right spot at the right time. We wound up south at the Olds River with cured roe or fish eggs on hooks. We could each get two Silvers a day at the Olds. They were hitting the eggs hard. One day we limited in less than an hour. We caught 56 Silvers in all and came home with over 300 pounds of filleted frozen salmon. Many of these Silvers were 15-17 pounds in weight, bright and shiny and did they ever give us a fight. It was a terrific trip.

Around December we discovered that the next Commandant of the Coast Guard job was coming down to two names, a Vice Admiral who I worked for my last year at Headquarters, and my present Vice Admiral boss. Both interviewed with the Secretary of Homeland Security. My present VADM boss said he had a good shot at it in spite of the fact that the other VADM had headed up the Katrina and Rita disasters and had a lot of face time with the President and the media. I did not want to be considered for Chaplain of the Coast Guard, a job also coming open June 2006. However, with the possibility of my present VADM boss becoming the next Commandant, I began to have a change of mind. He was a Christian who valued chaplains and it would be a pleasure to work with him for the next four years in Washington, D.C. Finally the Secretary's decision came in. The other VADM would become the next Commandant.

My son David's best friend Ryan joined the Marine Corps and went to boot camp in San Diego. We headed down for his graduation. It was very impressive. David began to think about the service too. I thought the graduation ceremony would put him over the edge. After careful consideration and prayer, he decided not to go in.

Much was happening with our other children about this time. Jonathan was fired from his job by the new management at Mulligan's right after he worked Christmas Day. It was a low blow. It worked out well though as he finally went to work training at an assistant manager position that had been offered the summer before. He proposed to Aleeya and they were planning an August wedding in South Lake Tahoe.

Lauren and Tyler moved north. They found it too expensive to continue living in Marin County where the median house was going for $990,000. They found an affordable house up in Marysville, WA and I helped them move up New Year's weekend in the middle of a huge rain storm and flooding.

David quit the Country Vet when Lauren left and found a job selling men's clothes at Macy's in Corte Madera. He also continued to keep a B average at junior college taking fire science classes. Briana was enjoying her new job in billing at the Barton Hospital in South Lake. Mae was becoming quite famous as an oil painter and even had one sold at the school auction for $115. Gail continued to work at the school and occasionally travel with me. Her income helped us keep the condo in Hawaii that was rented but not covering all our costs. She and I kept looking for our summer retirement residence. At first we wanted to go to Lake Chelan but with Lauren's move, we started thinking more and more about Western Washington State where many of our family resided.

Spring 2006, long time Charismatic Renewal leader and former Roman Catholic Priest Francis MacNutt was having a conference on healing in Dallas, TX. For years I had wanted to get back into the ministry of spiritual gifts. As a military chaplain, the opportunities to move in these gifts had not been as numerous as when I had been the civilian pastor of a church.

What brought this to a head for me was the demonic infestation of one of the civilian computer gurus at Alameda. He was a Christian who had picked up a powerful occult demon or demons while playing with Ouija boards. For years I had not believed that

Christians could be possessed with demons but this man changed my perspective. I tried to pray and lay hands on him and got nauseous. I knew I was over my head and needed others to help me set him free. I looked all over the San Francisco Bay Area and could not find one church that had a successful ministry in deliverance. Francis had such a ministry and a new book out on the subject. I decided to go and hear what he had to say.

I wanted to take Lauren with me. From the first moment that she had lost vision in her left eye, I had felt that it was an attack of the enemy. I asked her to go with me and she accepted. I had been in Seattle on business and we flew together to Dallas. She only stayed the first two days. Francis had offered us the opportunity to be prayed for by his ministry teams. Lauren and I both signed up. I fasted and prayed while they prayed for her. The eyesight in her left eye was not changed but she was healed of some resentment towards her older sister and a sense that God was punishing her for her sins. On Tuesday night she also prayed to be baptized in the Holy Spirit, a greater empowerment of the Spirit of God post-salvation that she felt she needed.

I also was prayed for and the healing team had prophecy for me that God was welcoming me home in a new way and that the second half of my ministry would be more powerful than the first half. I was really overwhelmed with the love and power of God in a way that lasted for days. I came home determined to spend more time just hanging out with God. I also experienced a new power to stop drinking and smoking again.

Gail and I started thinking and praying about a place to live in Coronado. We started with friends and the Coronado churches and got a couple of contacts. On one business trip I visited them both. One was small and one was big. Both were more than we could afford. After doing a budget, we determined we could only afford a monthly payment of $2700.00. The government only gave us $2426.00 and we were losing our Cost of Living Allowance from Alameda. It was going to be tight and Jonathan was getting married in August. One morning I woke up and sensed the Lord telling me to take the smaller condo in Coronado by the ferry landing. I called the owner Pete who worked for Fox News and he told me that he was just on his way to list the condo in the Coronado paper. Most places listed in the paper were rented the same day. He told me the condo was ours.

We decided to clean the huge house in Hamilton Field and it was quite a chore. Gail and I worked on it for weeks every evening. We really had to downsize our possessions. David informed us he was not going to move with us to San Diego and that he was moving in with a girl named April that we barely knew. We were not happy with his decision but realized we could do little about it. He would be on his own. We would not support him financially to live with a woman outside of marriage. We made the same decision with the other three children too. Like our other children, we did offer to continue helping with college tuition and books if he would stay in school.

We moved to Coronado, California the end of June. Our condo would not be ready until the middle of July so we had to live in hotels and Bachelor Officer Quarters (BOQ's) until then. Otis the dog and Myla the cat had to be boarded at the Coronado Vet. We could visit them and even take Otis out on certain days at certain times. We tried to run him at the Dog Beach near the Naval Air Station at North Island. There dogs were allowed off lease. Otis spent most of his time sniffing other dogs and got little exercise but at least he got out of the vet for awhile. We found another beach where the Navy Seals train that we could run him and very few people and dogs were around. He loved it and immediately settled into chasing every bird on the beach into the surf.

Once moved in, we began to settle into our new community. Our condo was strategically located by restaurants, shops, tourist attractions and a jogging/bike path around the water looking at the city. It was a lovely spot but much smaller than our house at Hamilton. We had to keep a lot of our possessions in storage.

Right after we moved in we had to go back north to South Lake Tahoe for Jonathan and Aleeya's wedding on Saturday August 5th. We decided to drive on the east side of the Sierra Mountains, an area we had not been in since seminary days. We were able to rent the Coast Guard condo there and arrived on a Wednesday and started getting ready. We used the condo to gather and have family meals. All of Gail and my family arrived except her sister Joan and my sister Suzanne, this included our parents. The rehearsal was Friday night at Baron Lake on the west side of South Lake Tahoe. In addition to the wedding rehearsal, we also baptized Aleeya. It was very moving for all of us.

Saturday finally came and we gathered back at Baron Lake for a 1 PM wedding. When we arrived we discovered that there was still much that needed to be done. All of our guests helped us get organized and set up. Finally the service began. All of Jonathan's siblings, brother-in-law and even his dad were in the service. It was a very moving and blessed event. We had a nice catered dinner and music to dance. Lauren and I sang a love song Garth Brooks did in the movie "Hope Floats". Many toasts were given to the new bride and groom. The next morning we all gathered again at the condo as Jonathan and Aleeya opened presents. They left the next morning for Cancun. It was sad to say goodbye to our family not knowing when we would all be together again.

Gail, Mae and I came back to Coronado to celebrate our 35th wedding anniversary and for Mae to start school the same day. Gail started to work in the school as she had done at Novato. I began to get into my new job that included supervising all the chaplains on all Navy surface ships, aircraft carriers and air wings. The job was really two full time jobs rolled into one. I worked for two three star admirals. I was overwhelmed most of the time and missing the user friendliness of Coast Guard ministry but glad and excited to be back in Navy khaki working with the warriors who protect our nation and fight our wars.

We found a good church at St Paul's United Methodist Church in Coronado. The pastor Neil was a surfer and mentioned surfing in almost every sermon. We liked him and the church. They even had a healing group that met on Wednesday nights run by a 94 year old man of God named Hal and his 92 year old wife Jenny. I went a few times and saw miracles almost every night. Sometimes Mae would go with me.

My predecessor told me he had no money to travel. I checked and found out I had $9K for travel unspent I would lose October 1. I started to travel once again going to Norfolk, Virginia and Washington State. This job was starting to look like my last one, visit the chaplains and Religious Program Specialists (RP's), mentor them and let their Commands know there is a senior chaplain looking over their shoulder who works for their Admiral boss. It is great work and I enjoy it.

I tried to get back into hunting with Otis and The Duck Boat (TDB). One of the problems with the military lifestyle is that you move every three years.

Once you figure out how to hunt an area, you get orders to move. It is very frustrating but you do get to sample hunting all over the country and the world. I even hunted in Spain. A Government Service (GS) employee at work, Rick, who was a little older than me and had a new Yellow Lab named Herne, started talking about hunting the Imperial Valley desert three hours east. We headed out there for doves in September where the temperature could get to 120 degrees. Otis could not believe I wanted to hunt there but he went along willingly. We would go and spend a night or two. We did well on doves but not so good on quail. It wasn't great but it was hunting and Otis learned how to retrieve yet another kind of bird.

I was still frustrated about having my TDB and not being able to use it. There was one lake but you could not use a gas motor. When duck season started in October we got out to that lake with Rick's electric motor on my TDB but did not do very good. I started thinking about selling my boat or hauling it up to Washington State and ask Tyler and Lauren to look after it for me.

October 1st the boys and I made our annual pilgrimage to Kodiak, Alaska for Silver Salmon fishing with Tyler's dad Tom. I had enough Alaska Airline miles for the boys and myself. We all flew from different cities and spent the night in Seattle with Lauren and Tyler to fly out the next day together with Tom. We stayed at the Coast Guard Guest House and fished the Olds River again with spinning reels and salmon eggs. Fishing was not as good as the last year but we managed to limit all four days, two apiece, and bring back 200 pounds of filleted salmon to split between us. I decided that I would not go again unless we had two separate rooms and two vehicles. It is just too much to get all five of us moving in the same direction harmoniously.

Rick and I started hunting a club up by Riverside, California that reminded me a little of my old club at Blackpoint. Otis got back into pointing pheasant and quail. I was worried that jogging on the beach every morning and chasing the beach birds would ruin him for hunting. It didn't, thank God. He seemed to know the difference. Rick and I were planning a trip to Nebraska after Christmas to hunt ducks, geese, pheasant and quail on some of the best hunting land in the United States with a Chaplain in DC. We would take both dogs and one vehicle and drive four days to get there and back hunting four days.

On December 22nd my mom and dad celebrated their 60th wedding anniversary. It was quite an accomplishment and my sister Suzanne and I wanted to honor them with a party at their home with all their friends. David was the only one coming to Coronado for Christmas so we planned to drive over with him Friday for the event on Saturday the 23rd and back on the 24th. It would make Christmas a hassle but we decided to go for it. I would bring the booze and Sue would do the rest. I tried to get all the other kids to come but they were all too busy with their own lives and living from paycheck to paycheck. At the last minute Briana decided to fly to Phoenix and called my folks with the good news. She was met with an announcement that there would be no room for her at their house or Sue's. She had never visited them in Phoenix in the over 14 years they had lived there. She called us bawling her eyes out at the insensitivity of her grandparents. The next day my parents called back asking her to still come and they would find a way for her to stay.

On the big day, we were all there setting up for a 1 PM-3 PM open house. Sue had done a terrific job.

The party came and went without a hitch. My nephew Ben came with his family from Washington State too. My folks seemed to have a good time. Afterwards we were all relaxing in the living room when a friend of Briana's dropped by with her boyfriend, an African American former professional football player. It did not sit well with my dad. Finally my dad said he was tired and that the party was over and would everyone please leave. I had too much to drink and told him simply to go to bed, we were all enjoying ourselves. He told me it was his house. Every one left and I stayed to help clean up. I was furious that my dad would order his family out of his house. We had words. My kids were not happy with their grandfather and it took me awhile before I visited them again.

Christmas came and went quickly as always. It was great to have David home but we missed the rest of our children. Since about September we had been dealing with the remodel of the condo that was going on outside. The entire complex was being redone with new siding, decks, gates, doors and windows. It was a huge job. They started pounding about 7:30 AM every morning including Saturdays. Often they were in the house too. We could not put up any Christmas decorations until the 22nd and none outside. Vehicles had to be out of the garages by 8 AM every morning. You could not have any pictures hanging on the walls. Dirt, dust and debris were everywhere. At one point, we had to take everything out of our garages. We felt like we were living in a war zone. Had we known the extent of the construction, we would not have rented the unit. Many moved out. We asked for and got half a month's rent reduced for the inconvenience and exasperation.

During this time I found out that the job I wanted in Hawaii as the Pacific Fleet/Pacific Command

Chaplain that the Navy Chief of Chaplain had promised me, was going to someone else. Also, the Navy Air Force side of my job was going to become a separate Captain billet and it was not going to me as I had requested. I contacted the Chief and he told me that he just wanted me to handle the Surface Force part of my job at the moment. I was very disappointed but resigned that this too must be part of God's will for my life. I had two carriers and an air station in my career and really knew the Air Force side of the Navy better than the Surface Force side. I decided to become the best Surface Force Chaplain yet. It would be good to be relieved of half of my responsibilities that were too much for one person to handle. I did not think that the Surface Force job would make me as competitive for Rear Admiral when the next board met in 2008 as the Pacific Fleet job would. Gail was glad that I would probably not be making Admiral as she did not want to move to DC and have me work until age 65, part of me agreed.

The Nebraska hunting trip got called off after Christmas due to heavy snow and winds in the mid-West. Rick and I decided to do our own trip to the Colorado River and Salton Sea looking for someplace to hunt ducks out of my TDB. We spent two days on the Colorado north of Yuma, Arizona, and though it was beautiful, there were few ducks and the water levels in the river were low ruining a prop on the boat. Next we went to the Salton Sea north of Imperial Valley above El Centro, California. The first day it was blowing too hard to get out but there were lots of hunters, blinds and ducks. I was greatly encouraged. The Sea is very low in the shallows and the mud is awful. Dangerous vents expel steam into the air.

Day two we got out and used a huge blind one group of hunters offered to us. They had gotten ducks there almost every weekend since opening in October. We hunted all afternoon and got several shots and three Spoonbill (Shoveler) ducks. I had finally found someplace to use my boat and hunt ducks only three hours from home. We came back all of January until the season ended hunting the Sea and Alamo River using Rick's fold-up boat too. Otis and Herne got lots of retrieves in the water including a goose. I had broken the code on hunting from San Diego, pheasants, quail and chukers at the Four Winds Club in Riverside and ducks and geese on the Salton Sea and Alamo River north of El Centro. Otis was becoming a hunting fool. Now it must be time to move again.

One sad experience during this time was Lauren's first pregnancy. She and Tyler called us Christmas Eve to tell us they were pregnant. We were ecstatic. Gail and I were both were really looking forward to grandchildren. Over a month later Lauren called again to say she had lost the baby. I was very saddened and really grieved. I cried with Lauren on the phone. Gail flew up and spent a week with her. Slowly we all got over the grief and got back to our busy lives. We still looked forward to meeting those young children of our children and being good grandparents to them.

Over the next few months the condo repair finally died down. I was on the road visiting my chaplains and RP's. Occasionally Gail would go with me. Most of the time she stayed back with Mae and tried to do as much substitute teaching as possible to make ends meet in expensive Coronado. When home I would begin each work day with a run with Otis on our beautiful beach where the Navy SEALS train. Weeks would go by and we would not leave Coronado Island. It was a nice existence but we missed our other children. I bought a DVD recorder and began

393

transferring our home movies from VHS to DVD to preserve them and keep up with the technology. I had been making home movies since the middle 70's beginning with 8 mm films.

During the arson fire of 1989 we lost all of our 8 mm films dating back before 1986. Those from VHS tapes from 1986 to 1989 were only poor copies that our families had given us back, copies we had made for them. Now I wanted to make copies in DVD format of everything we had for all my children to remember what they could of growing up in our household. As Gail and I taped and watched these family movies, we marveled that the children had been so small and the time had gone by so quickly. Where had those years gone? It seemed like only yesterday. People had told us that the child rearing days go fast and now we understood it too. I missed my young family and resolved to try anew to spend quality time with Mae, Gail and my coming grandchildren in the days ahead.

Our Chaplain Corps was top heavy. The Corps had too many Captains and would have an early retirement board (SERB) that year. I would be one of those looked at and considered. If selected I would have to retire by September 08. I would be 57 in June 2007 and would have 26 active years for retirement or 65% of base pay. If I was not picked up for the SERB, I could stay until 62, June 2012, and retire with 30 active years and 75% of base pay. I would also be eligible for early social security then and my United Methodist 35 year pension in June 2011. If I could finish five more years in the Navy, I did not think I would have to work again punching a clock and I could spend the rest of my days traveling, visiting my kids, grandkids, hunting, fishing, golfing and volunteering my time and gifts as the Lord led. Gail and I talked about retiring early and moving to Washington State to take a church or even taking one in Alaska, a place I always wanted to live. After prayer and silent retreat, I felt the Lord's leading to stay where I was, ride out the SERB and see what happened.

One day I got a call from Justin Cochetti at work. He called asking if I knew I had a new son-in-law? He then asked me for Briana's hand in marriage. I told him what I told Tyler a few years before when he asked for Lauren's hand. He had my blessing if Briana said yes, just don't hurt her. The presence of the Lord came into the room and fell on me. Gail and I had been praying for these two for years and for some unknown reason Justin had not been able to propose. Apparently he had the ring for months and was waiting for the right time. Finally he was able to do it. He told me he was very nervous and scared but wanted to ask me as he knew it was important to do. Years before, at a men's retreat I was speaking at with my four young men present, I had told Justin in front of all the men that I had been praying for my children's future spouses since they were small. I told Justin then that I did not know if he was the one I had been praying for. Now I knew. They were planning a June 08 wedding on the water in the San Diego area.

Jonathan and Aleeya visited us in Coronado. It was the first time we had them in our house as a married couple. It seemed strange to have them around us as husband and wife sleeping together in the same bed under our roof. We visited all the sites around San Diego and had a great time together. Shortly after that visit they called to say Aleeya was pregnant with our first grandchild, a little boy they planned to name Logan Jonathan. It is a tradition in our family that the first born son takes his dad's name as his middle name. Gail and I were moving into a new era in our lives, grandparents, and looking forward to it.

For our 36th wedding anniversary, Gail and I took a Carnival Cruise out of New Orleans to Costa Maya and Cozumel. It was our first cruise. After years of aversion to cruises due to six month deployments on haze gray ships to the Western Pacific and Arabian Gulf, Gail finally got me out there. We went with our long time friends the Braun's from enlisted Navy days. It was billed as a Gearing Class Destroyermen's Reunion but the only other sailor I knew was Mark. We flew in the night before and stayed with Chaplain Tim and his wife Judy who were stationed there. We had a nice stateroom with a window and the late dinner seating at the same table with the same people, including the Braun's, every evening. All the men at our table had been Navy Destroyermen.

The food was amazing, all you could eat of any item on the menu. We noticed many overweight and obese people on the cruise who were constantly over eating as if they were drawn to these cruises. At night the four of us would meet on the fantail to have drinks, smoke cigars and talk late into the evening. It was super. During the day we would lie in the sun out by the pool and sleep and or read. Breakfast and lunch could be taken many different ways and places including room service. We attended a couple of the shows that were good. At each of our stops we were only there for the day. Costa Maya we visited the Mayan ruins which were fascinating. In Cozumel we went to a beach resort, laid in the sun, swam and relaxed. It was only five days but we had a great time and would do it again.

Brian and Justin visited us from South Lake Tahoe and they decided that we would do the wedding June 8, 2008 at the Point Loma Sub Base club looking out at the ocean, a beautiful spot. We had a good time. That year we had visits from all our children and their significant other/spouse except Tyler. He was planning to come at Christmas. We really enjoyed David and April's visit. It was good getting to know her better. As always, our children and their significant others cannot sleep together in our home until married. Gail put some pressure on me to let Briana and Justin sleep together as they were engaged but I held my ground. It all worked out.

Hunting season started with doves in extreme heat in the Imperial Valley, about 120 degrees. It gets so hot that Otis cries. Rick and Hern joined us and we did well. Ducks started on the Salton Sea the middle of October. Our first weekend out in the Duck Boat the Sea was glass. We could not launch at the Red Hill Marina as the water had dropped significantly. We had to launch at Black Rock in the middle of nowhere. About the middle of the day the wind came up and before we knew it we had four foot swells and white caps. It took us two hours to get back to the launch and Rick hit his chair so hard it broke.

We started hunting a local named JJ's new Small Blind and doing well. We must have gotten about 40 ducks out of that blind. On the weekend David visited, Gail let me take him over for one day. We left very early and had to get back by dinner. It was six hours in the car but worth the trip. We had not been out for two years. We got eight ducks and had a blast, Otis retrieving all. I miss my sons at hunting season. We planned to all get together the end of January 2009 at Novato for the last weekend of duck hunting. I would haul the Duck Boat up.

About that time the wildfires hit Southern California. Over 500,000 were evacuated and 1500 homes burned including one of our Captain Chaplains. About 3,000 military families evacuated to four sites around San Diego. I helped arrange chaplain coverage at the sites and spent a couple of evenings there myself. Gail and I can relate to those who lose everything in fire.

Tyler and Lauren were planning to come for Christmas. Then Briana and David decided to come too. Gail asked Jonathan if he and Aleeya might be able to break away and before we knew it, all were coming. They all flew in the December 21st and flew out on the 25th as they had to work on the 26th. It was wild at our condo. David's best friend Ryan came over too from Yuma where he is serving with the Marines. We had ten at the condo. Gail decided to get some BOQ rooms and have them all sleep over there and leave their stuff so we could use the house. We spent the time together eating, drinking, planning games and watching football. We made a few trips but mostly just hung out. It was terrific having the kids all there for Christmas. It had been several years since that had happened.

Rick and I continued to hunt and did fairly well in JJ's blind on the Sea with the Duck Boat and floating the Alamo River in his small boat. We even got some Snow geese. It was a good season and we tried to make the best of it.

The middle of January 2008 I was on a business trip to Washington, DC and got a call from a woman at our church named Jane. The Sunday after Christmas I had preached at St. Paul's United Methodist Church in Coronado. During the prayer request time Jane had asked for prayer for her ear that she could not hear out of. I felt moved to touch her ear right there and ask Jesus to heal it in His name. She told me over the phone that when she was at home that night the Lord healed her ear and opened it. She said she had talked to the pastor Neil and he had told her to call and tell me. I told her she needed to tell the church and she said she had been telling everyone. The Lord is still alive and working and He never ceases to amaze me with His grace and power.

We were all awaiting the results of the Captain Early Retirement Board or SERB that had met in December. At a meeting one day one of the Captain Chaplains in the area told me he had just been called by the Detailer and he was going to be relieving me in the Surface Force job summer 2008. He went on to say that I would be going to Hawaii. I had just been in DC the week before with the Navy Chief of Chaplains but had heard nothing from him about moving early. The Detailer assumed that I had. That next week Gail, Mae, Otis and I drove to San Francisco and Monterey, CA for a United Methodist Chaplain's Conference that we have attended for over twenty-years off and on. We used the opportunity to stay in Novato at the Temporary Quarters there and visit with David, April, Jonathan and Briana. I took the boys hunting and we did well shooting both Canadian Geese and pheasants without the boat. I gave David my father's shotgun as I had given Jonathan mine from my dad. It was a good time and the Hawaii possibility came out though we tried to keep it quiet.

At the end of that visit the Detailer called asking me if I knew about my nomination to become the new Navy Region Hawaii and Surface Group Middle Pacific (MIDPAC) Chaplain in July. My first question back was, "Does that mean I am not SERB'ed?" He said he did not know but the Chief of Chaplains wanted me to go to Hawaii in July. I told Gail and the kids and we started to plan. We were leaving a year early which was hard on us but going to a great job and location for our last tour in the Navy. It looked like I would be allowed to retire with 30 years at age 62. We could also get the Hawaii condo ready for retirement and Mae would easily fit into the Polynesian culture. We had all but given up on ever getting stationed in Hawaii and suddenly it was back. God works in mysterious ways.

Shortly after that news, more came that was not so good. Lauren, who had lost vision in her left eye in 2005 due to a rare eye disease, was now having similar symptoms in her right eye. She raced to the University of Washington Medical Center and they told her they did not know what to do. Miraculously a new internationally known eye disease specialist was being hired there the next day, Dr. Van Gelden, and they would tell him about her situation. On his first day on the job, he brought Lauren in. He said she had a rare eye disease that attacks young near sighted women called Punctated Inner Choroidopathy or PIC. She probably had the same disease in the left eye three years ago. He had successfully treated PIC in other women through cold laser surgery and drugs and he thought he could help Lauren. He gave her the laser treatment immediately and put her on heavy medications.

I flew up there on business and arranged to take Lauren and Tyler to a Healing Room in Kirkland, WA. These rooms were started by a pastor in Spokane, WA and had spread to over 600 around the world. Sue and Harold joined us that night as the healing team of men and women laid hands on Lauren and Tyler and anointed them with oil. Lauren had a big release of anger she was carrying towards God. That night as she lay in bed she felt His peace, presence and His hands on her eyes. The next day we met again with the specialist Russ. He said the eye looked better and he was encouraged. We thanked God and I flew home.

In the days after, Lauren's eye continued to get worse. She hurried back to the specialist and he could not see what was going on. I went to the Lord in anguish and sensed Him tell me that he was healing

Lauren in His own time and way and to be patient. When I asked Him if I should try to change my Hawaii orders to get closer to Lauren, I sensed Him say the Hawaii orders where from Him and to go with them.

Soon Lauren could not function at work. There was only one medical option left, an experimental drug called Avastin that was having good results with Macular Degeneration when injected into the eye. It had never been used on anyone with PIC but the doctor thought it was worth a try. He said he would do it if it was his eye. Lauren decided with Tyler to have the injection and the wait began.

After the injection there was not much change and Lauren grew very discouraged as did all of us praying hard for her. Gail and I were at our Senior Leadership Symposium for all Navy Captain Chaplains in Albuquerque, New Mexico. The opening night Lauren called balling her eyes out. Gail and I were completely deflated and overwhelmed. Later the Navy Chief of Chaplains, RADM Bob, a good friend, came up to us asking how we liked the Hawaii orders. He told me he had given them to me, cutting our Naval Surface Force tour short by one year, because he knew we wanted to go to Hawaii and this would be the only chance for our last tour in the Navy. It was a kind gift from him.

We tried to act grateful and excited but our hearts were not in it. What we really wanted to do was ask Chaplain Bob to send us to Washington State instead. At one point Chaplain Bob asked all the chaplains present, about 125, to pray for Lauren and he began to cry in front of us all. We were moved by his concern and that of many of our long time colleagues who rallied around us and often prayed with us. Gail had a long conversation with Chaplain Bob's wife Evelyn about the pros and cons of moving closer to

Lauren at this time. Evelyn seemed to feel that we did not want to get too close and take away the blessing that God was working in Lauren's life by supporting her too much.

Right after the conference there was a radical change in Lauren's sight. It greatly improved and she was allowed to drive again. She said she could live normally with the vision she had. We were all praising the Lord. Many felt it was the experimental Avastin but I knew it was God. We began to plan again for our move to Hawaii. The joy did not last long however, quickly the improvement reversed and Lauren was worse off than before. Her doctor's said that they felt they had lost the battle for her eyes.

We were all completely devastated. I lay on my face before God every morning begging and pleading with Him in tears to give the order to heal her eyes as He had done with the Roman soldier's servant in Luke 7:7. I decided that I could not take the orders to Hawaii while my daughter up in Washington State was going blind. I asked Him if I could ask to have the orders changed if Gail agreed. I felt Him give me permission. I asked Gail's permission and she agreed. She said she had never had peace about going to Hawaii. My first priority was to stay in the Navy to retire in four more years with a 30 year retirement at age 62. If that was not possible in Washington State, I resolved to go to my United Methodist Bishop in Seattle and ask him for a church as soon as possible close to Marysville where Lauren lived.

The only Captain chaplain job in Washington State was the Regional Chaplain at Submarine Base Bangor where we had lived years before while on NIMITZ. I knew the chaplain and called him up asking if he would be interested in moving early to take my Hawaii orders so I could relieve him. After praying about it for a day, he and his wife graciously agreed. I then called my friend the Navy Chief of Chaplains, RADM Bob, and asked him to please get me to the Pacific Northwest for my last tour in the Navy. I said I would take any job up there. He told me he would look into it and get back to me. We did not tell any of our family what we were doing.

Lauren and Tyler started to interface with Service for the Blind in Seattle. They discovered many resources out there for the blind. Her company installed a new computer system for her that talks to you. She was able to resume her work. Her new car stayed in the garage.

On March 22nd we had something good happen. Our new grandson Logan Jonathan Waite was born to our son Jonathan and his wife Aleeya living in Carson City near South Lake Tahoe. He was normal size and healthy. Aleeya had to have him c-section. His pictures were very cute, blond and blue eyed like his dad. Logan gave us joy in the midst of despair for Lauren.

To add to our stress, many other things began beating us down at the same time. Gail had found a lump in her breast and I was experiencing pain in my stomach and passing blood. Gail's doctor set her up for tests and so did mine. To make matters even worse, on March 20th, coming home from a meeting at 5 PM, a young driver rear ended me at a metering light while getting on the freeway. He hit me so hard my full gas tank ruptured, my seat broke and he pushed me over a concrete barrier into oncoming traffic. I could have been easily killed. Somehow I was able to get to the side of the road and render assistance to the other driver. Both of our cars were totaled. My back had been injured but it took me twenty-four hours before I reported to the hospital. They said I had a bad case of whiplash. I began looking for a physical therapist.

A few weeks went by and no word from Chaplain Bob. I decided to email him and ask him if what was happening with our orders. He emailed me back and said nothing but he wanted to meet us for lunch when we came on a business trip to Hawaii in early May to discuss our future. Gail's test revealed no lump and my tests revealed nothing either. With therapy my lower back and neck were improving. I still had no peace to take the Hawaii orders and Lauren without sight. Gail had no peace to go either place. She was worried about mothering Lauren too much if we moved to Washington State and she did not want me to get out of the Navy early and take away about $1000 a month for the rest of our life in retirement. I began to get very worried about Gail. She was really rattled by all that was going on around us and was not coping well. I had never seen her like that. All the while I was lying on my face before the Lord every morning praying for Lauren and our many needs. I thought I kept hearing Him say He was healing Lauren in His own way and that he had our lives in His hands.

Gail, Mae and I made the trek to Hawaii the first week of May. We stayed at the Hilton Hawaiian Village and ate at the Hale Koa next door, the best of both worlds. On Sunday we attended the Protestant service at the Pearl Harbor Chapel where RADM Bob was preaching. He gave his testimony of being healed from Multiple Myloma Cancer. Afterward he and his wife Evelyn took Gail and me to lunch. Chaplain Bob began by telling Gail and I that he had gathered his staff and tried to find a way to get us to Washington State. They could not find a way to do it. He explained that he really needed me to take the Navy Region Hawaii job.

Gail and I had sensed before the meeting that

God would speak to us through the Bob and his wife and that we should listen to what they had to say. Once back to our room we felt no peace now going to our Bishop in Seattle and asking for a church. Somehow, someway, God was directing us to spend our last tour in the Navy in Hawaii with our daughter Lauren struggling with loss of her sight.

We began to make plans to continue with our move to Hawaii in July. I started looking for a new car to replace the Mustang. After much searching Gail found a new 2008 fire engine red Mustang convertible with 4500 miles that a Vietnamese man wanted to sell quickly for a loss. It was loaded and we loved it. I bought it in one day and we took our rental car back to the airport. We parked our new car at the chapel with a tarp on it as we left Hawaii for San Diego to finish up at Surface Force and move back in July.

As always, the last few weeks in San Diego were a flurry of activity. My hunting partner Rick Riley offered to take Otis while we waited for housing once in Hawaii. We would travel with Myla the cat that would stay in the MWR Kennel near Pearl Harbor. We shipped the Chevy Trailblazer and Rick let us continue to use his GMC Tahoe until we left. Rick and Jeanette were life savers for us.

Right before our move we had a wedding for our oldest daughter Briana at Point Loma Submarine Base on June 8th, a Sunday afternoon, to Justin Cochetti. Everyone started rolling in the week before from everywhere. On Saturday night we did the rehearsal at our condo followed by the Groom's Dinner at Il Fornaio right behind our condo. It was a very nice event. All our parents were there. Most of Justin's family came too. We pretty much took over the Crown City Inn on Orange in Coronado. The wedding was beautiful with the ocean in the background. Lauren was the matron of honor and she and I sang a song at the reception. It was our third wedding in three years. I rented a bus to take people home who drank too much. The next day we had our traditional brunch at the condo and decided to baptize our new grandson Logan. It was a conflicted affair with many different issues going on all at the same time. It all seemed to go off fairly well and Briana and Justin left for their honeymoon in the Bahamas.

We moved out of the condo June 27th and into the BOQ at Naval Amphibious Base Coronado. Otis went to Rick and Myla stayed at the vet until our flight. VADM Curtis awarded me the Legion of Merit for my work at Surface and Air Force over the last two years. It was an honor and Gail and Mae came to help me receive it in front of my peers at Surface Force. It was my highest award and one I had always hoped I would get some day. On my last day at Surface Force all the officers formed a gauntlet for me and held hand salute as I passed through them. At the end I saluted VADM Curtis and requested to, "Move to Hawaii", which he granted. Gail and Mae watched from above in our BOQ VIP room across the street.

16
Hawaii

We flew to Hawaii July 2nd. We were met by the Pearl Harbor Chaplains and RPs who gave us lei's and picked us up in the chapel van taking us to get my Mustang at the chapel via the MWR Kennel to drop off Myla. Gail and Mae went ahead to the Hilton Hawaiian Village where we had reservations. I checked into the Command and joined my family. The following day we met with housing who offered us a small house in Makalapa across the road from Naval Station Pearl Harbor. The Command had made us Key and Essential Personnel on the same level of priority as the Commanding Officers; otherwise we would be waiting for housing for months. We turned the small house down and immediately lost our Transient Lodging Adjustment or TLA to stay at the hotel. We would have to move out of the Hilton after ten days when our TLA ran out. From then on we would be living on our housing allowance. Gail was very disappointed as we had reservations at the Hilton for two months. After ten days we moved into the BOQ at Makalapa by Pearl Harbor.

Next housing offered us an older Hawaiian house on Pearl Harbor in an area called Hale Ali'i. For months Gail had been praying for a big old Hawaiian house for us to move into. This house was not exactly what she had in mind but we could make it work. We decided to take it and planned for an August move in.

During all this time Lauren's eyes continued to worsen. Her doctor kept telling her about a possible surgery that was only being done at Duke University in

North Carolina that she might be a candidate for. It was called Macular Translocation and was very invasive. At first Lauren decided not to try for the surgery but as what little sight she had diminished, she relented and decided to try for it. She was accepted and the surgery was scheduled for August 8th. She asked Gail to go with her.

One of the first Sundays in Pearl Harbor, I searched the web and found a United Methodist Church in Aiea. We attended and the pastor asked me to lunch the following day. Over lunch I told him about Lauren and he said that his sister-in-law worked at Duke University and lived in a three bedroom home there. He called and she said she would love to have Lauren and Gail stay with her when they came. They could even use her car. An Air Force AMAC flight came open to McCord Air Force Base the end of July and I sent Mae and Gail to Lauren's awaiting their trip to Duke.

During this time our two sons Jonathan and David also decided that they wanted to move from Northern California to Marysville, WA to be closer to Lauren. They packed up everything with Aleeya and Logan and headed north arriving about the same time as Gail and Mae. They rented a place close to Lauren and started looking for jobs. Gail and I were very relieved and happy that Lauren now had some immediate family close to her. I was very proud of my two sons and daughter-in-law.

Gail and Lauren flew to Duke and the surgery was completed. Mae stayed with family in the Seattle area. I immersed myself in my new job as Region Hawaii/MIDPAC Chaplain. After surgery Gail had to help Lauren lay in certain positions for hours each day for the first week. At their first post operation appointment the doctors felt that the surgery went well and that Lauren should get some sight back in her right eye in the months ahead. She may never drive a car again but they felt she should be able to live a normal life. We were all very relieved. Lauren would have to come back in a few months to have one more surgery to complete the Macular Translocation. They flew back to Washington State and Gail and Mae flew back to Hawaii with me.

Just before they arrived I got called from housing that housing had another house they wanted us to look at. It was a huge five bedroom and five bathrooms at Makalapa that was the same size as the Admiral housing. They said it was being rehabbed and would not be ready until September. We decided to take it. It was more like the housing Gail had been praying for over the last few months. Once we accepted the house at 37 Halawa Drive, housing then told us it might not be ready until October. Gail went over and talked to the foreman working on the house and found out it might not be ready until December. We were very disappointed but decided it would still be worth it in the end if we stayed for four years to retire as we had planned. I began to look for temporary housing until December and flew to San Diego to pick up Otis.

Looking at all the options, we decide to take a temporary (temp) house at the USMC Base at Camp Smith where Marine Forces Pacific (MARFORPAC) and Pacific Command (PACOM) where located. The houses were slated to be demolished in April 09. The one we selected was a four bedroom two bath and had a big lanai looking over Pearl Harbor and Hickam Air Force Base. It sat right on the edge of a rain forest high on the mountain. Wildlife and trails were all around. Otis would love it. I flew to San Diego for a conference and brought Otis back with me from Rick's.

We got Myla out of the MWR prison and moved in to the temp housing with temp furniture. Some of our friends at the BOQ also moved in next to us. It wasn't perfect but it was an improvement plus the animals were much happier.

There was a lot going on at work with the Navy Region and MIDPAC areas of responsibility. The admiral was a friend from the past but was leaving soon to take another Command. We also started to get ready for Lauren's second surgery at Duke. The first one had given her improved vision, 20/80, but it was double and at a 45 degree angle. The second one would correct the angle. Gail would go again, drop Mae at Beth's take Lauren to Duke and return. It would take about a month. She would also spend time with our children and new grandson plus our sisters and her dad who had taken a serious fall and had been in the hospital. She had started home schooling Mae because of all the trips. We had never done this with any of the other children.

I was trying to get into hunting on Oahu. There was only one place to go on the Leeward side, Kaena Point, where we had satellite tracking stations high on the hills. The state had planted some grouse, chukar and pheasant there. I met another officer, Lee, who had a German Shorthair and we stared making plans to go hunting. I needed a shotgun so when our friend Lenny came for a visit; I borrowed one from his gun safe in his Kailua home. Hunting licenses were also a problem but we finally met all the Hawaii regulations to get one. My hunting friend Lee and I went up to Kaena Point to scout out the area, run the dogs and shoot some clay pigeons.

Lee and I started hunting at Kaena Point with our shorthairs. We did pretty well the first couple of times. We even made friends with some of the local hunters who also had shorthairs. Everyone loved Otis and he was in true hunting form, his sixth season. I even took him to Kauai to hunt but we got rained out. Lenny hooked me up with some of his friends in Maui and I hunted there too but without Otis. Gail, Mae and I took the cruiser Lake Erie over for a weekend.

Gail had been gone for a month with Mae taking Lauren to Duke for yet another successful surgery. The day she returned I left for a week on a Guided Missile Destroyer for a missile defense shoot. We missed each other by a few hours. Lauren would need one more surgery in January. It looked like she would get some sight back.

Christmas we decided to go to Marysville, WA to be with most of our kids. Everyone would be there except Briana and Justin. Gail and Mae flew ahead and I joined them just before Christmas. When I left Honolulu the temperature was 80 degrees. When I landed in Seattle it was 16 degrees and lots of snow on the ground. Jonathan and Aleeya picked me up after 10 PM and took me to a Wal-Mart on the way to their house at midnight to get a hunting license. By 6 A.M. I was sitting in a duck blind with Jonathan and Tyler. The hunting was fantastic. We hunting five days in a row with my two sons and son-in-law in the cold and snow and killed many ducks and geese. My only regret was that I did not bring Otis. He would have loved it. My bag got lost coming over and so I had no winter clothes. I had to borrow clothes from all my sons. My bag finally showed up just before I flew back to Hawaii. We had a wonderful holiday time with most of our children, their spouses and our new grandson Logan.

January Lauren made one more trek to Duke but this time she went with her friend Nicole instead of Gail. It was supposed to be a simple procedure. When she got back things were looking good until her retina detached one Sunday morning. They rushed her to the hospital for emergency surgery. The doctors were able to reattach the retina but most of the gains she had made at Duke had been lost. It looked like she would spend the rest of her life with very little sight. She quit her job and went on disability. We were all very disappointed for her but continued to pray and hope for a miracle. She and Tyler were not doing well. They began to get some professional help and started to get more involved with their church where Lauren began to sing with their praise team.

January 9th, 2009 we moved into our new Makalapa house. It was fantastic and everything we had hoped it would be. Two days after moving in my sister Suzanne and her husband Harold showed up for a two week visit. It was hectic but we still managed to have a good time. Lauren came next for about a three week stay. We enjoyed having her with us and Hawaii seemed to heal her psyche. She returned though with more problems with her marriage.

Once hunting season was over, I started getting back into golf, taking some lessons. The other three 0-6 Navy Chaplains on Oahu and I began to golf together every Sunday afternoon. It was good fellowship and my game began to improve. I got a new admiral during this time and moved my office to the headquarters building out of the chapel. My position had not been part of the chapel for ten years but none of the previous captains had been willing to give up their big office at the chapel. I got tired of being mistaken as the chapel pastor and not being part of the admiral's staff so I moved into a smaller office on their third floor with a great view of the harbor. The first week I had many of the staff in my office who had never been there before. It was the right move.

The Chaplain Corps Flag Admiral selection list

finally came out and once again I was not selected for Rear Admiral (RDML) lower half or one star. In the Navy Chaplain Corps of about 860 active chaplains, we have 60 captains and only two admirals, a one star and a two star. Every three years we select one more RDML from the 60 captains. Since I have not worked for a four star admiral in what we call an Echelon II job such as Pacific Fleet, I did not expect to be selected. I even sensed God tell me a few weeks before the results came out that I would not be on it. Still I had a one in sixty chance and I knew some of the members of the board and had good Captain Fitness Reports. Gail was praying that I would not be selected because she did not want to move to Washington, DC and she did not want me to work until I was age 65 or older. If selected I would have become the one star Deputy Chaplain of the Navy and Chaplain of the Marine Corps for about three or four years. At the end of that time I would probably be nominated to become the two star Rear Admiral upper half (RADM) Chief of Chaplains, for three or four more years. Both of these positions are in Washington, DC.

A good friend of mine, Mark, was selected to become the RDML one star Deputy. We served together in Yokosuka, Japan and I even baptized one of his children on the cruiser Reeves when our friend Lenny was the Executive Officer (XO). Mark also went to seminary at Fuller as I did. Mark's father was a three star Vice Admiral (VADM) and his brother was also selected to RADM, two stars. Mark had also held some Echelon II positions. I congratulated him on the good news. I never really aspired to become the Chief of Navy Chaplains and did not think I had much of a chance but I would have done the job if God had called me to it. If I served until age 62, mandatory retirement for Navy Captains, I would have one more opportunity to become an admiral. Navy chaplain admirals can serve until age 68. I really did not want to work past age 62 and did not want to move from Hawaii to DC. I felt very blessed and honored to be a Navy Captain.

The first six months we were in our new base house we had 23 overnight visitors stay with us. It was exhausting but we felt that God had given us that great big house to offer hospitality to others. Two of the guests were the Navy Chief of Chaplains RADM Bob and his wife Evelyn, long time friends of ours. Bob had sent me to Hawaii to the job I held. Three of the other visitors were our son Jonathan, his wife Aleeya and our 14 month old grandson Logan. They stayed for ten days and Logan ran us all ragged chasing him around and keeping him out of trouble. He was into everything, turning buttons off and on and causing general havoc. When they finally left we really missed having our little grandson around. We looked forward to seeing more of them in retirement.

During this time Gail, Mae and I made several trips to Kauai and Maui Staying at various places. Gail decided to send Mae to Washington State for the second half of the summer. Gail followed her a couple of weeks later. I had the house to myself with Otis and Myla until mid August. Then I flew to Florida for our annual 0-6 and above Navy chaplain Senior Leadership Symposium (SLS) in St. Petersburg, Florida. Gail joined me from Seattle but got stuck and had to spend the night in Denver on the way. We had a nice hotel and enjoyed seeing all our long time friends in the Chaplain Corps.

Just before SLS we had our current chaplain one star not get his second star to become the Chief of Navy Chaplains. He had to retire early. Our two star RADM Bob was asked by the Chief of Naval Operations to stay on for another year so they could have another RDML

Chaplain Board in November 2009. It seemed to me many of the aspiring admiral chaplains, knowing they had another shot at promotion, spent the conference jockeying for position and recognition. By the end of the week I was sick of it all. I was quickly reaching the point where I had absolutely no interest in the politics of the Corps.

One job that I had always wanted to have was the Pacific Fleet/Pacific Command Chaplain working for two four star admirals in Hawaii. Gail, Mae and I loved Hawaii and never wanted to leave. Pacific Fleet and Pacific Command was the only other job I wanted. It was coming open March of 2010. I let the Chief of Chaplains know that I would like the job. Many other people who were more politically connected also wanted it. I let the powers to be know and put it into God's hands.

At Christmas Gail and I decided to surprise all our children who had gathered for Christmas Eve dinner at Gail's sister Beth's house in Seattle. We told them we were not coming because we had come the Christmas before and everyone was suppose to come to Hawaii that year but didn't. At the last minute Gail found cheap tickets and we flew Christmas Eve arriving in time for the dinner. We told no one we were coming. We called them from outside the house and told them to open the door. It was a grand reunion with all our children and their spouses and grandson. We stayed at the Smokey Point BOQ and did most of our gatherings at Lauren and Tyler's. Briana and Justin stayed at Lauren's. I even got some hunting in with my sons and son-in-law but it was not as good as the year before because no snow. We flew back New Year's Eve.

Lauren's situation suddenly got worse when her marriage began to fall apart. They had been having serious problems since February 2009. They tried but it did not work. It all came to a head with Tyler leaving in April 2010. We were all decimated. Gail flew to be with Lauren for a month. They wound up going together to Mexico to stay in a time share Lauren owned. During that trip Lauren met a man named Mike from Wisconsin. They struck up a close friendship and started Skyping on a regular basis. Soon they were visiting each other's homes. Mike was a divorced father of two boys who worked in sales for a welding supply.

Before we knew it, Lauren and Mike were in love. Lauren was being forced to declare bankruptcy as Tyler did and they were losing both of their homes. She was also losing Tyler's health care. She hired a lawyer to get some spousal support but the lawyer was not optimistic she would get anything. "Blood out of a turnip" was the term he used. Mike offered to pack Lauren out of her house and move her to WI until her divorce was over. He would also try to get her on his health care. They planned to get married.

Gail had met Mike but I had not. I visited Lauren on a business trip and got to meet and say hello to Mike on Skype through the computer. He seemed nice enough. We were just concerned she was moving way too fast. We wanted her to get through her divorce and then start to think again about marriage. It was not going to happen the way we wanted.

I came up one more time for Rear Admiral one star. I did not expect to make it but I did think I had a chance at the Pacific Fleet /Pacific Command Chaplain job. When the Chief of Chaplains visited in November he told me that he supported me in that request. I thought I might have it. Shortly after his visit the Pacific Fleet Admiral even asked for my biography.

When the new one star Rear Admiral Deputy Chief of Chaplains was selected, everyone was

416

surprised. The person they selected was a female. She would become the first female chaplain to make flag rank. Many of her male colleagues were shocked. I was not. Now I finally knew I was at what we call my 'terminal rank'. I would retire as a captain. I would have liked to make rear admiral if possible but was delighted that I had made captain. Many of my friends who were very good chaplains did not get that far. My goal was always to make commander and retire with 20 years. To make captain and retire with 30 active years was a great blessing and honor.

Shortly after this announcement the results also came out for the new Pacific Fleet and Pacific Command Chaplain job. It went to the chaplain who had the similar job in the Atlantic. I was disappointed to say the least. Now I was also in my 'terminal job'. I needed to extend on my orders for one year to reach mandatory retirement age of 62 and stay in Hawaii. I contacted the Detailers who had me put in a request through my rear admiral. He was glad to approve it and I got the extension. If I stayed healthy I would retire from the Navy with over 30 years of active service, over 34 total, in June 2012 at age 62. Thank you Jesus!

I began to think about real retirement. Would I be able to actually retire in June 2012? Gail and I wanted to take over our Waikiki condo and also buy a place in Washington State close to most of our children , grandson, sisters and dads. We began to crunch the numbers to see if it was possible. The recession had taken a toll on our investments. After doing a retirement budget and looking at all possible sources of retirement income, we decided that we would have to wait until July 2016 when I could begin receiving full social security benefits. We hoped that by then the economy and stock market would improve and our investments would come back. I didn't really want to keep working, I had been working since I was about 14, but I had to keep working if I wanted to retire in Hawaii and Washington State with any money to live on.

I needed to figure out what I was going to do for the next four years after Navy retirement. I held a Top Secret clearance until 2015 which was very marketable with the government and many military contractors. I felt that I had to continue in Christian ministry as that was my calling from the Lord and where my gifts were, especially preaching. I decided to ask the Bishop and Cabinet of the Pacific Northwest (PNW) Annual Conference for a church in June 2012. This was my original home conference that I had pastored in and come to the Navy from. I was still a member there in good standing and eligible for appointment to a church until I was 72. October of 2009 I was at a gathering of all the clergy in the PNW in Wenatchee, WA. I talked to my District Superintendent and the Bishop about an appointment to a church in June 2012. Both seemed very encouraging and hopeful.

My youngest daughter Mae started surfing with her older brother David when he visited. I started going out with her and got a lesson too, not bad for 59 years old. I even got up on my first try. Mae and I began to surf together at White Plains Beach. We would take our children there when they visited and get them a lesson too. I was only good for about an hour at a time. Surfing is exhausting, especially paddling out.

July 2010 I started a series of remarkable four trips. The first one was to Christian Healing Ministries School of Christian Healing II in Jacksonville, FL with Francis and Judith MacNutt. I took Lauren with me. She and I had attending the first one four years earlier in Dallas, TX. I took her hoping for healing of her eyes and to learn more about the healing and deliverance ministry. It was a week long course and she and I sat together up front every day where she could see a little. The talks and worship were amazing but the workshops made it a long day for Lauren.

We were staying at an inexpensive motel at the airport and taking the shuttle each day to the school. The place was packed with people from all denominations all over the world. Lauren wanted more personal ministry than teaching but we finally were able to have her prayed for. Her prayer group asked if she had ever lived overseas. Lauren got a mental picture of washing her hands in ritual water at one of the numerous Buddhist and Shinto shrines we had visited on our Japan tour. They felt that possibly someone overseas had put a curse on her and that could be related to her rare eye disease. They prayed to break it. She did not have any improvement in her vision but felt she had received some inner healing. They all wanted her to come back for the intensive three day prayer ministry done once a quarter.

I sensed at the end of the week that the Lord was telling me that I had spiritual post traumatic stress disorder (PTSD). This spiritual PTSD was a culmination of being involved in fulltime Christian ministry over a thirty-six year period involving many traumatic scenarios including two church splits, multiple military deployments in dangerous places of combat, ministry at the Pentagon and New York City in 9/11 and during Hurricanes Katrina and Rita. I sensed that I too needed to come back for the three day intensive prayer ministry, especially before I took another full time church in July 2012. Lauren and I made plans to return in 2011 together.

The second remarkable trip was one to Oberammergau, Germany with Rear Admiral (lower half) Jim, Medical Corps retired, my former Commanding Officer in Yokosuka, Japan. My dermatologist at the Pearl Harbor Medical Clinic, Dr. Klaus Rennert, was originally from Germany. As a young man he and his father had served the German Air Force, Luftwaffe, during the end of World War II. After the war he attended medical school and came to the United States. He tried private practice and eventually became a medical doctor in the United States Navy moving to Hawaii. After his discharge he continued in the clinic as a contract doctor and was now in his 80's working three days a week. We became good friends.

Klaus was once given a free ticket to attend the world renowned every ten year Passion Play in Oberammergau, Germany south of Munich in the mountains of Bavaria near Austria. In 1633 the Black Plague threatened the little Bavarian village and they all prayed God would spare them. Many other villages were completely wiped out. If God would spare them, the people of Oberammergau promised to put on a play of the last week of Jesus' earthly life every ten years. After that prayer, no one else died. Since that time, Oberammergau has put on this play every ten years except for once during the Nazi Regime. Klaus attended the first one in 1950 after World War II. He now wanted to pay back his free ticket and send me. I had always wanted to go but did not want to go alone. I put out a call to all my email Prayer Warriors to see if anyone else wanted to attend with me. My former boss and friend Admiral Jim said he would go. Gail had no interest in going to Europe for such a short trip.

I flew to Munich from Honolulu via an overnight in Denver and stop at Dulles Airport to meet Jim at the Munich airport where he had arrived from Florida. We took the train to Munich and shared an inexpensive room there that included breakfast. The first day we visited one of the many beer gardens.

Munich is a wonderful city. The second day we took a bus to Oberammergau to attend the play.

The entire town of Oberammergau is involved in putting on this play every ten years. Over 2700 people are in the play. You must possess a birth certificate from Oberammergau to participate in the play. The people of this town do everything including music, costumes, lighting, scripts and acting. It is one of the marvels of this world. The play goes from May to October five days a week to 5,000 people a performance from all over the world. It is all in German but not hard to follow if you know the Bible story. I was really touched by this dramatic live presentation of the last week of Jesus' earthly life, especially the crucifixion. It was so real. It went from 2:30 PM to 10 PM with a three hour dinner break. The people waiting on us in the restaurant for dinner were also in the play later in the evening. It was an experience I will never forget.

Our last day we continued to visit Munich and had dinner with a retired German Admiral and his wife that Jim knew from his NATO days. They gave us a tour and took us to a wonderful monastery for dinner. We got back late that night. I flew all the way home to Honolulu from Munich the following day. It took me 24 hours stopping in Dulles and San Francisco. Klaus had given me a gift of a lifetime. The next chance to attend this play would be in 2020.

The third remarkable trip was a 39th wedding anniversary present from Gail. She had booked us a cruise from Seattle to Alaska and back. We left on our wedding anniversary August 28th and returned a week later. Our friends Lenny and Jean went with us. We stopped in Ketchikan, Juneau, Skagway and Prince Rupert. It was absolutely beautiful. I had commercial fished these waters as a young man and had always wanted to share this part of the world with Gail. She got us a balcony room and we kept the door open most of the trip looking at the incredible scenery at all hours of the day and night. I also gained seven pounds eating everything I wanted for a week three times a day. We saw salmon jumping, eagles flying and hundreds of whales. It was amazing. My Bishop in Seattle had some United Methodist Churches in Alaska but I did not think I could talk Gail into letting me take one after Navy retirement. It was too far from our families and very cold in the winters.

The fourth remarkable trip was another one to Kodiak, Alaska with my two sons, son-in-law Justin and fourteen year old daughter Mae. For years I had taken my sons and son-in-law Tyler to Kodiak to fish for Silver Salmon the first week of October. It had been four years since we had done it. Justin and Mae had never been. Mae was the only one of my three daughters who really wanted to go. Her school Fall Break just happened to coincide with our plans.

I flew them all with Alaska Air miles. We came from three cities, Honolulu, Marysville and Sacramento and all arrived Saturday October 2nd. I got a big rental car at the airport and checked us into the USCG Guest House on the base. Sunday I attended worship at the chapel and the Protestant Chaplain Carl had us all over for a halibut and salmon dinner. The next morning we started to fish for Silvers, or Coho, on the Buskin River. Mae, Justin and David hooked Silvers early and all signs were pointing to a very successful day. Suddenly a huge Kodiak brown bear came down the hill fast at David and Jonathan. Mae and I were on the other side of the river with Justin.

Kodiak browns are some of the biggest bears in the world often reaching nine feet in height. We blew air horns, I shot Carl's loaned .357 Magnum hand gun, all to no avail, and we dropped all our gear and ran for our lives. The bear was close behind David and Jonathan and closing fast. Jonathan was carrying two of the fish we had just caught. I yelled at him to throw one to the bear. He did and the bear picked up the salmon and headed back. We waited at the car for him to leave the area and then went back for our gear. Our hearts were pumping solid adrenaline and we heaved a sigh of relief we were all safe. We decided to move to the other end of the river with hopes we would not see the bear again.

We continued fishing for another couple of hours and Mae hooked another big Silver salmon. Jonathan took it to the car and shortly after he and David fell in the icy river together. They took the car and headed back to the base to change. No sooner had they left than another monster Kodiak brown bear came up the stream at us. Mae was with Justin on one side of the river and I was directly across from them on the other bank. He started for me and then headed straight for Mae. Once again we blew air horns and I shot off the .357 but the bear did not seem concerned. He had Mae and Justin cornered and Justin kept yelling at me what to do. I did not know what to tell him. They crossed the deep river and got soaked. The bear followed homing in on salmon roe they were carrying in sacks on their belts. They shot up the steep hill in heavy woods and the bear turned back looking at me. Once again we waited for him to leave and then went and got all the gear we had left.

At this point we decided we had enough of Kodiak brown bears. The fish were in the Buskin but it was just too dangerous to continue fishing there. We tried our old favorite the Olds River and the Pasagshak River. We had no bites in either one. The following day we went back to them again with the same result. I was growing very discouraged and afraid we were going to come home with very few fish when I got a call from a young Coast Guard Petty Officer Brandyn who offered to take us out fishing on his boat. It was an answer to prayer.

Wednesday morning we went out with Brandyn in his 23 foot steel work skiff with a covered pilot house. We motored around to the other side of Kodiak and began to catch halibut, ling cod, yellow eye and black rock fish, all good eating. It was a beautiful sunny Alaskan day in some of the most gorgeous scenery in the world. Mae caught 15 fish by herself. One was a double. She hooked a rock fish that was swallowed by a huge ling cod as it was surfacing. We also pulled three snow crab pots. By the time we were done we had enough fish and crab to fill five coolers. It was a successful fishing trip in spite of the bears. We flew back in shifts to Anchorage, Seattle and Sacramento with our frozen coolers. Mae and I spent the night in Marysville to see my grandson Logan who was growing like a weed and talking up a storm. So ended my four remarkable trips July to October 2010. Thank you Lord for adventure, beauty, inspiration, safety, fun and time with my family and loved ones.

About this time I began to get several emails from my United Methodist Bishop in Seattle. The first one he sent I did not recognize the email address. I asked Gail who she thought it was and she said, "What is your Bishop's name?" I was blown away. In my 34 years of ordained ministry, I had never received a personal email or note from my Bishop. He had four influential United Methodist Bishops visiting Hawaii, he called them "heavy hitters", and he wanted to know if I would help them get the VIP Pacific Fleet Remembrance Tour of Pearl Harbor and the Arizona Memorial. I organized the outing and Gail helped me plan a lunch at our quarters after with their spouses. I invited another Navy Captain United Methodist and his spouse to join us.

The day of the tour, our new one star reserve Navy Chief of Chaplains, a Presbyterian pastor in Bakersfield, CA, was also in town and wanting a tour. I had them all go together. The reserve Rear Admiral really added to their tour with his Summer White uniform. Lunch at the house went great. They all stayed for hours. Afterward, they all told me they would speak to my Bishop about giving me a great appointment after Navy retirement. Later I learned from my Bishop they were all with him at a meeting and said, "If you don't give Doug a good appointment, we will". Once more, I was totally blown away.

My Bishop began to email me asking when I could come back home to the Pacific Northwest Annual Conference to take a local church appointment. He wanted me as soon as possible. I told him that I wanted to achieve my goal of thirty active years of Navy active duty for retirement. I would hit that mark in January of 2012 for a February 1, 2012 retirement date. With leave and house hunting time I could conceivably leave active duty the end of November 2011, move to Washington State and start with a new church in January 2012. He told me to put my retirement papers in and plan on it. He would appoint me in January 2012 and bring an interim pastor in from July 2011 until I came. Most United Methodist appointments begin July 1st of each year.

Just before Christmas we got a call from our oldest daughter Briana and she and Justin were going to have a baby girl named Zoey Mae. We were ecstatic. Briana is our oldest and she married in her 30's. If she was going to have children, she needed to get started.

Her due date was May 10, 2011. Gail promised to be there with her for the birth.

That hunting season my partner Lee with his dog Bella were out for most of the season. He broke his right arm running her on a leash with his bike. I picked up a new partner for a few weeks, Chris, who was an Air Force Lieutenant Colonel. He had a German Shorthair Pointer (GSP) male he bought and trained in Germany, solid liver. Otis hunted circles around him. Otis is the best hunting dog I had ever had or seen. Though in Hawaii, he got many pheasants up for me that I simply missed. I could not understand it. We did get a few. We bred Otis again to Kahlua on Ford Island. She got pregnant again with eleven puppies, same as the last time. They went for $1000 apiece. We got either our choice of the litter or the price of one pup. Gail said again, we could only handle one GSP at a time; they are just too high maintenance.

For the first time in three seasons, we decided to stay in Hawaii for the Christmas and New Year holidays. Our grown children were scattered in three other states and there was no way for all of us to get together. Christmas Eve we spent with our good friends Klaus and Patti. I preached the Coast Guard Lighthouse Christmas Eve Service and we went out to dinner and to another historic Hawaiian Church for a late candle light service. Christmas day was lonely as we had been with most of our children and grandson the last two years. It was nice though to relax and not be running around airports, getting rental cars and staying at the officer's quarters on some base.

The end of January 2011 Gail and I flew to Columbia, South Carolina for our last Navy Captain and above Professional Development Training Course (PDTC). It was located at our new Chaplain School now located with the Army and the Air Force at Fort

Jackson, SC. We had a great time with all of the chaplains and spouses we had known for almost 30 years. Many were retiring.

On the way to South Carolina we stopped for a few days at my mom and dad's at Sun City West in Arizona. They were both in their mid 80's and doing well except my mom's Alzheimer's had progressed. She still knew who we were but could not remember Gail's name or the names of our children and grandchildren. Dad was still sharp and seemed to able to take care of her. We worried about them but there was not much we could do. They chose many years ago to live apart from the rest of the family. We felt they would be OK for a few more years unless something happened to dad. I got to play golf with dad and made a CD of all of his financial arrangements in case we had to step in and help. He was planning on putting everything in a living trust for Sue and me to save the cost of probate at their death. I also talked him into a fire safe.

On the way back from the PDTC we stopped at Sacramento to see Briana and Justin for a few days. We wanted to see our oldest daughter pregnant with her daughter. It was a good visit and we had a lot of fun. It is always hard to say goodbye to our loved ones.

During the PDTC we learned that the Marysville, WA United Methodist Church were two of our sons live was coming open July 2011. I emailed the Bishop and told him we were interested. He emailed back that Marysville would be a good appointment but he had something larger and more strategically important to the Annual Conference he wanted me to consider. We tried to figure out what church that might be. During February we had two couples from the Annual Conference stay with us at different times and we tried to determine what church that might be. My guess was the Cornerstone Church in Covington, WA southeast of Seattle. It was a large fairly conservative United Methodist church. The pastor had started it 24 years ago and was due to transfer.

Jonathan, Aleeya and Logan came to visit us again in March. Jonathan had just been laid off from the restaurant he had been managing in Woodinville, WA. He was tired and needed a break. I set up the train set for Logan and we had a lot of fun. In five minutes Logan had the knack of spreading all of his toys all over the house. He was talking like crazy. Gail and I really miss him when they leave.

In the middle of that visit, I got a call one night from the Seattle United Methodist District Superintendent (DS). The Bishop and his Cabinet had met and decided they wanted to appoint me as the next pastor of the Covington Cornerstone United Methodist Church effective January 2011. I was very honored. Cornerstone was the second largest United Methodist Church of 245 in Washington, northern Idaho and Alaska. I would never have guessed they would offer me such an important church after being gone in the military for the past 27 years. I called the pastor and they had three Sunday morning services. On holidays such as Easter and Christmas the attendance was very large for a United Methodist Church in that part of the world. It seemed they were an amazing congregation who gave 10% of their gross offerings to missions over and above what they gave to the United Methodist Church. As a result, God had blessed them greatly. Their worship had a full praise band at each service. It sounded like a good fit for me.

Gail was not very excited. She envisioned me in a much slower paced congregation closer to our sons, daughter-in-law and grandson. She was concerned I would be working way to hard with three Sunday morning services. Mae just had her first real boyfriend Brandon and did not want to leave Hawaii. We decided to pray, fast and ask God what he wanted us to do. We had to get back to the DS on our decision the end of the week. We ended our prayer time at the old tiki bar on Sand Island, La Marinara. Over dinner we decided to say yes to Cornerstone. Gail found out one of her closest childhood friends, Claudette, and her husband had helped start the church. Right after we left the restaurant, a great earthquake hit Japan and a tsunami wave was on its way to Hawaii. We were all up most of the night. The tsunami did not really hit Pearl Harbor but it did take out the marina at La Marinara sinking over 20 boats and destroying the docks. The restaurant was not touched. Japan was crushed and many died and lost their homes.

I called the DS and said we would be honored to accept their nomination to pastor the Covington Cornerstone Church. She said the procedure then was for her to contact the church and set up a meeting between them and me. We set up the meeting for the evening of April 11, 2011. I flew to Seattle on the red eye Friday April 8th to spend some time with our family. The Cornerstone pastor and his wife were on the same flight coming back from a Hawaiian vacation. On Sunday April 10th, my two sons, Aleeya, Logan plus David's girlfriend Catelyn all joined me in visiting the Cornerstone 11 AM service. We did not tell them we were coming and tried to act like new visitors. We all loved it. Afterward we had a big family reunion in North Bend at my niece Justine's house. I visited my sister Sue in Monroe later in heavy rain. This move was going to take some getting used to after sunny and warm Hawaii.

The day April 11th I visited with the DS, Bishop and Cabinet at their Des Moines headquarters. I had dinner with the pastor Daniel and his wife Anita and met with the church Staff Parish Relations Committee at 7 PM. The DS brought me in and introduced me as their new pastor. They asked me many questions and I gave them my Christian testimony. I went out and they discussed me for a long time. I sat in the sanctuary and thought what I would do if they did not want me. I knew I was older than what they wanted in a new pastor. After a long time the DS came out to ask me how I felt. She said they wanted me as their pastor if I still wanted to come. I was very relieved and excited. I stayed at the pastor's house that night and called Gail to tell her the news. The next morning I met with a realtor and looked over the area we would be moving to. I flew home that night.

As the birth of Zoey got closer, Gail tried unsuccessfully to take a military flight from Hickam in Hawaii to Travis Air Force Base near Sacramento. She tried for four days and every flight was canceled. Finally she gave up and flew commercial. The plan was for her to be with Briana for the birth. Mae and I would come later in the month when she got out of school and we all hoped to fly back together on military air.

Gail stayed with Briana and Justine for three weeks before Zoey Mae Cochetti was born on May 24, 2011. Briana was very late and the doctors decided to induce her on the 23rd but were unsuccessful. Suddenly it looked like Briana was unable to dilate and Zoey was in distress. The doctors quickly took Briana into the ER to do an emergency C-Section birth. Neither Gail nor Justin was able to be present. They were all very disappointed. The good news was that Zoey was born healthy and Briana recovered quickly from the emergency surgery. Zoey was our first granddaughter.

After Mae finished school on May 26th, she and

I tried to take a military flight from Hickam to Travis AFB. After a few days we were able to get out. We spent about five days with Briana, Justin, Zoey and Gail in Roseville near Sacramento. Zoey was a joy to behold. She was so small and cute. She looked a lot like Briana when she was first born, dark hair and dark eyes. We all laughed as she kept sticking her feet straight out and her arms down by her side. The time passed quickly and Gail, Mae and I caught a C-17 flight back to Hickam from Travis. It was a tearful goodbye as always. We really missed them all.

That summer I decided I needed to write the story of my friend Dr. Klaus' life. He was brilliant, had met Adolph Hitler when he was eight, served in the Hitler Youth and became a Luftwaffe Messerschmitt pilot like his dad, was almost killed and captured by the invading Russian Army, walked out of post war Germany, came to America with nothing to become a doctor and self made millionaire, joined the United States Navy as a doctor, made Commander and was still working at a Navy medical clinic in his 80's. Klaus had many sayings but one hit me hard, "When an old man dies, a library burns".

I would visit Klaus in his office every Tuesday afternoon and tape the story of his life. Later I put it in writing. Before we knew it we had a book with pictures. We entitled it "God's Little Helper", a title Klaus used to talk about his work as a dermatologist. A local Hawaiian publisher put it into print and we began to give copies out. It was never intended to make money. Klaus attended a few book signings and spoke to a group of marines. I later did the same thing for my dad and father-in-law about their WWII war experiences. When an old man dies, his library should not burn completely. That is why I am writing this.

Gail decided to buy the second house she was

shown. It was about 2600 square feet and had been remodeled and in a safe gated community. We found out later it was also in Meridian Valley Country Club. The only down side was it had a flat roof. I was not excited about the roof but told Gail if she liked it to buy it. She did and I owned a home I never saw until a few months later. After being married for over 41 years I trusted Gail's judgment. Also, if she is happy, so am I.

Saturday October 1st we had all of our children, their spouses and grandchildren in Hawaii for Lauren's wedding to Michael Smith from Onalaska, Wisconsin. This was a second marriage for both of them. Mike brought his two children Cade and Mason, his parents, sister and her family. Lauren only had her siblings, their spouses and children. Lauren and Mike's family stayed at the Hale Koa Hotel in Waikiki. They had never been to Hawaii. Everyone else stayed at our house.

This was the second time in three years we had a wedding to put on just as we were moving. We got the Admiral's Cabin at White Plain's Beach and did the wedding on the beach at sunset. It was a beautiful setting. Our friend Klaus Rennert and his wife Patty also came with Mae's boyfriend Brandon . Brandon played the ukulele and did break dancing. Right after the wedding we baptized our newest grandchild, Zoey Mae Cochetti. Both services were done while standing in the surf at sunset. I had been blessed to officiate at the weddings of all of my children and to baptize my first two biological grandchildren. We held the reception at the cabin. It was all a very simple and fun affair. The week following we got all our family together for a hike and early October Thanksgiving dinner at the Makalapa house.

It was over before we knew it and we started gearing up for the movers and saying goodbye to all our

Hawaii and Navy friends. We shipped all of our possessions for hopefully the last time, moved out of our beautiful Hawaiian home and moved into our friends Lenny and Jean's lovely house in Kailua on the other side of the island. I would take Mae to school on my way to work each day and pick her up on the way home. She spent a lot of time at her boyfriend Brandon's house. This move was tough on her giving up her Hawaiian lifestyle, surfing and her boyfriend. It was tough on all of us. We loved Hawaii and did not want to leave but looked forward to our new home, job and being closer to family.

My last day in a Navy uniform was November 28, 2011. We had many goodbye lunches and dinners with the chaplains, civilian employees, the chapel, wardroom and the Federal Firefighters whose Bible study I attended for over three years. Gail and I decided we did not want to have a retirement ceremony. They were expensive, none of our close friends and family would be able to attend and we would rather spend the money on a retirement cruise. The command asked me if I would like to have a shadow box made as my retirement gift from the wardroom made up of all the officers. I said I would love to have one. They show case your career in a beautiful wooden display case.

The night of November 28th I took the red eye flight first class to San Francisco to pick up the SUV I had shipped there and my duck boat. My cousin Craig had graciously kept my duck boat in his warehouse in Salinas, CA for over three years while we were in Hawaii. I was looking forward to getting it back out duck hunting with my dog and sons.

A friend of many years from Navy Boot Camp, Reed, picked me up and helped me get the SUV. I drove to Craig's and spent the night. The next day I took him duck hunting at my old spot near Novato, CA. Afterwards I drove to Sacramento with my boat to spend a few days with Briana, Justin and Zoey. I eventually headed north stopping at our good friends Ceci and Tudor in Winston, OR and Lee in Portland on the way.

I rolled into our new home in a gated country club community and immediately found out my boat would fit in the garage. I took our express shipment of 1000 pounds the next day and got us all set up to live until our household goods arrived. I also picked up our second car, the Mustang convertible, I had shipped to Seattle. I was ready for the family to arrive.

I flew back to Hawaii to take Gail on our Hawaiian retirement cruise to four Hawaiian Islands. We went with our good Navy friends Mark and Lynn. Mae stayed with friends. On our second day out we got a call that Gail's older sister Joan had died of cancer at her home. We were devastated. Gail had hoped to come home and spend time with her sister nursing her during her final days. The family told us to stay on the cruise and they would have the service when we arrived in Seattle the end of the month. We did stay but the joy of retirement was gone the rest of our time in Hawaii.

We returned from the cruise and checked into the Hale Koa for our last five nights on the island. Mark and Lynn came with us and Mae too. On December 22nd we got our pets out of the kennel and caught the red eye to Seattle landing early in the morning of December 23rd. It was cold and raining. We were ready to start our new life back in the Pacific Northwest where we had started out for the Navy chaplaincy 27 ½ years earlier. What amazing things had transpired in those busy years. Thanks be to God!

17

Cornerstone Church

The church secretary Jan picked us all up at the airport and took us to our new home with the dog and the cat. Parishioner and staff member Trish brought us some food gifts from the new church. December 24th I made my preaching debut at Covington Cornerstone Church at three services. Over 750 attended. By the third service at 11 P.M., I could hardly stay awake. Gail went to her sister Beth's house with Mae. My sister Sue and her husband Harold came to the second service.

I did not start officially at the new church until the middle of January 2012. I used the few weeks of retirement to work on the new house and get the family settled. Right off the bat we had an ice storm and snow. The power went out and huge tree limbs came down breaking the deck rail. It was freezing cold out and I had to buy studded snow tires for the Mustang convertible and a chain saw. Thankfully we had a new generator we had purchased before we left Hawaii and had shipped to Jonathan. It helped us get through the power outage with our gas fireplace.

My first Sunday at the church was January 22nd. The Believe worship team decided to have a Hawaiian theme to make us feel welcome. They had lei's for everyone. I gave my testimony at the 9 and 10:30 A.M. services. Attendance was about 300 and another 100 children. It seemed like a great congregation. The entire church was modeled after the book The Simple Church. Everything in the church was grouped into Believe, Connect, Serve and Share categories. The church didn't do anything unless it fit into those four categories. It was very unique. I followed a pastor who had started the church 24 years before. He and his wife did a terrific job. I inherited a great staff of 10 talented individuals who love and serve the Lord.

I tried not to do anything too different from what they had been doing before I arrived. Their founding pastor had left in June 2011 and the church had a six month interim pastor before I arrived. They had lost some members in the process and giving had gone down a little. All and all, the church was in pretty good shape. I felt very blessed and fortunate to be their new pastor even though the weather was hard to take after Hawaii.

Because of the snow, Mae did not start school for quite a few weeks when the new semester started. We were concerned about how she would fit in to her new high school as an Asian. She told us that her school was loaded with Asians and we were very relieved. She also really liked the new church youth group that was preparing for a mission trip to Peru.

Jonathan, David and I got to do some duck hunting together the first month we were back. I would leave the boat at Jonathan's and we would put in at Marysville and hunt the slough there. We only got a few and one goose but had a great time getting back out together. I also joined a pheasant club in Ellensburg and we got out there a few times too. I really missed my sons.

Our family joined the social part of the new country club and Gail and I started having lunch there occasionally. It had the best view and food of any restaurant in town. They had a great golf course and club but it was way too expensive for us.

Mae finally got settled in school and made some friends. She also started attending the church youth group that she enjoyed. They were planning a mission trip to Peru in the summer to build houses in Ica. Mae and Gail went to Hawaii for spring break and Mae got some surfing in. We also took her to Westport to surf in a full wet suit off the Pacific Northwest coast in its icy water. She didn't like it but planned to go back.

We found we loved the house Gail had picked out. It was pretty and very comfortable. Gail and I decided to invite all our neighbors over for a thank you party for letting us join their neighborhood. Everyone came but one couple. We had learned to do this in Japan and had also done it in Coronado. I think it helped us establish relationships with our neighbors. Many of them had not spoken to each other in years.

Gail and I made a trip down to Sun City West to check on my folks. Mom's Alzheimer's had continued to downgrade her. I tried to get my dad to seriously consider moving north by us so we could help him. He seemed interested but got cold feet when we started making plans for him to come up and pick out a place while one of us stayed with mom. He said he would feel guilty picking something out without her but felt she could not travel. I thought he would remain there until something happened to one of them. Suzanne and I wanted to support them but did not want to do it there. They chose to be away and apart for the past twenty years. It had worked fine for them for many years. There was nothing more we could do except pray that dad would have a change of heart.

One blessing we had was having our grandson Logan come down one night a week and stay with us. He looked exactly like his dad did at that age. I found myself calling him Jonathan, Gail mom and myself dad. We had him for a week at our church Vacation Bible Study (VBS). He seemed to have a great time. Both Gail and Mae were leaders. He did have more energy than Gail and I could keep up with. When he finally went to sleep at night we collapsed in front of the television hardly able to move.

From the moment we arrived I started searching for a used truck and camper to pull my boat. I finally found the truck in Sedro Woolley at a Ford dealer. It was a 2006 F-150 super cab 4X4 with an eight foot bed and only 37,000 miles. A few months later I found the camper at an Apache dealer. It was a 2007 eight feet plus Pastime self-contained that could sleep five. Together they made a good looking combo. Gail and I took it out to the local KOA for a break in run. It was small but nice and hoped it would give us years of camping fun. We later took it to Westport with Mae and our son David for a great weekend of camping and surfing.

In October we had a Conference on Healing in the church with internationally known leader in healing, Mike Evans. I had wanted to do this conference in 2013 but my leaders insisted they were ready for it now. I had given them four chapters of Mike's book "Learning to do What Jesus Did: How to Pray for Spiritual, Emotional and Physical Healing". Mike said they should read this and make sure this was where they wanted to go before he came. They all agreed they wanted to go in this direction. It surprised me but felt it was the leading of the Lord.

Mike began on Friday night with a word of knowledge and many people were miraculously healed. The miracles continued on Saturday and culminated in a Saturday night healing service where many were healed. Mike also preached to the church on Sunday. This weekend brought the supernatural gifts of the Holy Spirit to our church. Many were very energized. Some were turned off. The result of the weekend was that we started new Healing Teams. We hoped to have Mike back in the future.

About this time my mother was found unresponsive in bed by my dad and he called 911. Mom was dehydrated and in bad shape but the hospital was able to revive her. Dad told the firemen that he had waited too long to move. From that day on he was ready to move. We started making plans to downsize his possessions; sell his house and move them to a faith based non-profit assisted living facility close to us that had memory care. We found one six miles away in Auburn, WA called Wesley Homes Lea Hill. It was also affiliated with the United Methodist Church and fairly new. I told dad it was one place I would move to. That seemed to do it for him and we started to make plans.

My sister Suzanne and I flew down and began getting ready to sell the house and move. We took loads of stuff to the library and Goodwill. We met with a realtor and put the house on the market. It sold in 24 hours. There was a bidding war and dad took the highest offer. We were amazed and decided that God wanted dad to move soon.

We flew back and Gail flew down again with Suzanne to pack them up and fly with them to Seattle. I flew down again to finish with the movers, clean up the house and drive dad's car the 1600 miles up to Auburn, WA. We move them into Wesley Homes Lea Hill and hoped life would be easier and better for both of them.

David graduated from college with a criminal justice two year degree and so Gail, Mae, David and I flew to Hawaii for the Thanksgiving holidays. We stayed at the Capello's house in Kailua on Oahu and used their cars. David and Mae did lots of surfing and I even got a golf game in with some of the chaplains I knew there. We got our vitamin D fix and headed home.

No sooner had we returned than my mom went back

in the hospital. She had a fever and diarrhea. Wesley Homes had the fire department take her to Saint Francis Hospital in Federal Way. Dad and I were with her that night. Sunday they told us to come back and take her home on Monday. When we arrived they told us that now they wanted her to go to a rehab facility to gain strength. We looked at a couple and made plans for the next day to move her. When we left her room for the last time she had a hoarse and sore throat. The next morning I got a call from the doctor that mom had died. They said she had respiratory distress and quit breathing. We had asked for a Do Not Resuscitate Order and they did not try to revive her.

I tried to find dad but could not. I called my sister Sue to tell her and then headed to Wesley Homes and the hospital. I found dad in her hospital room sitting there. He had just arrived after having registered his car. My sister arrived later with her daughter Nancy and her husband. We had prayer and left for lunch at our country club. It was December 11th. Mom had lived three weeks after moving from Arizona. On Friday the 14th we had a funeral service at Tahoma National Cemetery with a reception at our home. Many family and friends came. I did the service. Wesley Homes was great about finding my dad a new room outside of the memory care unit. He began to learn how to live without his wife of almost 67 years. I too was feeling the grief and out of sorts.

Right after the New Year I began to sense that the honeymoon was over at Cornerstone Church. We had been giving some time after the last song at the beginning of the service to see if God had a word of knowledge or prophecy to give us. We had an open microphone for those who wanted to use it. Slowly people started speaking up. Others found this very uncomfortable and some said they were going to leave, we were becoming too Pentecostal. I had a meeting with our Believe Team and some who were upset. As a result we decided to change that part of the service and have people bring me their words of knowledge or prophecy and I would read them if I felt they were appropriate. This seemed to help some but a few others left. I sensed that attendance was down.

I began to wonder if I was the right person for Cornerstone and asked the Lord to not let me continue if I was going to hurt the church. I believed that God had sent me to Cornerstone to add the dimension of the gifts and power of the Holy Spirit. Gail felt I should stay away from those topics and just preach the gospel. I believe that the gospel included the gifts and power of the Spirit. Jesus did not just preach about the Kingdom of God. He demonstrated the Kingdom's reality with the power of the Holy Spirit and the love of God.

Our Leadership Team decided to bring Mike Evans back again in April. I continued to preach on topics like the Baptism of the Holy Spirit, Overcoming the Enemy, the Gift of Healing and Inner Healing. Some told me they wanted me to continue in this direction, that Cornerstone needed it. Our Leadership Team also began to meet to vision together as to the direction we felt the Lord was leading us for the future. I had everyone over to the country club one Saturday for a visioning offsite session. It was great. We decided to continue to try and meet once a month for a while.

The second meeting we had did not go so well. It seemed that the conversation was scattered and disoriented. Our third meeting I shared my sense of call from the Lord to bring the gifts and power of the Holy Spirit to Cornerstone. Some leaders wanted to know if I was trying to make Cornerstone a charismatic church. I told them that I purposely did not like to use that term as it means many things to many people. We agreed to pray on our own and meet together in a month. The vision statement I had proposed with the staff's help at our staff retreat was 'to bring the power and love of God to everyone we meet'. One leader wanted to know what I meant by 'power'? I met with him a couple of days later and we talked about how all of this was new to Cornerstone and how I needed to be patient, like turning an aircraft carrier.

During all this time I was meeting with my dad about once a week for lunch and having him over for dinner and lunch plus going to the church. He was very very lonely and struggling to be single after so many years of marriage. Wesley Homes was great but he was not really making any close friendships and at night he was very lonely. Dad began to talk to my sister Suzanne about moving in with her. She lived in Monroe about an hour northeast. Her husband Harold was in construction and had been out of work for the winter. Dad felt that moving in with Sue would be good for him and help them out financially. It seemed like a good plan to me though I would miss having him close after so many years of being far apart. Sue and Harold had been coming down every Saturday too and taking dad swimming and having lunch with him.

Just before Easter I went back to Christian Healing Ministries in Jacksonville, Florida for their Level III School of Healing Prayer. I had done Level's I and II with Lauren hoping she would be healed. She did not want to do any more training. It was strange not having her there with me. I had a great Holy Spirit week in the sun soaking up the vitamin D every chance I got. In my estimation Christian Healing Ministries is the center of Christian healing on the planet. I always came away full of the Lord and full of new ideas and books.

After Easter we had Mike Evans for Healing Conference II. Attendance was not as good as the first conference but many leaders came from other churches. Many people were touched by the Holy Spirit. We flew Lauren out hoping that the Lord would miraculously heal her eyes. Mike and his assistant Chris prayed for her many times with no noticeable difference in her physical vision. On Sunday she sang a song in the service. All in all it was a good weekend. I was disappointed that more of our people and leaders did not take advantage of this important and exceptional training.

After this weekend more people decided they wanted to leave our church. I found this very hard to take. A few came in to talk to me and tell me why they were leaving. Others said nothing, just left. At the same time we were gaining some new attendees who were attracted to what we were doing. Gail attended a women's tea and everyone at her table had come in the past four months. Fortunately our income was keeping up with our expenses.

About this time I decided that I was finally ready to really retire. Gail and I crunched the numbers again and discovered that in the summer of 2014, when I turned 64, we could retire and financially keep places in Hawaii and Washington State. As much as I loved preaching on Sunday and ministering to people in the gifts and power of the Holy Spirit, pastoring a church is very hard work and I found I was growing tired of doing it six days a week. The evening meetings and politics were driving me nuts.

The straw that broke the camel's came when I wanted to take some of the staff to a huge church in Redding, CA called Bethel. Bethel Church is on the leading edge of worship and ministering in the power of the Spirit of God. I asked my Staff Parish Relations Committee to fund this trip for the other staff. They refused saying that they did not see how this contributed to the future of the church. Needless to say, I was very disappointed at their short sightedness.

I started asking the Lord if I could retire summer of 2014. I had told the church and myself that I would not leave until the Lord told me I could. One day I was doing a quarterly day of prayer with the Lord and Otis at Dash Point State Park close to where we live. I was relaxing in the presence of the Lord, saying and doing very little while enjoying the sun and the beauty of the Puget Sound and the forest. I sensed the Lord telling me that if I wanted to retire, it was OK with him. I sensed him telling me that I had been working full time long enough and if I wanted to stop, I had his permission. I never want to quit serving the Lord and ministering to his people in the power and love of his Spirit. I did look forward to not punching a time clock any more.

Things at the church came to a head at a Leadership visioning meeting in June. We had been meeting for about six months trying to discover the vision Jesus had for us in the future. We had been working with a facilitator for a few weeks and had seemed to reach a consensus on a vision we could all agree to. Just then, one of our leaders wanted to talk about the elephant in the room, all the people who had left. We wound up talking for the next hour about how some people thought the church was becoming too charismatic and that was causing people to leave. We ended by saying we would vote on whether to keep going this direction at our next Leadership meeting. Many of us went home sick to our stomachs including me.

The next night I could not sleep and got up to pray asking God about the turmoil at the church. I thought I heard him say, "This is from me, for my purposes and I do not want you to do anything". I did feel that if I let Leadership take a vote, it would amount to a confidence vote on me and could split the church. I decided I needed to get the District Superintendent involved. I called her and she called a meeting of the Staff Parish Committee (SPR). Looking back it was probably the worst thing I could have done.

SPR is the committee that is supposed to deal with relationships between the congregation and the pastor. They met without me and I was briefed by the District Superintendent the next day. They seemed to feel that the problems were: 1) that the staff had a morale and communication problem. 2) that our Youth Director had taken over a lot of my responsibilities. 3) that the people who were leaving believed that the only thing I wanted to talk about and emphasize was healing. They recommended that we get a coach for the staff and I to meet with. I tried not to get defensive and just listen. I had no problems with getting a coach for the staff.

I met with SPR the following week and we talked about all of these issues. I decided to write a letter to the church. In it I explained that healing was not the most important thing to me and that my goal was to have Prayer Teams set up for the future. It went out and I got many emails of support from members of the congregation.

The staff met with the coach, an ordained PHD from Seattle University. During the two hour session, it became clear to him that we do not have a communication problem. The problem he saw was the polarization theologically of the congregation. Some of the people do not think healing and the gifts of the Holy Spirit are for today. Others think they are and want more of them. I left wondering how this was all going to turn out. I believed a lot of this was an attempt by our spiritual enemy to destroy Cornerstone Church and my ministry. I kept thinking back to the words I thought I heard the Lord say in prayer that this was from Him for His purposes.

Not long after this DS called another meeting with the SPR Committee. The first hour they met without me with one of the female staff members. They said later they wanted to hear her side of how the exodus of families had affected her ministry. She had lost a lot of volunteers and children. Then they met with me and I sent her home.

It was one of the most hurtful SPR Committee meetings I have ever experienced. They all seemed to say that I was a brilliant preacher but that I was not a very good pastor. They felt I was out of touch with the congregation and staff and needed a coach. I wanted to resign and go home. I had my defensive shields down and was not expecting such a frontal attack. I was deeply hurt and wanted to quit. They only members of SPR who would have supported me were not present due to other commitments. I told them that I did think we needed a coach as the problem was theological with some of the congregation, a minority, and me. I did not think the problem was as serious as they did. I told them I had been through similar situations in the past and we weathered it. They were not convinced. We ended on a stalemate note.

I did not feel God's peace to resign yet from Cornerstone. I wanted one more year to get Mae through high school. I set my sights on July 1, 2014 as my final retirement date from the United Methodist Church. I would be 64. I was not sure I would make it that long. The DS had told me that if more people left, the Cabinet might make me resign.

The rest of the summer went well for Cornerstone. We had a great Fourth of July Block Party, made $12K on the youth fireworks stand, had a super Vacation Bible Camp, a terrific youth mission trip and an amazing Church Camp and serve experience at Lazy F near Ellensburg. We went to one service at 9:45 AM for the summer and seemed to be attracting new families. Those who felt I was not doing a good job seemed to be quiet and no more families left the church.

On the way back from Lazy F, I pulled off Snoqualmie Pass Interstate 90 at exit 62 on the shoulder of the exit to check something on the camper. Some man in a Honda Pilot SUV with two young children in back told the State Patrol later he fell asleep and ran right into the back of my truck and camper just as I got back in the cab. If it would have been seconds earlier he would have killed me. It was a miracle I had no one else with me, not even my dog Otis. I believed my spiritual enemy was trying to kill me and God protected me and others. I had just baptized many people in the river at Lazy F Camp. The enemy hates me and all I stand for but the Lord Jesus and his Father God are my helper and protector. They send many angels to protect me and mine. Thank you Lord!

The sleepy driver totaled his SUV and my truck. He also did damage to my camper. I had a mild concussion and whiplash to my head, neck and back. I could not believe this had happened. My truck might have saved the lives of him and his children. It could have been far worse for them if they had continued off into the forest. I was able to drive the truck home with help and get the camper off. USAA towed my truck and I got Apache Campers to come and get my camper. We left for summer vacation at Lake Chelan with most of our children and grandchildren three days later. That vacation was a blur to me as I was very sore and on pain medications.

That fall I was praying and fasting asking God for clear direction about leaving Cornerstone Church and retiring from the active ordained ministry. I was reading the prophet Jeremiah Chapter 42 where he asked the Lord for an answer and it took days for it to come. I was also doing lots of work with the chiropractor and physical therapist trying to recover physically from the accident.

In October the District Superintendent asked me to meet her for coffee. She told me she thought Cornerstone Church was troubled and that if the numbers kept dropping, the Bishop and Cabinet would not ask me to return in June. I told her that if the numbers came back up that I may not ask to return. She could not believe I said that. I cherish the freedom my Navy retirement gives me to be myself. If I had to depend on the United Methodist Church for financial survival, I would have been very intimidated and vulnerable to their abuse.

When I got home Mike Evans called saying that I was on his mind. I told him all that was going on with the church and it was hard not to feel like I had failed. Mike said that he had a similar experience with a church and that God had sent me to Cornerstone to bring the Holy Spirit's power and gifts and I had done what He wanted me to do. I was not a failure. He said Seeker Churches like Cornerstone Church often dropped in numbers when the Holy Spirit's power and gifts were introduced and could take three to five years to start coming back up. The Bishop and Cabinet were only giving me 21 months. That was unbelievable. My heart was aching about Cornerstone.

Ten days later the DS called to say that she had met with the SPR Committee, they respected me, loved my preaching but did not think the numbers would come back up. She said I would not be reappointed in June of 2014. The church and the Cabinet blamed me for attendance and giving being down. I was heartbroken. Was this my answer from the Lord I was praying for about retiring? I knew all of this was the enemy trying to destroy the great ministry that was going on in the power of the Holy Spirit. True Christian ministry is spiritual warfare and when you begin to move in the power and authority of the Holy Spirit to destroy the work of the enemy, you will experience that war on many levels.

When my Leadership Chairman and his wife heard what some of the church leaders and the Bishop were doing to me, they were so angry they resigned and left the church. I understood but missed their support. They were two of the few key leaders who supported me and my ministry.

The next week my retired Navy Captain friend and Hawaiian neighbor Lee and his German Shorthair Pointer (GSP) Bella joined Otis and I for a two day drive to Eureka, South Dakota (SD) for the Veteran Pheasant Hunt. My friend retired Navy Captain Lenny had invited me to this hunt for years but I had not been able to make it until now. The year before we were going to go and I had to move my folks from Phoenix to Washington State. The Veteran Hunt took place the first week of November. These retired senior officers would rent a house in Eureka for the month of November and arrive in shifts with their GSP's and other dogs.

Lee and I arrived with our dogs with four other hunters and five GSP's. The dogs had the run of the house. There were three Navy Captains including me, one commanded submarines and one commanded cruisers, one Air Force Colonel fighter pilot, a two star submarine Rear Admiral and a Surface Force Navy Commander.

Lee and I hunted for six days and headed home. The pheasant hunting was not as good as years past. My dog Otis did a terrific job although I almost lost him at one point when I lost my electronic collar transmitter and he disappeared in a huge field. He was ten and his hearing was going. We found him later at the truck where he had returned when he could not find any of us. He is a very smart dog. He made many points and retrieves, the best dog there in my opinion.

This trip helped me cope with what was going on at the church. I grew up and love to hunt pheasants with the dogs and good friends. Closing the day at the side of a corn field with the sun setting blood red and my great dog on point over a big wild Chinese Pheasant, invigorates my soul.

I returned home to meet again with the SPR Committee. They wanted to know what my retirement plans were going to be July 2014. I told them this was not about me but about how they were going to tell the church that they did not want me back. I walked out and never attended another meeting until I left the church.

Our annual church meeting was coming up where the District Superintendent presides, some leaders give reports of the year and the pastor's salary is voted on. I had asked them not to give me a raise. I was making enough.

I asked DS to announce at that meeting that I would not be reappointed. She refused saying she would do it after. I think that decision was a big mistake. I gave my reports of those who had left and joined the church. We had taken in over 20 new members as the year before and there were many things to celebrate. It was hard to talk about these things knowing that I was not coming back and not able to tell the church and with many enemies present knowing it all. I have always said that pastoring a church is one of the hardest and most rewarding jobs there is. In that job you have a target on your back and face the full force of the enemies attacks against the Kingdom of God who he hates.

We had a men's retreat at Mount Rainier that weekend. None of the leaders who did not support me attended. Twenty men did attend and it was a good event though I was very quiet and some men noticed. The year before we had fifty men. Later they would find out the burden I was carrying and unable to share. There are some great people at Cornerstone. As in many churches, those great people are sometimes not in any positions of leadership. Why is it that antagonistic people often do fill those positions?

The DS sent out an email letter to the Leadership of Cornerstone saying that I would not be reappointed in June. I told the staff and some were very sad, some were not. I had antagonists on the staff that caused me a lot of pain and trouble. I think they resented the fact that I was not the preceding pastor. Two of them resigned and some peace finally came to the office. I had not realized how oppressive the office had become. There was no happiness there.

The following day the DS's email letter went out to the church. Many were in shock. My cell phone and email got a work out all day and night. Many people were livid at some of our leaders, the Bishop and Cabinet. The majority of the church supported my ministry and did not want me to go. Many lives had been touched and changed by the Holy Spirit in a short amount of time. I told some of those who talked to me that this was a spiritual war and to not hate those involved.

That following Sunday I preached two sermons on Mark 15, the crucifixion of Christ, a series I was doing on Mark. It was one of the toughest sermons I ever preached. The opposition of the enemy was so strong I could hardly stand up there and speak. By the grace of

God I was able to finish.

That afternoon Gail, Mae and I headed to Hawaii for a Thanksgiving week of vacation. Gail was very angry at the church for taking away from our last year of our daughter in high school and for the pain this was causing Mae. Mae lettered in five sports that year, judo, swimming, diving, gymnastics and track. She was the Captain of the Diving Team in her first year doing it. She is an amazing athlete and artist. All my children and my wife are amazing people. Thank you Jesus for each of them and for putting them in my life!

Hawaii is a very healing place for Gail and I and our children. We love it there and planned to spend much time in the years ahead. Thanksgiving Day we had a big dinner at the Hale Koa armed forces hotel with our friends Dr. Klaus and Patty Rennert and Jean and Lenny's daughter Catie. At that dinner I started drinking again with a Mai-Tai after two and a half years of not drinking. This happened to me in Hawaii once before after I had not had a drink for years. I have a weakness for Mai-Tai's in Hawaii. I started again because I felt that I was having pride about not drinking towards others as if I was better than they were.

When we returned home we found out that there was a meeting called for the church Sunday afternoon with the District Superintendent. The church was fasting Saturday for that meeting. I joined in the fast but decided I would not attend the meeting.

The church meeting was very angry and contentious. My supporters were furious and my antagonists were very negative about how I relate to people. The church was polarized and divided. Once again the enemies work was evident.

I had told the church the Sunday following that I did not agree with the Cabinet's decision to have me removed and that there was no crime or immoral act that I had committed to make it happen. A rumor was going around the community that I had committed some crime or immoral act and was being removed for that. One woman, wife of one of my leaders, was so angry at my comments on Sunday she sent a terrible email to many members of the church saying that I was a liar, a terrible person and that she would not come to church as long as I was there. The enemy was having a hay day.

That Christmas season I felt like all the joy in my life had been ripped away. When people asked me how they could pray, I told them to pray that my joy would return. Every Sunday it was extremely difficult to stand up in front of the church and preach. I decided to quit going to meetings where people attended who were antagonistic towards me. Why should I put myself through that pain? I kept up all my other duties including preaching, counseling, hospital visits, men's breakfasts and meeting with the staff.

One of the chief antagonist leaders made an appointment to talk to me. He wanted to blame me for all that happened because he felt I had been disrespectful to the District Superintendent at one of the SPR meetings. I told him that I felt he did not have my back but had thrown in with the Annual Conference he did not like or trust and now he would have to live with the results.

The District Superintendent called and said that the Bishop wanted to see me to give some pastoral care. I called his secretary and made an appointment deciding I would take Gail. When we arrived at his office, he asked me why we were there. At that point I should have gotten up and walked out. I explained to him we were there because his District Superintendent said he wanted to see me. He had no idea why we were there. It was unbelievable. He had just written a book on leadership.

Gail was able to express some of her anger at the Bishop and to his credit he listened. She said that he had us retire early from the military in Hawaii and brought us with a high school junior to a new place where we knew no one and then threw us under the bus. He of course did not remember that he had asked us to retire early. I expressed some of my frustration with his DS and some of the antagonist leaders at Cornerstone. He listened, offered me another church if I wanted it and we left.

Some of my good friends from the civilian and military ministry heard about what was happening and asked me to stay in the ministry. They believed this was an attack from the enemy and that he was trying to take me off the spiritual battlefield. I told them that I never wanted to quit serving the Lord and was open to whatever the Lord wanted me to do next. Some felt this was happening to move my ministry out of the church and into the world. I got a call from a good friend of mine, Glen Evans, who has a ministry in Honduras. Glen asked me to bring my healing ministry there with his people. I began to pray about it.

Gail and I started to fast and pray and ask the Lord whether or not we should take another church. The Bishop and the Cabinet were waiting for our response. According to the Methodist Discipline, our book of laws, I had to let them know if I was retiring 120 days before or April 1st. I decided to wait as long as possible and make them sweat a little. The DS kept asking.

While this was going on the Cabinet picked my replacement and had him meet with the SPR Committee without letting me know, in violation of the Discipline. He was pastoring a little church in southern Washington. He was young and had a wife and two children with a baby on the way. He never had a large church. I knew he would be over his head with this church.

I really wanted to send the new pastor the book "When Sheep Attack" which I felt accurately described my experience at Cornerstone. Mike Evans told me to just walk away and leave the church in the Lord's hands. I decided to listen to Mike. I did talk to the new pastor on the phone, tried to answer all of his questions without naming names and prepared a long turnover file like we did in the military.

During this time Gail felt I needed to talk to someone besides her. I started looking for a psychologist through my insurance or the VA. I met with two and decided on the second one. He had some kind of disability, was young with a family and was a Christian. We hit it off. He and his family had even been in a church where the pastor had been removed because of a few antagonists. He told me that I was burned out and staggering towards the finish line. He said I was going from the freeway at 70 MPH to an exit at 25 MPH. He wanted me to talk to others I knew who had retired and ask them how they did it. The ones I talked to all said to stay busy at first, something I planned to do.

I went on one of my days of prayer, silence and fasting that I try to do every quarter. For the first time I thought I heard the Lord say that it was OK with Him if I retired from active Christian ministry. Gail and I crunched the numbers with all of our retired sources of income and decided that we could probably retire July 2014 but it would be tight. We decided we would tell the Bishop, Cabinet and the church that we would retire.

I sent a letter to the Bishop and Cabinet to arrive April 1st, in compliance with the Discipline, announcing my retirement. I was ending my status as an active United Methodist minister that I had held for 38 years. It was a love/hate relationship. I loved some of the structure and security but did not like the liberal theology of the majority of those in power in the Pacific Northwest.

I decided to tell the church I was retiring and would be spending my summers in our Kent residence and our winters in Hawaii. It happened the same Sunday that the SPR Committee told the church who their new pastor was. They wanted to show a video to the church about him and I told them they could. The video spent a lot of time talking about his wife and how wonderful she was. Gail felt it was a slam on her. I would not let them show any more video's about him until after I was gone. Some of my antagonists thought I was being awful and selfish.

Gail seriously thought about not attending Cornerstone any more but continued to support me by going. Mae continued to go to Youth Group off and on but we worried she would hear from one of the youth some of the terrible things their parents were saying about her dad. Fortunately it did not happen. Mike Evans told me that because of the way his last church had treated him over the Holy Spirit, his grown children were so traumatized that they did not attend church anymore. He said that church went to being full in a huge sanctuary to just a 100 or so in an empty building as the years passed. I wondered what would happen to Cornerstone.

We began to prepare for retirement July 2014. I planned to preach until the middle of June and take the last two weeks as vacation. I continued to work a normal schedule except I did not attend evening meetings any more. We even took in a bunch of new members just a few weeks before I left. In the thirty months I was there, we took in over 70 members and baptized a lot of babies and people. The year before I came to Cornerstone they took in zero members. The income came in too, paying the bills though many people who supported me began to withhold their giving. I encouraged them to give to our seminarian Marc or find some other way to support many of the good things we were doing such as the Youth Group. Some said they would stay with the church only until I left.

One opportunity for continued ministry after Cornerstone came up in the way of the website www.howtoheal.org. This site had been started by my good friend, Hal Weeks, in his 90's while at St. Paul's Church in Coronado, CA. The site was anointed by God and used by His Spirit to help many people. Hal eventually died and the site just sat there unattended. I inquired about it and found that friends of Hal had kept it up but someone wanted to buy it. I told them I was interested in keeping it going and they said I could have it.

I took the site over and began added my own information on healing and some of my past sermons plus keeping Hal's information. I wanted to honor him. Once up I started getting calls from all over the world and the United States, about one a week. Gail did not like my involvement with this site. She was worried it made us too public, mostly an ego trip for me and opened me up to potential lawsuits in the future. I talked to Mike Evans about it and he said I should not do it if Gail was not behind me. Over the thirty years I was in the active military I had put her through a lot and I should listen to her concerns now. I did and parked the site. I planned to give it back to the family to sell. After a while, I picked it back up again. I tried to sell it and give the money to Hal's wife but no one wanted it.

Gail and I continued to make plans for retirement. Mae was going off to college in Hawaii and David was getting married. Those two things would keep us busy at first. We decided we wanted to go on an RV trip and visit our daughters and their families in CA and WI. Briana had her second child, a boy named Liam Brystin, on May 6th. Gail was there for the birth. I flew down a week or so later.

We decided that our camper was just too small to travel in for weeks at a time. We started attending RV shows and looking at many trailers. We found the size and floor plan we wanted and then began to look for a used one. We found one close to home, 25 feet with a couch slide out and a rear kitchen with dinette. It had a queen size forward walk around bed and a big bathroom with a tub. The trailer was a 2010 Nash that had hardly been used. We dickered and got a good price and great financing. Then we sold the camper on Craig's List. We made plans to camp with our kids/grandson in WA and to travel and visit our kids/grandkids in CA and WI.

There is a great bunch of pastors in Maple Valley, Black Diamond, Hobart and Covington that I met with weekly while I was at Cornerstone. Not one of them was United Methodist. Every spring we went on a two night overnight at a log mansion in Cle Elum. I loved these guys. We would hike, golf, shoot clay pigeons, play cards, eat, watch movies, talk and sleep. It was great. On our last retreat day we prayed for each other and laid hands. Sometimes there was a word from the Lord, a prophesy. When they prayed for me, one of the pastors said the Lord was telling him for me, "Go where you are celebrated, not where you are tolerated". That word really resonated with me. I had been tolerated by some at Cornerstone too long. It would be wonderful to have my ministry with the Holy Spirit be celebrated. I would really miss these pastors and their fellowship. I had never experienced anything like it. Often we would pray together for thirty or more minutes at a time.

I felt the Lord calling me to Honduras. My good friend and former DC pastor Glen Evans had started a ministry there to the poor when he retired. His ministry was a 200 acre farm out in the middle of the Honduras forest. It was called Art for Humanity. He had also started a school, The Learning Center or TLC, to teach young Honduran women how to start businesses for themselves in the countryside of Honduras. These women had to be high school graduates, single, not pregnant, poor and have a recommendation from a missionary there. Volunteers came from all over the Western world to teach them. They raised coffee and were trying to raise fish and other plants to support themselves. They were solar powered. Glen is brilliant, hard working, creative and inventive.

Glen had asked me to come and bring my healing ministry to the girls. Someone was celebrating my ministry instead of tolerating it. I had some church travel money left and decided to use it before I retired. I flew to the capitol of Honduras, Tegucigalpa, and Glen met me. The cities of Honduras are some of the most dangerous in the world. Violent gangs run rampant. Business owners wear guns and have armed guards at the door. Murders are common. Glen wants his girls to have businesses outside of the murderous cities.

We drove out into the bush of Honduras for two hours on roads that are barely tolerable. We arrived at TLC and Glen gave me a tour. All food is cooked on a wood heated oven/grill that goes back to the 19th Century. The entire time I was there I did not have any meat though Glen said chicken and fish are sometimes served.

I decided to use the first four chapters of Mike Evans book/manual "Learning to do What Jesus Did: How to Pray for Spiritual, Emotional and Physical Healing". I asked Mike if I could copy it for them and he said yes. Mike always began his seminars by asking of there was someone who was experiencing physical pain to come forward. I felt led of the Spirit to do the same. The girls were expecting me to be a speaker like all the others Glen brought there, teaching on business stuff. When they learned of my topic, they were very interested. All of them reminded me of my high school senior Mae.

When I asked if there was anyone who had pain, a girl came forward who had recent surgery and was in pain. I asked if I could lay my hands on her and say a prayer for healing. She said yes. As I prayed she began to cry. I asked her what was happening. She said that the pain was gone. The girls went wild. None of them felt they had seen a miracle before.

I asked if there was anyone else who had pain. They said there was a girl still in bed with a toothache hurting too much to come to class. I asked them to go and get her. When she came I asked her if we could pray for her and lay hands on her. She said yes. As I prayed she began to cry too. I asked her what has happening and she said that the pain was gone. She began to hug me. Once again the girls went crazy. Thank you Jesus! He is so good.

I continued to teach on Mike's four chapters and met individually with many over the next couple of days. These girls were so simple and unsophisticated that God was able to move upon them in a powerful way like I had never seen before. We in developed countries have much to learn about being simple before God to see our prayers answered immediately.

I flew home on top of the world to face my last few Sundays at Cornerstone and the beginning of full retirement. The Honduras trip had really boosted me spiritually in a time of real pain and depression. God was still alive and working through me. His Spirit and His gifts are real and for today. I felt some leaders at Cornerstone had just chosen to shut Him out by having me removed.

While all of this was going on, we were getting ready for Mae to graduate and go to college in Hawaii and for David to get married to Catelyn Grieve in September. Mae got accepted at all three colleges on Oahu and decided to go to the smaller one, Chaminade, and take interior design. She got a scholarship from them and one from her art school in Seattle. She is an amazing athlete and artist. She graduated from Kentwood High School the day before my last sermon at Cornerstone on June 15, 2014. Like all my children, I was very proud of her. It is not easy being the child of a Navy Chaplain and United Methodist Minister. All my children have done it exceptionally well. Thank you kids!

The church wanted to have some kind of retirement going away party for me. I told them I wanted nothing, just like when I retired from the Navy. This was not a happy celebratory time for me. The Bishop, Cabinet and some antagonist parishioners had forced me to retire at least two years early. I did not want to have any celebration with them.

For my last sermon I gave my testimony. I have always tried to make it my first and last sermon like Pastor Don McCauley used to do. I gave an invitation and two people received Christ. I also baptized the baby of a new young couple. Unknown to me many in the church who supported me had put together a video talking about how my ministry of the Holy Spirit had changed their lives for the better. It was very moving to me and much appreciated. God had done some amazing things at Cornerstone during those thirty months. As painful as it was, it was probably worth it.

Gail, Mae and Lauren were there with me. The band asked me to play with them my last Sunday. I would really miss them. They were the best Christian band I had ever been with. Afterward the church had a chocolate chip cookies and milk reception and many people hugged and thanked me.

Two weeks later, on July 1, 2014, I was officially retired from everything. The Pacific Northwest Conference of the United Methodist (UM) Church was meeting at the Puyallup Fair Grounds and having a retirement ceremony for all retiring clergy. They wanted me to write something up for my picture on the big screen. I wanted nothing to do with them and told them I did not plan to attend.

Annual Conference had always been a miserable time for me and I dreaded it. I always felt like the only Republican at the Democratic National Convention. Everything they did was full of Democratic ultra-liberalism they call progressive just like the Democratic Party. It took me weeks to spiritually recover from attending. It was a great relief to stay home.

I had been a member of that conference for 38 years. They ordained me and had given me two churches to serve plus made it possible for me to become a Navy Chaplain for almost thirty years. Now they were going to pay me a retirement check for the rest of my life. For these things and the many wonderful people I had met through them, I thanked God. For the rest, I was more than ready to say goodbye. Now on to retirement and hopefully some much needed spiritual and psychological healing. I put Cornerstone in God's hands and walked out the door.

18
Retirement

July 1, 2014 I began the final chapter of my amazing life and ministry with the Lord. They call it retirement and if you live long enough and are blessed you can experience it. We had planned a lot of camping trips in our new trailer and at first it felt like I was on an extended vacation. I kept wondering when I was going to have to go back to work. I was fun camping with some of our children and grandchildren in our new 2010 trailer. We really liked it.

We had our normal family vacation at Lake Chelan but Briana and Lauren did not come this year with their families. I did not bring the Duck Boat with me this year to cut down on some of my stress and drama. I played a lot of golf with my sons and brother-in-law Steve which I always enjoy. Shortly after that Gail and Mae went to Hawaii to check Mae into her dorm for her first year at Chaminade University in Honolulu. Our last child was finally in college. She was taking Interior Design and doing lots of surfing.

I stayed home and worked on many projects around the house such as restaining the deck, repairing the ceiling over the fireplace from a leak and moving the TV over the fireplace. I went on a diet and lost some weight. Gail came back and we were finally empty nesters. How would we do 24/7 together without the kids? I was still having my dad over once a month for a few nights and Gail and her sister were taking care of their dad Burdette. We had to move Burdette from an assisted living to a home that offered more care. He was aging fast.

September 11th I woke up to swelling on my left

knee. I had done a normal two mile run with Otis the day before with no problems. I had even been thanking God how I could still run after 64 years. I waited a few days and the pain and swelling did not go away. I finally went to the ER. They x-rayed it and could find nothing. The doctor sent me to the orthopedist who told me to work with physical therapy.

I had been working with a psychologist to prepare me for retirement months before I retired. I recommend this to others going through the same thing. He had me call all my retired friends who all told me to stay busy. We started very busy. We had been camping, working on the house and sending Mae off to college. The next thing on our slate was David's wedding to Cate September 20th.

They asked me to officiate as I had all the other weddings and baptisms and I agreed. We hosted the rehearsal and groom's dinner at our home and had the country club cater. All our children came with their spouses and children. It was mass drama at our home. I hauled the trailer over to make room for everyone. Mae came home from college. This was the fifth wedding we had been involved with our children. One more to go we hoped. It was a great celebration at the Edmonds Community Center. Both our dads were there and all our grandchildren. When our immediate family gets together there are 16 of us as of this writing not counting grandparents or siblings and their families, quite a gaggle and always lots of drama.

Right after the wedding Mae went back to college and Gail and I prepared for a six week RV trip in our trailer. We planned to visit our girls in California and Wisconsin and hunt in South Dakota. We left on October 1st and traveled eleven states and 5,000 miles in those six weeks. Only twice did we stay more than one night in the same place while traveling, Crater Lake and Eagle Lake near Susanville, CA. Most travel days we traveled about 250-300 miles. Gail would drive on the freeways for an hour or so a day to give me a break. At both of our daughters we set up the trailer at their homes and stayed in it nine nights. The grandkids loved to come, visit and even stay with us in the trailer.

While on the road my knee got progressively worse. I tried unsuccessfully to get physical therapy while in Wisconsin. I finally decided I could not go on the South Dakota hunt and we headed home a week early so I could try to get surgery. From about the middle of October we had trouble finding places to stay on the road that had hook ups and wifi/cable. Most everything in that part of the world closes in mid October because of freezing weather. It took some detective work each day but we managed. We learned to bring our water hose in at night.

One of the hardest parts of the trip for me was driving through South Dakota with Otis, now eleven, my shotgun, license and not go hunting in those beautiful pheasant fields. It turned out to be a blessing to have left early as the next week the snow fell and all travel was affected. We would have been seriously compromised. Snow was falling on Snoqualmie Pass our last night coming over the Cascades before home.

We got home the first week of November and I began to try and set up arthroscopic surgery on my knee. The doc did a scan and found I had torn my left meniscus. Surgery was set for December 11th. They put me on a cane, ice and a tens unit. Nothing helped and I could hardly sleep at night. They would not give me pain meds.

While this was going on I was trying to volunteer as a chaplain at the VA in Seattle. I did not care where I volunteered and tried the USO and the Red Cross. When I contacted the VA I was put in touch with their senior chaplain who said he wanted me as a volunteer chaplain. I would have been happy to push the book cart but was ecstatic to be able to be a chaplain to the vets, my favorite people. The USO and the Red Cross never got back to me. I prayed that the Lord would put me where he wanted me.

I got all my training done for the VA and started visiting patients in the nursing home, hospice and spinal cord injury units. I was on a cane and looked like a wounded vet like them. The majority opened up to me immediately and let me into their lives. I loved visiting and praying with them. It was like being back in the military. All the chaplains graciously made me feel part of the team. I loved giving back and got more out of it than I gave.

Mae came home from college for Christmas and on December 11th I had my surgery. Finally I got some pain meds. Soon I lost my cane and started walking normally but with pain and discomfort. On my follow up with ortho the doc told me to go back to normal activity but low impact. Running was now in the past.

Gail's Dad was getting progressively worse and needing more and more care. On December 18th we got the call from her sister Beth that he had died. We hurried over and spent time praying with family in the room. He was a great father-in-law, dad and grandpa and will be dearly missed. He was one of our heroes from WWII and lived to be 92. We had his service after Christmas at their church in Seattle, Sandpoint UMC, on January 3rd. I helped by doing his obituary. I also provided copies of his war stories that I had completed while on our RV road trip. He was married to two women for over 30 years each, an amazing man. Now Gail is the matriarch of her family.

We had a great Christmas holiday, one of the first I could remember when I was not working. At the same time Gail and I were getting ready to move to our condo in Waikiki and rehab it. We had owned the condo for 10 years and for the last 8 we had rented to a young marine couple. We sent them a letter of eviction that they called the nicest they had ever got.

One day during a big wind storm one of our large Scotch Pines came crashing down on top of our flat roof right over our bedroom. We were out of the house at the time but our animals were not. When we came home they were seriously traumatized, especially the cat that had been sleeping on our bed. It took days to get the tree people over to take down the tree. By the grace of God it did not go through the roof and I covered the damage with a tarp to protect from the rain. Gail said it did not go through the roof was because we had a stronger flat roof. I always gave her a bad time about that flat roof but maybe she was right.

When the tree finally did get taken off we had lots of firewood. We also decided to take the second tree that was bigger down and my neighbor offered to split the considerable cost. Huge pieces of wood were everywhere. It took a lot of finagling but we finally got all the wood taken away.

Mae went back to college and Gail and I flew to Honolulu on January 13th. Gail's friend Jean picked us up to get our Mustang we had shipped and to take us to the condo. We told the workers when we were arriving. They were supposed to have started work and removed the wallpaper and popcorn ceiling. When we opened the door it was like a combat zone. Dust and filth were everywhere. We brought only our suitcases, my golf clubs and a blow up bed.

Jean did not want us to stay and invited us to their Kailua home but I was stubborn and said that I wanted to stay at the condo. I had owned that condo for 10 years and never spend a night in it. I was determined we would make it work. Gail and I pulled up the carpeting and found a place to put the bed. We spent our first night and the next morning the workers arrived. Apparently they thought we were coming later in the week.

We immediately entered into the extensive remodel of our condo. That week they ripped out all the carpeting and remudded all the walls. The next week they started putting in crown molding, sanding and painting. Mud dust got on everything. Fortunately we had already remodeled the bathrooms so we had them and the lanai as our living spaces, closet and sanctuary. We had stored some things in our locker when I had retired from the military so we had some plates, silverware, pots, pans and other items to set up house plus some lawn chairs. Our former tenants left us some lanai chairs to use too.

The first items we bought were a cable box, router/modem and a new TV. We would escape all day from the time the workers arrived at about 9:30 in the morning, go shopping, walking on Magic Island, exercise and read at the condo pool or the Hale Koa Armed Forces Hotel that was a 10 minute walk away. At night we would sit on our lanai, cook dinner, drink wine, enjoy the fantastic view of the city, mountains and sea plus watch our favorite taped shows and news on TV. When we bought the condo, besides the right price we wanted a great view and to be close to the Hale Koa where we could use our military benefits.

Our construction team was headed by a man named Bill who called his business The Repair Shop. For years he had done minor repairs for us on the condo. We had asked him if he could do a remodel and he said he could. We had no idea that this was his principal business and that he had many people working for him rehabbing condos all over Oahu. We were constantly seeing new people come and work who we had never seen before. They were all hard workers, very talented, neat and respectful. We became close to all of them.

The weeks went by and we saw our laminate wood flooring installed, large leaf Polynesian fans installed, crown molding put up, everything painted multiple times, the kitchen torn out and new cabinets put up, new lighting, plugs and switches, new and old appliances put in place and new furniture delivered covered with plastic. I installed the new TV on the wall with a shelf that hid the wiring. Our master bedroom was the first room completed and after much shopping we chose a dark wood bedroom set from Costco. We had to deliver it ourselves and the construction workers helped us and set it up. It was so great to be back in a real bed.

Gail always seems to have low self esteem when it comes to picking out colors, artwork and decorating everything. Mae is taking Interior Design at a university close to the condo so I suggested we hire one of her professors to help us. We did, she charged us $60 an hour and she was worth every penny. She really only met with us once at the condo. We got some great advice, direction and proceeded to do most of the rest ourselves with some emails, texts and pictures to her. Mae also had some great ideas from her creative artistic gifts.

As soon as I could get insurance, I began physical therapy (PT) on my left knee. It was sore most of the time. I tried swimming, walking and doing exercises. I began to meet with PT once a week. They tried to get me to develop my quads that had atrophied during the injury and surgery. I did these exercises every day and they started to help.

Just as I did at the Seattle VA Hospital, I tried to start volunteering at the Honolulu VA that is housed at

Tripler Army Hospital. I contacted the VA Chaplains with a letter from the head of the Seattle VA Chaplains and they were not interested. A Navy Chaplain friend told me to try the head Army Chaplain, a Colonel, at the hospital. I did and he immediately started the process for me to become a Red Cross volunteer working with them. He was leaving soon so he expedited my entry process. Within weeks I was visiting active duty, vets and their families in the ICU and PCU units at the hospital. Like the Seattle VA, I would introduce myself as a volunteer chaplain, retired as a Navy Chaplain, ask if I could visit with them and close with a prayer, few turned me away. It really gives my life a boost to go there every week. I often tell people, if you think you are having a tough week, just go make rounds at the hospital. You will be thanking God for your many blessings when you finish.

Gail thinks I am an unhappy person. I got off Paxil on the RV trip just to see how I did. Gail thought the stress had come down in my life to the point that I would not need it. At her insistence, I have used Paxil for several years to soften the low grade depression, dysthymia, that some feel I have, including me. I would tell doctors that my wife liked me better with Paxil and that is why I used it. Well the stress did not come down during or after the RV trip and Gail kept reminding me that I was acting very unhappy and that was affecting her. I decided to go back on Paxil. Also, I ran into a book on happiness.

Dennis Prager is an author, speaker and radio talk show host who wrote a book on happiness called "Happiness, A Serious Problem". I heard him speak on the topic briefly one day by chance on the radio and decided to get the book for myself and my dad who Gail and I feel is also very unhappy. I am now in the process of reading and digesting this book and decided that I wanted to work harder at being happy instead of unhappy. It is a daily battle and Dennis' book is helping me understand this very important topic.

In our third month of the condo rehab, Gail and I decided we needed a break. We called the Navy MWR cabins on Kauai at Barking Sands also called Pacific Missile Range Facility (PMRF) where the DOD develops our intercontinental missile technology. In my last Navy Chaplain assignment before retirement, I would come to PMRF quarterly to provide religious ministry to the small Navy contingent there and their families.

PMRF is very isolated on the end of Kauai with amazing beautiful private beaches with cabins. We called and got a cabin right on the beach for four nights, the only nights available for the month. It brought back a lot of memories flying into Lihue airport and driving the hour south to the base. My good friend Dr. Klaus Rennert let us use his car that he keeps at the Lihue airport for his condo in Princeville to the north. While at the isolated cabin we just relaxed, ate, drank, enjoyed real furniture and a kitchen, slept, read, watched TV and walked the beaches looking for shells. In the winter months, rare Sunrise Shells can be found on Barking Sands beaches. We have found several over the years and made them into necklaces for our children and grandchildren. Walking the beach together looking for shells is very therapeutic.

We came back to Oahu refreshed and launched into the final weeks of rehabbing the condo. Our kitchen cabinets finally arrived and then the beautiful granite countertops and back splash. We finally unwrapped our new furniture from the Navy Exchange and began to enjoy the condo for the very first time. We bought a bed and mattress at Costco, a second bedroom set at Salvation Army and a dining table and chairs on

Craig's List. All of a sudden the concrete bunker started looking like a place where people were living. Our comfort level went up accordingly. Weekly Gail was in the thrift shops all over the island finding us things we needed at great cost savings. We started with four suit cases and a blow up bed and suddenly we had a condo full of furniture with all the trimmings.

When I retired from the Navy Gail and I took a seven night Hawaiian Cruise on Norwegian Cruise Lines, NCL, from Honolulu. We decided to do this instead of an expensive full blown retirement ceremony and reception. It was December 2011 and it rained the entire week and about the second day out we were telephoned that Gail's older sister Joan had died of cancer. It was not our best trip.

While rehabbing the condo we decided to check and see if we could get a break on the same seven night NCL cruise. We were able to get a great deal with a Hawaiian residence discount for a big handicapped balcony room. We decided to take another break from the rehab and just go and relax. The weather was perfect and the only thing we did in the four Hawaiian ports was go shopping at the thrift stores. The rest of the time we just ate, drank, lay by the pool, read and watched the sunsets on our balcony. It was great.

I had a free Delta plane ticket that I had to use before August of 2015. I was saving it in case there was some emergency at home I needed to attend to. I almost went when the trailer was broken into. While on the cruise, I sensed the Lord tell me to use it to bring my 88 year old WWII vet dad back to Hawaii for some warmth and sun away from the wet and cold of Washington in the spring. I was saving it for his funeral but decided it would be better to enjoy him in our new condo. My sister also needed a break from being his caretaker. To my surprise, dad accepted my invitation. I think the rain and cold was getting to him. I knew it would be hard for him so I talked him into a first class ticket. I would fly over and get him and we would both fly together back in first class. I hoped he could then fly back by himself in first class and my sister could pick him up. I flew to Washington on Tax Day April 15th.

I arrived late and my neighbors the Lampe's picked me up. The house after three months looked like someone was home. I walked in to the eerie uninhabited space and began to bring the house back to life. When I got to the guest bathroom and started to turn the toilet water on, my stocking feet suddenly were wet. I looked down and the floor was wet, not a good sign. I looked all over and could not discover where the water had come from. I walked into the guest bedroom and suddenly I was in a completely soaked carpet. Water was dripping from a cracked ceiling onto Gail's Hawaiian chair. All wood touching the carpet was waterlogged. I could not believe my eyes. What a mess.

About that time Gail called looking for me. She had told me before I left not to call her with any drama in Washington. Drama was everywhere in our Kent house. I told her what I found. We were devastated. The next morning I called the restoration people and told them the new roof they had just put on was leaking all over my house. I then had an appointment with my orthopedic surgeon, my knee was killing me, and I went and picked up Otis in my truck. He was really glad to see me.

That night the roofers found the leak and the restoration people began tearing our guest room apart down to the studs. In so doing they found some black mold on the wall behind the guest bath where a past leak had occurred. Gail's grandmother's antique footboard was ruined.

I spent the next few days working on the house. Otis went right back to all his old routines. East Kent seemed like a quiet backcountry small town compared to Honolulu. The weather was beautiful, Mount Rainier was out in all its glory and the flowers were blooming at the house. I discovered I had missed our country club home. The northwest is a beautiful place when the sun is out.

While home I met with my orthopedic surgeon about my left knee. It was not getting better despite all the physical therapy I was doing. He suggested a shot of a fluid made from chicken combs that he said had good results. The shot cost $2K and took weeks to get approved through my Tricare health insurance. I decided to try and get it in Hawaii through the VA when I got back there.

I left the house in the hands of the restoration people, had my neighbor Bill Johnson take me to the airport and met my sister Sue with my 88 year old dad. I pushed him through security in a wheel chair and we climbed into our first class seats. We ate and drank for six hours all the way to Honolulu International. It is the only way to travel with an aging parent.

As soon as I got back to Hawaii I meet with the VA orthopedic surgeon. I told him what my surgeon said about the chicken comb shot. He said the VA policy was to try cortisone first. I had him give me the shot right then and the pain I had since my meniscus tear September 2014 immediately left. It has not returned since. Thank you Jesus!

Dad stayed with us for two weeks. We rented him a transportation chair and tried to do something fun every day. He spent the rest of the time sitting on the lanai looking at the world go by in Honolulu. He loved it. I gained a new appreciation for how difficult it is for my sister to take care of him all the time. I put him on the plane first class back to Seattle by himself and Sue picked him up. I think it was a good trip for him. I thank God that he moved me to use that ticket to go and get my dad. If I hadn't, I would never have discovered the leak in the roof and maybe our whole house would have flooded. Thank you Lord!

Gail and I had a break for a week and then Mae moved out of the dorm back with us and Briana came for ten days with her growing family. We had lots of fun but seven people in a two bedroom condo were exhausting. Our car broke down and we lost our parking spot to construction at the same time. We had to rent a van for over a week to get around.

Briana and her family left and we started getting ready to leave the condo for a few months. Our dream had been to make our condo available to civilian clergy that we knew for rest and renewal. When we were civilian clergy we had very little extra income for such a retreat. God had blessed us and enabled us to be able to offer this blessing to others. Two clergy contacted us with requests for August and November. We began to make plans for them and others to come in the future.

June 1st Gail, Mae and I flew back to Seattle and our home in Kent. The neighbors picked us up at the airport. The first thing Gail and I did was to pick up our cat Myla and dog Otis at David and Cate's. They did a great job of taking care of them. We could not do our condo in Hawaii without them.

The workers finished our guest room repairs from the leak in the new roof just before we arrived. Lenny and Jean came and spent a night in that room a few days later and came back for the U.S. Open at Chamber's Bay near Tacoma, WA. Lenny always works the Open's. I attended Friday with my neighbors and watched the best golfers in the world.

We picked up the trailer and noticed that they had missed a gouge in the linoleum floor. I worked with my USAA insurance to file another claim. We then went camping at Dosewalips State Park on the Olympic Peninsula with our old Navy friends Mark and Lynn Braun in their new Class A Motor Home. We had fun but our trip ended early when I was called by former parishioners Scott and Kathy Ridge that their 30 year old Navy pilot son Cory did not wake up from a family party and was dead. They wanted me to do the committal service at Tahoma National Cemetery in my uniform. It was very sad and lots of Navy brass came from Whidbye Island Naval Air Station. I was honored to be there for them.

The next service I did was the closing of Avon United Methodist Church in Mt.Vernon, WA, my former parish. Before we left Hawaii I was called by the Puget Sound District Superintendent that Avon was closing and the eleven people still there wanted me to do the last service on June 28th. I worked with Keith Johnson's sister Shirley Benson. We planned a funeral service for the church with lots of publicity and a nice reception after.

The Mt. Vernon Skagit Valley Herald called and did an interview with me that made the Saturday paper. Sunday morning I was there with my dad, Gail, Jonathan and his family and David with Cate. The place was packed with many former pastors, two who were still active. I talked to former parishioners and friends I had not seen in years. I preached on Romans 8:28, "Good Happens". It was very sad to close the church that had ministered to Skagit Valley for 131 years and 40 pastors. I was number 35. It was my first sermon since I retired July 2014, a year earlier.

As soon as I got back from Hawaii, I started visiting patients again at the Seattle VA Hospital in Seattle.

The chaplains there all welcomed me back with open arms. I would go every Monday and stay for four hours just like I did at Tripler in Hawaii with the Army Chaplains and the Red Cross. I wound up visiting mostly on the cancer oncology ward. Most of the patients were glad to see me and let me pray with them for healing. It was good to be a chaplain again once a week. I also ate lunch with the VA Chaplains each time I went.

Another thing I started doing was play nine holes of golf Monday nights with my neighbor Bill Johnson. We play super twilight at Druid's Glen that is very challenging. We also talked our other neighbor Tom Lampe into joining us.

Gail and I decided to take a new German Shepherd Pointer (GSP) pup that we later named Gus. He was the only pup in the litter from our dog Otis' breeder Mary in Northern California. His head looked liver like Otis but he had a much whiter body. It seemed he had some kind of overbite so they were not able to use him for show and wanted me to have him for hunting as Otis got older. We picked him up at the airport and took him home. From the beginning he was full of energy jumping and licking everyone and everything in his path. He ran around with his tail sticking straight up in the air all the time. He bugged the cat continually and she growled at him and gnawed this head. He constantly chewed on Otis' ears. He would put up with it to a point and then turn and give Gus a big growl that would send him scampering away. Everyone loved Gus' happy go lucky way.

Fourth of July we camped at Twanoh State Park on Hood's Canal right across from Gail's sister Beth's family cabin. We had a lot of fun. The following weekend I attended a Cub Scout Camp Out at Jim Creek Naval Installation in Arlington, WA with

Jonathan, Aleeya and Logan. It was good to be with them for the weekend camping in a tent.

The end of July I left on a fishing trip to River's Inlet British Columbia Canada with my former Cornerstone staff member Chuck. Chuck had made this trip every year for 20 years in his old 1974 twenty-seven foot Bayliner boat. Each year they had caught trophy King Salmon weighing anywhere from 30 to 67 pounds. He had invited me before but this year I decided to take him up on it. We would go with three other friends of his, five total.

We left on Sunday after Chuck got done with church and drove to Port Hardy on Vancouver Island taking the ferry once we crossed the Canadian border. That night we just slept in the boat on the side of the road. Monday morning we put the boat in the water and headed for River's Inlet about 80 miles north across open ocean. The sea state cooperated and we made good time arriving before dark. I slept in the bow with DJ the 38 year old son of Chuck's best friend John. DJ slept loudly all night long in those close quarters and I could not sleep even though I used ear plugs.

We would start fishing every morning at 0415 trolling with herring on five poles. We fished hard for three and a half days and caught only Humpy "Pinks" and a couple of Coho "Silvers". One of the Silvers we ate. The food was amazing. One night we all ate two crabs each that we had caught. I had to leave early for our Chelan family reunion flying back in a float plane. They stayed for another two weeks.

We saw only a few 30 to 50 pound trophy Kings being caught. The year before Chuck had caught one every day and some days had caught more. I was disappointed but the surroundings were beautiful. It reminded me of when I commercial salmon fished in Alaska as a young man. On the way to the float plane on my last day I caught a small 10 pound King that I took home.

While I was flying home my family was headed to our friends Marilee and Ray's condo at Chelan. Every year they let us use it. Lauren flew in with her family and Briana drove up with hers. By Sunday night we were all together along with Beth and Steve and their family plus Justine and hers, 24 total. It was great to all be together again. Lauren was very pregnant. We had smoke from the close forest fires that was very bad. Steve and I tried to play golf at the local course. The grandkids and cousins played hard every day. David and Cate had to leave Monday. Jonathan and his family left Wednesday. The rest of us stayed until Friday. The smoke eventually cleared a little.

Gail and I did some camping with the kids at various State Parks and got ready to head to Boston for a cruise and wedding. Jean and Lenny's son John was getting married and we found a cruise to New England and Nova Scotia going the week before. Gail and I had always wanted to see that part of America and Canada. We asked my good friend retired Navy psychiatrist Lou and his wife Lisa to join us from Atlanta and they accepted. We all met on the boat the day of the cruise. The cruise went first to Portland, ME where we had lunch at John's pizza restaurant. The next stop was Bar Harbor, ME where we took a small boat to the beach and toured that beautiful place. Next day we came to St. John, NB where we rented a car and visited sites. Last stop was Halifax, Nova Scotia where it rained. We took our first paid tour there. The following two days at sea we came back to Boston. We had dinner every night together with Lou and Lisa, many happy hours on our balcony and some great shows.

Once back to Boston, we left Lou and Lisa, rented a car and headed to Manchester-by-the-Sea and John's wedding. We stayed at the Corner Inn there that night. The following day we flew home after getting lost and visiting a good Coast Guard friend Brett who had made Captain and was the CO of the base there. We did not know he was the CO until we arrived.

We enjoyed being in our home again but had booked another trip to North California to see Briana and her family. They had just moved from Portola to Nevada City, CA. Briana is a medical coder and works about four hours a day from home before her kids get up and when they are at school and napping. Her husband Justin has a new job in solar that take him away all week. We enjoyed Briana, Liam, Zoey and eventually Justin came home once again. Each time we took one of these trips it costs us $50 a day to board the dogs.

I had planned to take Otis hunting in South Dakota one more time. He was now twelve but looking very good. I was giving him Fish Oil pills. I had tried to take Gus but my trainer said he was too young and I might ruin him with loud gunshots and a possible tangle with a pheasant. I just needed to be patient and let him be a puppy. Next year he would be an awesome hunter.

This time I was going by myself with Otis. I decided to drive the 1400 miles in three days instead of two stopping at Missoula and Miles City, MT at night on the way. I arrived the first day of hunting with various military retirees at a house we rent in Eureka, SD. We went out my first afternoon and Otis went on point and I got my first rooster. We hunted hard the next six days with as many as eight guys and as many dogs. Otis was by far the best dog in the field. I had to be sure and not let him get over exhausted. He was amazing. My knee held up too walking the equivalent of two 18 hole golf courses a day. I shot a few pheasants and missed many more. Wild pheasants explode like missiles when they take off and are very hard to hit.

I had fun but felt there were just too many guys there. Dogs and hunters were sleeping everywhere. I need to find a new way to hunt wild birds where I do not have to drive so far and can include my sons. The first week I was in South Dakota, Gail was in HI with Beth and her daughter Audrey. They enjoyed the condo and Mae was doing very well and enjoying college.

Gail and I finally got back together again and drove to my sister Sue's for a reunion of my dad's living brother and sister, Bob and Bev. Bev flew up from California with her son Mark. My cousins Craig and Brad Waite came too with Craig's wife Shawn. We had a nice evening at Sue's catching up with cousins and letting the three siblings see each other again, maybe for the last time in this life.

Lauren's baby was due November 14th and Gail flew back to be with her. She delivered her first live baby; a little girl named Hadley Lauren Smith, on November 21st about 2100 hours in LaCrosse, WI. Lauren wanted to go natural but ended up having a C-section. Hadley, they did not know it was a girl until the birth, was healthy, 7 pounds 9 ounces and 19 ¾ inches long. We were all thrilled, our second granddaughter. Finally Lauren had her baby girl she so wanted. Gail was there to help. I decided to fly there on December 2nd and fly back with Gail on December 9th.

There were now 17 of us in our immediate family, four grandsons and two granddaughters with two of our children who had no children yet. I stayed a week just like we did at Briana's. It was great to be with Hadley and Lauren as I had done with my other three biological grandchildren right after their births. It is a granddad bonding time. We did very little every day except try to help Lauren and hang out with our new granddaughter. It is always hard to leave again knowing we would not see them for many months. We hate being so far away from our children and their families.

We arrived back from Wisconsin in time to meet Mae coming home for Christmas Break from Chaminade University in Honolulu, HI on December 11th. I had not seen her since August. The next morning she and I took my truck and cut our nine foot Christmas tree for the living room as we do every year together. I have done this with all our children over the years as we were able. This year we decorated it sparingly, as it was just going to be the three of us again, and I hung the outside lights as I always do. Christmas Eve we had all our Washington family including our two sons and their families and Gail's sister Beth and her family and her sister Joan's son Joseph. My daughter–in–law Aleeya also brought her dad visiting from California. We had a great party and sang Christmas carols by the tree and fireplace. We missed our two oldest daughters and their families in Wisconsin and Northern California.

I did a little duck hunting with my sons and prepared to return to our new condo in Hawaii. Mae noticed that Gus had very bad breath and I decided to take him to the vet. The vet saw that his bottom teeth were missing except for the two incisors that were crooked and puncturing the top of his pallet. We called our breeders and one met me at the dog dentist in Seattle. The dentist said Gus was in serious trouble, it would cost $5K to fix and he could not be a hunting dog. My breeders agreed to take him back and try to fix him or give me another pup. I gave Gus to her after the dentist appointment and we all cried for a couple of days. He had become part of our family.

My son David agreed to take Otis and Myla again

for the winter when we left for Hawaii. Jonathan had agreed to take Gus but now we did not have to worry about him. On January 6th we flew back to Hawaii with Mae. I had not been back to the condo for over seven months. Gail had been back twice in that time with Mae, her sister and niece. I had really missed Hawaii. It was so good to be back. In December we had let our first pastor and his family use the condo for a couple of weeks, This was a dream we had to let full time civilian Christian workers, pastors and missionaries use the condo for just a $200 cleaning deposit for rest and relaxation. We knew what it was like to be in full time Christian ministry with typical low pay. We wanted this to be a way to tithe our blessings and give back to others. The condo looked great and no worse for the wear.

The condo pool and weight room was being renovated that year and we had no place to work out or swim. The year before we had lived at the pool and weight room with all of the renovation going on. We visited the Hale Koa and found out that they were no longer letting retirees join the fitness club there. We could still use their big family pool but it was about a 15 minute walk away. We checked with the YMCA and were informed it was closed. We checked with 24 Hour Fitness and discovered it was cost prohibitive to join and no pool except at one far away. We wrote a letter to the condo association asking for assistance to find a pool and work out facility to use while they had ours closed and they turned us down.

We began our daily walk to the point at Magic Island and then I began to swim at the Hale Koa pool for about 30 minutes of laps. I was trying to lose weight and I needed the cardio work out. Often we would come back to the hotel again later in the day to lay by the pool and read. Once a week I tried to use our single car to go hit some golf balls and I got out a few times with some active duty and retired chaplains, our contractor and his son and partner and our Kent next door neighbors who came to spend a week with us for their Spring Break. My golf game was not good. One of our neighbors, Ann, was the Big Ten Women's Champion in college and our country club Women's Champion in Kent. She offered to give me some lessons and I readily agreed. In about 45 minutes she showed me what I was doing wrong and I began to hit the ball a lot straighter and further.

My good friend and former Luftwaffe pilot and U.S. Navy doctor, Klaus Rennert, had retired from the Navy Makalapa Medical Clinic in his 80's and had a stroke in June of 2015. He was now 88 and moving slowly. His short term memory was not what it used to be. He had a condo in Princeville, Kauai but had not been there since the stroke. Gail suggested I take him over there. The man managing his condo picked us up and took us to the condo where we found his car still able to start. We stayed there a few days and returned. I had to use a wheelchair for him at the airport.

Our daughter Mae was back at Chaminade University about two miles away and living at the dorm. She was in her second year and had gotten straight A's in the fall semester. She was changing her major from Interior Design to Art and planned to transfer to the University of Hawaii (UH) the next fall. UH had a terrific art program. Without asking us, Mae went out and bought a moped and was driving it around without a helmet. We were very concerned for her safety but she would not discuss it. We offered to buy her a car, Klaus' on Kauai, but she was not interested. Later she said we could get it for the fall. We prayed every day that God and his angels would protect her.

Such is our life in retirement. My friends and the

psychologist had said to stay busy and Gail and I have certainly done that. Life has been very busy with two homes in two places and five children and grandchildren in four states. We love camping and traveling in the mainland. I also enjoy hunting with my sons, grandson and dogs there. I visit the veterans in the hospital weekly and try to golf weekly in WA and HI. Gail and I love spending our winters in the sun away from the cold and rain. We hope and pray we can stay healthy and keep doing all these things into our 80's.

God has blessed us abundantly and we are very glad to be able to share those blessings with others. I know I deserve nothing from Him but he continually chooses to bless me anyway. His love, patience and kindness are truly amazing. I keep trying to spend time with Him daily, fast and set aside a few hours with Him in silence one day a week. Gail also does daily devotions and we both write in our journals daily. We try to attend worship services somewhere every Sunday and give financially to many Christian causes and organizations.

I started writing this autobiography while on deployment on the USS Abraham Lincoln in the Arabian Gulf 2000-2001. I wanted to write it so my kids and grandkids could see the grace of God in my life and hopefully be drawn to Him through it. I hope many others will read it and be drawn to Him as well. My life has not been perfect but it has been wonderful. Most of what has been written on these pages would not have come to pass if I had not invited Him into my life the spring of 1971. He has always been with me, as He is with you, but when I invited him into my heart that night with my dog Jasper in the woods at Woodinville, He came to live in me. There is a huge difference from having God with you and having Him in you. I would have self destructed my life without Him in me. Thank you Lord and help those who read these words invite you to live in them as well. By the grace of God you took this sinner and gave him a beautiful life. Thank you Lord! I look forward to spending eternity with you and hopefully all of my loved ones and friends in paradise forever.

Made in the USA
Lexington, KY
11 August 2016